Communications in Computer and Information Science   **1070**

Commenced Publication in 2007
Founding and Former Series Editors:
Phoebe Chen, Alfredo Cuzzocrea, Xiaoyong Du, Orhun Kara, Ting Liu,
Krishna M. Sivalingam, Dominik Ślęzak, Takashi Washio, Xiaokang Yang,
and Junsong Yuan

More information about this series at http://www.springer.com/series/7899

Juan Antonio Lossio-Ventura ·
Nelly Condori-Fernandez ·
Jorge Carlos Valverde-Rebaza (Eds.)

Information Management and Big Data

6th International Conference, SIMBig 2019
Lima, Peru, August 21–23, 2019
Proceedings

 Springer

Editors
Juan Antonio Lossio-Ventura 🔘
Stanford University
Stanford, CA, USA

Nelly Condori-Fernandez 🔘
University of A Coruña
A Coruña, Spain

Jorge Carlos Valverde-Rebaza 🔘
Visibilia
São Paulo, Brazil

ISSN 1865-0929   ISSN 1865-0937 (electronic)
Communications in Computer and Information Science
ISBN 978-3-030-46139-3   ISBN 978-3-030-46140-9 (eBook)
https://doi.org/10.1007/978-3-030-46140-9

This Springer imprint is published by the registered company Springer Nature Switzerland AG
The registered company address is: Gewerbestrasse 11, 6330 Cham, Switzerland

Preface

SIMBig has been positioning itself as one of the most important conferences in South America on topics related to data science, artificial intelligence, machine learning, big data, data mining, natural language processing (NLP), semantic web, multilingual text processing, biomedical NLP, health informatics, among others.

SIMBig 2019, the 6th edition of the International Conference on Information Management and Big Data, aimed to present new methods of fields related to data science for analyzing and managing large volumes of data. The SIMBig conference series brings together national and international actors in the decision-making field to reveal new technologies dedicated to analyzing data. SIMBig is a convivial place where participants present their scientific contributions concerning full and short papers. This book presents the entire proceedings of the papers presented at SIMBig 2019[1], which was held in Lima, Peru, during August 21–23.

Keynote Speakers' Resumes

Sophia Ananiadou, from the University of Manchester, UK, provided an overview of recent developments in neural information extraction at the National Center for Text Mining to support biomedical applications, including applications ranging from pathway construction, database curation, semantic search, and systematic review development. She presented two systems: (a) LitPathExplorer, a visual text analytics tool that integrates advanced text mining, semi-supervised learning, and interactive visualization, to facilitate the exploration and analysis of pathway models; and (b) RobotAnalyst, a web-based screening system combining machine learning and text mining for document prioritization.

Later, Vipin Kumar, from the University of Minnesota, USA, focused on climate change. He stated that climate and earth sciences have recently undergone a rapid transformation from a data-poor to a data-rich environment. In particular, a massive amount of data about earth and its environment is now continuously being generated by a large number of earth-observing satellites as well as physics-based earth system models running on large-scale computational platforms. These massive and information-rich datasets offer huge potential for understanding how the earth's climate and ecosystem have been changing and how they are being impacted by humans' actions. This talk also discussed various challenges involved in analyzing these massive data sets, and opportunities they present for both advancing machine learning as well as the science of climate change in the context of monitoring the state of the tropical forests and surface water on a global scale.

---

[1] https://simbig.org/SIMBig2019/.

Michael Franklin, from the University of Chicago, USA, presented the big challenges in data science. He stated that the emergence of data science has led to a flourishing of initiatives, centers, degrees, programs, and organizational units at educational and research institutions around the world. The demand for data science know-how from students, parents, scientists, and employers is strong and getting stronger. However, the interdisciplinary nature of the topic and the lack of a consensus around its definition raise challenges for its implementation in the modern university setting. Many ongoing efforts treat data science as simply a combination of topics from existing fields. While such an approach has obvious practical advantages, Michael believes that the challenges raised by data science imply that it should be more productively pursued as a new discipline in its own right. In this talk, he tried to frame this larger question with a goal of initiating a discussion to identify the intellectual opportunities and research questions that could lie at the heart of a new discipline of data science.

Nigam Shah, from Stanford University, USA, talked about Stanford Medicine's Program for Artificial Intelligence (AI) in Healthcare and their mission of bringing AI technologies to the clinic, safely, cost-effectively, and ethically. They used their experiences in deploying the predictive model to improve access to palliative care services, he discussed potential solutions to issues relating to model correctness, interpretability, fairness, and equity as well as issues such as autonomy of decision making and fiduciary responsibility. Drawing on their experience in running a clinical consult service for generating evidence from the collective experience of patients, he discussed the challenges as well as potential solutions to use aggregate patient data at the bedside.

Finally, Ravi Kumar, from Google, USA, discussed the problem of estimating the difficulty of parking at a particular time and place; which is a critical sub-component for any system providing parking assistance to users. He described an approach to this problem that is currently in production in Google Maps, providing inferences in cities across the world. He presented a wide range of features intended to capture different aspects of parking difficulty in order to study their effectiveness both alone and in combination. He also presented various model architectures for the prediction problem. Finally, Ravi presented the challenges faced in estimating parking difficulty in different regions of the world, and the approaches taken to address them.

March 2020   Juan Antonio Lossio-Ventura
                                                                      Hugo Alatrista-Salas

Organization

General Organizers

Juan Antonio Lossio-Ventura — Biomedical Informatics Research, Stanford University, USA

Hugo Alatrista-Salas — Universidad del Pacífico, Peru

Local Organizers

Michelle Rodriguez Serra — Universidad del Pacífico, Peru

Cristhian Ganvini Valcarcel — Universidad Andina del Cusco, Peru

SNMAM Track Organizers

Jorge Carlos Valverde-Rebaza — Visibilia, Brazil

Alneu de Abdrade Lopes — University of São Paulo, Brazil

DISE Track Organizers

Nelly Condori Fernandez — Universidade da Coruna, Spain

Denisse Muñante Arzapalo — ESTIA, France

Carlos Gavidia Calderon — University College London, UK

ANLP Track Organizers

Marco Antonio Sobrevilla-Cabezudo — University of São Paulo, Brazil

José Eduardo Ochoa Luna — Universidad Católica San Pablo, Peru

Félix Arturo Oncevay-Marcos — University of Edinburgh, UK

PSCBig Track Organizers

Julian Salas Piñon — Universitat Oberta de Catalunya, Spain

Miguel Nuñez Del Prado — Universidad del Pacífico, Peru

DLTA Track Organizers

Jorge Guerra Guerra — Universidad Nacional Mayor de San Marcos, Peru

Armando Fermín Pérez — Universidad Nacional Mayor de San Marcos, Peru

DSRS Track Organizers

Victor Hugo Ayma Quirita	Universidad de Lima, Peru
Walter Aliaga Aliaga	Universidad del Pacífico, Peru
Waldo Elio Ibarra Zambrano	Universidad San Antonio Abad del Cusco, Peru
Victor Andres Ayma Quirita	Pontificia Universidad Católica del Perú, Peru

SIMBig Program Committee

Nathalie Abadie	COGIT IGN, France
Amine Abdaoui	Stack Labs, France
Pedro Marco Achanccaray Diaz	Pontifical Catholic University of Rio de Janeiro, Brazil
Elie Abi-Lahoud	University College Cork, Ireland
César Antonio Aguilar	Pontifica Universidad Católica de Chile, Chile
Marco Alvarez	University of Rhode Island, USA
Sophia Ananiadou	NaCTeM, The University of Manchester, UK
Erick Antezana	Norwegian University of Science and Technology, Norway
Smith Washington Arauco Canchumuni	Pontifical Catholic University of Rio de Janeiro, Brazil
Victor Hugo Ayma	Universidad de Lima, Peru
Jérôme Azé	LIRMM, University of Montpellier, France
Pablo Barceló	Universidad de Chile, Chile
Riza Batista-Navarro	NaCTeM, The University of Manchester, UK
Nicolas Béchet	IRISA, Université de Bretagne-Sud, France
Patrice Bellot	Aix-Marseille Université, CNRS, LSIS, France
César Beltrán Castañón	Pontificia Universidad Católica del Perú, Peru
Jose David Bermudez Castro	Pontifical Catholic University of Rio de Janeiro, Brazil
Mohamed Ben Ellefi	LIS, Aix-Marseille Université, France
Lilian Berton	University of São Paulo, Brazil
Jiang Bian	University of Florida, USA
Albert Bifet	LTCI, Télécom ParisTech, France
Selen Bozkurt	Stanford University, USA
Sandra Bringay	LIRMM, Paul Valéry University, France
Jean-Paul Calbimonte Pérez	University of Applied Sciences and Arts Western Switzerland HES-SO, Switzerland
Hugo David Calderon Vilca	Universidad Nacional Mayor de San Marcos, Peru
Guillermo Calderón Ruiz	Universidad Católica de Santa María, Peru
Ricardo Campos	Polytechnic Institute of Tomar, LIAAD, INESC TEC, Portugal
Thierry Charnois	LIPN, CNRS, University of Paris 13, France
Davide Chicco	Peter Munk Cardiac Centre, Canada
Diego Collarana Vargas	Fraunhofer IAIS, Germany

Rafael Rossi	University of São Paulo, Brazil
Luca Rossi	Southern University of Science and Technology, China
Jose M. Saavedra	Orand, Chile
Fatiha Saïs	Paris Saclay University, France
Rafael Santos	Instituto Nacional de Pesquisas Espaciais, Brazil
José Segovia-Juárez	INIA, Peru
Selja Seppälä	University College Cork, Ireland
Arnaud Sallaberry	LIRMM, Paul Valéry University, France
Nazha Selmaoui-Folcher	PPME, University of New Caledonia, New Caledonia
Matthew Shardlow	Manchester Metropolitan University, UK
Pedro Nelson Shiguihara Juárez	Universidad Peruana de Ciencias Aplicadas, Peru
Gerardo Sierra-Martínez	Universidad Autónoma de México, Mexico
Diego Silva	Universidade Federal de São Carlos, Brazil
Thiago Silva	Federal University of Technology, UTFPR, Nigeria
Aurea Rossy Soriano Vargas	University of Campinas, Brazil
Newton Spolaôr	State University of Western Paraná, Brazil
Victor Stroele	PPGCC, UFJF, Brazil
Ran Sun	Stanford University, USA
Claude Tadonki	MINES ParisTech, PSL Research University, France
Alvaro Talavera López	Universidad del Pacífico, Peru
Andon Tchechmedjiev	IMT Mines Alès, France
Maguelonne Teisseire	Irstea, UMR, TETIS, France
Paul Thompson	The University of Manchester, UK
Thibaut Thonet	University of Grenoble Alpes, France
Camilo Thorne	Elsevier, Germany
Ilaria Tiddi	Open University, UK
Jose Leomar Todesco	Federal University of Santa Catarina, Brazil
Andrew Tomkins	Google, USA
Juan Manuel Torres	University of Avignon, France
Turki Turki	King Abdulaziz University, Saudi Arabia
Willy Ugarte	Universidad Peruana de Ciencias Aplicadas, Peru
Paola Valdivia	University of São Paulo, Brazil
Alan Valejo	University of São Paulo, Brazil
Jorge Carlos Valverde-Rebaza	Visibilia, Brazil
Edwin Villanueva	University of São Paulo, Brazil
Sebastian Walter	Semalytix GmbH, Germany
Carlos Vázquez	École de technologie supérieure, Canada
Julien Velcin	ERIC Lab, University of Lyon 2, France
Maria-Esther Vidal	Universidad Simón Bolívar, Venezuela
Boris Villazon-Terrazas	Fujitsu Laboratories of Europe, Spain
Sebastian Walter	Semalytix GmbH, Germany
Florence Wang	LIRMM, France
Guo Yi	University of Florida, USA
Osmar Zaïane	University of Alberta, Canada

Amrapali Zaveri	Maastricht University, The Netherlands
Karine Zeitouni	University of Versailles-Saint-Quentin, France
Chryssa Zerva	The University of Manchester, UK
Hong Zheng	Stanford University, USA
He Zhe	Florida State University, USA
Pierre Zweigenbaum	LIMSI-CNRS, France

SNMAM Program Committee

Alan Valejo	University of São Paulo, Brazil
Alexandre Donizeti	Federal University of ABC, Brazil
Aurea Soriano Vargas	State University of Campinas, Brazil
Brett Drury	Scicrop, Brazil
Conceição Rocha	INESC TEC, Portugal
Diego Furtado Silva	Universidade Federal de São Carlos, Brazil
Huei Diana Lee	State University of Western Paraná, Brazil
Hugo D. Calderon Vilca	National University of San Marcos, Peru
Leissi Castañeda León	University of São Paulo, Brazil
Luca Rossi	Southern University of Science and Technology, China
Mathieu Roche	CIRAD, TETIS, University of Montpellier, France
Newton Spolaôr	State University of Western Paraná, Brazil
Nils Murrugarra	University of Pittsburgh, USA
Oscar Cuadros	University of São Paulo, Brazil
Pablo Fonseca	University of Montreal, Canada
Paola Llerena Valdivia	Inria Saclay, France
Pascal Poncelet	University of Montpellier, France
Pedro Shiguihara Juárez	Universidad Peruana de Ciencias Aplicadas, Peru
Rafael Giusti	Federal University of Amazonas, Brazil
Rafael Rossi	Federal University of Mato Grosso do Sul, Brazil
Rafael Santos	National Institute for Space Research (INPE), Brazil
Ricardo Campos	Polytechnic Institute of Tomar, LIAAD, INESC TEC, Portugal
Ricardo Marcacini	Federal University of Mato Grosso do Sul, Brazil
Sabrine Mallek	Université de Lorraine, France
Shima Kashef	Shahid Bahonar University of Kerman, Iran
Thiago de Paulo Faleiros	University of Brasilia, Brazil
Thiago Henrique Silva	Federal University of Technology in Paraná, Brazil
Victor Stroele	Federal University of Juiz de Fora, Brazil
Willy Ugarte	Universidad Peruana de Ciencias Aplicadas, Peru

DISE Program Committee

Joao Araujo	Universidade Nova de Lisboa, Portugal
Yudith Cardinale	Universidad Simon Bolivar, Venezuela
Alejandro Catala	Universidad de Santiago de Compostela, Spain
Vanea Chiprianov	University of South Brittany, France

Maria Fernanda Granda	Universidad de Cuenca, Ecuador
Itzel Morales-Ramirez	Infotec, Mexico
Manuel Munier	Université de Pau et des Pays de l'Adour, France
Jose Antonio Pow-Sang	PUCP, Peru
Glen Rodriguez	UNMSM, Peru
Daniel Rodriguez	Universidad de Alcalá, Spain
Silvia Lizeth Tapia Tarifa	University of Oslo, Norway
Jovan Varga	Universitat Politècnica de Catalunya, BarcelonaTech, Spain
Otto Parra	Universidad de Cuenca, Ecuador

ANLP Program Committee

Fernando Emilio Alva Manchego	University of Sheffield, UK
Fernando Antônio Asevedo Nóbrega	University of São Paulo, Brazil
Leandro Borges dos Santos	University of São Paulo, Brazil
Shay Cohen	University of Edinburgh, UK
Paula Christina Figueira Cardoso	Federal University of Lavras, Brazil
Nathan Siegle Hartmman	University of São Paulo, Brazil
Roque Enrique López Condori	Institute for Research in Computer Science and Automation, France
Shashi Narayan	University of Edinburgh, UK
Thiago Alexandre Salgueiro Pardo	University of São Paulo, Brazil
Márcio de Souza Dias	Federal University of Goiás, Brazil
Francis M. Tyers	UiT Norgga árktalaš universitehta, Norway

PSCBig Program Committee

Ali Tosun	University of Texas at San Antonio, USA
John Marsh	SUNY Polytechnic Institute, USA
Nihat Altiparmak	University of Louisville, USA
Hisham Kholidy	SUNY Polytechnic Institute, USA

DSRS Program Committee

Victor Hugo Ayma	Universidad de Lima, Perú
Walter Aliaga	Universidad del Pacífico, Perú
Pedro Achanccaray	ICA, Pontifical Catholic University of Rio de Janeiro, Brazil
Jose Bermudez	ICA, Pontifical Catholic University of Rio de Janeiro, Brazil

Patrick Happ   LVC, Pontifical Catholic University of Rio de Janeiro,
                                Brazil
Gilson Costa   Rio de Janeiro State University, Brazil

DLTA Program Committee

Serguei Popov   Moscow State University, Russia
Augusto Bernuy Alva   National University of San Marcos, Peru
Joachim Taiber   ETH Swiss Federal Institute of Technology,
                                Switzerland
Jose Carlos Alvarez   National University of San Marcos, Peru
Jong Hyuk Park   Seoul National University of Science and Technology,
                                South Korea
Ilse Villavicencio   National University of San Marcos, Peru
Nour El-Deen Mahmoud   Cairo University, Egypt
Nora La Serna Palomino   National University of San Marcos, Peru

Biomeds Program Committee

Davide Chicco   Peter Munk Cardiac, Canada

Organizing Institutions

Universidad del Pacífico, Peru[1]
Stanford University, USA[2]

Collaborating Institutions

Springer[3]
Universidad Andina del Cusco, Peru[4]
University of Florida, USA[5]
Universidad Nacional Mayor de San Marcos, Peru[6]
Labóratorio de Intêligencia Computacional, ICMC, USP, Brazil[7]
Université de Montpellier, France[8]
Visibilia, Brazil[9]

---

[1] http://www.up.edu.pe/.
[2] https://www.stanford.edu/.
[3] http://www.springer.com/la/.
[4] http://www.uandina.edu.pe/.
[5] https://www.ufl.edu/.
[6] http://www.unmsm.edu.pe/.
[7] http://labic.icmc.usp.br/.
[8] https://www.umontpellier.fr/.
[9] http://visibilia.net.br.

Sponsoring Institutions

Google[10]
Telefónica del Perú[11]

---

[10] https://www.google.com.
[11] https://www.telefonica.com.pe/.

Contents

Anomaly Detection and Levels of Automation for AI-Supported System Administration

Anton Gulenko, Odej Kao$^{(\boxtimes)}$, and Florian Schmidt

TU Berlin, 10587 Berlin, Germany
{anton.gulenko,odej.kao,florian.schmidt}@tu-berlin.de

Abstract. Artificial Intelligence for IT Operations (AIOps) describes the process of maintaining and operating large IT infrastructures using AI-supported methods and tools on different levels. This includes automated anomaly detection and root cause analysis, remediation and optimization, as well as fully automated initiation of self-stabilizing activities. While the automation is mandatory due to the system complexity and the criticality of QoS-bounded responses, the measures compiled and deployed by the AI-controlled administration are not easily understandable or reproducible in all cases. Therefore, explainable actions taken by the automated systems are becoming a regulatory requirement for future IT infrastructures. In this paper we present a developed and deployed system named ZerOps as an example for the design of the corresponding architecture, tools, and methods. This system uses deep learning models and data analytics of monitoring data to detect and remediate anomalies.

Keywords: AIOps · Predictive fault tolerance · Anomaly detection

1 Introduction

The complexity of systems is growing to a level, where it is impossible for human operators to oversee and holistically manage the systems without additional support and automation. Uninterrupted services with guaranteed latencies and response times are, however, a mandatory prerequisite for many data-driven and autonomous applications. Therefore, downtimes and malfunctioning components may have a crucial impact. On the other hand, the software-defined technology on all layers of the infrastructure stack opens new possibilities to control not only the server landscape, but also the connected frontend devices and the communication paths. This optimization potential can be utilized to increase the dependability and the reliability of the overall system.

The large service providers are aware of the need for always-on, dependable services and already introduced additional intelligence to the IT-ecosystem, e.g. by employing network and site reliability engineers, by deploying automated tools for 24/7 monitoring, and AIOps platforms for load balancing, capacity

© Springer Nature Switzerland AG 2020
J. A. Lossio-Ventura et al. (Eds.): SIMBig 2019, CCIS 1070, pp. 1–7, 2020.
https://doi.org/10.1007/978-3-030-46140-9_1

planning, resource utilization, storage management, and threat detection. This decision-making in combination with advanced virtualization techniques allows a significant progress regarding reliability, serviceability, and availability: checkpointing, migration, restarts, scale-out/scale-down, rerouting, and resource reservations are much more flexible and easier to deploy, independent from the underlying hardware infrastructure and not limited to a certain site. The next piece of the puzzle aims at rapidly decreasing the reaction time, in case an urgent activity of a system administrator is necessary – e.g. due to performance problems (tuning), to component/system failures (outages, degraded performance), or due to security incidents. All these examples describe situations where the system operates outside of the normal (expected or pre-defined) parameters. Thus, the system exposes an anomaly that must be registered, recognized, and remediated before it leads to a component or a system failure. Many anomalies are straightforward to detect and handle; for example component outages and interrupted services have a massive impact and trigger a lot of indicators to be noticed by the administrators. More sophisticated malfunctions, such as stressed CPUs, leaks of main memory or storage space, increased network latency are far more complex to be detected, taking the number of involved cores, networks, and software systems into account. Usually, these effects propagate horizontally and/or vertically leading at some point of time – if not detected and remediated – to an interrupted service noticed by an administrator. Finding the cause for the observed symptoms and then repairing the cause requires valuable time, and in the worst case visible to the customer due to a service downtime or due to a significantly reduced QoS. Therefore, much effort was spent in recent years to speed-up this process by developing and deploying advanced mechanisms for monitoring the systems, aggregating and analyzing the data, detecting the root cause, and finally remediating it.

2   Background

The rules of automation for an AI-supported IT infrastructure management should help IT operators to find a common ground for discussion of the AIOps paradigm. These rules clearly define policies, benefits and boundaries of automated administration tools. In 1978, Sheridan and Verplank [11] provided one of the first listings of rules and levels of autonomous operation in the context of undersea teleoperators. The list contains ten rules:

Level 1: the operator defines the task, which the computer executes.
Level 2: the computer helps determining the options.
Level 3: the computer determines and suggests options. The operator can modify the recommendations.
Level 4: the computer selects and parameterizes the action and the operator decides if it should or should not be executed.
Level 5: the computer selects the action and executes it if the operator approves the action.

Level 6: the computer selects the action and informs the operator in case the operator wants to cancel the action.
Level 7: the computer executes the action and reports to the human operator.
Level 8: the computer executes the action and reports only if the operator asks.
Level 9: the computer executes the action and reports to the human operator only if the computer decides the operator should be told.
Level 10: the computer executes the action autonomously and does not report to the human operator.

These rules describe a wide spectrum of human-controlled, computer-assisted, computer-controlled, up to an autonomous mode of operation. Endsley developed a similar hierarchy for expert systems to supplement human decision-making in [1,2]. Another combination of rules for automation and architecture was provided by IBM in 2002 coining the term of autonomic computing [3,8]. The five levels range from a basic, fully manual level up to an autonomic level with an interplay between autonomic components and business rules and policies without human intervention. The levels named managed, predictive, and adaptive do not specify the applied technology, so they are transferable into the current world of AIOps. A valuable extension is given on the alignment with the business goals, as the authors describe the impact of autonomic computing on the processes, tools, skills, and benchmarks. One of the core contributions in the autonomic computing initiative is the introduction of the self-X paradigm. Originally, four properties – self-configuring, self-healing, self-optimizing, and self-protecting – were presented, each of them addressing a capability of an autonomic system to deal with an induced modification. The need for change can be caused by manually initiated demands or by monitoring the environment and responding to degraded performance, security attacks, or system malfunctions. In the following, we use the levels of automation proposed by Sheridan and Verplank for describing automation in IT infrastructures.

3 Application Scenarios

The AIOps paradigm includes a large set of typical activities such as runtime optimization, remediation/recovery after malfunctioning, software updates, security upgrades, and sizing (scale-up/-down) tasks. Applying a fully automated operation is possible in all these cases, however the cost of false decisions and consequences varies significantly.

Runtime Optimization. The runtime optimization and sizing aims at keeping the QoS parameters within predefined bounds, e.g. the response time is less than x seconds, the CPU load is lower than y%, or the free hard disk capacity does not fall below z%. The typical activities such as adding/removing nodes, replicating the database, resizing storage volumes, may have impact on the overall system performance, but usually not on the functionality reducing the risk significantly. Therefore, the level 5 automation is the standard in the majority of the productive infrastructures. The level 6 automation may be useful for optimization cases triggered by unusual circumstances, e.g. by DDoS attacks. The optimization can switch the strategy from up-scaling to reconfiguring the balancing frontends to block suspicious traffic.

Updates. System updates are frequent operations on all layers of the IT infrastructure. Mobile devices are typically updated automatically without user interaction (level 5). A step towards level 6 is implemented by initiating an automatic rollback to the last known working setup in case of update failure. Server and other core components are challenging to update due to the individual configuration and the necessary interaction. Level 4 is therefore the standard approach. Level 5 is reached in combination with a testing and deployment pipeline, where the updates are verified prior migrating to the production lines. Deployment frameworks like Kubernetes allow gradual updates of multiple components with fast rollback.

Reliability, Availability, Security. A guaranteed continuous service within predefined QoS parameters is the main pre-requisite for IoT applications. Thus, reliability and availability need as much real-time automation as possible. Automating the anomaly detection in IT infrastructures using AI-methods (deep learning, time series analysis) is currently a hot topic in the academia and industry. These approaches correspond to at least level 5 automation, or – depending on the deployed policy – to level 6. Automatic remediation is examined as well, where the system evaluates existing recovery and remediation options and applies the selected operation until the anomaly disappears or the set of feasible options is exhausted. Even higher levels are targeted by the idea of self-healing and self-stabilizing systems, where the system is able to generate a feasible remediation work-flows autonomously, but there are no implemented solutions yet.

4   ZerOps: A System for Anomaly Detection and Remediation

The AIOps demonstrator ZerOps provides a self-stabilization pipeline consisting of components for monitoring, streaming data analytics, and of an AI-controlled remediation/recovery engine [6]. The implementation is based on OpenStack and Kubernetes and is experimentally evaluated using two real-world domains: a core network NFV scenario based on the virtual IP multimedia subsystem Clearwater and a streaming edge cloud service with low latency demands following a real-time messaging protocol. The detection of anomalies before causing a failure is a key requirement for AIOps systems. Inspired by Kephart and Chess [9] work about autonomic computing, Fig. 1 shows the self-sustainable AIOps loop. Monitoring data are continuously collected from the monitored system, then analyzed in order to extract and maintain a knowledge base, and finally used to select, plan and execute remediation workflows in anomaly situations.

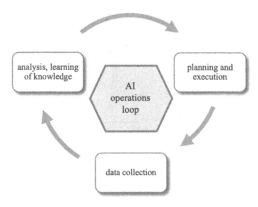

Fig. 1. High-level steps of the self-sustainable AIOps loop [9].

Ghosh et al. [4] confine anomalies to a fuzzy deterioration zone between the normal and failed state of individual system components. Thus, anomalies can manifest themselves as changes of individual or combined system metrics like increased latency, decreased throughput, unusual CPU or disk I/O utilization patterns, and many others. The ZerOps system continuously monitors a large number of indicators to determine whether the monitored infrastructure components are exposing abnormal system metric levels or patterns. The collected data include time series metrics from multiple sources across the technological stack. Operating systems deliver real-time resource utilization data for the entire host, or for individual processes. Both physical and virtual hosts deliver these generic data, which are completely independent of the actual workload of the system. Other sources of data are more application and network protocol specific, like the HTTP response latency or number of incoming requests per second. In order to reduce network bandwidth overhead and the data analysis latency, the data are analyzed and pre-aggregated directly at the source, while keeping the computational overhead within predefined bounds.

The data are analyzed using machine learning methods. A fully supervised approach relies on injection and learning of all possible anomalies and thus can be implemented straightforwardly. However, anomaly injections inside a productive system impact the QoS perceived by clients, and all expected anomalies must be known beforehand, which is generally not the case [5]. Thus, collecting labeled training data within the actual production environment remains as challenge. Besides supervised machine learning approaches, which require data of all anomalies, the applied unsupervised approach requires only data of the running system without artificially injected anomalies in order to detect the "normal" state and identify all data points that do not fit into the learned model as abnormal. Thus, the requirement for labeled training is abandoned and we solely assume that anomalies occur far less frequently than normal operation corresponding to the level 5 expectations.

Level 6 automation additionally requires a fully unsupervised machine learning model adaptation of thresholds or cluster borders to the current system load situation [7,10]. This can be achieved by online adaption to concept drifts of the machine learning models.

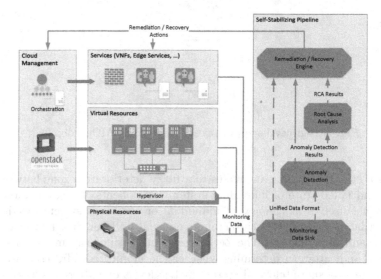

Fig. 2. Architecture of an OpenStack cloud infrastructure with a self-stabilizing pipeline.

Detected anomalies can be either the source or the symptom of horizontally or vertically propagating failures. Therefore, in a largely distributed infrastructure with high dependency between system components, the identification of the root cause (root cause analysis – RCA) during an anomaly scenario is essential [12]. We propose to utilize results from the anomaly detection models to either directly determine root causes or to obtain valuable indications to reduce the set of possible root cause nodes to enable reduction of complexity and time efficient analysis for the next analysis steps.

The proposed rules of automation above level 2 require the system to either suggest or autonomously execute countermeasures in case of detected anomalies. Thus, the remediation engine requests monitoring data to apply time series pattern matching methods (see Fig. 2). Combining the results of anomaly detection, RCA, and pattern matching enables the system to determine whether a similar situation has been previously encountered. In this case, the system can provide automatic selection of options to an expert user based on executed remediation workflows in the past. The probability of fixing the anomaly, and the execution time of the workflow are important factors in this selection process.

5 Summary

The AIOps platforms aim at supporting system operators to holistically control large, complex IT infrastructures with attached QoS requirements found in many current and future domains. The monitoring components, methods for data analytics and machine learning as well as the knowledge repositories with patterns for detecting and remediating anomalies allow the development and deployment of tools and frameworks for largely autonomous control of infrastructures and implementation of the self-X vision established in the last decade. We presented a developed demonstrator utilizing unsupervised machine learning to detect anomalies, identify the root cause, and finally deploy remediation workflows to stabilize the overall system and prevent the anomaly from turning into failure. The future work will be focused on verifying the scope of the defined rules in different IT domains, and to improve the precision and reaction time, if necessary. Moreover, we are experimentally evaluating the demonstrators in real-world environments in order to adapt the models to the characteristics of productive infrastructures.

References

1. Endsley, M.R.: The application of human factors to the development of expert systems for advanced cockpits. In: Proceedings of the Human Factors Society Annual Meeting, vol. 31, pp. 1388–1392. SAGE Publications, Los Angeles (1987)
2. Endsley, M.R.: Level of automation effects on performance, situation awareness and workload in a dynamic control task. Ergonomics $42(3)$, 462–492 (1999)
3. Ganek, A.G., Corbi, T.A.: The dawning of the autonomic computing era. IBM Syst. J. $42(1)$, 5–18 (2003)
4. Ghosh, D., Sharman, R., Rao, H.R., Upadhyaya, S.: Self-healing systems survey and synthesis. Decis. Support Syst. $42(4)$, 2164–2185 (2007)
5. Gulenko, A., Wallschläger, M., Schmidt, F., Kao, O., Liu, F.: Evaluating machine learning algorithms for anomaly detection in clouds. In: 2016 IEEE International Conference on Big Data (Big Data), pp. 2716–2721. IEEE (2016)
6. Gulenko, A., Wallschläger, M., Schmidt, F., Kao, O., Liu, F.: A system architecture for real-time anomaly detection in large-scale NFV systems. Procedia Comput. Sci. **94**, 491–496 (2016)
7. Hundman, K., Constantinou, V., Laporte, C.: Detecting spacecraft anomalies using LSTMs and nonparametric dynamic thresholding. In: Proceedings 24th ACM SIGKDD Conference on Knowledge Discovery, pp. 387–395. ACM (2018)
8. IBM: An architectural blueprint for autonomic computing. IBM White Paper 31, 1–6 (2006)
9. Kephart, J.O., Chess, D.M.: The vision of autonomic computing. Computer **1**, 41–50 (2003)
10. Schmidt, F., et al.: IFTM - unsupervised anomaly detection for virtualized network function services. In: 2018 IEEE International Conference on Web Services (ICWS), pp. 187–194 (2018)
11. Sheridan, T.B., Verplank, W.L.: Human and computer control of undersea teleoperators. Technical report, MIT Man-Machine Systems Lab (1978)
12. Solé, M., Muntés-Mulero, V., Rana, A.I., Estrada, G.: Survey on models and techniques for root-cause analysis. arXiv preprint arXiv:1701.08546 (2017)

Characterization of Salinity Impact on Synthetic Floc Strength via Nonlinear Component Analysis

Hang Yin[✉], Patrick Carriere, Huey Lawson, Habib Mohamadian, and Zhengmao Ye

College of Science and Engineering, Southern University, Baton Rouge, LA 70813, USA
{hang_yin,patrick_carriere,huey_lawson,habib_mohamadian,
zhengmao_ye}@subr.edu

Abstract. Many complex mechanisms are inherently engaged in flocculation processes with nonlinear nature. The strength of synthetic flocculates or natural flocculates may be relevant to numerous factors as well. It will be expensive and virtually impossible to determine an exact influential list among various factors via trial and error experiments exclusively. The objective is to develop an analytical scheme for decision making about the relevant influential list at least cost. Multivariate statistical methods are actually capable of differentiating dominating factors. There is no existing research outcome being documented about applications of either principal component analysis (PCA) or nonlinear component analysis (NCA) to the whole area of flocculation and coagulation research, essentially optimization has been never achieved indeed. Compared with PCA, NCA is more versatile to solve large dimensional nonlinear multivariate problems with a potential to reach infinite dimensionality. NCA is thus proposed in a preliminary study to figure out feasibility of challenging research to extract dominating factors associated with the mechanical behavior of flocs. Without convincing evidence so far on specific utmost factor in the floc strength studies, the scale of adjustable salinity has been intentionally chosen as the first principal component to interpret variations observed in the simulation results, together with interconnections to other major principal components. Based on the pioneering methodology proposed, some interesting results are well obtained and documented. At the same time, there is no technical difficulty unquestionably to extend the proposed NCA approach to multivariable and high-dimensional nonlinear cases.

Keywords: Flocculation · Flocculate strength · Salinity · Principal component analysis (PCA) · Nonlinear component analysis (NCA)

1 Introduction

Flocculation and coagulation are two major processes for solid and liquid separation. The floc arises from the flocculation process when fine particulates are gradually accumulated to clump together. There are a vast variety of factors affecting floc strength, including salinity, pH scale (acidic, alkaline, neutral), particles (concentration, size and turbidity), mineral precipitates (e.g. aluminium salt, iron salt, aluminium or iron hydroxide),

© Springer Nature Switzerland AG 2020
J. A. Lossio-Ventura et al. (Eds.): SIMBig 2019, CCIS 1070, pp. 8–20, 2020.
https://doi.org/10.1007/978-3-030-46140-9_2

biological matters (e.g., bacteria, fungi, virus), organic substances (e.g. humus, oils), geometries (e.g. surface porosity, roughness, microstructure, nanostructure), physical properties (e.g. temperature, pressure, humidity), hydro-dynamics (e.g. velocity variability, flowrate), and so on. Dilute suspensions could also give rise to colloidal dispersions and interactions with remarkably complex nature. In fact it leads to a complicated nonlinear multivariate analysis problem [1, 2]. Among these factors, there is no doubt that the salinity effect is one of commanding factors being involved. Its impact on the synthetic floc strength will be analyzed as a typical case study.

In order to experimentally test the strength of flocs and mineral, some state-of-the-art techniques have been adopted to observe the deformation mechanism under various load levels even at nanoscale. For instance, the effect of loading on the nanoscale deformation modes has been investigated under repeated nanoindentation loading on muscovite with a sharp indenter tip, so as to analyze the deformation mechanisms at nanoscale on a basis of hardness and elastic modulus normal to the basal plane. The testing curves show nonlinear characteristics upon loading and unloading such as the closed hysteresis loops. The transition from the high Young modulus to low bulk modulus occurs due to 3D confinement surrounding an indenter tip in the plastic shakedown process [3, 4].

To avoid or to minimize laborious, expensive, risky and time-consuming processes in the relevant civil engineering studies, and to be away from instrument-specific, field-specific and technology-specific conditions, the multivariate model could serve as a promising solution. It ranges from the classical multivariate regression model to popular principal component analysis (PCA), as well as to more powerful nonlinear component analysis (NCA) and independent component analysis (ICA). Even though no application of PCA on mechanical behaviors of the floc strength has appeared in literatures, various cases of successful research have been conducted across related fields. For instance, failures occur frequently at wastewater treatment sites, which cause terrible environmental implications. The reliable and versatile PCA helps to group soils independently of classifications to distinguish the appropriate soils for sustainable long-term effluent irrigation and to locate influential parameters for actual characterization [5]. PCA is also proposed for sensor fault detection to monitor the structure health such as cracks on the underground structure. The useful results could be extended to micro-crack detection of the concrete [6]. The decision-making of drought quantification depends on various statistical aspects. The multivariate PCA technique has been applied to hydrological drought monitoring. A typical Streamflow Drought Index (SCI) has been expanded to multivariate index at multiple time scales. In general the first principal component can be used to interpret majority of regional variations [7]. Reliable data acquisition of soil permeability in fact is vital for soil-water research. An accurate prediction model will be beneficial to identify those key soil parameters without high cost and length time needed. From PCA analysis on over 90 samples examined with 16 parameters at 37 sites, five variables are determined to be of strong correlation with soil permeability in a preliminary study [8]. PCA can be also applied to characterization of biomedical samples. In Raman spectroscopic study, PCA has been carried out to differentiate diverse tissue samples using scatter plots together with artificial intelligence techniques [9].

PCA always provides convincing outcomes for linear feature extraction. Limitation of PCA however lies in data analysis of nonlinear high dimensional spaces. Especially for nonlinear problems in high dimensional or even infinite dimensional cases, PCA itself could be sometimes vulnerable. As an alternative, with the involvement of a nonlinear kernel, kernel PCA is capable of extracting nonlinear features. NCA has the priori advantage with the possibility to extract more principal components than linear PCA. NCA classification also works pretty well with a relatively limited number of principal components compared with feature space dimensionality. To each the same classification performance, much fewer nonlinear principal components are needed than those in the linear case [10]. Another ICA approach is also powerful for nonlinear cases. It covers the steps of centering, whitening and independent optimization. ICA has the merit of minimizing statistical dependence of all components. It has been applied to spatial object recognition problems in remote sensing areas [11].

2 Instrumentation and Data Normalization

All natural floc samples are directly collected from the Atchafalaya Bay in Gulf of Mexico. The natural floc and synthetic floc samples are both tested at Lab using a UTM (Universal Testing Machine) together with a patent licensed compression cell. The dynamic nature of cohesive sediments has a strong impact on the mechanical properties of clay flocs in aqueous environment. Testing samples have been prepared with aqueous clay suspensions and instant ocean salt solution for floc generation. The applied suspension has a constant clay concentration of 0.4 g/L. The flocculation of suspended clay particles occurs in the stirring bath of the Particle Size Analyzer (PSA). The clay to clay collision continues upon stirring. Three targeting salinities for synthetic flocs are 2, 10 and 30 PSU respectively, while the natural floc acts as the sample reference instead. For each clay flocs group, over a dozen individual flocs are examined to provide a sufficient sample population for further statistical analysis. A sketch of instrumentation and experimental setup is shown in Fig. 1.

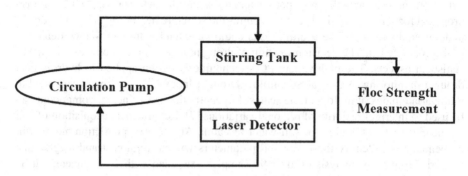

Fig. 1. Sketch of flocculation generation systems

In Fig. 1, the stirring tank is used for sample preparation. Synthetic floc samples are prepared inside by mixing the Na-mont suspension with the guar gum in water with different salinities. Using a Laser detector, when formed flocs are traveling along the circulation pipes, the particle size is measured and plotted until floc size distribution is determined to be stable. The circulation pump forces water inside to continuously flow in order to avoid sedimentation. Then selected individual floc samples will be collected which are transported through a pipette to a universal testing machine for floc strength measurement. For each test, the compressive load and displacement are both recorded for analysis subsequently to determine breakage strength. Rather than the costly nano-scale contact mechanics based approach being developed, promising nonlinear component analysis has been employed for the first time to analyze the floc compression curves in this study. A typical testing result for each clay floc group is plotted in Fig. 2, representing a sufficient set of sample population. To conduct the further statistical analysis, data normalization is necessary.

$$x_i = \frac{z_i - \bar{z}}{s} \tag{1}$$

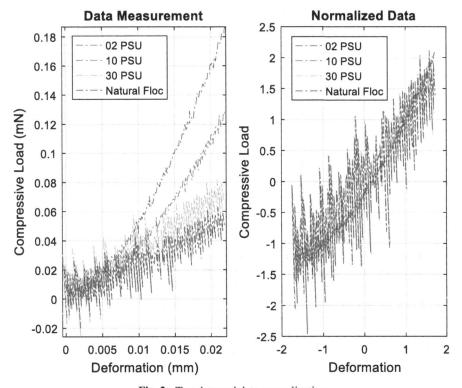

Fig. 2. Test data and data normalization

The normalized data are computed as a ratio of difference between the ith observation data and the sample mean to the sample standard deviation based on all conducted measurements, as shown in (1) where z_i refers to the ith set of observation data and x_i refers to the ith set of normalized data; z_bar refers to the sample mean and S refers to the sample standard deviation. The typical normalized data are also shown in Fig. 2.

From Figs. 1 and 2, among four sets of data, the compressive load-deformation curve of the natural floc (roughly 36 PSU) collected from the Gulf of Mexico is much less deterministic than those synthetic flocs of 2, 10 and 30 PSU. The randomness reflects that highly nonlinear mechanical behaviors occur in the floc strength study.

3 Nonlinear Component Analysis

PCA is unsupervised numerical dimensionality reduction technique to examine the underlying variability of multi-dimensional data. PCA generates the orthogonal transformation of the coordinate system for visualization of experimental data in terms of sample arrays. Some handful principal components are sufficient to describe complex data structure in new axes. Data rotation is implemented to maximize the variance. High dimensional data are projected into a low dimensional subspace. The underlying variables of experimental data could be extracted by solving eigenvalue problems [9]. For a set of N centered observations x_i ($i = 1, 2, ..., N$) in the feature space, PCA in fact implements diagonalization for the covariance matrix C_{PCA} in (2).

$$C_{PCA} = \frac{1}{N} \sum_{i=1}^{N} x_i x_i^T \qquad (2)$$

It is conducted by solving the eigenvalue Eq. (3):

$$\lambda v = C_{PCA} v = \frac{1}{N} \sum_{i=1}^{N} (x_i \cdot v) x_i \qquad (3)$$

where λ is an eigenvalue of C_{PCA} and v is the correspondent eigenvector. x_i is the centered data and C_{PCA} is a positive definite matrix in general. The solutions lie in a span of $x_1, x_2, ..., x_{N,}$, which is formulated in (4).

$$\lambda(x_i * v) = (x_i * C_{PCA} v) \text{ for } i = 1, 2, ..., N \qquad (4)$$

For high-dimensional feature extraction of the nonlinear behaviors (e.g. mechanical properties) with respect to the actual flocculation processes, principal components of various features are in fact nonlinearly related to the complex mechanical behavior itself. The nonlinear kernel approach is proposed to deal with this tough engineering issue for the first time. The nonlinear kernel PCA could extract the more substantial features than the linear PCA for both classification and prediction purposes, in typical nonlinear feature space of high dimensionality and even up to infinite dimensionality. With the centered data ($\sum_{i=1}^{N} \Phi(x_i) = 0$), $i = 1, 2, ..., N$, NCA is able to implement diagonalization on the covariance matrix C_{NCA} in (5).

$$C_{NCA} = \frac{1}{N} \sum_{i=1}^{N} \Phi(x_i) \Phi(x_i)^T \qquad (5)$$

The eigenvalue Eq. (6) is now to be solved.

$$\lambda V = C_{NCA} V = \frac{1}{N} \sum_{i=1}^{N} (\Phi(x_i) \cdot V) \Phi(x_i) \qquad (6)$$

where λ is an eigenvalue of C_{NCA} and V is the correspondent eigenvector. $\Phi(x_i)$ is the centered data and C_{NCA} is a positive definite matrix in general. Solutions lie in a span $\Phi(x_i)$, $\Phi(x_2)$, ..., $\Phi(x_N)$ where Φ defines a nonlinear function. The nonlinear kernel function is defined as an inner product in the feature space being denoted as (7).

$$k(x_i, x_j) = <\Phi(x_i), \Phi(x_j)> \qquad (7)$$

NCA has been applied to project data in a higher dimension space to lower dimension space without necessity of explicit mapping. It can even reach infinite-dimensional cases. Without loss of generality, three typical nonlinear kernel functions are selected: Gaussian kernel, Laplace kernel and Cauchy kernel, respectively. The three kernel functions are formulated as (8–10).

$$k_G(x, y) = e^{-\|x-y\|^2/2\sigma^2} \qquad (8)$$

The Gaussian kernel is an exponential kernel in which sigma acts as an adjustable parameter to be set. It depends on the tradeoff between nonlinearity and sensitivity.

$$k_L(x, y) = e^{-\|x-y\|/\sigma} \qquad (9)$$

The Laplace kernel is another exponential kernel in fact. It can suppress sensitivity against the sigma parameter variations.

$$k_C(x, y) = \frac{1}{1 + \|x - y\|^2/\sigma^2} \qquad (10)$$

The Cauchy kernel instead follows the Cauchy distribution. It provides the long-range influence and sensitivity over the high dimensional space. The focus of the article is however to demonstrate feasibility of new NCA engineering practices on the synthetic floc strength study. Details on comparing merits and drawbacks of three typical nonlinear kernels will be discussed in another subsequent article.

4 Numerical Simulations

Numerical simulation results based on the NCA approach are depicted in Fig. 2 to Fig. 7, respectively. The 1st nonlinear principal component (PC1) always represents a coordinate direction with the greatest variation, which is of the maximal variance. The 2nd nonlinear principal component (PC2) represents a direction with the maximal variation still remained in the data which is orthogonal to PC1. The PC3 is orthogonal to both PC1 and PC2, the PC4 is orthogonal to PC1, PC2 and PC3, and so on.

In Fig. 3, the scores (eigenvalues) corresponding to the first 10 nonlinear principal components via kernel NCA have been shown, representing the 10 latent nonlinear factors with strongest correlation to mechanical properties, such as the salinity, pH scale, organic substance, biological matter, mineral precipitate, geometry, and so on. For the natural floc curve tested, the variance of PC1 to PC10 drops gradually but no PC is exceptionally high indicating that the strength of the natural floc depends on a number of factors instead of individual one. On the other hand, up to 6 PCs (PC1 to PC6) could contribute to over 60% of the total data variation. Thus the emphasis should be put on six prevailing factors for the floc strength analysis. It is however unconvincing to claim the superiority list of these factors without the scientific proof. The proposed approach is to adjust the scale of salinity in the synthetic flocs (2 PSU, 10 PSU, 30 PSU) while the natural floc (36 PSU) serves as the reference. PC1 always contributes the most to the variation. Apparently additional variations on PC1 of synthetic flocs (2 PSU, 10 PSU, 30 PSU) come from major changes on salinity, as no other factors differ from those of the natural floc (36 PSU). The largest difference on the scale of salinity also gives rise to the highest mismatch on PC1 between synthetic floc (2 PSU) and natural floc (36 PSU). The PC curves of two synthetic flocs (2 PSU and 10 PSU) are similar while the curve of the synthetic floc (30 PSU) resembles that of the natural floc (36 PSU). Based on data of PC1 to PC5, the curves become sharper when the scale of salinity moves further away from the reference level of the natural floc due to the superior role of salinity on the mechanical behavior. Influential factors might also be intrinsically coupled together, variations of some other PCs could occur accordingly. It depicts evidently that NCA could be successfully applied to the nonlinear floc strength analysis. When changes on some other influential factors are also involved besides the salinity, an identical NCA methodology could be applied while several PCs will be accessed simultaneously to determine the exact priority list among all the corresponding influential factors.

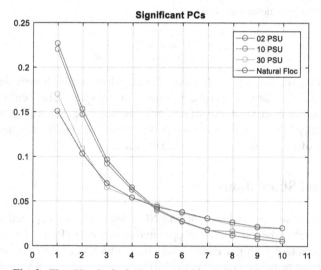

Fig. 3. First 10 principal components via nonlinear kernel PCA

The NCA study also reveals internal correlations among multiple PCs. A simple way is to examine 3 dominating PCs in the 3D plots. Despite of the fact that the nonlinear kernel type selection is out of scope of this work, which acts as another part of future research, the Gaussian kernel, Laplace kernel and Cauchy kernel have all been used so that some differences could be visually observed. In Fig. 4, 3D results (PC1 vs PC2 vs PC3) based on Gaussian kernel and Laplace kernel are quite similar but the 3D result based on Cauchy kernel exhibits a remarkable difference. Higher deviation on scale of salinity being artificial tuned (2 PSU) from that of the natural floc leads to more deterministic curve. The smaller mismatch (30 PSU) leads to more stochastic pattern similar to that of the natural floc. From PC1 to PC3, the variation level will decrease step by step.

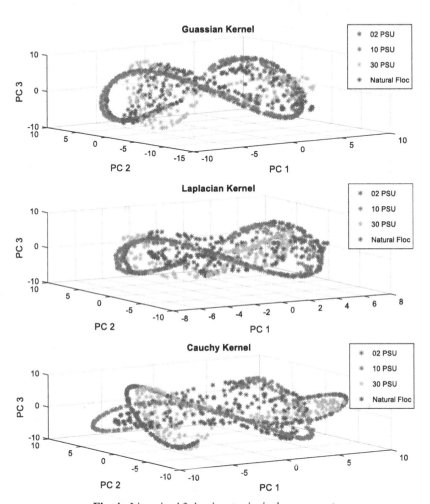

Fig. 4. Linearized 3 dominant principal components

For PC1 to PC6 instead, corresponding to individual constant significant eigenvalues, contour curves can be plotted which represent projection of the principal component vectors onto the 2D plane in the linear space. These contour curves are orthogonal to the corresponding principal component (eigenvector) in fact. For example, contour curves for the synthetic floc (2 PSU) are shown in Fig. 5 and contour curves for the natural floc (36 PSU) are shown in Fig. 6. The unique variations of patterns provide another evidence of the salinity impact on the floc strength.

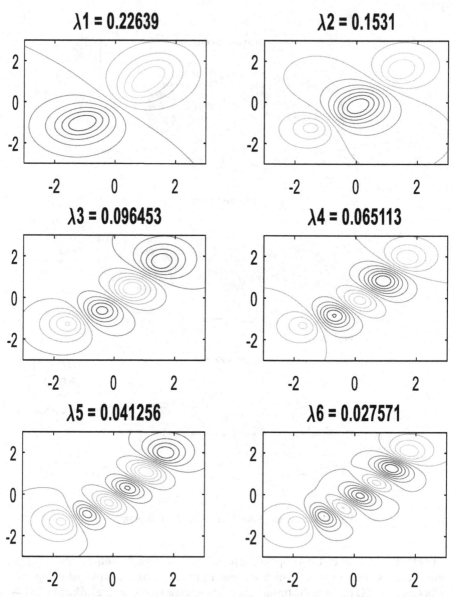

Fig. 5. Projection 2D contours of eigenvectors (PCs) – 2 PSU

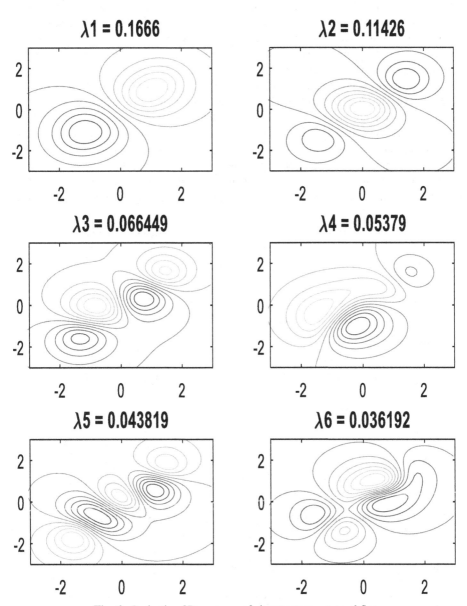

Fig. 6. Projection 2D contours of eigenvectors – natural floc

5   Scatter Plot Analysis

Classification and prediction are two potential and challenging engineering practices for all the research, especially when at least 5 or 6 influential factors are all taken into account. Some interesting results have been obtained by comparing PC1 to PC4 in the 2D scatter plots. The simulation data arise from diverse sets of experimental data at several scales of salinity. The scatter plot is shown in Fig. 7. The first 4 leading PC scores (eigenvalues) are plotted in pair, such as PC1 vs PC2, PC1 vs PC3, and PC3 vs PC4. It could be extended to more complex cases of arbitrary number of factors with no extra technical effort at all. From Fig. 7, four sets of data of synthetic flocs (2 PSU, 10 PSU, 30 PSU) and natural floc (36 PSU) can be distinguished clearly in each of 6 plots. Each set of data could be grouped as a single cluster. The distance between any 2 clusters also reflect the mismatch on the scale of salinity. With large amount of data, classification can be easily made using NCA and scatter plots immediately. Meanwhile without the priori hypotheses needed, some future on-site sample data can be analyzed directly and quickly

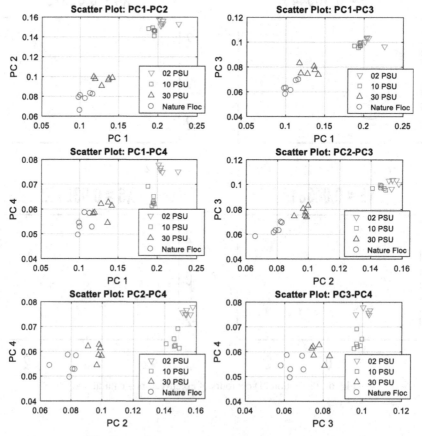

Fig. 7. Nonlinear component analysis - scatter plots

via the proposed NCA approach, possibly in real time, so that the range of influential factors (e.g. salinity) will be determined for accurate model prediction instantly.

6   Conclusions

A reliable nonlinear multivariate approach has been presented to characterize the deformation mechanism of flocculation in this preliminary study, where the reachable scale of salinity has been deliberately used as the first principal component on the synthetic floc strength research. Comparisons on mechanical properties between the natural floc strength and synthetic floc strength at different salinity scales have been made. Among a plenty of variables that actually affect the mechanical property of flocs, a number of controlling factors with strong correlation should be captured for classification and redundancy removal. Experimental methods are obviously lengthy, burdensome and costly. Nonlinear component analysis instead has the capability of significant dimensionality reduction for nonlinear problems in the high dimensional space. Thus some powerful parameters in the low dimensional linear space are used to manifest the physical phenomena occurred in the high dimensional nonlinear space. Impact of salinity scale variations on the floc strength has been explored which has verified the feasibility of the NCA methodology. Interesting results from scatter plots are helpful for both classification and prediction purposes potentially. The proposed approach can be extended to the highly nonlinear cases at the large dimensional space in a straightforward way.

References

1. Shainberg, I., Levy, G.: Flocculation and dispersion. In: Encyclopedia of Soils in the Environment, pp. 27–34. Elsevier Ltd (2005)
2. Theng, B.K.G.: Formation and Properties of Clay-Polymer Complexes, vol. 4, 2nd edn, p. 511. Elsevier, Amsterdam (2012)
3. Yin, H., Zhang, G.: Nanoindentation behavior of muscovite subjected to repeated loading. ASME J. Nanomech. Micromech. 1(2), 72–83 (2011)
4. Yin, H., Zhang, G.: Cyclic nanoindentation shakedown of muscovite and its elastic modulus measurement. In: Proulx, T. (ed.) Proceedings of the Society for Experimental Mechanics Series, MEMS and Nanotechnology, Proceedings of Annual Conference on Experimental and Applied Mechanics, vol. 4, pp. 83–92. Springer, New York (2011). https://doi.org/10. 1007/978-1-4614-0210-7_12
5. Dawes, L., Goonetilleke, A.: Using multivariate analysis to predict the behaviour of soils under effluent irrigation. Water Air Soil Pollut. 172(1–4), 109–127 (2006). https://doi.org/10. 1007/s11270-005-9064-z
6. Stoffels, N., Sircoulomb, V., Hermand, G., Hoblos, G.: Principal component analysis for fault detection and structure health monitoring. In: 7th European Workshop on Structural Health Monitoring, 8–11 July 2014, Nantes, France, pp. 1751–1758 (2014)
7. Arabzadeh, R., Kholoosi, M., Bazrafshan, J.: Regional hydrological drought monitoring using principal components analysis. ASCE J. Irrig. Drain. Eng. 142(1), 20 (2016)
8. Yulianti, M., Sudriani, Y., Rustini, H.: Preliminary study of soil permeability properties using principal component analysis. In: IOP Conference Series: Earth and Environmental Science, vol. 118, pp. 1–5 (2018)

9. Ye, Z.: Artificial intelligence approach for biomedical sample characterization using raman spectroscopy. IEEE Trans. Autom. Sci. Eng. **2**(1), 67–73 (2005)
10. Schölkopf, B., Smola, A., Müller, K.: Nonlinear component analysis as a kernel eigenvalue problem. Neural Comput. **10**(5), 1299–1319 (1998)
11. Ye, Z., Mohamadian, H., Ye, Y.: Independent component analysis for spatial object recognition with applications of information theory. In: Proceedings of IEEE World Congress on Computational Intelligence, Hong Kong, pp. 3640–3645, 1–6 June 2008

Recurrence Plot Representation for Multivariate Time-Series Analysis

Dennys Mallqui$^{(\boxtimes)}$ and Ricardo A. S. Fernandes

Federal University of São Carlos, São Carlos, SP 1355-905, Brazil
dennys.mallqui@gmail.com, ricardo.asf@ufscar.br

Abstract. The analysis of time-series is a productive field, which is applied in different areas such as finance, bio-medicine, neurology, among others. However, one of the main challenges is the identification of non-linear patterns. Thus, the apparent chaotic behavior of a time-series can mean the manifestation of a dynamic system. Often, these phenomena are recurrent, meaning that certain regions of their available state space are frequently visited along of time. For this reason, the use of recurrence plots (RPs) and Recurrent Quantification Analysis (RQA) are used to extract features of time series that allow their better understanding and facilitate prediction tasks (classification, regression and novelty detection). However, to successfully apply this transformation in the aforementioned tasks, it is necessary to obtain the best combination of three parameters: time lag (τ), embedding dimension (m) and recurrence rate (RR). In other studies to find these parameters it is necessary to apply the prediction process for each possible combination, which represents a high computational cost. We propose to use a measure that seeks to maximize the entropy with the lowest possible randomness to calculate $RP_{[\tau,m,RR]}$ before the application of the prediction. In this way, reduce the computational complexity, where we initially validate these claims using Bitcoin's multidimensional time-series, with results that surpass the accuracy of previous studies.

Keywords: Recurrence plot · Recurrent Quantification Analysis · Time series · Chaos theory · Multivariate classification · Bitcoin

1 Introduction

The analysis of time-series for pattern recognition is an important field of research, which is applied in different fields of study such as financial data, biomedical signals, music mining and so on. Thus, the analysis tasks can be grouped into curve fitting or function approximation, forecasting, segmentation or classification and clustering as is detailed in [16]. One of the challenges encountered in the treatment of time-series is the identification of non-linear patterns, which are present in dynamic systems or stochastic processes [6,12,16].

This work has been supported/funded by KPiQa and Xertica companies.

© Springer Nature Switzerland AG 2020
J. A. Lossio-Ventura et al. (Eds.): SIMBig 2019, CCIS 1070, pp. 21–34, 2020.
https://doi.org/10.1007/978-3-030-46140-9_3

Often, these phenomena are recurrent, meaning that certain regions of their available state space are frequently visited along of time [6].

Recurrence plots (RPs) and Recurrent Quantification Analysis (RQA) are tools of analysis of data that was initially introduced to understand the behavior of a dynamical system in phase space [27]. In recent studies [6,7,12,16–18] these methods have been used with success to study patterns in the dynamics of a time-series system. According [9] it is possible to calculate the phase-space representation of a time-series X_t using a time lag or delay (τ) and embedding dimension (m) by computing the Delay Vectors (DVs) described in Eq. 1.

$$DV(i) = [X_{i\text{-}m.\tau}, X_{i\text{-}(m\text{-}1).\tau}, ..., X_{i\text{-}\tau}] \tag{1}$$

In this sense, the recurrence plots can be calculated by considering the Eq. 2, such as defined by [18]:

$$RP_{i,j} = \begin{cases} 1, & \|DV(i) - DV(j)\| \leq \varepsilon \\ 0, & otherwise \end{cases} \tag{2}$$

where ε is the distance metric threshold of two sampling points $DV(i)$, $DV(j)$. After that, the percentage of recurrence or recurrence rate (RR) is defined as a percentage of points where the distance function is less than ε between the total points. Thus, it is possible to represent the RP as three parameters $RP_{[\tau,m,RR]}$.

The application of RP presents high complexity when working with multivariate time-series, since the function of similarity between the embedded vectors can be complex to calculate. Also, an open problem is the identification of the most appropriate values of $RP_{[\tau,m,RR]}$ for time-series analysis (univariate and multivariate).

RP matrix exhibits global characteristic (typology) and local patterns (texture) as is mentioned in [16]. In the same study, the authors claims, that texture component is formed by single dots, diagonal lines as well as vertical and horizontal lines (using graphic information), while typology information which is characterized as homogeneous, periodic, drift and disrupted (using RQA measures). Thus, from the generated components, it is possible to analyze them to identify the inherent patterns in time series with chaotic behavior.

For instance, in [17] is used RP for image representation from multivariate time-series and using Convolutional Neural Networks (CNN) for identify patterns. In a similar study, [10] conduct an experiment for classification of DNA sequences where multivariate time-series are transformed in images by RP matrix and applied fractal dimensions (FD) for pattern detection. In other studies [2,9,18], the authors use RQA measures for novelty detection and drift signal identification. In addition, the RQA measures such as determinism (DET), laminarity (LAM) and DIV (1/Maximum length of diagonals) help to detection of change or classification. There are studies that propose the use of other measures to extract nonlinear patterns more efficiently in time-series. Thus, in [12] the authors used the Hotelling T^2 statistic for detection of dynamic transitions and compared to the use of RQA traditional measures. After that, in [7], it is proposed a Principal Singular Value Proportion (PSVP) measure to detect the complexity and periodicity of systems.

Although the use of texture analysis and typology have presented success in the above-mentioned studies, a serious problem still exists, which is the computational cost. This is because, for calculate RP matrix ($RP_{[\tau,m,RR]}$) is necessary to select adequately time lag or delay (τ), embedding dimension (m) and recurrence rate (RR). In [14], it is used minimum of the time-delayed mutual information as a reasonable value for τ and, in [8], it is selected the minimum embedding dimension m based on the false nearest neighbor algorithm. However, these methods were proposed for univariate time-series, with which the discussion of their obtaining in multivariate signals is still open. For this reason, studies in which predictions are made from the extracted RP and RQA features, iterate to find the optimal $RP_{[\tau,m,RR]}$ [6,7,16,17], which implies a high computational cost.

Based on the context previously presented, this study seeks to focus on feature extraction for multivariate time-series using RP and RQA transformation, where a novel methodology will be sought to obtain the most appropriate values of delay (τ), embedding dimension (m) and recurrence rate (RR) for RP matrix calculation ($RP_{[\tau,m,RR]}$) without the need to iterate in the application of predictions, reducing the computational cost of this set of methods. For this, we propose to use a novel RQA measure that seeks to maximize the entropy with the lowest possible randomness inspired by [3]. Finally, once RP matrix is generated and the extraction of features is realized, we will proceed with the application of machine learning models for the identification of patterns on the transformed data and evaluate their contribution to tasks of classification using a Bitcoin time-series study conducted by the authors previously [23].

2   Experiment

An overview of the methodology is presented in Fig. 2, where the following steps are shown: (a) preparation and partition of the data set of the Bitcoin multivariate time-series; (b) unsupervised features extraction using the RQA measures generated from RP matrix calculation using the proposed method; (c) training a machine learning model using the transformed data and; (d) results evaluation and comparison with other studies (Fig. 1).

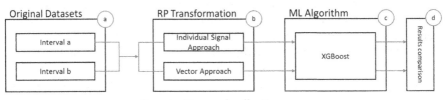

Source: Personal collection.

Fig. 1. Methodology overview

2.1 Data Collected

A set of real-world multivariate time-series data was selected to validate the effectiveness of the proposed methodology. Thus, in this preliminary phase, it was selected the case study of Bitcoin trend prediction (daily exchange rate against US dollar). For traders or general users, the greatest challenge is the Bitcoin exchange rate volatility. Thus, as mentioned by [29] and [19], in comparison with the traditional currencies, the Bitcoin presents a volatility approximately twice greater referring to its value of exchange rate. For example, Fig. 2 shows a comparison between the price volatility of the Bitcoin and the gold. However, as mentioned by [1], the author claims that the volatility of Bitcoin can not be a reason that invalidates it as a currency, but it is a motivation for users to seek solutions to reduce their risk [23].

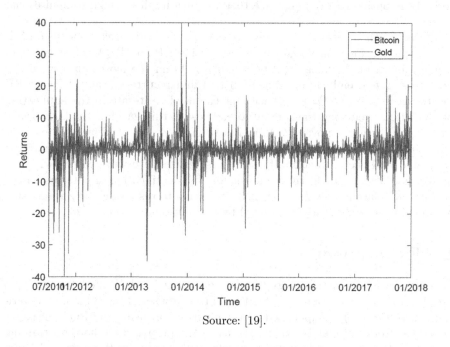

Source: [19].

Fig. 2. Daily return series of Gold and Bitcoin (2012–2018)

The sorts of information can be categorized into *internal* (Bitcoin historical transaction data) and *external* (international economic factors or public recognition). Thus, in the data sets are considered Blockchain information (*internal*) that potentially includes Open, High, Low and Close (OHLC) Bitcoin prices, the volume of trades, total transaction fees, number of transactions, cost per transaction and average hash rate (measure about level of transaction peaks), as suggested by [4,25]. As *external* information are considered international economic indicators where several possible indicators were analyzed, such as crude oil future prices, gold future prices, S&P500 future, NASDAQ future and DAX index [28]. In addition, it was considered public recognition data extracted from Google Trends and Wikipedia Searches, as used by [13,20,21]. Finally, using *internal* data was constructed technical indicators commonly used by traders, as proposed by [26].

2.2 Data Partition

Such as used in [23], it is considered two data sets: (i) from 2013 to 2016 (named as *interval a* with 1066 instances), which considers 80%/20% for training/test; and (ii) from 2013 to 2017 (named as *interval b* with 1462 instances), which considers 75%/25% for training/test.

2.3 Attribute Selection

It is considered the same attributes used on a previous study published by the authors [23]. Thus, in addition to technical indicators (Table 1) is included the most relevant attributes from Blockchain (Tables 2 and 3), Economic indices (Table 4) and Social trends (Table 5) through information gain score.

Table 1. Attribute selection - technical indicators for interval a and b

Attribute	Details
OBV	On Balance Volume: $OBV_t = OBV_{t-1} + \theta \times V_t$
SMA_5	Simple Moving Average: $SMA_5 = (\sum_{i=1}^{5} C_{t-i+1}/5)$
$BIAS_6$	Average deviation: $BIAS_6 = (\frac{C_t - SMA_6}{SMA_6}) \times 100$
PSY_{12}	Psychological Line: $PSY_{12} = (A/12) \times 100$
ASY_5	Average of return (5 days): $ASY_5 = (\sum_{i=1}^{5} ASY_{t-i+1})/5$
ASY_4	Average of return (4 days): $ASY_4 = (\sum_{i=1}^{4} ASY_{t-i+1})/4$
ASY_3	Average of return (3 days): $ASY_3 = (\sum_{i=1}^{3} ASY_{t-i+1})/3$
ASY_2	Average of return (2 days): $ASY_2 = (\sum_{i=1}^{2} ASY_{t-i+1})/2$
ASY_1	Average of return (1 days): $ASY_1 = ASY_{t-1}$
Open. Price	Opening price in the same day of prediction

Source: Personal collection.

In these tables, V_t is the volume of trade of the Bitcoin at time t, θ is a step function, A is the number of rising days in the last n days, and WMA represent Weight Moving Average.

Finally, it was obtained the multivariate time-series with 19 attributes for trend prediction of daily Bitcoin exchange rate (classification task). In the following sections, it will be detailed two approaches that have been applied to extract the features of multivariate time-series.

Table 2. Attribute selection - blockchain data for interval a

Attribute	Details
Transaction fees $D-2$	Voluntary fees paid by users to miners with time lag of 2 days
Hash rate average $D-2$	Average daily hash rate with time lag of 2 days
Minimum Price $D-5$	Minimum daily exchange rate with time lag of 5 days
Hash rate average $D-7$	Average daily hash rate with time lag of 7 days
Number of trx $30-Day\ WMA$	WMA of number of transactions in last 30 days

Source: Personal collection.

Table 3. Attribute selection - blockchain data for interval b

Attribute	Details
Maximum Price $D-5$	Maximum daily exchange rate with time lag of 5 days
Minimum Price $D-5$	Minimum daily exchange rate with time lag of 5 days
Closing Price $D-5$	Closing daily exchange rate with time lag of 5 days
Volume of trades $D-5$	Volume of exchange transaction with time lag o 5 days
Hash rate avg $30-Day\ WMA$	WMA of daily hash rate average in last 30 days

Source: Personal collection.

Table 4. Attribute selection - economic indicators for interval a and b

Attribute	Details
DAX index $30-Day\ WMA$	WMA of daily DAX index price in last 30 days

Source: Personal collection.

Table 5. Attribute selection - public recognition for Interval a and b

Attribute	Details
Google trends $W-4$	Google trend score with time lag of 4 weeks
Wikipedia trends $D-1$	Number of Wikipedia searches with time lag of 1 day
Wikipedia trends $30-Day\ WMA$	WMA of Wikipedia searches in last 30 days

Source: Personal collection.

2.4   RQA Transformation - Individual Signal Approach

In this stage, the approach to the treatment of multivariate time series is to individually analyze each of the signals that comprise it, generating for each one its corresponding RP and from it extracting RQA measurements that will finally be used for classification tasks. First, a time window is determined to create segments of each of the signals in isolation, each segment is calculated every 7 days (time step) considering a time window of 120 days backwards (window time). In each segment, the most suitable delay (τ) value is calculated from the method proposed by [14]. Then, Figs. 3 and 4 show the distribution of the optimal τ values for each attribute, where it was select the average value represented by the 50th percentile in each case.

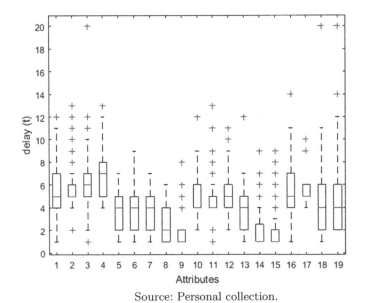

Source: Personal collection.

Fig. 3. Optimal delay (τ) selection – interval a

As a next step, to obtain the most appropriate value of embedding dimension (m) and threshold (ε) for appropriate recurrence rate (RR), is proposed a novelty measure inspired by [3]. As mentioned by [24] the concept of entropy contains a concept of disorder, with which in consideration of the authors, it is sought to obtain the recurrent structure that presents a greater quantity of possible variations so that this allows to have more possibilities of identification of patterns. At this point, the proposed indicator is positively related to the amount of entropy that is detected by the RP matrix generated from a segment of the time-series. However, the exaggerated disorder can mean a randomness in the data which would invalidate any subsequent attempt to extract patterns in

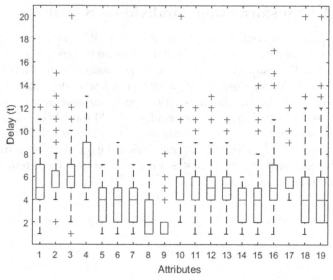

Source: Personal collection.

Fig. 4. Optimal delay (τ) selection – interval b

them. The indicator should be negatively related to the amount of randomness and, for this purpose, it will be used such as proposed by [7] (Principal Singular Value Proportion – PSVP). As mentioned by [3], in the arts, the most successful works of Abstract Expressionism show a random distribution of spray and splash pigment controlled by the artist's sense of visual order. Therefore, the Eq. 3 tries to measure the balance between the amount of information or the disorder and order, therefore, we proposed the name of the measure as the Art Score (AS).

$$AS = \frac{ShannonEntropy}{PSVPscore} \qquad (3)$$

In addition, with the same segmentation to obtain the optimal delay, it is used to test combinations of embedding dimension (m: 1, 2, ..., 10) and recurrent rate (RR: 5%, 10%, ..., 25%) in order to obtain the highest AS value and, consequently, the optimal threshold (ε), as shown in Figs. 5 and 6 for OBV attribute.

In Fig. 5, the best result of AS in *interval a* is obtained by combination 5 ($m = 1$ and $RR = 25\%$). In a similar way, for *interval b*, the best result was obtained with the combination 5 ($m = 1$ and $RR = 25\%$). In summary, for each signal, it is tested multiple combinations of delay (τ), embedding dimension (m) and recurrence rate (RR) values as show in Table 6.

After that, with optimal τ, m and RR values, the RP matrix is calculated (best $RP_{[\tau,m,RR]}$) for each signal. Then, it is generated seven RQA measures for each one: recurrent rate (RR), determinism (DET), L average (Lavg), L maximum (Lmax), laminarity (LAM), transitivity (Trs) and PSVP.

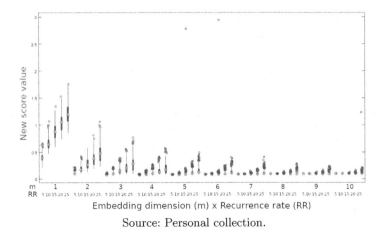

Source: Personal collection.

Fig. 5. Embedding dimension (m) and recurrent rate (RR) – OBV (interval a)

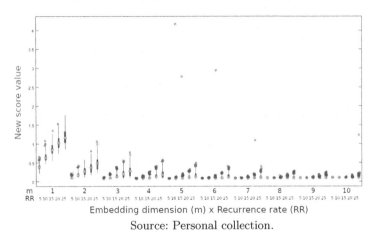

Source: Personal collection.

Fig. 6. Embedding dimension (m) and recurrent rate (RR) – OBV (interval b)

Table 6. Hyper-parameter combinations – recurrence matrix

Parameter	Values tested
Delay (τ)	1, 2, ..., 5
Embedding dimension (m)	1, 2, ..., 10
Recurrence rate (RR)	5%, 10%, ..., 25%

Source: Personal collection.

Because 133 variables are obtained in the individual processing of each of the 19 signals (19 × 7 features), which will be used for the algorithm proposed by [11], XGBoost. Thus, a selection is made based on the importance score obtained by the model, using cross-validation method (10 folds). As a result, 38 features are selected for *interval a* and 45 features are selected for *interval b*.

2.5   RQA Transformation - Vector Approach

As proposed by [5], it was used the *vector recurrence* concept. In the Eq. 2, $DV(i)$ and $DV(j)$ are d-dimensional vectors and the norm in R^d of vector difference is calculated. In addition, it is possible to consider any sort of norm in R^d like Euclidean or Mahalanobis distance. Thus, for this experiment, Euclidean norm is used with the same combinations presented in Table 6.

Once the optimal parameters for RP matrix ($RP_{[\tau,m,RR]}$) calculation have been determined, the corresponding matrix is generated and the following RQA measurements are extracted 14 features: recurrence rate (RR), determinism (DET), average diagonal length, maximum diagonal length, laminarity (LAM), transitivity (Trs), PSVP, diagonal entropy, average vertical length, maximum vertical length, average white vertical length, maximum white vertical length, global clustering and assortativity.

Finally, the information is compressed from 19 attributes to 14 attributes for *interval a* and *interval b*

3   Machine Learning Algorithm

Because for the individual transformation approach it was necessary to use XGBoost to obtain the ranking of the features and in order to compare both approaches, the algorithm proposed by [11] was used to generate the predictive models. In addition, the results of previous studies [22] were added using the original time-series (19 attributes), where the models used are based on Artificial Neural Networks (with prefix "*nn*") and Support Vector Machines (with prefix "*svm*").

4   Results

In order to validate the prediction capacity of the unsupervised transformations, the Area Under the ROC Curve (AUC) metric is used as proposed by [15]. Thus, the values obtained by individual approach detailed in Sect. 2.4 (with prefix "*gbm_individual*") and vector approach mentioned in Sect. 2.5 (with prefix "*gbm_vector*") are compared.

In addition, all stochastic classification models were executed 50 times and, in Figs. 7 and 8, are shown the average results obtained for *interval a* and *interval b*, respectively.

Finally, in *interval a* the best result is obtained by *individual approach* and in *interval b* the best score is presented by *vector approach*, where both proposed methods in present study surpass previous results.

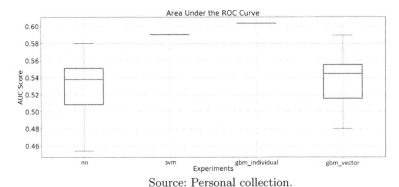

Source: Personal collection.

Fig. 7. Classification performance – AUC score (interval a)

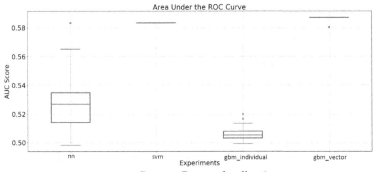

Source: Personal collection.

Fig. 8. Classification Performance – AUC score (interval b)

5   Conclusions and Future Research

The use of the proposed measure can improve the identification of patterns in time series, extracting characteristics in an unsupervised way, improving the results in the classification tasks and at the same time reducing the computational cost presented in previous studies. Therefore, we can infer that it is possible to use these transformations for future experiments that encompass tasks of identification of change of concept, regression and clustering.

Likewise, in addition to the transformations that use typology information (RQA measures), we consider that there is a great opportunity to take advantage of the texture features (RP images) due to its expressiveness to expose patterns in the signals as shown in Fig. 9. Moreover, they could eventually improve the results obtained for the Bitcoin time-series and others in general as postulated by [17].

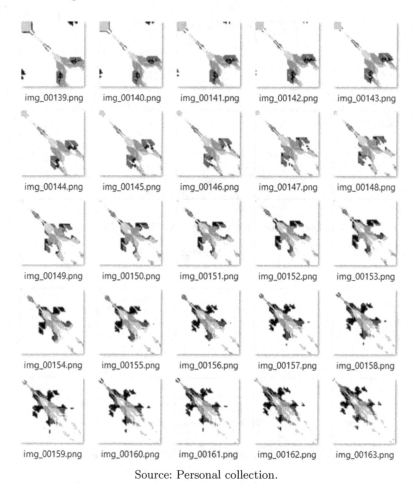

Source: Personal collection.

Fig. 9. RP Texture RGB – Slide windows of 120-90-60 days (interval b segment)

References

1. van Alstyne, M.: Why Bitcoin has value. Commun. ACM **57**(5), 30–32 (2014)
2. Altmann, E.G., Kantz, H.: Recurrence time analysis, long-term correlations, and extreme events. Phys. Rev. E **71**(5), 056106 (2005)
3. Arnheim, R.: Entropy and Art: An Essay on Disorder and Order. University of California Press, California (1974)
4. Balcilar, M., Bouri, E., Gupta, R., Roubaud, D.: Can volume predict bitcoin returns and volatility? A quantiles-based approach. Econ. Model. **64**, 74–81 (2017)
5. Bandt, C., et al.: Analysis of bivariate coupling by means of recurrence. In: Dahlhaus, R., Kurths, J., Maass, P., Timmer, J. (eds.) Mathematical Methods in Signal Processing and Digital Image Analysis. Understanding Complex Systems. Springer, Heidelberg (2008)

6. Beim Graben, P., Sellers, K.K., Fröhlich, F., Hutt, A.: Optimal estimation of recurrence structures from time series. EPL **114**(3), 38003 (2016)
7. Bian, S., Shang, P.: Recurrence quantity analysis based on singular value decomposition. Commun. Nonlinear Sci. Numer. Simul. **46**, 1–13 (2017)
8. Cao, L.: Practical method for determining the minimum embedding dimension of a scalar time series. Physica D **110**(1–2), 43–50 (1997)
9. Carrión, A., Miralles, R.: New insights for testing linearity and complexity with surrogates: a recurrence plot approach. In: Webber, C.L., Ioana, C., Marwan, N. (eds.) Recurrence Plots and Their Quantifications: Expanding Horizons. SPP, vol. 180, pp. 91–112. Springer, Cham (2016). https://doi.org/10.1007/978-3-319-29922-8_5
10. Cattani, C., Pierro, G., Cattani, C., Pierro, G.: On the fractal geometry of DNA by the binary image analysis. Bull. Math. Biol. **75**(9), 1544–1570 (2013)
11. Chen, T., Guestrin, C.: Xgboost: A scalable tree boosting system. In: Proceedings of the 22nd ACM SIGKDD International Conference on Knowledge Discovery and Data Mining, pp. 785–794. ACM (2016)
12. Chen, Y., Yang, H.: Multiscale recurrence analysis of long-term nonlinear and nonstationary time series. Chaos, Solitons Fractals **45**(7), 978–987 (2012)
13. Ciaian, P., Rajcaniova, M.: d'Artis Kancs: the economics of Bitcoin price formation. Appl. Econ. **48**(19), 1799–1815 (2016)
14. Fraser, A.M., Swinney, H.L.: Independent coordinates for strange attractors from mutual information. Phys. Rev. A **33**(2), 1134 (1986)
15. Hanley, J.A., McNeil, B.J.: The meaning and use of the area under a receiver operating characteristic (ROC) curve. Radiology **143**(1), 29–36 (1982)
16. Hatami, N., Gavet, Y., Debayle, J.: Bag of recurrence patterns representation for time-series classification. Pattern Anal. Appl. **22**(3), 877–887 (2018). https://doi.org/10.1007/s10044-018-0703-6
17. Hatami, N., Gavet, Y., Debayle, J.: Classification of time-series images using deep convolutional neural networks (2018)
18. Hu, M.I.N., Zhou, S., Wei, J., Deng, Y., Qu, W.: Change-point detection in multivariate time-series data by recurrence. WSEAS Trans. Comput. **13**, 592–599 (2014). Plot 2 Related Works 3 Problem Formulation
19. Klein, T., Pham Thu, H., Walther, T.: Bitcoin is not the new gold – a comparison of volatility, correlation, and portfolio performance. Int. Rev. Financ. Anal. **59**, 105–116 (2018)
20. Kristoufek, L.: BitCoin meets Google Trends and Wikipedia: quantifying the relationship between phenomena of the Internet era. Sci. Rep. **3**, 1–7 (2013)
21. Li, X., Wang, C.A.: The technology and economic determinants of cryptocurrency exchange rates: the case of Bitcoin. Decis. Support Syst. **95**, 49–60 (2017)
22. Mallqui, D.: Predicting the direction, maximum, minimum and closing price of daily/Intra-daily bitcoin exchange rate using batch and online machine learning techniques. Master's thesis, Universidade Federal de São Carlos (2018)
23. Mallqui, D., Fernandes, R.: Predicting the direction, maximum, minimum and closing prices of daily Bitcoin exchange rate using machine learning techniques. Appl. Soft Comput. **75**, 596–606 (2018). https://doi.org/10.1016/j.asoc.2018.11.038
24. Marcolli, M.: Entropy and Art: the view beyond Arnheim (2015). http://www.its.caltech.edu/~matilde/SlidesEntropyArt.pdf
25. Mcnally, S.: Predicting the price of Bitcoin using Machine Learning. Ph.D. thesis, National College of Ireland (2016)
26. Qiu, M., Song, Y.: Predicting the direction of stock market index movement using an optimized artificial neural network model. PLoS ONE **11**(5), 1–11 (2016)

27. Romano, M.C., Thiel, M., Kurths, J., Von Bloh, W.: Multivariate recurrence plots. Phys. Lett. **330**(3–4), 214–223 (2004)
28. Vassiliadis, S., Papadopoulos, P., Rangoussi, M., Konieczny, T., Gralewski, J.: Bitcoin value analysis based on cross-correlations. J. Internet Bank. Commer. **22**(S7), 1 (2017)
29. Yermack, D.: Is Bitcoin a real currency? An economic appraisal. National Bureau of Economic Research (NBER) Working Papers 19747 (2013)

Detecting Anomalies in Time-Varying Media Crime News Using Tensor Decomposition

Hugo Alatrista-Salas[(⊠)], Pablo Lavado, Juandiego Morzan,
Miguel Nuñez-del-Prado, and Gustavo Yamada

Universidad del Pacífico, Av. Salaverry 2020, Lima, Peru
{h.alatristas,p.lavadopadilla,j.morzans,m.nunezdelpradoc,
yamada_ga}@up.edu.pe

Abstract. Nowadays, the mass media surround us in many forms. Newspapers, radio and TV reports about many topics, including the crime committed in a region. Indirectly, the media provide statistics about crime incidents, and policymakers could focus their attention on the unusual number of crime news (*c.f.*, regular events) for evaluating and proposing new public policies. In the present work, the Tensor decomposition is used to detect an unusual amount of crime news. To achieve this goal, two rejection criterion techniques were compared. Also, several image binarization techniques were used to validate our proposal. Our result can be used to detect an unusual amount of crime news as a proxy of unusual crime activity.

Keywords: Tensor decomposition · Event detection · Crime

1 Introduction

Crime is a worldwide concern. For instance, the United Nations makes reports about crime tends through his United Nations Office on Drugs and Crime agency[1]. There are also independent global initiatives to report crime statistics, *e.g.*, Numbeo[2] is an independent organization not influenced by any governmental organization, which produces a crime index based on citizens surveys. The drawback of these studies and reports is the number of resources that organizations must concentrate to obtain data for processing it and make these reports. However, media continuously reports - through newspapers, radio and TV - about crime incidents, which can be used as a source of information to build crime statistics. Some works are highlighting and communicating the interest, as well as, the importance of data mining techniques for crime analysis [2,6,11]. Accordingly, data analytics is a handy option to extract knowledge from data for facilitating police work, saving money and time costs.

---

[1] http://www.unodc.org/.

[2] www.numbeo.com.

© Springer Nature Switzerland AG 2020
J. A. Lossio-Ventura et al. (Eds.): SIMBig 2019, CCIS 1070, pp. 35–45, 2020.
https://doi.org/10.1007/978-3-030-46140-9_4

In this respect, governments are interested in analyzing peak crime statistics, which are not typical. Therefore, anomaly detection is defined as the process of detecting patterns in data that do not follow expected behaviour. Popular anomaly detection techniques rely on spectral methods, which project high dimensional data onto a lower subspace where unusual occurrences are evident. Nevertheless, much data presents a multiway structure not accounted for this task. Thus, anomalies may appear imperceptible while using traditional techniques [5]. Hence, tensor-based solutions for anomaly detection appear showing better performance in real case studies [4].

In the present effort, several characteristics of newspapers, radio and TV news were analyzed through a tensor decomposition. Later, to detect the abnormal presence of crime news, a rejection-criterion measure based on Median Absolute Deviation (MAD) was proposed. Later, we compare our proposal with a standard measure based on mean/std.dev. Finally, to validate the anomaly detection, several image binarization techniques, were compared with our proposal.

The present work is organized as follows: Sect. 2 describes related works, while Sect. 3 introduces the proposed methodology. Then, Sect. 4 outlines our experiments on a crime news dataset. Finally, Sect. 5 concludes this work and proposes new research avenues.

2   Related Works

We have found in the literature some efforts to deal with crime information extraction. For instance, Chen *et al.* [2] propose a data mining framework for the identification of five different types of entities: people names, addresses, vehicles, narcotics names and physical features. In the first place, they use linguistic rules to identify noun phrases. In the second place, a set of feature scores were computed for the expressions using pattern matching and lexical look up. Finally, they predict the entity type for each phrase based on a feedforward/backpropagation neural network. This approach proves to have a better identification for a person (74.1%) and narcotics names (85.4%) while having lower scores for addresses (59.6%) and personal properties (46.8%).

Hassani *et al.* [6] review different applications of data mining in crime, finding relevance in the development of crime over time and the role that data mining can play in the analysis, detection, and prevention of crime. For instance, extraction of valuable information from unstructured data, crime hot spots detection, link crime incidents, detection of specific criminal activities, and even detection of criminal networks. To achieve these purposes, authors describe specific tasks such as entity extraction, clustering, classification association rule mining and social network analysis. Consequently, to accomplish these tasks, they discuss algorithms such as Decision Trees, Support Vector Machines, Naive Bayes Rule, Neural Networks. They found that in different data mining applications, classification techniques are the most popular, where algorithms such as SVM and Neural Networks are often the typical choice.

Concerning the use of tensors, Mu et al. [11] argue that Tensor analysis is the result of new computing processing capabilities never seen before, which enable us to analyse and mine high data volumes. He describes different domain applications for Tensor factorisation and decomposition. The Tensor application ranges from Psychology, chemistry, neuroscience, signal processing, bioinformatics, computer vision and web mining. In a particular domain, Mu *et al.* [11] propose an Empirical Discriminative Tensor Analysis to forecast crime incidents in Northern city. The basic idea of this method is to combine several four-order tensors containing latitude, longitude, time and other characteristics, such as residential burglary, social events, offenders data, etc. Then, authors compare three different techniques based on four-order tensor namely (1) Empirical Discriminative Tensor Analysis (*EDTA*), (2) three-way discriminative locality alignment (*TWDLA*), and (3) Offline Tensor Analysis (*OTA*). Authors used geo-referenced data from 2016 - divided in 20×20 grid cells to represent the whole studied area in Boston - to predict crime in 2017. Finally, the authors show that ETDA outperforms other methods.

In the present effort, we rely on Tucker decomposition over a 3-dimension tensor to represent the textual information about crimes extracted from newspapers, radio and television to detect anomalous abnormal of crime news.

3 Methodology

This subsection describes the methodology followed to measure media influence on the population's crime perception. Five main stages are proposed:

1. Dataset acquisition: for this effort, a dataset containing about 262 000 crime news was built. This dataset contains the descriptions and other attributes of interest (*e.g.*, type of crime, the monetary cost of the news, total audience reached by the news) from a set of crime-related news published in Spanish between the years 2013 and 2017 in Peru. A more extensive dataset description is provided in Table 1. This dataset was provided by the iMedia company[3].

2. Data Pre-processing: regarding the pre-process, three tasks were performed: Data Scaling, Grouping, and Label Encoding. For the *Data Scaling* task, we rely on Min-Max Scaling [4]. In this case, each attribute is scaled separately, and their values are transformed to a scale between 0 and 1. Once attributes are on the same scale, regarding the *grouping* task, those variables sharing the same meaning are grouped. Finally, for *Label Encoding*, textual labels variables are coded with discrete values.

3. Tensor Model: for tensor processing, we use a three-mode tensor containing media source dimension, crime news characteristics and temporal component. Then, Tucker Decomposition [8] is applied to obtain three 1-rank latent components. In our case, the temporal component is analysed, since we seek to detect anomalies in those days in which a vast amount of criminal news is generated. More specifically, variables are grouped into three dimensions: (1)

---

[3] iMedia framework: http://www.iMedia.pe/monitoreo-medios-tradicionales.

Table 1. Crime dataset description

Variable	Description	Data type
Crime	The type of crime the news talks about	String
	Namely, theft, threats, abuse, sexual offense, kidnap, extortion or fraud	
Duration	The amount of time (in seconds) taken to address the news on air	Integer
	For radio and tv news format only	
Surface	The total surface the news occupies in the newspaper	Float
	For written press only	
Page	The page number in which the news is located in the newspaper	String
	For written press only	
Height	The height of the news article in the newspaper	Float
	For written press only	
Width	The width of the news article in the newspaper	Float
	For written press only	
Press section	The newspaper section in which the news is located	String
	For written press only	
Title	The title of the news	String
News format	The type of format in which the news is delivered	String
	Namely written press, tv or radio	
Valuation	The economic cost of publishing or delivering the news	Float
Audience	The amount of people to who received the news	Integer
Text	The textual description or transcription of the news	String
Media source	The media source in which the news is published or delivered	String
Date	The date in which the news was published or delivered	Date

temporal dimension; (2) media source dimension (newspapers, radio and TV); and, (3) characteristics dimension, namely crime, surface, seconds, valuation, sentiment, and news format (c.f., Fig. 1).

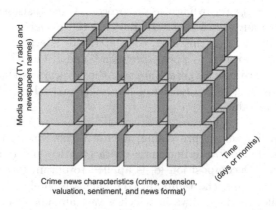

Fig. 1. Three order tensor representation

4. Anomaly Detection: once events were represented in time, we must capture the unusual ones. To perform this task, we rely on Statistical Characterization. The goal is to identify if there is a difference between events classified as anomalous and non-anomalous. Thus, a first approach for establishing activity limits is the mean and standard deviation. However, the shortcomings of this approach have been explained in [9]. Therefore, we use the Median Absolute Deviation (MAD) to compute the rejection criterion. The MAD calculation can be summarised in four steps: (1) compute the median value of the data series; (2) calculate the deviation of all data points to the median value; (3) compute the median value of the deviations; and, (4) multiply the obtained value by a constant dependent on the distribution (usually 1.4826, assuming normality and disregarding abnormality introduced by outliers). Once the MAD is computed, it is possible to establish a rejection criterion using Eq. 1.

$$\frac{x_i - M}{MAD} > |\pm c| \tag{1}$$

Where x_i refers to data point i, M to the data points median value and c is the rejection threshold (3 = very conservative, 2.5 = moderately conservative and 2 = poorly conservative). Thus, any value exceeding the specified threshold of $c = 2.35$ will be treated as an anomaly.

5. Anomaly Validation: to validate our approach, we compare the MAD with the image binarization techniques, such as Binary, Binary Inverted, Trunc, Nozero, Nozero Inverted [14]. The idea behind the comparison with binarization techniques is that an image can be represented as a histogram, which tells us the intensity of each pixel from 0 to 255 in a grey-scale image. Analogously, the intensity of each pixel in an image can be contrasted to the value of the temporal component of the tensor in a day. In image processing, the binarization or thresholding technique work in the following manner: if the pixel value is higher than a threshold value, it is assigned one value (*e.g.*, True), else it is assigned another value (*e.g.*, False). In this effort, the "True" output value will be considered as "anomalous activity". Besides basic techniques, the Otsu algorithm [12] was performed. This algorithm allows to separate or classify an image in two parts foreground and background, in our case, normal and abnormal news amount. The algorithm takes as input the 1-rank temporal component. Then, a threshold is computed for separating foreground or background. The best threshold is the one allowing the sum of foreground and background spreads is at its minimum. Finally, the Adaptive algorithm [3] was also used for the binarisation task. This algorithm calculates the threshold for small regions of the image. So we get different thresholds for different regions of the same image, and it gives us better results.

To perform the validation, we use the MAD results as ground truth and the results of the binarization methods as the predicted values. Then, both results were compared day-by-day to verify if the binarization method predicts unusual events. Later, we compute the standard quality measures such as accuracy and F1.

4   Experiments

The present section describes the experiment performed and the results obtained.

4.1   Anomaly Detection

For this effort, we use a dataset composed by the written press, verbatim transcription of radio news, and verbatim transcription of TV news recovered from years 2013 and 2017. First, we collect filtered crime news based on a list of keywords in the iMedia framework (*c.f.*, Sect. 3).

The obtained dataset contains 262 000 crime-related news and it was curate using `nltk` library for Python. Note, the length of the articles in the written press, news on radio and TV are different (in square centimetres and seconds respectively), they represent a similar concept. To homogenize these values, a Min-Max normalization was applied for each concept. In this manner, surface and seconds - represented by their 0–1 rang values are grouped under the same variable called *extension*. Next, for all dataset, we count the number of positive, negative and neutral words through a widely-used Spanish dictionary[4] [10,13,16,18] and we label each news as positive, negative or neutral in a new column called *sentiment*. Later, we encode textual labels such as crime type, media source, sentiment, and news in a numerical shape. Finally, other variables representing a similar concept among the three sources, but having different names and magnitudes, were standardised through a Min-Max normalisation. After pre-processing, we keep 183 400 news for the overall dataset, which does not contain missing data.

Towards the goal of detecting an unusual amount of crime news, the following variables were used: crime type, extension, valuation, media source, sentiment, news format, and date.

As described in the methodology, we model the news from radio, TV and written press using a Tensor for applying Tucker decomposition. Again, the advantage to using a Tensor is to take into account other rich variables, such as crime type, extension, valuation, media source, sentiment, news format, and date, in the unusual number of news identification. Therefore, we rely on tensor to model all the variables together. Once the decomposition was performed, we took the temporal dimension to identify abnormal values. To do that, we use two methods: (1) the median; and, (2) the Median Absolute Deviation MAD.

A graphical comparison between the median and the MAD (by column) for years 2013 to 2017 (by line) is depicted in Fig. 2. The limit between the white area (non-anomalous events) and the gray area (anomalous events) is given by the rejection criterion computed by each approach. Indeed, news (blue line) belonging to the gray area are considered as anomalous events. It is crucial to notice that the MAD technique transform the temporal dimension of the tensor to capture the unusual events better.

---

[4] https://github.com/autoritas/RD-Lab/tree/master/resources/Afffectivity/.

Regarding the Fig. 2, we can deduce that the MAD technique is more restrictive than the median-based one. These results are impressive if we want to analyse events that happened on a specific day deeply. For instance, in the year 2017, around the 120th day, the peak corresponding to investigations around a corruption involving a former Peruvian president.

4.2 Anomaly Validation

In [15], the authors compared their proposal with the Otsu algorithm. Following the same idea, we use several algorithms of image segmentation (binarization), which aims to slice a 1-rank temporal component (*i.e.*, "the image") into two classes anomalous and typical amount of crime news (*i.e.*, the object from the background). The idea behind this validation is to compare our proposal (anomaly detection using MAD) with the binarization algorithm results.

To measure the efficiency of our approach, we detect the anomalies using the binarization techniques, and we compare it with the anomalies found by our approach. Table 2 shows standard measures like the accuracy and the F1-measure computed by each year and by the seven binarisation techniques. We can notice that the best result for the year 2013 is provided by Otsu method. For the rest of the years, the Binary Inverted way brings us the best performance. In all cases, the F1-measure is high. This effect can be seen in the confusion matrices depicted in Fig. 3 representing the correct (anomalies) and the misclassified instances (non-anomalies) for each year and the best binarization algorithm. For example, in Fig. 3a), the dark diagonal squares represent a high number of instances correctly classified, while other squares represent a low number of misclassified instances. On the opposite, Fig. 3c) shows a considerable number of anomalies classified as false and a small number of right instances correctly classified. This effect can be explained by the fact that we have unbalanced classes, *i.e.,* much news considered as non-anomalies news versus a few news recognised as unusual.

Table 2. Summarizing of thresholding techniques on crimen dataset

Technique	2013		2014		2015		2016		2017	
	ACC	F1	ACC	F1	ACC	F1	ACC	F1	ACC	F1
Binary	0.6011	0.4692	0.1420	0.1277	0.2316	0.1802	0.1315	0.2324	0.1452	0.0602
Binary Inverted	0.0202	0.0396	**0.8579**	0.4090	**0.7683**	0.2975	**0.8684**	0.1428	**0.8547**	0.5691
Truc	0.2832	0.4311	0.1065	0.1925	0.1280	0.2270	0.1397	0.2451	0.1178	0.2107
Tozero	0.9797	0.9613	0.1420	0.1277	0.2316	0.1802	0.1315	0.2324	0.1452	0.0602
Tozero Inverted	0.0317	0.0401	0.8524	0.3720	0.7629	0.2689	0.8657	0.1090	0.8493	0.5454
Otsu	**0.9798**	0.9613	0.5409	0.2149	0.6049	0.2995	0.4493	0.1728	0.3671	0.0796
Adaptive	0.6011	0.4692	0.5355	0.2129	0.5422	0.2695	0.4794	0.1810	0.4410	0.0892

4.3 Additional Findings

Once our proposal was compared with binarisation techniques in the literature, two additional methods were used to highlight the pertinence of our proposal.

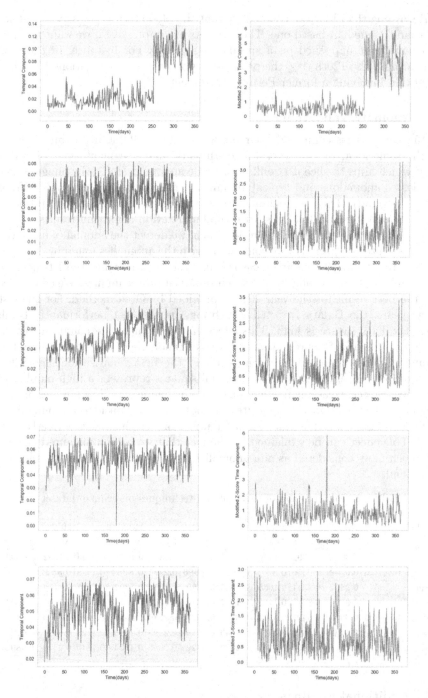

Fig. 2. Anomaly detection for years 2013 to 2017 (from top to bottom) through median (left hand) and MAD (right hand) techniques (Color figure online)

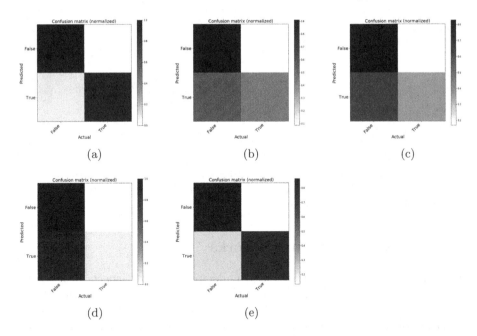

Fig. 3. Confusion matrix for: (a) Year 2013 and Otsu method; (b) Year 2014 and Binary Inverted method; (c) Year 2015 and Binary Inverted method; (d) Year 2016 and Binary Inverted method; (e) Year 2017 and Binary Inverted method

First, we analysed the correlation of the number of news and the temporal component extracted from the temporal tensor component depicted in Fig. 5. This figure confirms that a correlation between the number of news and the temporal component of the tensor exist.

Besides, the influence of the amount of crime news over crime perception was measured. To this end, the National Survey of Budget Programs (ENAPRES[5]) dataset was used to capture the perception of citizens concerning crime. This dataset contains 529 490 records belonging 22 questions about crime victims behaviour. We are interested only in questions regarding security perception. Figure 4 shows the temporal component of the tensor and the crime perception extracted from ENAPRES aggregated by month during the period 2013 to 2017.

Furthermore, in Fig. 5 we can see that there is a correlation between the temporal component of the tensor and the perception of crime in Peruvian citizens measured in the number of times in which a citizen was the subject of an incident associated with insecurity for 2016. In that respect, we can point out that the temporal component of the tensor can be seen as an empirical indicator of perception of vulnerability in citizens.

---

[5] Web site ENAPRES: https://webinei.inei.gob.pe/anda_inei/index.php/catalog/614/vargrp/VG114.

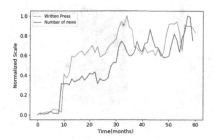
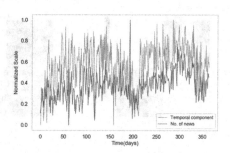

Fig. 4. Crime perception vs the tensor temporal component (by months from 2013 to 2017)

Fig. 5. Number of news vs the tensor temporal component (by days in 2016)

5   Conclusions and Future Works

The news is a source of information to understand several aspects in a country, including criminality and citizen security. In that sense, by reporting daily criminal facts, the news act as a thermometer allowing the quantification or evaluation of illegal activities in a given territory. News not only contains the description of the facts (crime) but includes rich information like the price of the news, the importance of the news represented in the number of the page it appears, among others. The question is, how to exploit this rich information, which varies in time, and for different sources (written press, radio and TV) to detect unusual activities associated with crime?. In this article, we present a complete process to identify anomalies through the use of tensors. For this, two techniques were compared: (1) the method based on the mean and the standard deviation; and, (2) the method based on Median Absolute Deviation (MAD). Both ways were tested on a corpus containing news about crime recovered from written press, radio and television. Then, we compare our proposal with seven binarisation techniques (image segmentation). Finally, we correlate the temporal component of the tensor with the results of a monthly survey about crime perception. Our results highlight the interest of using MAD to capture atypical events if we are interested in analysing specific peaks of unusual crime activities. Furthermore, our approach can be used as an empirical indicator of perception of vulnerability in citizens.

Concerning future directions, we wish to use and compare other tensor decomposition techniques, such as PARAFAC or pTucker [7], or non-negative tensor factorization method [1,17]. Also, we intend to use other public corpora to validate our approach.

References

1. Anandkumar, A., Ge, R., Hsu, D., Kakade, S.M., Telgarsky, M.: Tensor decompositions for learning latent variable models. J. Mach. Learn. Res. **15**, 2773–2832 (2014). http://jmlr.org/papers/v15/anandkumar14b.html

2. Chen, H., Chung, W., Xu, J.J., Wang, G., Qin, Y., Chau, M.: Crime data mining: a general framework and some examples. Computer **37**(4), 50–56 (2004)
3. Dani, M.-C., Jollois, F.-X., Nadif, M., Freixo, C.: Adaptive threshold for anomaly detection using time series segmentation. In: Arik, S., Huang, T., Lai, W.K., Liu, Q. (eds.) ICONIP 2015. LNCS, vol. 9491, pp. 82–89. Springer, Cham (2015). https://doi.org/10.1007/978-3-319-26555-1_10
4. Fanaee-T, H., Gama, J.: Tensor-based anomaly detection: an interdisciplinary survey. Knowl.-Based Syst. **98**, 130–147 (2016)
5. Gupta, M., Gao, J., Aggarwal, C.C., Han, J.: Outlier detection for temporal data: a survey. IEEE Trans. Knowl. Data Eng. **26**(9), 2250–2267 (2014)
6. Hassani, H., Huang, X., Silva, E.S., Ghodsi, M.: A review of data mining applications in crime. Stat. Anal. Data Mining: ASA Data Sci. J. **9**(3), 139–154 (2016)
7. Hayashi, K., et al.: Exponential family tensor factorization for missing-values prediction and anomaly detection. In: 2010 IEEE International Conference on Data Mining, pp. 216–225, December 2010
8. Kolda, T.G., Sun, J.: Scalable tensor decompositions for multi-aspect data mining. In: 2008 Eighth IEEE International Conference on Data Mining, pp. 363–372, December 2008
9. Leys, C., Ley, C., Klein, O., Bernard, P., Licata, L.: Detecting outliers: do not use standard deviation around the mean, use absolute deviation around the median. J. Exp. Soc. Psychol. **49**(4), 764–766 (2013)
10. Molina-González, M.D., Martínez-Cámara, E., Martín-Valdivia, M.T., Perea-Ortega, J.M.: Semantic orientation for polarity classification in Spanish reviews. Expert Syst. Appl. **40**(18), 7250–7257 (2013)
11. Mu, Y., Ding, W., Morabito, M., Tao, D.: Empirical discriminative tensor analysis for crime forecasting. In: Xiong, H., Lee, W.B. (eds.) KSEM 2011. LNCS (LNAI), vol. 7091, pp. 293–304. Springer, Heidelberg (2011). https://doi.org/10.1007/978-3-642-25975-3_26
12. Otsu, N.: A threshold selection method from gray-level histograms. IEEE Trans. Syst. Man Cybern. **9**(1), 62–66 (1979)
13. Perez-Rosas, V., Banea, C., Mihalcea, R.: Learning sentiment lexicons in Spanish. In: LREC, vol. 12, p. 73 (2012)
14. Sahoo, P., Soltani, S., Wong, A.: A survey of thresholding techniques. Comput. Vis. Graph. Image Process. **41**(2), 233–260 (1988). http://www.sciencedirect.com/science/article/pii/0734189X88900229
15. Sapienza, A., Panisson, A., Wu, J., Gauvin, L., Cattuto, C.: Detecting anomalies in time-varying networks using tensor decomposition. In: 2015 IEEE International Conference on Data Mining Workshop (ICDMW), pp. 516–523. IEEE (2015)
16. Sidorov, G., et al.: Empirical study of machine learning based approach for opinion mining in tweets. In: Batyrshin, I., González Mendoza, M. (eds.) MICAI 2012. LNCS (LNAI), vol. 7629, pp. 1–14. Springer, Heidelberg (2013). https://doi.org/10.1007/978-3-642-37807-2_1
17. Takeuchi, K., Tomioka, R., Ishiguro, K., Kimura, A., Sawada, H.: Non-negative multiple tensor factorization. In: 2013 IEEE 13th International Conference on Data Mining, pp. 1199–1204, December 2013
18. Urizar, X.S., Roncal, I.S.V.: Elhuyar at TASS 2013. de TASS (2013)

A Fuzzy Linguistic Approach for Stakeholder Prioritization

Yasiel Pérez Vera[1](✉) (iD) and Anié Bermudez Peña[2] (iD)

[1] La Salle University, Arequipa, Peru
yasielpv@gmail.com
[2] University of Informatics Science, Havana, Cuba
abp@uci.cu

Abstract. A factor considered relevant to achieve a successful project is stakeholder management. The stakeholder prioritization process is usually carried out by the project manager manually using techniques such as interviewing, brainstorming and checklists. These techniques do not take into account the uncertainty introduced by the evaluations of multiple experts in the stakeholder classification process. The objective of this research is to propose a fuzzy linguistic approach for stakeholder prioritization. To do this, a study is made about the stakeholders prioritizing process, as well as the techniques to manage information with uncertainty of the information. The steps of the proposed approach for stakeholder prioritization based on the linguistic 2-tuple model are described. An illustrative example is shown where the stakeholder prioritization is applied to a project to determine who the stakeholder is more important than another. The proposal is based on the computing with words paradigm that you can obtain more interpretable results firstly unifying the assessments of multiple experts into linguistic 2-tuple values and applying an accurate aggregation process. The correct classification of stakeholders allows prioritizing and attending to those that are most important for the project, allowing actions to be taken to avoid the negative impact and improve the positive impact.

Keywords: Fuzzy linguistic · Project Management · Stakeholders prioritization

1 Introduction

The failure of a project is directly related to the impression that the stakeholders have on the value of the project and the correct way of managing the relations between the stakeholders. The lasts public results in The CHAOS Report [1] clearly reflect that only 29% of software projects are considered satisfactory, the rest does not complete successfully. This study examines the aspects that are considered relevant to achieve a successful project and the great majority is directly related to the management of stakeholders [2].

The term stakeholder was developed by Edward Freeman in 1984, where he defined stakeholders as groups or individuals that may affect or be affected by the achievement of the company's goals [3]. According to the author, these groups should be considered as

© Springer Nature Switzerland AG 2020
J. A. Lossio-Ventura et al. (Eds.): SIMBig 2019, CCIS 1070, pp. 46–60, 2020.
https://doi.org/10.1007/978-3-030-46140-9_5

an essential element in the strategic planning of the organization [4]. The management of stakeholders in a project includes the processes necessary to identify them, analyze their expectations and impact on the project, and develop appropriate management strategies to enhance their participation. A correct identification, classification and prioritization of stakeholders helps the project manager to focus on the relationships necessary to ensure project success [5].

The stakeholder prioritization process is usually carried out by the project manager using techniques such as interviewing experts, brainstorming and checklists [6]. There are several methods [7–10] that use different attributes to prioritize stakeholders. It is not possible or viable to choose a method as the best or the most effective since it is the characteristics of the project, the work team and the stakeholders themselves that determine it.

These methods are based on a subjective assessment of experts on the possession of attributes by the stakeholders that is usually qualitative. This introduces a certain degree of uncertainty in the prioritization process since each expert has a different appreciation on the subject. Another difficulty is that it does not establish any mechanism for the treatment of the valuations of multiple experts, which leads to loss of time and information to achieve a convergence between valuations. When this level of uncertainty is not taken into account and the appropriate methods are used for its processing, there is a loss of information that affects the accuracy of the result.

To overcome such limitations this paper proposes a new approach for the stakeholder prioritization process, which provides a flexible evaluation framework capable of gathering assessments taking into account the uncertainty of the experts' criteria. The uncertain information will be managed by a fuzzy linguistic approach [11] that implies the necessity of Computing With Words (CWW) processes [12, 13]. It is remarkable that this approach not only obtains accurate and understandable results but also it will calculate the priority by a multi-step aggregation procedure whose outcomes will be accurate and interpretable.

This paper is structured as follows. Section 2 reviews the main characteristics of stakeholder prioritization process and traditional solving methods. Subsequently Sect. 3 revises approaches to deal with uncertain information and select the suitable for those problem. Section 4 introduces the new approach for stakeholder prioritization based on the linguistic 2-tuple model for dealing with uncertain information. Section 5 shows an illustrative example and Sect. 6 concludes the paper. Finally, Sect. 7 introduces future work to generalize the proposed approach.

2   The Stakeholder Prioritization Process

Techniques for stakeholder prioritization are aimed at grouping the stakeholders of a project according to their characteristics, functions, expectations, interests and influences. Once their quantitative and qualitative information has been identified and collected, the stakeholders are classified in order to guarantee the efficient use of the effort to communicate and manage their expectations. This allows the project manager to concentrate on the relationships necessary to ensure the project success [14].

Several techniques are based on a series of attributes and the possession or not of these attributes to establish the categories that segment the spectrum of stake-holders of the project. The attributes or characteristics are given by the interrelation of the stakeholders with the project or with other stakeholders [15].

Among the attributes that take into account the techniques of stakeholder prioritization are: interest in the success (or not) of the project, level of decision, power it exercises over the project, the urgency of the requests made to the project and belonging to the organization. As part of the investigation, some techniques for the stakeholder classification are analyzed [16–20].

Generally, techniques for classification of stakeholders have evolved from simple methods and with few attributes more complex methods. Techniques Gardner [16] Savage [17] Clarkson [18] and Friedman [20], they are biased in the stakeholder analysis since only raise the relationship between two variables, leaving address key aspects of the relationship between stakeholders and the project.

The Mitchell Prominence Model [19] defines the stakeholder classification based on a diagram in which relate the variables power, legitimacy and urgency. The power is the ability of the stakeholder to influence the project; legitimacy refers to the relationship and actions of the stakeholder with the project in terms of desirability, property or convenience; and the urgency refers to the immediate attention to the stakeholder's requirements by the project.

According to several investigations [21–25], this model is one of the most discussed and used in the world. This model is considered to be operable, since it allows the stakeholders identification to the extent that the amount of power, legitimacy and urgency they possess can be assessed. Due to the characteristics and advantages provided by the use of the Mitchell technique for the stakeholder classification in the projects, it is decided to choose it as the base method in the investigation.

In [7] the identification, prioritization and classification of stakeholders is done using Mitchell's prominence model. In [9] a method for the prioritization of stakeholders based on operations with fuzzy sets is described. The proposed method defines eleven attributes measured at different scales that profile each stakeholder. Once the values are normalized, the fuzzy operations of union and intersection of sets are applied, obtaining a numerical value that serves to order the stakeholders. This proposal does not classify the stakeholders, it only prioritizes them by adding the assessments made by experts, once normalized, of the defined attributes.

In the analyzed researches, techniques are proposed that do not take into account the uncertainty management that provides the human perception of the characteristics of each stakeholder in the project. Nor is there an opportunity for several experts to give their opinion on the stakeholder classification.

3 Management of Uncertain Information in Decision Analysis Processes

This section firstly reviews the decision analysis process to provide the means for managing uncertain information; secondly presents a revision about the fundamentals and use of the 2-tuple linguistic representation model.

3.1 The Decision Analysis Process

The decision analysis [26] is a suitable approach for evaluation and prioritizing processes. Its main purpose is to support the decision-making process by providing the relevant and effective elements to the decision makers in a rational, intuitive and ordered mode. It supplies methods for organizing decisions by firstly establishing the set of appraised elements in the evaluation framework, then gathering the information and finally, computing a final assessment for each element. These phases are depicted in Fig. 1.

Fig. 1. The decision analysis scheme.

The stakeholder prioritization process is usually considered a multi-attribute and multi-expert decision-making problem since several experts give their opinion on various attributes of stakeholders in the projects.

There are different models to perform the CWW processes. Initially, in the fuzzy linguistic approach, the so-called classics were used: a model based on the extension principle and the symbolic one. The first is considered accurate, but difficult to interpret, although it can be interpreted at the expense of its accuracy. However, the second is easily interpretable, but presents information loss in their computational processes [27]. To overcome these limitations other symbolic computational models have been proposed that improve the accuracy of classical computational models, some of the most widespread being the 2-tuple linguistic model [11], the virtual linguistic model [28] and the proportional 2-tuple linguistic model [29].

The 2-tuple model is easy to understand and maintains a fuzzy representation of the linguistic information where its results are assigned a syntax and semantics. This linguistic model is feasible for the treatment of the uncertainty associated to the prioritizing of the stakeholders on the projects. To guarantee the accuracy of the 2-tuple model, it is necessary to use a set of labels symmetrically and evenly distributed. It is also important to highlight that this model is widely used in problems of evaluation, classification, prioritization and ordering of alternatives [11, 26, 30–33].

In the coming subsection is described the 2-tuple linguistic representation model that will be used in the management of uncertain linguistic information to prioritize the stakeholders.

3.2 2-Tuple Linguistic Representation Model for CWW

This computational model was presented in [11] with the aim of improving the accuracy of CWW, in addition to expressing in a symbolic way any result in the universe of discourse. This model has subsequently been used satisfactorily for the treatment of multi-granular linguistic information, unbalanced linguistic information and heterogeneous information (numerical, interval and linguistic).

Let $S = \{S_0, \ldots, S_g,\}$ be a set of linguistic terms, and $\beta \in [0, g]$ a value obtained by a symbolic operation. The symbolic translation of a linguistic term $S_i \in \{S_0, \ldots, S_g,\}$ is a numerical value defined in $[-0.5, 0.5)$ that represents the "information difference" between a quantity of information $\beta \in [0, g]$ obtained of a symbolic operation and the index of the closest linguistic term [11].

From this concept, a new model of representation for linguistic information was developed, which uses a 2-tuple as a basis for representation. Each 2-tuple is represented by (S_i, α) where $S_i \in \{S_0, \ldots, S_g,\}$ corresponds to the linguistic term and $\alpha \in [-0.5, 0.5)$ which symbolizes the numerical value that constitutes the distance from the original result $\beta \in [0, g]$ to the index of the nearest linguistic term S_i.

To obtain the linguistic 2-tuple that expresses the information contained in β, in [11] it is proposed to use the formula $\Delta(\beta) = (S_i, \alpha)$, where $i = round(\beta)$ and $\alpha = \beta - i$. It should be noted that Δ is bijective and that therefore $\Delta^{-1} : \langle S \rangle \to [0, g]$ is defined as $\Delta^{-1}(S_i, \alpha) = i + \alpha = \beta$; leaving the 2-tuple in $\hat{S}$ identified with a numerical value in the interval $[0, g]$. Bearing this in mind, to convert a linguistic term into a linguistic 2-tuple, a value of 0 must be added as a symbolic translation, leaving $S_i \in S \to (S_i, 0) \in \hat{S}$.

The comparison of linguistic information represented by 2-tuples is done according to a lexicographic order. Let (s_k, α_1) and (s_l, α_2) two 2-tuples, each representing a quantity of information, so if $k < l$ then $(s_k, \alpha_1) < (s_l, \alpha_2)$, if $l < k$ then $(s_l, \alpha_2) < (s_k, \alpha_1)$. If $k = l$ then the 2-tuple greater will depend on the value of its symbolic translation. If $\alpha_1 < \alpha_2$ then $(s_k, \alpha_1) < (s_l, \alpha_2)$, if $\alpha_2 < \alpha_1$ then $(s_l, \alpha_2) < (s_k, \alpha_1)$ and if $\alpha_1 = \alpha_2$ then $(s_k, \alpha_1) = (s_l, \alpha_2)$ [11].

Aggregation consists of obtaining a collective value that expresses the information of a set of marginal values. The result of an aggregation operation must be consistent with the representation of the input values, therefore, the result of the aggregation of 2-tuples must be a 2-tuple. Below we review some aggregation operators on 2-tuples that were defined in [11].

The arithmetic mean (AM) is an aggregation operator to determine the balance point or center of the set of values. For a set of 2-tuples $x = \{(s_1, \alpha_1), \ldots, (s_n, \alpha_n)\}$, the extension for 2-tuples model of this operator is obtained as follows in Eq. 1.

$$\bar{x}^e(x) = \Delta\left(\frac{1}{n} \sum_{i=1}^{n} \Delta^{-1}((s_i, \alpha_i))\right) = \Delta\left(\frac{1}{n} \sum_{i=1}^{n} \beta_i\right) \tag{1}$$

The weighted average (WA) allows the values x_i to have different importance, for which each value x_i must have an associated weight w_i that emphasizes its importance. So, for a set of 2-tuples $x = \{(s_1, \alpha_1), \ldots, (s_n, \alpha_n)\}$ with a vector of weights associated with each 2-tuple, $W = (w_1, \ldots, w_n)$, the extension for this operator is obtained as shown in Eq. 2.

$$\bar{x}^w(x) = \Delta\left(\frac{\sum_{i=1}^{n} \Delta^{-1}(s_i, \alpha_i) \cdot w_i}{\sum_{i=1}^{n} w_i}\right) = \Delta\left(\frac{\sum_{i=1}^{n} \beta_i \cdot w_i}{\sum_{i=1}^{n} w_i}\right) \tag{2}$$

In the ordered weighted aggregation (OWA) operator, the weights are not associated to a predetermined value but to a determined position. So, if you have a set of 2-tuples $x = \{(s_1, \alpha_1), \ldots, (s_n, \alpha_n)\}$ and $W = (w_1, \ldots, w_n)$ is your associated weight vector such that $w_i \in [0, 1]$ and $\sum w_i = 1$, the extension of the operator is obtained as shown in Eq. 3, where β_j^* is the j-th highest value of the $\Delta^{-1}(s_i, \alpha_i)$.

$$OWA(x) = \Delta\left(\sum_{j=1}^{n} w_j \cdot \beta_j^*\right) \tag{3}$$

This model allows a simple process without loss of information where the result of the process is always expressed in the initial linguistic domain. This allows to improve the accuracy of its results by not having to carry out approximation operations. This computational model is precise when the representation of the semantics of linguistic labels is performed with triangular functions [32].

4 An Approach for Stakeholder Prioritization Based on the Linguistic 2-Tuple Model

In this section is presented a new approach for stakeholder prioritization based on the linguistic 2-tuple model that deal with uncertain information. This approach has three steps that are described in further detail in the following sections.

First, all the elements of the approach are defined, including the experts, the stakeholders and its attributes. Then, the evaluation of the experts will be collected for each of the attributes defined for each stakeholder. Next, the evaluation of the experts to be used in the CWW linguistic model will be converted to 2-tuples. Then, the aggregation phase is followed, first by experts, where a collective evaluation will be obtained for each attribute for each stakeholder. Next, the collective evaluations will be aggregated by attribute, obtaining a single evaluation for each stakeholder that expresses the collective evaluation of all the experts for all the attributes. With a 2-tuple for each stakeholder, we proceed to order them using the 2-tuple comparison operators analyzed in the previous section. As an output of this approach, we will have a ranking list of project stakeholders that takes into account the uncertainty of the information provided by multiple experts.

4.1 Definition of Approach's Elements

All the elements of the approach are defined in the first step.

- Let $T = \{t_j | j \in (1, \ldots, p)\}$ be a set of project stakeholders.
- Let $C = \{c_k | k \in (1, \ldots, q)\}$ be a set attributes to evaluate for the stakeholder prioritization with de weighting vector $W^c = \{w_k^c | k \in (1, \ldots, q)\}$, $w_k^c \in [0, 1]$ with $\sum_{k=1}^{q} w_k^c = 1$.
- Let $E = \{e_l | l \in (1, \ldots, r)\}$ be a set of experts with de weighting vector $W^e = \{w_l^e | l \in (1, \ldots, r)\}$, $w_l^e \in [0, 1]$ with $\sum_{l=1}^{r} w_l^e = 1$. Each expert e_l will be evaluate each attribute c_k for each stakeholder t_j using the evaluation vector $x_l^{jk} = \{x_1^{11}, \ldots, x_r^{pq}\}$.
- Let $S = \{s_i | i \in (0, \ldots, g)\}$ be a set of ordered linguistic terms where the representation of the semantics of linguistic labels is defined with triangular functions and $s_{i1} < s_{i2}$ for all $i1 < i2$. The evaluations of the experts x_l^{jk} are expressed using the set of linguistic terms S.

4.2 Recollection of Expert's Evaluations by Attribute and Its Conversion to 2-Tuple

Once the elements of the approach have been defined, preferences must be gathered as in Table 1. Each expert provides her/his evaluation over attribute by means of evaluation vector described previously.

Table 1. Expert evaluations by attribute

Stakeholders	Attributes	Expert e_1	...	Expert e_l
t_1	c_1	x_1^{11}	...	x_l^{11}
	...	...	...	...
	c_k	x_1^{1k}	...	x_l^{1k}
...	...	...	...	...
t_j	c_1	x_1^{j1}	...	x_l^{j1}
	...	...	...	...
	c_k	x_1^{jk}	...	x_l^{jk}

Then, it is obtained the linguistic 2-tuple from de evaluation provided by the experts for each attribute for each stakeholder. The Table 2 show the transformation.

Table 2. 2-Tuple expert evaluations by attribute

Stakeholders	Attributes	Expert e_1	...	Expert e_l
t_1	c_1	$(S_i, a)_1^{11}$	...	$(S_i, a)_l^{11}$
	...	...	...	...
	c_k	$(S_i, a)_1^{1k}$	...	$(S_i, a)_l^{1k}$
...	...	...	...	...
t_j	c_1	$(S_i, a)_1^{j1}$	...	$(S_i, a)_l^{j1}$
	...	...	...	...
	c_k	$(S_i, a)_1^{jk}$	...	$(S_i, a)_l^{jk}$

4.3 Aggregation of Evaluations by Expert and Attribute

The main objective of this step is to obtain a collective assessment based on individual assessments through the use of aggregation operators. It is carried out from the individual evaluation of the experts on the set of attributes by stakeholder to obtain a global evaluation for each attribute by stakeholder. Since each expert has an associated weight vector indicating the importance of his evaluation, the WA operator described in Sect. 3.2 is used to aggregate the expert evaluations as show in Table 3.

Table 3. Collective evaluation by attribute

Stakeholders	Attributes	Collective evaluation
t_1	c_1	$(S_i, a)^{11}$
	...	...
	c_k	$(S_i, a)^{1k}$
...	...	...
t_j	c_1	$(S_i, a)^{j1}$
	...	...
	c_k	$(S_i, a)^{jk}$

Later, it is obtained an evaluation for each stakeholder from the collective assessment by attribute obtained previously through the use of aggregation operators. Since each attribute has an associated weight vector indicating its importance, the WA operator described in Sect. 3.2 is used to aggregate the attribute collective evaluations as show in Table 4.

Table 4. Evaluation by stakeholder

Stakeholders	General evaluation
t_1	(S_i, a)
...	...
t_j	(S_i, a)

As the final evaluation of the stakeholder is obtained through a 2-tuple, its ordering is very simple using the 2-tuple comparison operator described in Sect. 3.2. As a result of this step, a ranking list of project stakeholders that takes into account the uncertainty of the information provided by multiple experts is obtained. This list provides the stakeholder's priority above the rest of the project stakeholders.

5 An Illustrative Example

The stakeholder prioritization can be applied to any project to determine who the stakeholder is more important than another stakeholder. In this example the project to analyze has four stakeholders: employees (Stakeholder 1), product owner (Stakeholder 2), government (Stakeholder 3) and managers (Stakeholder 4). The set of attributes to evaluate for each stakeholder is defined in C = {Coercive power, Utilitarian power, Normative-social power, Social legitimacy, Organizational legitimacy, Temporal sensitivity and Criticism} with weighted vector $W^c = \{0.17, 0.17, 0.16, 0.1, 0.1, 0.15, 0.15\}$. These attributes are described following.

There are several attributes that describes the stakeholders, among which is the Mitchell prominence model [19]. In this research, power variable is associated with the disposition or possibility of obtaining coercive power (CP) through physical force or weapons, utilitarian power (UP) by means of technology, money, knowledge, logistics, raw materials and normative-social power (NSP) as prestige, esteem, charisma.

Legitimacy is considered as the presumption or generalized perception that the actions of a stakeholder [19]. Legitimacy can be measured based on the attributes: organizational legitimacy (OL) and social legitimacy (SL). Where the first expresses the attribution of a degree of desirability of the actions of the stakeholder at the organizational level and the second at the social level.

The urgency variable is defined as the degree to which stakeholders consider their claims to the project important [19]. In this context, they differentiate the degree of emergency possession according to the possession of two attributes: temporal sensitivity (TS) that is the degree of unacceptability on the part of the stakeholder in the delay of the manager in addressing their claims and criticism (C) manifests itself in the importance that stakeholders consider having their claims or issues.

A set of 5 linguistic terms is defined so that the experts issue their evaluation of the different attributes for each stakeholder. Let $S = \{s_0 = Very\ Low;\ s_1 = Low;\ s_2 = Moderated;\ s_3 = High;\ s_4 = Very\ High\}$ with $s_i < s_j$ for all $i < j$ as show in Fig. 2.

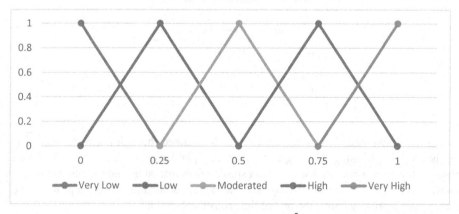

Fig. 2. Linguistic term set S^5

The experts committee is composed by three experts: the project manager (Expert 1), the SCRUM master (Expert 2) and the business analyst (Expert 3). The weighted vector associated to the experts is defined as $W^e = \{0.4, 0.35, 0.25\}$. The Table 5 show the expert's evaluation recollected for each attribute by stakeholder.

Table 5. Expert evaluations by attribute

Stakeholders	Attributes	Expert 1	Expert 2	Expert 3
Stakeholder 1	CP	Very Low	Very Low	Very Low
	UP	Low	Very Low	Very Low
	NSP	High	Very Low	Low
	SL	Moderated	Very Low	Moderated
	OL	Moderated	Very Low	Moderated
	TS	Low	Very Low	Very Low
	C	High	Very Low	Very Low
Stakeholder 2	CP	Very High	Very High	Moderated
	UP	High	High	Very High
	NSP	Very High	High	Very High
	SL	Very High	High	Very High
	OL	Very High	High	Very High
	TS	Very High	High	Very High
	C	High	High	Very High
Stakeholder 3	CP	Low	Moderated	Very Low
	UP	Low	Moderated	Moderated
	NSP	Moderated	Moderated	Low
	SL	Moderated	Moderated	High
	OL	Moderated	Moderated	Moderated
	TS	Low	Moderated	High
	C	High	Moderated	High
Stakeholder 4	CP	High	Very High	Low
	UP	High	High	Very High
	NSP	High	High	High
	SL	High	High	Very High
	OL	High	High	Very High
	TS	Very High	High	Very High
	C	High	High	Very High

Then, the evaluation of the experts must be transformed into the linguistic representation of 2-tuples in order to be able to process this evaluation. Once transformed into 2-tuples, the evaluation is aggregated. The WA operator is used since it is considered that the evaluations of the experts have different relevance expressed in the weighted vector. Table 6 shows the evaluations of stakeholders by the experts transformed into 2-tuples and the result of the aggregation process by experts.

Table 6. 2-Tuples experts' evaluation and collective evaluation for attribute

Stakeholders	Attributes	Expert 1	Expert 2	Expert 3	Collective evaluation
Stakeholder 1	CP	$(s_0, 0)$	$(s_0, 0)$	$(s_0, 0)$	$(s_0, 0)$
	UP	$(s_1, 0)$	$(s_0, 0)$	$(s_0, 0)$	$(s_0, 0.4)$
	NSP	$(s_3, 0)$	$(s_0, 0)$	$(s_1, 0)$	$(s_1, 0.45)$
	SL	$(s_2, 0)$	$(s_0, 0)$	$(s_2, 0)$	$(s_1, 0.3)$
	OL	$(s_2, 0)$	$(s_0, 0)$	$(s_2, 0)$	$(s_1, 0.3)$
	TS	$(s_1, 0)$	$(s_0, 0)$	$(s_0, 0)$	$(s_0, 0.4)$
	C	$(s_3, 0)$	$(s_0, 0)$	$(s_0, 0)$	$(s_1, 0.2)$
Stakeholder 2	CP	$(s_4, 0)$	$(s_4, 0)$	$(s_2, 0)$	$(s_4, -0.5)$
	UP	$(s_3, 0)$	$(s_3, 0)$	$(s_4, 0)$	$(s_3, 0.25)$
	NSP	$(s_4, 0)$	$(s_3, 0)$	$(s_4, 0)$	$(s_4, -0.35)$
	SL	$(s_4, 0)$	$(s_3, 0)$	$(s_4, 0)$	$(s_4, -0.35)$
	OL	$(s_4, 0)$	$(s_3, 0)$	$(s_4, 0)$	$(s_4, -0.35)$
	TS	$(s_4, 0)$	$(s_3, 0)$	$(s_4, 0)$	$(s_4, -0.35)$
	C	$(s_3, 0)$	$(s_3, 0)$	$(s_4, 0)$	$(s_3, 0.25)$
Stakeholder 3	CP	$(s_1, 0)$	$(s_2, 0)$	$(s_0, 0)$	$(s_1, 0.1)$
	UP	$(s_1, 0)$	$(s_2, 0)$	$(s_2, 0)$	$(s_2, -0.4)$
	NSP	$(s_2, 0)$	$(s_2, 0)$	$(s_1, 0)$	$(s_2, -0.25)$
	SL	$(s_2, 0)$	$(s_2, 0)$	$(s_3, 0)$	$(s_2, 0.25)$
	OL	$(s_2, 0)$	$(s_2, 0)$	$(s_2, 0)$	$(s_2, 0)$
	TS	$(s_1, 0)$	$(s_2, 0)$	$(s_3, 0)$	$(s_2, -0.15)$
	C	$(s_3, 0)$	$(s_2, 0)$	$(s_3, 0)$	$(s_3, -0.35)$
Stakeholder 4	CP	$(s_3, 0)$	$(s_4, 0)$	$(s_1, 0)$	$(s_3, -0.15)$
	UP	$(s_3, 0)$	$(s_3, 0)$	$(s_4, 0)$	$(s_3, 0.25)$
	NSP	$(s_3, 0)$	$(s_3, 0)$	$(s_3, 0)$	$(s_3, 0)$
	SL	$(s_3, 0)$	$(s_3, 0)$	$(s_4, 0)$	$(s_3, 0.25)$
	OL	$(s_3, 0)$	$(s_3, 0)$	$(s_4, 0)$	$(s_3, 0.25)$
	TS	$(s_4, 0)$	$(s_3, 0)$	$(s_4, 0)$	$(s_4, -0.35)$
	C	$(s_3, 0)$	$(s_3, 0)$	$(s_4, 0)$	$(s_3, 0.25)$

Next, the collective evaluation by attribute is aggregated to obtain a general evaluation by stakeholder. The WA operator is used in the aggregation process as it is considered that the attributes of the stakeholders have different relevance expressed in the weighted vector. Then, the 2-tuple comparison operator is used to establish the stakeholder's order as it's shown in Table 7.

Table 7. Evaluation by stakeholder

Stakeholder	General evaluation	Order
Stakeholder 1	$(s_1, -0.2)$	4
Stakeholder 2	$(s_3, 0.4965)$	1
Stakeholder 3	$(s_2, -0.161)$	3
Stakeholder 4	$(s_3, 0.202)$	2

5.1 Comparison Between the Proposed Approach and Existing Approaches for Stakeholder Prioritization

Table 8 shows a comparison between the proposed approach and the existing techniques for the stakeholder prioritization that were analyzed in Sect. 2. It is used as comparison criteria between the different stakeholder prioritization approaches: the use of several attributes, the management of the uncertainty of the information provided by the experts, the use of multiple experts for the stakeholder evaluation and if the approach allows the information's aggregation to obtain a unique assessment.

Table 8. Comparison between approaches for stakeholder prioritization

Criteria	Stakeholder prioritization approaches					
	Clarkson's approach	Friedman's approach	Gardner's approach	Savage's approach	Mitchell's approach	Proposed approach
Use of several attributes	No	Yes	Yes	Yes	Yes	Yes
Management of the uncertainty	No	No	No	No	No	Yes
Use of multiple experts	No	No	No	No	No	Yes
Aggregation of the information	No	No	No	No	No	Yes

6 Conclusions

Prioritization of project stakeholders is an important task because the success of a project depends largely on stakeholders. The handling of the uncertainty of information provided by the experts is an aspect to be taken into account in this process, since the more accurate be the information, the more accurate decisions can be taken with respect to the stakeholders. Current methods are not efficient in handling the uncertainty and assessment of multiple experts of stakeholder prioritization. In this paper, we have proposed a linguistic approach for stakeholder prioritization to overcome these limitations, by using the linguistic 2-tuple fusion model. The proposal is based on the CWW paradigm that allows obtaining more interpretable results firstly unifying the assessments of multiple experts into linguistic 2-tuple values and latter applying an accurate aggregation process that makes possible to generate a more exact priority for the stakeholder in the project.

7 Future Work

As future work, the approach presented for stakeholder prioritization could be extended to use other more accurate and adjustable aggregation operators to this problem. It could also be taken into account that each expert could express their evaluations in different domains of expression, like numerically, in an interval way or based on a set of linguistic labels of different cardinalities. An extension of the proposed approach would be presented as a solution to the treatment of heterogeneous information unifying the different domains of expression of expert evaluations.

References

1. The Standish Group: Standish Group 2015 Chaos Report - Q&A with Jennifer Lynch. https://www.infoq.com/articles/standish-chaos-2015. Accessed 13 Dec 2016
2. Pico López, Ó.: Los Stakeholders como actores estratégico-instrumentales en los proyectos de la Nueva Gestión Pública (2016). http://digibuo.uniovi.es/dspace/handle/10651/38421
3. Freeman, R.E.: Strategic Management: A Stakeholder Approach. Cambridge University Press, Cambridge (2010)
4. Figuerola, N.: Procesos y Técnicas en la Gestión de los Interesados. https://articulospm.files.wordpress.com/2013/09/procesos-y-tc3a9cnicas-en-la-gestic3b3n-de-los-interesados.pdf
5. Schwalbe, K.: Information Technology Project Management. Cengage Learning, Boston (2015)
6. Project Management Institute: A Guide to the Project Management Body of Knowledge. Project Management Institute, Inc., Pennsylvania (2017)
7. Parent, M., Deephouse, D.: A case study of stakeholder identification and prioritization by managers. J. Bus. Ethics 75, 1–23 (2007). https://doi.org/10.1007/s10551-007-9533-y
8. Bendjenna, H., Charre, P., Eddine Zarour, N.: Using multi-criteria analysis to prioritize stakeholders. J. Syst. Inf. Technol. 14, 264–280 (2012). https://doi.org/10.1108/13287261211255365
9. Majumdar, S.I., Rahman, M.S., Rahman, M.M.: Stakeholder prioritization in requirement engineering process: a case study on school management system. Comput. Sci. Eng. 4, 17–27 (2014). https://doi.org/10.5923/j.computer.20140401.03
10. Elsaid, A., Salem, R., Abdul-Kader, H.: A dynamic stakeholder classification and prioritization based on hybrid rough-fuzzy method. J. Softw. Eng. 11, 143–159 (2017). https://doi.org/10.3923/jse.2017.143.159
11. Herrera, F., Martínez, L.: A 2-tuple fuzzy linguistic representation model for computing with words. IEEE Trans. Fuzzy Syst. 8, 746–752 (2000). https://doi.org/10.1109/91.890332

12. Martinez, L., Ruan, D., Herrera, F.: Computing with words in decision support systems: an overview on models and applications. Int. J. Comput. Intell. Syst. **3**, 382–395 (2010). https://doi.org/10.1080/18756891.2010.9727709
13. Zadeh, L.A.: What is computing with words (CWW)? In: Zadeh, L.A. (ed.) Computing with Words, pp. 3–37. Springer, Heidelberg (2013). https://doi.org/10.1007/978-3-642-27473-2_1
14. Mainardes, E.W., Alves, H., Raposo, M.: A model for stakeholder classification and stakeholder relationships. Manag. Decis. **50**, 1861–1879 (2012). https://doi.org/10.1108/00251741211279648
15. van der Duin, P.: Foresight in Organizations: Methods and Tools. Routledge, Abingdon (2016)
16. Gardner, J.R., Rachlin, R., Sweeny, A.: Handbook of Strategic Planning. Wiley, Hoboken (1986)
17. Savage, G.T., Nix, T.W., Whitehead, C.J., Blair, J.D.: Strategies for assessing and managing organizational stakeholders. Executive **5**, 61–75 (1991). https://doi.org/10.5465/AME.1991.4274682
18. Clarkson, M.E.: A stakeholder framework for analyzing and evaluating corporate social performance. Acad. Manag. Rev. **20**, 92–117 (1995)
19. Mitchell, R.K., Agle, B.R., Wood, D.J.: Toward a theory of stakeholder identification and salience: defining the principle of who and what really counts. Acad. Manag. Rev. **22**, 853 (1997). https://doi.org/10.2307/259247
20. Friedman, A.L., Miles, S.: Developing stakeholder theory. J. Manag. Stud. **39**, 1–21 (2002)
21. Poplawska, J., Labib, A., Reed, D.M., Ishizaka, A.: Stakeholder profile definition and salience measurement with fuzzy logic and visual analytics applied to corporate social responsibility case study. J. Clean. Prod. **105**, 103–115 (2015). https://doi.org/10.1016/j.jclepro.2014.10.095
22. Samboni Navarrete, A.P., Blanco Torres, J.G.: Herramientas de gestión de interesados utilizadas en las etapas de planeación y control de proyectos. Bibl. USB Cali T658404 S187h CD-ROM (2015)
23. Arévalo, A.U., Requena, R.: Considerations of the stakeholder approach. Punto Vista. **4**, 8 (2013)
24. Bernal, A., Rivas, L.A.: Modelos para la identificación de stakeholders y su aplicación a la gestión de los pequeños abastecimientos comunitarios de agua. Rev. Lebret. **4**, 251–273 (2012)
25. Acuña, A.: La gestión de los stakeholders. Análisis de los diferentes modelos. Grupo Investig. RSE Sist. Inf. Univ. Nac. Sur. 1–12 (2012)
26. Martínez, L.: Sensory evaluation based on linguistic decision analysis. Int. J. Approx. Reason. **44**, 148–164 (2007). https://doi.org/10.1016/j.ijar.2006.07.006
27. Rodríguez, R.M.: Un nuevo modelo para procesos de computación con palabras en toma de decisión lingüística (2010)
28. Xu, Z.S.: Goal programming models for obtaining the priority vector of incomplete fuzzy preference relation. Int. J. Approx. Reason. **36**, 261–270 (2004)
29. Wang, J.-H., Hao, J.: A new version of 2-tuple fuzzy linguistic representation model for computing with words. IEEE Trans. Fuzzy Syst. **14**, 435–445 (2006)
30. Espinilla, M., Palomares, I., Martinez, L., Ruan, D.: A comparative study of heterogeneous decision analysis approaches applied to sustainable energy evaluation. Int. J. Uncertain. Fuzziness Knowl.-Based Syst. **20**, 159–174 (2012)
31. Wei, G., Zhao, X.: Some dependent aggregation operators with 2-tuple linguistic information and their application to multiple attribute group decision making. Expert Syst. Appl. **39**, 5881–5886 (2012). https://doi.org/10.1016/j.eswa.2011.11.120

32. Zulueta, Y., Martell, V., Martínez, J., Martínez, L.: A dynamic multi-expert multi-criteria decision making model for risk analysis. In: Castro, F., Gelbukh, A., González, M. (eds.) MICAI 2013. LNCS (LNAI), vol. 8265, pp. 132–143. Springer, Heidelberg (2013). https://doi.org/10.1007/978-3-642-45114-0_11

33. de Andrés, R., García-Lapresta, J.L., Martínez, L.: A multi-granular linguistic model for management decision-making in performance appraisal. Soft. Comput. **14**, 21–34 (2010)

Automatic Speech Recognition of Quechua Language Using HMM Toolkit

Rodolfo Zevallos[1,3]($\boxtimes$) ⓘ, Johanna Cordova[2] ⓘ, and Luis Camacho[1] ⓘ

[1] Pontifical Catholic University of Peru, Av. Universitaria 1801, Lima 15088, Peru
rjzevallos.salazar@gmail.com, l.camacho@pucp.pe
[2] National Institute of Oriental Languages and Civilisations, Paris, France
johanna.cordova@inalco.fr
[3] National University of Callao, Av. Juan Pablo II 306, Bellavista, Peru

Abstract. In this paper, we present the implementation of an Automatic Speech Recognition system (ASR) for southern Quechua language. The software can recognize both continuous speech and isolated words. The ASR was developed using Hidden Markov Model Toolkit (HTK) and the corpus collected by SIM-INCHIKKUNARAYKU. A dictionary provides the system with a mapping of vocabulary words to sequences of phonemes; the audio files were processed to extract the speech feature vectors (MFCC) and then, the acoustic model was trained using the MFCC files until its convergence. The paper also describes a detailed architecture of an ASR system developed using HTK library modules and tools. The ASR was tested using the audios recorded by volunteers obtaining a 12.70% word error rate.

Keywords: Quechua · Endangered languages · ASR · HTK · HMM

1 Introduction

The Quechuan languages are amongst the most spoken indigenous languages of America. In Peru, 13.9% of the population have Quechua as their first language, and over 22% reported a Quechuan ethnic background[1]. Although the language is official in the regions with the most speakers, it has little visibility, and despite recent efforts by the Peruvian State to develop services in native languages, the number of speakers is decreasing. One of the reasons why speakers are abandoning their language in favour of Spanish is their perception that Quechua is unsuited to modernity and without economic value. Indeed, historically an oral language, Quechua is still little used in its written form and is almost absent from digital uses, which limits its scope. The moving into the digital scope would thus be a way of supporting States' initiatives for fundamental access to public services in native languages and a crucial step towards the revitalization of these languages.

---

[1] 2017 National Census, https://www.inei.gob.pe/.

This project was supported by CONCYTEC CIENCIACTIVA of the Peruvian government through grant 164-2015-FONDECYT and by PUCP through grant 2017-3-0039/436.

© Springer Nature Switzerland AG 2020
J. A. Lossio-Ventura et al. (Eds.): SIMBig 2019, CCIS 1070, pp. 61–68, 2020.
https://doi.org/10.1007/978-3-030-46140-9_6

In this paper, we aims to develop an Automatic Speech Recognizer (ASR) for Southern Quechua, based on Markov's Hidden Models (HMM). This statistical approach is the most widely used method for processing low-resourced languages [13, 14]. The objective of our work is to provide the Quechua speakers with an interface between oral and written communication and to provide the research field with the basic building blocks to develop more complex tools that would broaden the prospects for using Quechua on a daily basis.

2 Background and Related Works

Only a few groups in Latin America and abroad have been working recently for the last years on language technology for Peruvian native languages. The Institute of Andean Amazonian Language and Literature (ILLA)[2] has compiled electronic dictionaries for Quechua, Aymara and Guarani. The group Hinantin[3] at the Universidad Nacional San Antonio Abad del Cusco, has developed, among other things, a text-to-speech system for Cusco Quechua and a Quechua spellchecker plug-in for LibreOffice. Rios [15] developed a language technology toolkit of high quality for Southern Quechua, including the first Quechua dependency treebank.

The SIMINCHIKKUNARAYKU[4] project is led by a community of activists researchers whose vision is that the future of the languages of America depends not only on the preservation efforts, but also on the polyglotism of all citizens, regardless of ethnicity. They have developed: HUQARIQ, a tool for collecting speech corpus; QILLQA, a corpora repository [11]; SIMINCHIK, 97 h of Southern Quechua speech corpus and the corresponding transcribed text [17]; and 2,500 h of non annotated corpus.

To our knowledge, there was no Quechua speech dataset before the one compiled by SIMINCHIKKUNARAYKU.

3 The Quechuan Languages

Quechua is a linguistic family of South America whose languages are spoken by about 7–8 million people, mainly in Peru, Ecuador and Bolivia [8]. According to Torero's classification, this family is divided into two branches, called Central Quechua (QI) and Peripheral Quechua (QII) [16]. The first is a complex set of varieties currently spoken in the central Andes of Peru. The second is subdivided into three subgroups A, B and C, and covers a geographical area that extends as far north as Colombia and as far south as Argentina. In this work, we will focus on the most widespread and widely spoken variety, Quechua IIC, or Southern Quechua. This subgroup is itself composed of 3 mutually intelligible variants: Ayacucho-Chanca, Cusco-Collao and Santiagueño. As part of the SIMINCHIK project, audio and text corpora were collected for two of these variants: the QUECHUA CHANCA, mainly spoken in the Peruvian department of Ayacucho and surroundings, and the QUECHUA COLLAO, spoken in in the Peruvian departments of Cusco and Puno, and in Bolivia. We will then focus on these two variants in our continued work.

---

[2] http://www.illa-a.org/wp/.

[3] http://hinant.in.

[4] https://siminchikkunarayku.pe.

3.1 Quechua Phonology

Writing System. Quechua is written with a Latin alphabet. In Peru, the graphical system for Quechuan languages is officially determined by a "Quechua pan-dialectal alphabet"[5]. Quechua's graphical and spelling systems are phonological, that is, each letter or digraph corresponds to exactly one phoneme, and the word spelling is regular. Table 1 shows the alphabet for Southern Quechua.

Table 1. Alphabet for Southern Quechua

Vocals	Consonants	Semi-cons.
a, i, u	ch, h, k, l, ll, m, n, ñ, p, q, r, s, sh, t,'	w, y

Phonological Features. The main phonological feature that differentiates the two variants CHANCA and COLLAO is the occurrence of glottalized and aspirated stops on the occlusive consonants (/ch/, /k/, /p/, /q/, /t/): while this feature is distinctive in Quechua Collao, it is not used in Quechua Chanca. Thus, QUECHUA CHANCA has a total of 15 consonants, most of them voiceless, as shown in Table 2. The glottal and an aspirated version of each occlusive for QUECHUA COLLAO leads to a total of 25 consonants for this variant. Voiced consonants from the Spanish phonemic inventory are also used in the many borrowings.

Table 2. Consonants in the phonemic inventory of QUECHUA CHANCA (IPA)

	Bil	Alv	Pal	Vel	Uvu	Glo
Plosive	p	t	t͡ʃ	k	q	
Nasal	m	n	ɲ			
Fricative		s				h
Lat. Approx.		l	ʎ			
Approximant		ɹ				
Semi-consonants	w		y			

Both quechua dialects are trivocalic: the distinctive vocalic phonemes are /a/, /i/, /u/. Though, in QUECHUA COLLAO, when immediately preceding or following the voiceless uvular stop /q/, /i/ is realized [e] or [ɘ], and /u/ is realized [ɔ] for articulatory reasons. Another phonetic difference between Chanca and Collao is in the realization of the phoneme /q/: while it is pronounced as a stop [q] in Collao, it is realized as a fricative [χ] in Chanca.

---

[5] Ministerial Resolution 1218-1985-ED.

3.2   Quechua Morphology

Southern Quechua is agglutinative, with suffixes only, and concatenative: each suffix is added to the previous one without morphological changes in the root or in any of the suffixes. The order of the suffixes varies somewhat from one dialect to another but is stable within a given dialect.

Most roots are monosyllabic or bisyllabic. A syllable is a phonemic unit composed of a nucleus, which is here always a vowel (V) and of margins, which are here consonants (C). Thus, the phonological scheme that describes any Quechua root is the following: (C)V(C)-CV(C) [5].

4   Experiments

4.1   System Description

The Quechua speech recognizer developed is based on a triphone model and was designed and tested using Markov's Hidden Models (HTK) tool.

The Quechua Dictionary. The statistical approach used in the creation of the Quechua speech recognizer is based on phonemes. As we previously mentioned, the official spelling of Quechua is phonological; it is therefore very simple to build a dictionary of phonemes from Cerrón-Palomino's dictionary [5].

Speech Corpus. The corpus used for the construction of the Quechua speech recognizer was the one collected by SIMINCHIKKUNARAYKU. It has 97 h of audio recorded and transcribed, in the two dialects previously mentioned.

We sampled the total data set, obtaining 8 h of training data and a 2 h test corpus, for a total of 16,340 instances. The audio for the training corpus was recorded by 9 collaborators (3 men and 6 women), and the test corpus by 2 collaborators (one male and one female). The Table 3 shows the number of collaborators and statements in the training and test data.

Table 3. Number of participants and emissions for the training and testing stage

Stage	Numbers of participants	Utterances
Training	9	11,831
Test	2	4,509
Total	11	16,340

Some audios contained music and Spanish parts. In order to filter the content and split the speech at word level, we used a voice detector based on pyAudioAnalysis [9]. The processed audio files were adjusted to single-channel, 16 kHz sampling, 16-bit precision coding and WAV format.

Records must then be encoded to extract the characteristic vectors. The HCopy tool is responsible for producing coded files (feature vector files).

4.2   System Architecture

The Quechua speech recognizer has a 3-stage architecture: pre-processing, training and testing. In the pre-processing stage, we use the audios and transcripts made by the volunteers to create MFCC files (which contain the data relative to the audio signal) and the main MLF file, which contains all the transcripts. For the training stage, we use the MFCC and MLF files, the Quechua dictionary, the language model and a prototype for the construction of an acoustic model. At the final stage, the performance of the model is evaluated with the test set. Figure 1 shows the general architecture of the system.

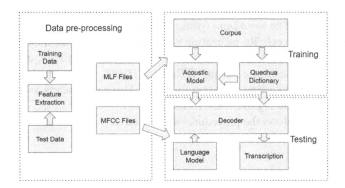

Fig. 1. Quechua speech recognition architecture

4.3   Language Modeling

Given the high presence of rare words in morphologically rich languages such as Quechua, we use singleton pruning rate κ of 0.05 as proposed by [3], to randomly replace only a fraction κ of words that occur only once in the training data with a global UNK symbol.

We built a modified Kneser-Ney model interpolated from 5-g to word level, getting a perplexity of 298.79. A vocabulary intersection analysis revealed a 63.46% intersection between the validation set and the training set vocabulary. This rather high value of perplexity and low intersection of vocabulary reveals the morphological richness of this language family. A more exhaustive inspection of the vocabulary showed that 64.42% of the words have a frequency of one.

5   Acoustic Models

Different sets of parameters have been tried to check the performance of every arrangement. The base model consists of 5-state HMM in which the first and last states are non-emitting states similar to that presented by Alegre [1]. The model has in each vector of ellipse 39 length, which represents the static vector of (MFCC_0 = 13) plus the delta coefficients (+13) and the acceleration coefficients (+13). These vectors are extracted from the coded data files. The initialization of means and variances has been done manually for the HMM topology because there are no boot data available (boot data are the data files that have been completely tagged at the data recording stage). After having the HMM prototype file, we must process it using the HCompV tool, which calculates the global averages and variances of the HMM model. The HCompV tool automatically updates the prototype file with new parameters, which will be our starting file for the new estimate. The HERest tool uses the Baum-Welch algorithm to update the states with new parameters (mean, variance and transition probabilities). For each required context-dependent model, the appropriate monophone was cloned and then all of the resulting models were retrained on data using context dependent transcriptions. The next step is to add the word limit. The word limit (pause) is responsible for adding silence between words in continuous speech. Re-estimation is applied again to update model parameters. For the monophonic models, the model is re-estimated using HERES, and for the triphones models, it is re-estimated using HERest and HHEd, which calculate the optimal values of the parameters using Gaussian mixtures. These parameters are re-estimated repeatedly using the training data until it converges.

The experiment follows the procedures mentioned in [7, 12].

6 System Test

The test stage is responsible for generating transcripts of new recordings, for this we use the test data, with a total of 4,509 instances recorded by two collaborators (male and female).

To generate the new transcripts, we must use the HVite tool that is designed to get the recognition files in the Master Label File (MLF) format.

In order to process the test data, the Hvite tool needs the MFCC files of the new recordings, the trained acoustic model, the dictionary and the language model.

7 Results and Discussion

For the comparative analysis between the original transcript and the output sentence of the speech recognizer, which is obtained using the HVite tool, we use the HResults tool, which provides comparative statistics.

Equations (1) show the formula for analyzing the results.

$$\text{Accuracy} = \frac{N - D - S - I}{N} \times 100\% \tag{1}$$

Where N is the total number of labels in the reference transcripts with correct recognition, D is the number of removal errors, S is the number of substitution errors, and I is the number of insertion errors.

Equation (2) shows the calculation of the word error rate which is a criterion for evaluating speech recognition systems.

$$\text{Word Error Rate} = 100 - \%\text{Accuracy} \tag{2}$$

Table 4. Comparative recognition results for different models

Model Set	WER
Monophone aligned (13 MFCC)	19.60
Monophone tied (13 MFCC)	14.52
Gaussian triphone aligned (13 MFCC)	13.41
Gaussian triphone tied (13 MFCC)	12.70

Table 4 gives the recognition performance using monophone aligned (13 MFCC), monophone tied (13 MFCC), Gaussian triphone aligned (13 MFCC), Gaussian and triphone tied (13 MFCC). There are several points to note about these results. Firstly, the overall accuracy is better even for a highly constrained grammar based on the test set itself. This reflects the inherent difficulty of the task. Secondly, the general trend is that increasing the complexity of the models improves performance. Finally, the training data set was deliberately restricted to reduce the overall time needed to train a system. However, even if all of the available data had been used, it seems unlikely that the performance would have exceeded that obtained on the training set. Hence, a closer look was taken at the data. Spontaneous speech is very different from read speech. It contains frequent false starts, repetitions, hesitations, poor articulation, and this problems included missing silence at the beginning and/or end and truncated words at the beginning.

8 Conclusion and Future Work

This paper presents an automatic speech recognition system for Quechua language based on HTK HMM Toolkit. The results show significant improvements in the WER (reductions from 19.60 to 12.70%) using a Gaussian triphone HMM acoustic model. Although no direct comparison with other published results is possible, it seems that our performance is slightly lower than that proposed by Chuctaya [6] with DTW and KNN. The highly agglutinating nature of language is a challenge for tasks based on word morphology, such as n-gram language modeling, POS labeling, speech recognition, among others. Similar challenges can be found in ASR systems for typologically similar languages such as Turkish [4] or Basque [12]. This system can be used in applications where small vocabulary Quechua speech recognition is required. Moreover, this research work could form the basis for further research in Quechua ASR systems.

An immediate future work is introducing neural networks instead an HMM acoustic model. The new model is to reproduce the work of Graves [10] including extensions made by Amodei [2], that means to introduce neural networks in each stage of the process and use Knowledge Transfer described by Zhao [18] to build a model capable of learning several languages, in this case Basque and Quechua.

References

1. Alegre, F.: Aplicación de rna y hmm a la verificación automática de locutor. IEEE Lat. Am. Trans. **5**(5), 329–337 (2007)
2. Amodei, D., et al.: Deep speech 2: End-to-end speech recognition in English and Mandarin. In: International Conference on Machine Learning, pp. 173–182 (2016)
3. Botha, J.A.: Probabilistic modelling of morphologically rich languages (2015)
4. Carki, K., Geutner, P., Schultz, T.: Turkish LVCSR: towards better speech recognition for agglutinative languages. In: 2000 IEEE International Conference on Acoustics, Speech, and Signal Processing, vol. 3, pp. 1563–1566. IEEE (2000)
5. Cerrón-Palomino, R.: Quechua sureño diccionario unificado quechua-castellano castellano-quechua [unified dictionary of southern quechua, quechua-spanish spanish-quechua]. Biblioteca Nacional del Perú, Lima (1994)
6. Chuctaya, H.F.C., Mercado, R.N.M., Gaona, J.J.G.: Isolated automatic speech recognition of quechua numbers using MFCC, DTW and KNN
7. Dua, M., Aggarwal, R., Kadyan, V., Dua, S.: Punjabi automatic speech recognition using htk. Int. J. Comput. Sci. Issues (IJCSI) **9**(4), 359 (2012)
8. Durston, A., Mannheim, B.: Indigenous Languages, Politics, and Authority in Latin America: Historical and Ethnographic Perspectives. University of Notre Dame Press, South Bend (2018)
9. Giannakopoulos, T.: pyAudioAnalysis: an open-source python library for audio signal analysis. PloS One **10**(12), e0144610 (2015)
10. Graves, A., Jaitly, N.: Towards end-to-end speech recognition with recurrent neural networks. In: International Conference on Machine Learning, pp. 1764–1772 (2014)
11. Melgarejo, N., Camacho, L.: Implementation of a web platform for the preservation of american native languages. In: 2018 IEEE XXV International Conference on Electronics, Electrical Engineering and Computing (INTERCON), pp. 1–4. IEEE (2018)
12. Odriozola, I., Serrano, L., Hernaez, I., Navas, E.: The AhoSR automatic speech recognition system. In: Navarro Mesa, J.L., et al. (eds.) IberSPEECH 2014. LNCS (LNAI), vol. 8854, pp. 279–288. Springer, Cham (2014). https://doi.org/10.1007/978-3-319-13623-3_29
13. Rabiner, L.R.: A tutorial on hidden markov models and selected applications in speech recognition. Proc. IEEE **2**, 257–286 (1989)
14. Rabiner, L.R., Juang, B.H., Rutledge, J.C.: Fundamentals of Speech Recognition, vol. 14. PTR Prentice Hall, Englewood Cliffs (1993)
15. Rios, A.: A basic language technology toolkit for quechua. Procesamiento del Lenguaje Natural **56**, 91–94 (2016)
16. Torero, A.: Los dialectos quechuas. Univ, Agraria (1964)
17. Zevallos, R., Camacho, L.: Siminchik: A speech corpus for preservation of southern quechua. In: Proceedings of the Eleventh International Conference on Language Resources and Evaluation (LREC 2018). European Language Resources Association (ELRA), Paris, France (2018)
18. Zhao, Y., et al.: Cross-language transfer speech recognition using deep learning. In: 11th IEEE International Conference on Control and Automation (ICCA), pp. 1422–1426. IEEE (2014)

Implementation of an Indoor Location System for Mobile-Based Museum Guidance

Dennis Núñez-Fernández[✉]

Universidad Nacional de Ingeniería, Lima, Peru
dnunezf@uni.pe

Abstract. In this work we proposed an indoor location system that makes use of a mobile phone and WiFi signal levels to determine the location of a person in the museum "Eduardo de Habich" at the Universidad Nacional de Ingeniería, Peru. Therefore, by determining the location, additional information such as recommendations, multimedia, an more could be shown to each user in order to have a better user experience. The main advantage with similar indoor location systems such as Beacons or RFID technology is that the proposed system does not require additional hardware as it only uses pre-installed WiFi hotspots. The experimental tests show promising results, achieving a location accuracy of 93.61%, which is useful for similar navigation tasks.

Keywords: Indoor location system · WiFi signal · Bayesian filter · Mobile phone · User experience

1 Introduction

Current navigation systems like Global Positioning System (GPS) or Global Navigation Satellite System (GLONASS) offer high accuracy in outdoor environments, but in indoor areas they provide low position accuracy [1]. For this reason, the implementation of indoor location systems has attracted the interest of researchers due to the demand for these systems in several real applications like immersive experiences, asset tracking, proximity marketing, indoor navigation, controlling robots in a warehouse, augmented reality, and more.

Up to date, there exist several approaches for indoor location systems [2] such as radio frequency identification (RFID), wireless local area networks (WLAN), Bluetooth among others [3,4]. Regarding WiFi based indoor location systems, in [5] a precise WiFi-based indoor location system using Monte Carlo (MC) filter is proposed, however, the system is intended for tracking trajectories with a high precision, which it is not suitable for our project since the divided regions are not so smalls. In [6], an indoor positioning system for smart buildings is used, but the system makes use of RFID technology, which results in additional costs. In a more recent work, [7] describes a novel system that uses machine learning techniques,

© Springer Nature Switzerland AG 2020
J. A. Lossio-Ventura et al. (Eds.): SIMBig 2019, CCIS 1070, pp. 69–75, 2020.
https://doi.org/10.1007/978-3-030-46140-9_7

nevertheless the system is intended for centimeter level location and relies on visible-light technology. In another recent work [8], an easy and understandable method is proposed in order to improve IoT localization in smart buildings across heterogeneous devices via a Markov-Chain model, however the system achieves a localization accuracy of 87.2% for a hexagonal region of 3.5 m cell radius. In addition, indoor Google Maps [9] provides guidance in buildings, but its accuracy is not enough, according to our experience.

In this paper, a system for indoor location for museum guidance is proposed, which is intended for the museum "Eduardo de Habich" at the Universidad Nacional de Ingeniería, Peru. In contrast with indoor location systems that relies on external devices like RFID hardware or Bluetooth beacons (which result in additional costs), the proposed system does not require additional equipment. In this way, making use of a mobile phone and pre installed access points, our indoor location system is able to provide a good position accuracy and the information related to its location.

2   Proposed Method

2.1   Overview

The presented system performs interior localization of museum visitors in real-time on a mobile phone using WiFi signal. This system works on devices with low computational resources. With the purpose to achieve response time and power computational requirements, a simple but effective estimator is employed, which is a Bayes recursive estimator (also called Bayes filter).

The proposed methodology has two phases: offline phase and online phase. At online phase, WiFi levels are captured several times per region, obtaining an RSSI table per region, later the RSSI data is divided into training and testing datasets for performance evaluation, then the normalized histograms are calculated and cleaned via Gaussian curve, finally the localization system is evaluated. At online phase, the Bayesian filter is implemented in an Android mobile device.

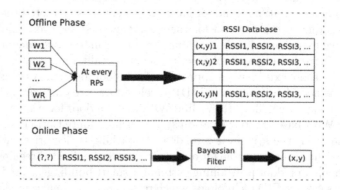

Fig. 1. Diagram for the proposed indoor location system

This filter uses the captured WiFi levels and the cleaned RSSI database to predict the most likely region. Figure 1 shows the diagram of our methodology.

2.2 Data Recolection

First, the main areas of the museum "Eduardo de Habich" at the Universidad Nacional de Ingeniería are identified and divided into regions larger than 2 × 2 m and less than 5 × 5 m. Figure 2 shows such a distribution.

Then, the WiFi information such as SSID, MAC and RSSI are recollected via a custom application in Java for Android devices. Therefore, 150 samples in each region (at different times during three non consecutive days/nights) are captured. Later, no stable APs and far APs are filtered, so, only the best APs are selected for the final dataset.

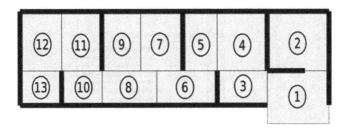

Fig. 2. Division of the museum into regions

2.3 Pre-processing

In this step, the samples are randomly shuffled, and divided in 80% for training and 20% for testing in order to evaluate the performance of our estimator. Then, the normalized histograms are extracted from the training dataset (for each AP and region). However, this original training database is composed of noisy samples which are affected by reflections and scattering (see Fig. 3).

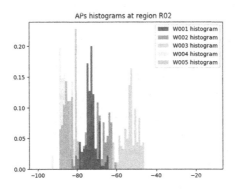

Fig. 3. Sample of the original histograms

Many papers related to RSSI based indoor location assume its Gaussian probability density function (PDF) [10,11]. This is justified by the relation to PDF of radio-receiver's noise or together to influence of average white Gaussian noise radio-channel which is modelled by a Gaussian PDF. Therefore, original histograms are cleaned by approximating each one to a Gaussian PDF. In Eq. (1), the formulation of a Gaussian PDF is shown, which is defined by two parameters: μ (mean) and σ (standard deviation).

$$f(x|\mu,\sigma^2) = \frac{1}{\sqrt{2\pi\sigma^2}}e^{-\frac{(x-\mu)^2}{2\sigma^2}} \tag{1}$$

Figure 4 depicts one sample of the original and cleaned histograms, which are presented as continuous Gaussian curves. As we can see, this new normal distribution fills the missing values of the original RSSI histogram and readjust the noisy values which were disturbed by strong reflections and scattering.

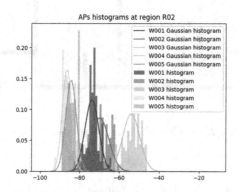

Fig. 4. Sample of the original and cleaned histograms

Finally, construction of one AP table for each access point is performed. In this way, the AP table will be made up of the union of the Gaussian histograms of different regions with the same AP. Table 1 show its structure.

Table 1. AP table for access point j (Wj)

Region	Gaussian histograms
Region 1	Wj Gaussian histogram at Region 1
Region 2	Wj Gaussian histogram at Region 2
	...
Region N	Wj Gaussian histogram at Region N

2.4   Bayesian Filter

In order to achieve response time and computational requirements, a straightforward and effective estimator is used, it is based on the Bayes recursive estimator [12]. This is able to infer the posterior using sensed and prior knowledge (see Eq. (2)). Being A the event we want the probability, and B the new evidence that is related to A. Therefore, the posterior $P_{(A|B)}$ is calculated by the likelihood $P_{(B|A)}$ (probability of observing the new evidence) and the prior $P_{(A)}$ (probability of our hypothesis without any additional prior information). $P_{(B)}$ is the marginal likelihood, which is the total probability of observing the evidence.

$$P_{(A|B)} = \frac{P_{(B|A)} P_{(A)}}{P_{(B)}} \tag{2}$$

Algorithm 1 describes the implementation of the Bayes-based estimator. This takes the AP tables and current WiFi measurement as inputs, and return the estimated region and its probability. Thereby, the algorithm recursively calculates the probability of the posterior region (line 11), then the probability (line 12) and predicted region (line 13) are calculated. The Algorithm 1 was implemented in Python for evaluation of performance of the Bayes estimator, and implemented in Java for real-time inference on an Android mobile phone.

Algorithm 1. Bayes Estimator Algorithm

1: $N = number\ of\ regions;\ R = number\ of\ routers$
2: $W_r = AP\ table\ for\ router\ r$
3: **procedure** BAYESESTIMATOR$(w_1, w_2, ..., w_R)$
4:     # Start with uniform distribution
5:     $priorW_{1,2,..,R} = [1/N; 1/N; ...; 1/N]_{Nx1}$
6:     $probability = (100/N)\%$
7:     **while** probability $< 95\%$ **do**
8:         # Perform Bayes
9:         **for** r from 1 to R **do**
10:             $posteriorW_r = norm(priorW_r \times W_r[:, w_r])$
11:             $prob_r = max(posteriorW_r)$
12:             $pred_r = where(posteriorW_r == prob_r)$
13:         **end for**
14:         # Find the highest probability
15:         $probability = max(prob_{1,2,..,R})$
16:         $r\_best = where(prob_{1,2,..,R} == probability)$
17:         $prediction = pred_{r\_best}$
18:         # Update the new prior
19:         **for** r from 1 to R **do**
20:             $priorW_r = posteriorW_{r\_best}$
21:         **end for**
22:     **end while**
23:     Return $prediction, probability$
24: **end procedure**

---

3 Experimental Results

In order to obtain the performance and another metrics for the indoor localization system, we evaluated it on the testing dataset. The results are defined by the overall accuracy and the confusion matrix (see Fig. 5). This matrix for the proposed system shows a high accuracy for the diagonal values and low accuracy for the others, it means that the system has a high accuracy per class/region. Also, the accuracy of the indoor location system is about 93.61%.

	R01	R02	R03	R04	R05	R06	R07	R08	R09	R10	R11	R12	R13
R01	0.95	0	0	0	0.01	0.02	0	0	0	0.01	0	0.01	0
R02	0	0.91	0	0	0.02	0.01	0	0.02	0	0	0	0.04	0.01
R03	0.01	0	0.95	0	0.01	0	0	0.03	0	0.01	0	0	0
R04	0	0	0	0.94	0	0.01	0.02	0	0.01	0	0	0.02	0
R05	0	0.04	0	0.03	0.9	0	0	0.02	0	0.01	0	0.01	0
R06	0.01	0	0.01	0	0	0.92	0	0.01	0.03	0	0.02	0.01	0
R07	0	0	0	0.02	0	0	0.94	0	0.01	0.01	0	0	0.03
R08	0.01	0	0.01	0	0.02	0	0	0.92	0	0.02	0	0.02	0
R09	0	0	0.01	0.01	0.01	0	0.01	0	0.93	0	0.01	0.01	0
R10	0.01	0.02	0	0	0.01	0	0	0	0	0.96	0	0	0
R11	0	0.02	0	0	0.02	0	0	0.01	0.01	0	0.94	0	0
R12	0	0.01	0	0.02	0	0	0.01	0	0	0	0	0.95	0.01
R13	0	0.01	0.01	0	0	0.01	0	0	0	0.01	0	0	0.96

Fig. 5. Confusion matrix for the proposed system

For the evaluation of the system, our Android application was tested on a Samsung J2 with Android 6.0.1. This is conducted in different regions and for several positions. As expected, the system correctly predicted the locations in all regions. Figure 6 shows some results of this test. As we can see, our system correctly predict the location with a probability above 94%.

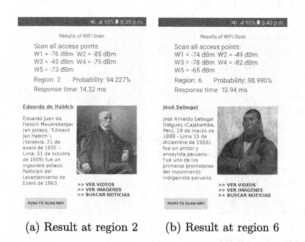

(a) Result at region 2   (b) Result at region 6

Fig. 6. Online results on an Android mobile phone

4   Conclusions

This paper introduced the implementation of a WiFi based indoor location system to guide visitors at the museum "Eduardo de Habich" at the Universidad Nacional de Ingeniería, Peru. With the aim to accomplish a high positioning accuracy, a fast response time and low computational power consumption, the proposed system makes use of a simple and effective Bayes recursive estimator. Experiments show promising results, obtaining an accuracy of 93.61% and a response time of 14 ms. Thus, the proposed methodology is not limited to this work, but can also be applied to similar localization tasks such as robot control, immersive experiences, asset tracking, augmented reality, among others.

References

1. Motte, H., Wyffels, J., De Strycker, L., Goemaere, J.-P.: Evaluating GPS data in indoor environments. Adv. Electr. Comput. Eng. **11**(3), 25–28 (2011). https://doi. org/10.4316/AECE.2011.03004
2. Sakpere, W., Adeyeye Oshin, M., Mlitwa, N.B.: A state-of-the-art survey of indoor positioning and navigation systems and technologies. South Afr. Comput. J. **29**(3), 145–197 (2017)
3. Zafari, F., Gkelias, A., Leung, K.: A survey of indoor localization systems and technologies. arXiv:1709.01015v3 (2019)
4. Brena, R.F., García-Vázquez, J.P., et al.: Evolution of indoor positioning technologies: a survey. J. Sens. **2017**, 21 (2017)
5. Dhital, A., Closas, P., Fernández-Prades, C.: Bayesian filters for indoor localization using wireless sensor networks. In: 5th ESA Workshop on Satellite Navigation Technologies and European Workshop on GNSS Signals and Signal Processing (NAVITEC). Noordwijk, vol. 2010, pp. 1–7 (2010)
6. Moreno-Cano, M.V., Zamora-Izquierdo, M.A., Santa, J., Skarmeta, A.F.: An indoor localization system based on artificial neural networks and particle filters applied to intelligent buildings. Neurocomput. **122**, 116–125 (2013)
7. Li, X., Cao, Y., Chen, C.: Machine learning based high accuracy indoor visible light location algorithm. In: 2018 IEEE International Conference on Smart Internet of Things (SmartIoT), Xi'an, pp. 198–203 (2018). https://doi.org/10.1109/SmartIoT. 2018.00043
8. Lin, K., Chen, M., Deng, J., Hassan, M.M., Fortino, G.: Enhanced fingerprinting and trajectory prediction for IoT localization in smart buildings. IEEE Trans. Autom. Sci. Eng. **13**(3), 1294–1307 (2016)
9. Indoor Google Maps. http://maps.google.com/help/maps/indoormaps/. Accessed Jan 2014
10. Chruszczyk, L.: Statistical analysis of indoor RSSI read-outs for 433 MHz, 868 MHz, 2.4 GHz and 5 GHz ISM bands. Int. J. Electron. Telecommun. **63**(1), 33–38 (2017)
11. Kaji, K., Kawaguchi, N.: Design and implementation of WiFi indoor localization based on Gaussian mixture model and particle filter. In: 2012 International Conference on Indoor Positioning and Indoor Navigation (IPIN), Sydney, NSW, pp. 1–9 (2012)
12. Park, J.-G., et al.: Growing an organic indoor location system. In: Proceedings of the 8th International Conference on Mobile Systems, Applications, and Services (MobiSys 2010), pp. 271–284. ACM, New York (2010)

TensorFlow for Doctors

Isha Agarwal[1] , Rajkumar Kolakaluri[1] , Michael Dorin[1(✉)] ,
and Mario Chong[2]

[1] University of St. Thomas, St. Paul, MN 55105, USA
mike.dorin@stthomas.edu
[2] Universidad del Pacífico, Lima, Peru

Abstract. Machine learning has advanced substantially in the past few years, and there are many generic solutions freely available to classify text and images. The solutions are so straightforward to set up and run that having a software background is no longer necessary to perform machine learning experimentation. These systems are being adapted in many ways, and it seems only natural that those in the medical field may wish to see how machine learning might help with their research. This research examines if off-the-shelf machine learning systems are suitable for research by medical professionals who do not have software backgrounds. If all doctors who wish to experiment with machine learning could have an adequate system available, the impact on research could be substantial. This investigation applies a commonly available machine learning practice lab to medical images. As part of this investigation, we evaluated the TensorFlow for Poets (TFP) tutorial from Google Code Labs with openly available medical images provided by Kaggle Inc. While we would not recommend our test results as a basis for diagnosing medical conditions, the results were encouraging enough to suggest that using off-the-shelf systems can offer a promising opportunity to expand machine learning research into those with medical, but not software backgrounds.

Keywords: TensorFlow · Machine learning · Image classification

1 Introduction

In our world there is an increasing availability of quality medical treatments for various diseases. While the pharmaceutical field continues to provide strong remedies for common ailments, it is of the utmost importance to diagnose patients early and get them the remedies they need. In first world countries it is much easier to find a doctor with adequate diagnostic technology for "one's disease". However, in developing countries where doctors are sparse and the availability of cutting-edge technology is limited, there needs to be a way to provide patients more timely diagnoses of life-threatening diseases. The purpose of this study is to research how off-the-shelf systems can allow non-technological

Supported by the University of St. Thomas.

J. A. Lossio-Ventura et al. (Eds.): SIMBig 2019, CCIS 1070, pp. 76–88, 2020.
https://doi.org/10.1007/978-3-030-46140-9_8

medical professionals access to the technology they need to quickly and effectively diagnose patients. This study will examine the use of the lab "TensorFlow for Poets" in diagnosing brain tumors, breast cancer, malaria and pneumonia. We hypothesize that it is possible for non-technical medical personnel to use off-the-shelf software and readily available hardware for providing diagnoses services or performing research. The purpose of this study is to explore this potential.

2   Relevant Existing Research

2.1   Brain Tumors

There have been numerous studies investigating the use of machine learning techniques in connection with diagnosis of brain tumors. These can be broadly divided based on whether they use unsupervised or supervised machine learning algorithms. [45] use an unsupervised fuzzy clustering approach to automate brain tumor segmentation. In the papers that use supervised learning, there are a growing number of studies that use convolutional neural networks (CNN) of tumor segmentation. Amongst these examples, the best results are those by [33]. Their experiment used CNN with small ($3*3$) filters on the Brain Tumor Segmentation Challenge 2013 dataset and achieved DICE scores (Duration, Team Performance Integrity, Commitment, and Effort) of 0.88, 0.83 and 0.77 on whole tumor, core tumor and active tumor regions respectively. An interested reader can refer to [22] and [1] for surveys of papers that use machine learning algorithms in the context of brain tumors.

2.2   Breast Cancer

There has also been lot of research performed on using machine learning techniques for detection and diagnosis of breast cancer. Broadly speaking, detection refers to determination of the location of suspect lesions and diagnosis refers to predicting whether a lesion is benign or malignant [45]. For doing any of these tasks, image data acquired from various sources such as digital mammogram [18,23], ultrasound [10,26], magnetic resonance imaging [3,43], microscopic images [17,27], and infrared thermography [6,38] is used for training the algorithms. Machine learning techniques such as K-Nearest Neighbor [14], Support Vector Machines [24], Deep Learning [25], Decision Trees [35], and Logistic Regression [26] have been applied on images from these sources, and many papers report metrics such as accuracy, specificity, and sensitivity to be much better than 90% for their methods. For example, [23] aim to classify potential micro-classifications using support vector machines on digital mammogram data and they report that 100% accuracy was achieved. [43] successfully used a special type of neural network, again on digital mammogram data, to classify tissue as normal, benign or malignant. A detailed survey on the use of machine learning algorithms on image data in the context of breast cancer can be found in [45].

2.3   Malaria

The fundamental way to diagnose malaria is in a laboratory [13], where parasites and infected red blood cells are counted manually by a trained microscopist. There is no way to measure the efficiency and correctness of such diagnoses and this may sometimes lead to severe complications. Therefore, it is important to find or develop a more reliable and efficient method to diagnose malaria. A diagnosis can be divided into the following steps:

- Determining the presence of the parasite.
- Identifying the species of the parasites.
- Identifying the life-cycle-stages of the parasites.

[19] present a technique for identifying the life stages and species of parasites using microscopic images of thin stained blood smears. The paper used an Artificial Neural Network and achieved classification accuracy of 97.76% in recognizing stages and sensitivity of 93.2% in recognizing the species. [4] introduce a deep belief network (DBN) to classify peripheral blood smear images into parasite or non-parasite classes. They achieved an F-score of 89.66%, sensitivity of 97.6%, and specificity of 95.92%. Their paper is the first application of a DBN for malaria parasite detection. [34] develop an unsupervised malaria screening technique using stained thin smear images with overall sensitivity of 100% while capturing malaria cases and specificity between 50% and 88% for all species. [41] propose a novel binary parasite detection scheme that is based on a modified K nearest neighbor. [15] performed a computer aided pattern recognition of malaria parasitemia along with its stages. It uses color, textural, and morphological information as input. [28] present techniques based on segmentation of red blood cells (RBCs) and parasites in HSV (hue, saturation, value) color space to segment parasites in stained images.

2.4   Pneumonia

The research on using machine learning techniques for diagnosing pneumonia is not as extensive as for diagnosis of other diseases such as brain tumors and breast cancer. In a recent paper, [36] use a 121-layer convolutional neural network (CNN) on a publicly available X-ray dataset that is labelled and consists of more than 100,000 frontal view X-rays. They compare the performance of their CNN with that of four radiologists and show that the CNN's performance is statistically better than that of the radiologists. They also show that the CNN achieves an AUROC (area under the receiver operating characteristic curve) of 0.768, which is better than 0.633 and 0.713 by [42] and [44] respectively. In another study, [33] use transbronchial biopsies to extract RNA (ribonucleic acid) sequence data and use a logistic regression to classify the sample. They achieve AUROC of 0.86, specificity of 86% and sensitivity of 63%. Taking a completely different approach, [32] use support vector machines on lung sounds to diagnose pneumonia. Their technique achieves classification accuracy of 86%.

3   Background Diagnosis

3.1   Brain Tumors

There are various tests that are performed to find or diagnose a brain tumor; to detect the type of tumor; to find out if it has spread to other parts of the body; to determine if it is indeed a brain tumor or instead some kind of cancer which has spread to the brain from another part of the body; and, to figure out the best possible treatment for a particular patient [11].

When ordering these tests, a doctor may consider multiple factors about the patient, such as symptoms, the patient's medical history, the type of tumor suspected, the patient's age, and the patient's current health. Generally, a brain tumor is diagnosed by a neurologist, and the first step of the diagnosis is magnetic resonance imaging (MRI). In case the MRI result is positive, a biopsy or surgery is performed [2].

3.2   Breast Cancer

Often women with breast cancer usually do not observe any signs or symptoms. Therefore, regular breast cancer screening is recommended to help find it at an earlier stage and, therefore, can be treated more easily. There are many tests available to diagnose breast cancer and these tests provide different pieces of information, such as whether this cancer has spread to any other part of the body and which treatment would be most effective for a patient. Not all tests are required for a single person. In addition to an MRI, other tests may be required to diagnose breast cancer [37].

Diagnostic mammography is recommended when a patient is having symptoms of breast cancer or if there is any problem detected in breast cancer screening. Such issues include abnormal breast, nipple discharge, or maybe a new lump. This is more like a detailed x-ray where multiple images are captured for better results. A biopsy is the only technique that gives definitive results. In this process, the tissue is extracted from the affected area and examined with the help of a microscope [39].

3.3   Malaria

Malaria is caused by Plasmodium parasites spread by infected female Anopheles mosquitoes. Its signs and symptoms such as fever, chills, sweats, headaches, muscle pains, nausea and vomiting are not specific and can be seen in other diseases like flu or viral infection. Doctors may need other information from the patient including their medical history, occupation, and recent travel. There may be other signs of malaria which lead to full diagnosed through testing [12].

According to the American Centers for Disease Control, thick and thin blood smears are the most common and reliable way to diagnose malaria. In this process blood is stained with an agent and examined under a microscope for malaria parasites. The thin smear test can be helpful in identifying the type of Plasmodium species causing the infection along with the count of infected red blood cells. Regularly two sets of both tests are performed and there is still a high probability that no parasite is found, as the number of parasites fluctuates greatly [8].

3.4 Pneumonia

Pneumonia is an infection in the lungs, which can be caused by bacteria, fungi, or viruses. Its common symptoms, cough, fever, chills, loss of appetite, low energy, and fatigue are quite similar to the cold or flu, and therefore pneumonia is not always diagnosed easily. It can be diagnosed on the basis of the patient's medical history, a physical exam, or through diagnostic tests [7].

Physical exams listen to the lungs of the patient using a stethoscope to check if they are functioning normally without making any crackling and bubbling sounds while the patient is inhaling. Diagnostic tests are performed after the physical exam. If a doctor suspects that the person has pneumonia, they can recommend some lab tests to verify their suspicion and learn more about the infection. These tests provide different information related to pneumonia, such as the presence of bacteria, lung inflammation, the type of bacteria, and the affected lung area [30].

A chest x-ray is one of the most popular methods for diagnosing pneumonia. It is helpful to display pus or blood in the lungs. Chest x-rays cannot give any information about the bacteria causing pneumonia. A complete blood count measures various blood counts and can indicate if infection or inflammation is present, but it cannot specifically verify the presence of pneumonia. Sputum culture and gram stain are used to identify the bacteria causing the problem. A small amount of sputum is collected from the patient, stained, and examined under a microscope. Also, culture is performed on the sample using Petri dishes and growing agents. From there, the type of bacteria can be identified easily. This can be helpful in determining which antibiotic is more effective for a particular patient [30].

4 Background on TensorFlow for Poets

TensorFlow is a machine learning system which operates in different enviornments. TensorFlow provides a variety of intuitive workflows, and user-friendly application programming interfaces (API) for both beginners and experts to create machine learning models in numerous languages. TensorFlow is flexible for experimentation, and can efficiently run on various platforms ranging from mobile devices to supercomputers. This enables developers to more easily go from model building and training to deployment. This also expands the availability and utility of TensorFlow to a large audience [20].

TensorFlow for Poets (TFP) is based on transfer learning, where instead of starting from scratch, one starts from a model that has already trained on another problem [21]. The same model is used, but the model is retrained to differentiate a small number of classes based on a new application. In contrast to deep learning from scratch, transfer learning can be done quicker.

TensorFlow For Poets makes extensive use of ImageNet. ImageNet [16] is a database created for the purpose of providing images to researchers. According to the ImageNet website, the image database organized in a human-annotated manner and there are more than 14 million images available. The ImageNet project uses sophisticated algorithms to organize and annotate multimedia data. The availability of this large-scale image database greatly helps researchers and data scientists.

5 This Investigation

As previously mentioned, the goal of this investigation was to determine if machine learning tools could be used "off-the-shelf" for medical diagnosis or medical research. We followed the steps specified in the TensorFlow for Poets lab, just as a person with no relevant machine learning experience would do. However, instead of downloading and using the images of flowers, we downloaded and used medical images of brain tumors [9], breast cancer [40], malaria [31], and pneumonia [29] made available on from the Kaggle.com website. For retraining the network, we set the Linux shell variables exactly as indicated in the "Tensorflow for Poets lab".

As described by Browniee's tutorial on k–Fold Cross–Validation [5], we divided the data into groups separating a test data set from the training data. On the training data we used 10,000 training steps on brain tumor, malaria, and pneumonia images. However due to the quantity and size of the breast cancer images an increased training time required, so for this analysis, the number of training steps was reduced to 5,000. This is because the quantity of tumor types and number of magnification levels required an increase in analysis time.

For our test data set, a minimum of 10% of the images were separated for validation against the trained data set. For brain tumor images, malaria, and pneumonia, the test was setup as a binary "yes" or "no" problem for both the training and the testing. TensorFlow was tasked with determining if a condition was present.

The breast cancer testing was conducted with eight different tumor types each having four zoom magnifications. This test was also binary, as we checked for one type of tumor against all other types of tumors combined. For example, for the condition of adenosis, at each zoom magnification we compared adenosis to all the remaining types to measure how successful the determination of a particular tumor type would be. For each image type and magnification, a separate training and validation was setup. The system that ran the tests is based on a Core Due 2 processor and had a GTX-970 GPU.

6   Results

A confusion matrix, commonly used in machine learning, is a table visually showing the performance of an algorithm. In this study a confusion matrix was created to demonstrate model accuracy for the brain tumor, malaria, and pneumonia analysis. Regarding Breast Cancer, we show the model accuracy for different conditions under 40X, 100X, 200X, and 400X magnifications. The overall summary of how accurate all of the non-breast cancer models were is show in Table 2.

Table 1. Confusion matrix brain MRI images

Confusion matrix brain MRI images			.
Total = 26		Predicted class	
		Yes-brain tumor	No-brain tumor
Actual class	Yes-brain tumor	12 (TP)	3 (FN)
	No-brain tumor	3 (FP)	8 (TN)
Model accuracy = 77%		Misclassification rate = 23%	

Beginning with the brain tumor data, images were separated before the learning process began which had been classified as positive or negative for having a brain tumor. We then used the script provided the TFP laboratory to see how TensorFlow would classify the images. The results can be found in Brain Tumor section of Table 2. The confusion matrix for the Brain MRI Images can be found in Table 1 showing with the resulting model accuracy of only 77%.

Breast Cancer validation was done using the same procedures, but as there were many more files and many more types of tumors, the validation images were separated as a particular type of tumor or not that particular type of tumor. As before, we used the script provided in the TFP lab to classify the images. Table 3 shows the verification summary results for each condition. Conditions which had more data available, had better results.

Moving to the Malaria validation, there were more than 1,300 non-malaria validation images and more than 1,200 malaria positive validation images. The results are in Malaria section of Table 2. The Malaria confusion matrix can be found in Table 4. Overall the model accuracy was better than most, but this is likely due to the amount of data available.

With 483 images, pneumonia had a reasonable number available for final validation. Overall there were 401 classified to have Pneumonia and 82 classified as being without pneumonia. The model accuracy is shown in Table 2. Table 5 has the confusion Matrix for pneumonia.

Table 2. Project validation

	No-brain tumor image	Yes-brain tumor image
Validation images	11	15
No condition	8	3
Yes condition	3	12
Model accuracy	73%	80%
	No-malaria image	Yes-malaria image
Validation images	1298	1369
No condition	1269	252
Yes condition	29	1117
Model accuracy	98%	81%
	No-pneumonia image	Yes-pneumonia image
Validation images	82	401
No condition	77	13
Yes condition	5	388
Model accuracy	94%	97%

Table 3. Validation summary of BreakHist data

	40X		100X		200X		400X	
Adenosis	13	57%	9	39%	7	32%	8	38%
Non-Adenosis	10		14		15		13	
Ductal_Carcinoma	131	76%	56	31%	104	58%	46	29%
Non-Ductal_Carcinoma	41		124		75		112	
Fibroadenoma	21	41%	14	27%	9	17%	27	57%
Non-Fibroadenoma	30		38		44		20	
Lobular_Carcinoma	5	16%	0	0%	1	3%	2	7%
Non-Lobular_Carcinoma	26		34		32		25	
Mucinous_Carcinoma	0	0%	5	11%	4	10%	2	6%
Non-Mucinous_Carcinoma	41		39		35		32	
Papillary_Carcinoma	15	52%	6	21%	5	19%	1	4%
Non-Papillary_Carcinoma	14		22		22		27	
Phyllodes_Tumor	10	45%	5	45%	4	18%	8	35%
Non-Phyllodes_Tumor	12		6		18		15	
Tubular_Adenoma	13	42%	13	43%	11	39%	6	23%
Non-Tubular_Adenoma	18		17		17		20	

Table 4. Confusion matrix malaria cell images

Confusion matrix malaria cell images			
Total = 2667		Predicted class	
		Yes-malaria	No-malaria
Actual class	Yes-malaria	1117 (TP)	252 (FN)
	No-malaria	29 (FP)	1269 (TN)
Model accuracy = 89%		Misclassification rate = 11%	

Table 5. Confusion matrix - pneumonia images

Confusion matrix - pneumonia images			
Total = 483		Predicted class	
		Yes-pneumonia	No-pneumonia
Actual class	Yes-pneumonia	388 (TP)	13 (FN)
	No-pneumonia	5 (FP)	77 (TN)
Model accuracy = 96%		Misclassification rate = 4%	

7   Discussion

Figures 1 and 2 illustrate how the results do not indicate that following the procedures of our experiment would always lead to a quality medical diagnoses. However, some interesting aspects still stand out. Firstly, the experiments with the most image data had a higher success rate than the categories with fewer items. Malaria and Pneumonia had many images which gave low misclassification rates. In the categories of breast cancer, ductal carcinoma had the most image samples, and also had the lowest misclassification rate.

Though the success rates were not at the diagnosis quality level, they are encouraging for future research. One step that was bypassed in this analysis was proper preparation of the data. A doctor or scientist will have the medical background to properly identify good data and remove bad data. It is important that process has good data or good results cannot be expected. Preparing and scrubbing out the bad data is vital process which would lead to better results.

Further research is needed to determine exactly how the system could accurately and inaccurately diagnose medical conditions. With these results, actions could be put in place to help the system work more accurately therefore decreasing inaccuracies. It is necessary to create a research team that includes medical personnel, procedural technicians, software engineers, and cultural experts. Medical personnel are needed to manually check if the system-diagnosed data was accurate. Procedural technicians (i.e. fMRI and ultrasound technicians) would be integral to the staff as they could explain common errors in the images and the positioning of the patients themselves. Software engineers are necessary to run data and better the systems. Cultural experts could keep the team on task reminding the team to stay with locally accessible technology. A project manager is also recommended to help divide responsibilities and keep the team motivated for a given time line. This complete team would be best suited to providing the accuracy and care this study requires.

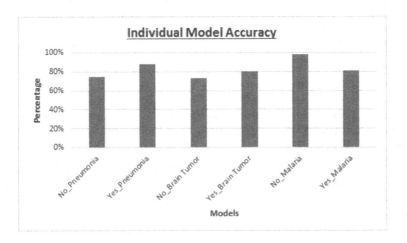

Fig. 1. Individual model accuracy

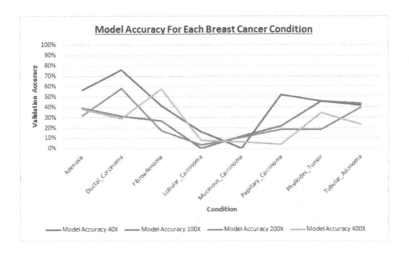

Fig. 2. Model accuracy for each breast cancer condition

8   Conclusion

This paper shows the simplicity and practicality of using readily available tools to perform research for those who do not have a software or data science background. Using publically available image data of brain tumors, breast cancer, malaria, and pneumonia, this paper investigated the reliability of applying off-the-shelf machine learning to medical diagnoses. While the accuracy of results are not currently recommended for actual medical usage, the results are encouraging to believe such technology will be useful in this way in the future. The raw data used in this study, when paired with large amounts of a diseases image data, showed a contextualy low misclassification rate. Future studies on using off-the-shelf machine learning tools in the medical field are to encouraged.

References

1. Akkus, Z., Galimzianova, A., Hoogi, A., Rubin, D.L., Erickson, B.J.: Deep learning for brain MRI segmentation: state of the art and future directions. J. Digit. Imaging **30**(4), 449–459 (2017)
2. Aswathy, S., Dhas, G.G.D., Kumar, S.: A survey on detection of brain tumor from MRI brain images. In: 2014 International Conference on Control, Instrumentation, Communication and Computational Technologies (ICCICCT), pp. 871–877. IEEE (2014)
3. Bhooshan, N., et al.: Potential of computer-aided diagnosis of high spectral and spatial resolution (HISS) MRI in the classification of breast lesions. J. Magn. Reson. Imaging **39**(1), 59–67 (2014)
4. Bibin, D., Nair, M.S., Punitha, P.: Malaria parasite detection from peripheral blood smear images using deep belief networks. IEEE Access **5**, 9099–9108 (2017)
5. Brownlee, J.: A gentle introduction to k-fold cross-validation (2018). https://machinelearningmastery.com/k-fold-cross-validation/. Accessed 4 July 2019
6. Calderón-Contreras, J.D., Chacón-Murguía, M.I., Villalobos-Montiel, A.J., Ortega-Máynez, L.: A fuzzy computer aided diagnosis system using breast thermography. In: 2015 IEEE 12th International Symposium on Biomedical Imaging (ISBI), pp. 105–108. IEEE (2015)
7. CDC: Causes of pneumonia (2020). https://www.cdc.gov/pneumonia/causes.html
8. CDC: Treatment of malaria: Guidelines for clinicians (2020). https://www.cdc.gov/malaria/diagnosis_treatment/clinicians1.html
9. Chakrabarty, N.: Brain MRI images for brain tumor detection (2019). https://www.kaggle.com/navoneel/brain-mri-images-for-brain-tumor-detection, Accessed 4 July 2019
10. Chmielewski, A., Dufort, P., Scaranelo, A.M.: A computerized system to assess axillary lymph node malignancy from sonographic images. Ultrasound Med. Biol. **41**(10), 2690–2699 (2015)
11. Mayo Clinic: Brain tumor (2020). https://www.mayoclinic.org/diseases-conditions/brain-tumor/symptoms-causes/syc-20350084
12. Mayo Clinic: Malaria (2020). https://www.mayoclinic.org/diseases-conditions/malaria/symptoms-causes/syc-20351184
13. Coleman, R.E., et al.: Comparison of field and expert laboratory microscopy for active surveillance for asymptomatic plasmodium falciparum and plasmodium vivax in western thailand. Am. J. Trop. Med. Hyg. **67**(2), 141–144 (2002)
14. Cunningham, P., Delany, S.J.: k-nearest neighbour classifiers. Multiple Classif. Syst. **34**(8), 1–17 (2007)
15. Das, D.K., Ghosh, M., Pal, M., Maiti, A.K., Chakraborty, C.: Machine learning approach for automated screening of malaria parasite using light microscopic images. Micron **45**, 97–106 (2013)

16. Deng, J., Dong, W., Socher, R., Li, L.J., Li, K., Fei-Fei, L.: ImageNet: a large-scale hierarchical image database. In: 2009 IEEE Conference on Computer Vision and Pattern Recognition, pp. 248–255. IEEE (2009)
17. Fernández-Carrobles, M.M., Bueno, G., Déniz, O., Salido, J., García-Rojo, M., González-López, L.: A CAD system for the acquisition and classification of breast TMA in pathology. Stud. Health Technol. Inform **210**, 756–60 (2015)
18. Gardezi, S.J.S., Faye, I., Sanchez Bornot, J.M., Kamel, N., Hussain, M.: Mammogram classification using dynamic time warping. Multimed. Tools Appl. **77**(3), 3941–3962 (2017). https://doi.org/10.1007/s11042-016-4328-8
19. Gitonga, L., Memeu, D.M., Kaduki, K.A., Kale, M.A.C., Muriuki, N.S.: Determination of plasmodium parasite life stages and species in images of thin blood smears using artificial neural network. Open J. Clin. Diagn. **4**(02), 78 (2014)
20. Google (2019). https://www.tensorflow.org/about. Accessed 7 July 2019
21. Google (2019). https://codelabs.developers.google.com/codelabs/tensorflow-for-poets/. Accessed 7 July 2019
22. Havaei, M., et al.: Brain tumor segmentation with deep neural networks. Med. Image Anal. **35**, 18–31 (2017)
23. Khan, S., Hussain, M., Aboalsamh, H., Bebis, G.: A comparison of different Gabor feature extraction approaches for mass classification in mammography. Multimed. Tools Appl. **76**(1), 33–57 (2017)
24. Kudo, T., Matsumoto, Y.: Chunking with support vector machines. In: Proceedings of the Second Meeting of the North American Chapter of the Association for Computational Linguistics on Language Technologies, pp. 1–8. Association for Computational Linguistics (2001)
25. LeCun, Y., Bengio, Y., Hinton, G.: Deep learning. Nature **521**(7553), 436 (2015)
26. Lo, C.M., Moon, W.K., Huang, C.S., Chen, J.H., Yang, M.C., Chang, R.F.: Intensity-invariant texture analysis for classification of BI-RADS category 3 breast masses. Ultrasound Med. Biol. **41**(7), 2039–2048 (2015)
27. Loukas, C., Kostopoulos, S., Tanoglidi, A., Glotsos, D., Sfikas, C., Cavouras,D.: Breast cancer characterization based on image classification of tissue sections visualized under low magnification. Comput. Math. Methods Med. **2013**, 3 (2013)
28. Makkapati, V.V., Rao, R.M.: Segmentation of malaria parasites in peripheral blood smear images. In: 2009 IEEE International Conference on Acoustics, Speech and Signal Processing, pp. 1361–1364. IEEE (2009)
29. Mooney, P.: Chest x-ray images (2018). https://www.kaggle.com/paultimothymooney/chest-xray-pneumonia. Accessed 4 July 2019
30. National Heart, Lung, and Blood Institute: Pneumonia (2020). https://www.nhlbi.nih.gov/health-topics/pneumonia
31. National Library of Medicine: Malaria cell images dataset (2019). https://ceb.nlm.nih.gov/repositories/malaria-datasets/. Accessed 4 July 2019
32. Palaniappan, R., Sundaraj, K., Ahamed, N.U.: Machine learning in lung sound analysis: a systematic review. Biocybern. Biomedi. Eng. **33**(3), 129–135 (2013)
33. Pankratz, D.G., et al.: Usual interstitial pneumonia can be detected in transbronchial biopsies using machine learning. Ann. Am. Thorac. Soc. **14**(11), 1646–1654 (2017)
34. Purwar, Y., Shah, S.L., Clarke, G., Almugairi, A., Muehlenbachs, A.: Automated and unsupervised detection of malarial parasites in microscopic images. Malaria J. **10**(1), 364 (2011)
35. Quinlan, J.R.: Induction of decision trees. Mach. Learn. **1**(1), 81–106 (1986)
36. Rajpurkar, P., et al.: ChexNet: radiologist-level pneumonia detection on chest x-rays with deep learning. arXiv preprint arXiv:1711.05225 (2017)

37. Roth, M.Y., Elmore, J.G., Yi-Frazier, J.P., Reisch, L.M., Oster, N.V., Miglioretti, D.L.: Self-detection remains a key method of breast cancer detection for US women. J. Women's Health **20**(8), 1135–1139 (2011)

38. Schaefer, G., Nakashima, T.: Strategies for addressing class imbalance in ensemble classification of thermography breast cancer features. In: 2015 IEEE Congress on Evolutionary Computation (CEC), pp. 2362–2367. IEEE (2015)

39. Smith, R.A., et al.: American cancer society guidelines for breast cancer screening: update 2003. CA: Cancer J. Clin. **53**(3), 141–169 (2003)

40. Spanhol, F., de Oliveira, L.S., Petitjean, C., Heutte, L.: A dataset for breast cancer histopathological image classification (2015). https://www.kaggle.com/ankur1809/breakhist-dataset. Accessed 4 July 2019

41. Tek, F.B., Dempster, A.G., Kale, I.: Parasite detection and identification for automated thin blood film malaria diagnosis. Comput. Vis. Image Underst. **114**(1), 21–32 (2010)

42. Wang, X., Peng, Y., Lu, L., Lu, Z., Bagheri, M., Summers, R.M.: ChestX-ray8: hospital-scale chest x-ray database and benchmarks on weakly-supervised classification and localization of common thorax diseases. In: Proceedings of the IEEE Conference on Computer Vision and Pattern Recognition, pp. 2097–2106 (2017)

43. Weiss, W.A., Medved, M., Karczmar, G.S., Giger, M.L.: Residual analysis of the water resonance signal in breast lesions imaged with high spectral and spatial resolution (HISS) MRI: a pilot study. Med. Phys. **41**(1), 012303 (2014)

44. Yao, L., Poblenz, E., Dagunts, D., Covington, B., Bernard, D., Lyman, K.: Learning to diagnose from scratch by exploiting dependencies among labels. arXiv preprint arXiv:1710.10501 (2017)

45. Yassin, N.I., Omran, S., El Houby, E.M., Allam, H.: Machine learning techniques for breast cancer computer aided diagnosis using different image modalities: a systematic review. Comput. Methods Programs Biomed. **156**, 25–45 (2018)

An Efficient Set-Based Algorithm for Variable Streaming Clustering

Isaac Campos$^{(\boxtimes)}$ [iD], Jared León [iD], and Fernando Campos [iD]

Department of Informatics, Universidad Nacional de San Antonio Abad del Cusco,
Cusco, Peru
{isaac.campos,jared.leon,fernando.campos}@unsaac.edu.pe

Abstract. In this paper, a new algorithm for Data Streaming clustering is proposed, namely the SetClust algorithm. The Data Streaming clustering model focuses on making clustering of the data while it arrives, being useful in many practical applications. The proposed algorithm, unlike other streaming clustering algorithms, is designed to handle cases when there is no available a priori information about the number of clusters to be formed, having as a second objective to discover the best number of clusters needed to represent the points. The SetClust algorithm is based on structures for disjoint-set operations, making the concept of a cluster to be the union of multiple well-formed sets to allow the algorithm to recognize non-spherical patterns even in high dimensional points. This yields to quadratic running time on the number of formed sets. The algorithm itself can be interpreted as an efficient data structure for streaming clustering. Results of the experiments show that the proposed algorithm is highly suitable for clustering quality on well-spread data points.

Keywords: Data streaming clustering · Variable clustering ·
Disjoint-set operations · Data structures for clustering

1 Introduction

Clustering is probably the most important unsupervised machine learning problem. While there are several models of clustering, the vast majority of them require working with the entire set of points to be clustered [1,10]. A particular clustering model called *Data Stream Clustering* allows streaming algorithms to cluster points while they arrive. However, the Data Stream Clustering problem focuses on finding clusters given a priori knowledge of the number of clusters [13].

The proposed algorithm (SetClust) tries to solve a very similar problem, the Variable Streaming Clustering. The problem, as in the Data Stream model, handles the case where the data arrives one point at a time; but in this case, there is no a priori knowledge of the number of clusters to be formed. Because of this, the algorithm not only tries to make clustering of the data but also tries to discover the correct number of clusters *online*, i.e., the number of clusters

© Springer Nature Switzerland AG 2020
J. A. Lossio-Ventura et al. (Eds.): SIMBig 2019, CCIS 1070, pp. 89–96, 2020.
https://doi.org/10.1007/978-3-030-46140-9_9

predicted by the algorithm can considerably change depending on the structure of the data. The algorithm tries to keep the number of predicted clusters as small as possible at any moment.

The experimental part was conducted using synthetic datasets from [7,8,11] aiming to evaluate the performance on well spread clusters and some other closer clusters. The experimental procedure consisted of evaluating the performance of the proposed algorithm and 3 other Data Stream Clustering algorithms on the datasets.

The paper is organized as follows: Sect. 2 briefly mentions the tool needed to construct the algorithm and some related work on the topic. Then, the SetClust Algorithm is described in Sect. 3. Section 4 explains how the experiments were performed and the achieved results. Section 5 offers a brief discussion on the algorithm and the relation hyperparameters have with the data. Finally, the conclusions are presented in Sect. 6.

2   Background

Below, we mention the data structure needed to develop the SetClust algorithm, then the evaluation metric used for testing clustering quality, and finally we mention 3 algorithms that are later used in the experimental comparisons.

Union-Find Disjoint Sets Operations. This data structure [9] allows keeping track of sets of elements storing minimal information about them. The structure allows two kinds of operations: (1) Make a query to know whether two elements are in the same set, and (2) Join two sets into one single set (see [6] for more).

V-measure. This metric is an entropy-based measure which explicitly measures how successfully the criteria of homogeneity and completeness have been satisfied. V-measure is computed as the harmonic mean of distinct homogeneity and completeness scores (see [14] for more on this).

Clustream. This Data Streaming Clustering Algorithm is based on micro-cluster structures that store information about a streaming. The algorithm has two phases: an online phase in which the streams are processed and an offline phase in which the clusters are created using k-means (see [2] for more on this).

ClusTree. This Data Streaming Clustering Algorithm is a self-adaptive index structure that keeps the summarized information about the stream. Also, this algorithm adds aging to the data to eliminate unnecessary information (see [12] for more on this).

DenStream. This Data Streaming Clustering Algorithm is based on densities, the reason why it can take arbitrary cluster shapes during the execution. This algorithm can easily deal with outliers (see [5] for more on this).

3   The SetClust Algorithm

From now on, the terms "cluster" and "set" will be used independently: we use the term set to denote the minimum unit of grouped information, and the term cluster to denote a collection of one or more sets joined together by the same label.

At any time, each set is represented by the following information: (1) label of the set, (2) arithmetic mean of the points that belong to the set, (3) standard deviation of the points, (4) sum of element-wise squared points and (5) the number of points. Also, the disjoint-set structure mentioned in Sect. 2 is built over all the sets. Of course, for each point that arrives, we also must store the label of the set it belongs to. With this information, we define three operations that represent the action to be taken depending on the situation: element aggregation, set linking, and set absorption. The three operations are described below.

Element Aggregation. The purpose of the element aggregation operation is to add the information of a point to a set. This is achieved in the following way: given a point $p \in \mathbb{R}^d$, find the set with the nearest mean $\mu_i \in \mathbb{R}^d$ having a standard deviation $\sigma_i \in \mathbb{R}^d$. Then, we take the number $c \in \mathbb{R}^+$ as hyperparameter. The point p is added to the set if the following inequation holds:

$$\|(p - \mu_i)./(\sigma_i \cdot c)\|^2 < 1 \tag{1}$$

Where $./$ is the element-wise division. The intuition behind this condition is that a point is to be added to the set if it lies inside c standard deviations of an ellipsoid with center μ_i. The extension of the ellipsoid in each dimension is given by σ. Given this condition, there are two possible scenarios. First, the point does not belong to the set. In this case, a new set is created having a unique element: the single point. The mean of the set is the point itself, and the standard deviation is initially fixed to σ_{ini} being this last a hyperparameter. At every moment, the standard deviation of each set is at least σ_{ini}. Then, the information about this point is added to the disjoint-set structure. Second, the point belongs to the set. In this case, the information of the set should be updated, i.e., update the mean, standard deviation, and the number of elements[1]. Both calculations have a running time complexity of $O(d)$, being d the dimension the points lie in. The overall complexity of the element aggregation operation is $O(rd)$, being r the number of current formed sets.

Set Absorption. The set absorption operation is responsible for converting two close sets into a single one when discovering that one can be included inside another. The operation goes as follows: given two sets with means and standard deviations μ_i, σ_i and μ_j, σ_j respectively and the hyperparameter c, the two sets must become a single one if one set, when extended c times by its standard deviation is included into the other set extended c times by its standard deviation

---

[1] These operations should be done online without traversing through all the elements.

in *all* its components. Formally, the set absorption must be performed if the following inequation holds:

$$|\mu_i - \mu_j| + c \times \sigma_j <^d c \times \sigma_i. \tag{2}$$

Where $<^d$ represents the minor operator on *every* component (see Fig. 1 for a one dimensional example).

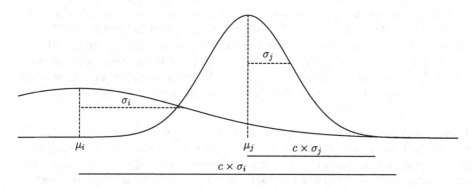

Fig. 1. One dimensional example of two sets satisfying the absorption condition. Set with mean μ_j is inside the acceptance border of set with mean μ_i.

When the absorption condition is met, we proceed to merge both sets re-calculating its information to form a new set[2]. The absorption operation is done until no two sets meet the absorption condition. It is possible that after joining two sets the need for making more absorption operations increase since the number of elements that belong to the last modified set also change. The absorption of a set has a running time complexity of $O(r^2 d)$. Depending on the implementation, we might need to traverse all sets once for every verification of the condition[3]. This operation has a good effect on the algorithm since every time it is used, the number of sets decreases by one.

Set Linking. The goal of the set linking operation is to determine whether two sets are close enough to be considered a single *cluster*. Given two sets with means μ_i, μ_j and standard deviations σ_i, σ_j respectively, we say that both sets are linked if the following inequation holds:

$$\|(\mu_i - \mu_j)./(\sigma_i \cdot c)\|^2 < 1 \tag{3}$$

---

[2] We need to calculate the new mean, standard deviation and the rest of the information in constant time.

[3] If we take advantage of the fact that only the last formed set can make instability, we can achieve an overall worst-case running time complexity of $O(rd)$.

Here, we use the previously defined hyperparameter c. Intuitively, the condition tests whether the mean of a set satisfies the element aggregation condition for another set.

Once determined if two sets will be linked, a *union* operation of the disjoint-set structure is performed on their labels, meaning that both sets belong to a single cluster. Doing the operation in this way, we allow the algorithm to link sets that create complex cluster forms, not just spherical.

The set linking operation is performed after the set absorption operation because if two sets satisfy the absorption condition, then they satisfy the linking condition with high probability. We restrict linking sets that can be absorbed by any other to reduce the number of clusters. Depending on the implementation, this operation can be performed in almost linear time in the number of sets[4].

It is important to clarify that, whenever a new point arrives, the algorithm tries to perform the three operations (element aggregation, set absorption, and set linking in that order) to the whole structure. The three operations are independently executed one after the other. As mentioned before, the worst-case running time complexity of the operations are: $O(rd)$, $O(rd)$ (at most $O(r)$ times), and $O(\alpha(r)rd)$ respectively. If we assume $\alpha(r)$ to be a small constant, the overall complexity of the algorithm when adding a point is $O(r^2d)$.

When two or more sets are linked, they are considered to belong to the same cluster. This property was specifically chosen for the algorithm as it has an advantage: linked sets can form non-spherical cluster shapes. It is quite easy to see that when two or more sets are joined into a single one, the shape of the final set is "pseudo elliptical". However, when two of these sets link each other, then the resulting shape can be more sophisticated. The linking process can continue until exotic shapes are formed. This last behavior helps the algorithm to achieve better cluster quality since it can make more suitable cluster shapes of the data.

At any moment, we can know if two elements belong to the same cluster with the help of the disjoint-set structure. Also, at any moment, the algorithm can return a list of the labels of the points seen so far. The algorithm can also return the entire structure containing all the information used completely to define the sets and clusters to continue doing clustering if necessary. A high-level pseudocode of the SetClust algorithm is shown in Algorithm 1.

Whenever a new point arrives, an element aggregation operation is performed. This can yield into creating a new set or adding the new point to a previously existing set. In any case, the modified or newly created set is taken as a possible candidate for the absorption operation. If the absorption condition is met, then the absorption operation is performed. The process of verifying the absorption condition and performing the absorption operation continues until no absorption operation can be done. Then, the same set is taken as a candidate

---

[4] As in the previous case, if we take advantage of the fact that only the last formed set can make instability, we can perform this operation in worst-case running time complexity of $O(\alpha(r)rd)$, where α is the inverse Ackerman function. For any practical situation, the function is never greater than 4.

for the linking operation, checking for the corresponding condition as in the previous case. If the condition is met, then the set linking operation is performed only once.

Algorithm 1: The SetClust Algorithm

---

1 **while** *point p arrives* **do**
2   *Element Agregation(p)*
3   Let *A* be the set where *p* belongs
4   **while** *an absorption can be performed with A* **do**
5   *Set Absorption*(A)
6   **if** *a link can be performed with A* **then**
7   *Set Linking*(A)

---

4 Experiments

For the experiments, six synthetic datasets were selected from [7,8,11]. Each dataset contains several points in some specified dimension together with its correct label. Relevant information about the datasets is shown in Table 1.

Table 1. Information about the synthetic datasets used for the experiments

Dataset	Dimension	Number of elements	Number of clusters
Dim512	512	1024	16
Dim1024	1024	1024	16
A1	2	3000	20
A2	2	5250	35
A3	2	7500	50
S1	2	5000	15

The first two datasets contain several Gaussian clusters. Clusters are well separated. The next three are incrementally included; i.e., A1 is included in A2 and A2 is included in A3. These datasets have low dimension and are not so spread as the previous two. The reason for including this type of datasets is to test the performance of the algorithm in an outlier scenario. The last dataset, S1, contain some non-spherical (amorphous) cluster shapes. The purpose of this dataset is to test how algorithms handle this kind of scenarios.

The experimental procedure was performed as follows: for every dataset and algorithm, we performed a grid search to find good hyperparameters. The evaluation of the clustering quality was performed using the V-measure metric [14], which gives a score between -1 and 1. Table 2 shows the results of this procedure. Each numerical value of the table contains the best score seen by the current algorithm on the current dataset. The best score achieved on every dataset (every column) is highlighted in bold.

Table 2. Results of the experiments

	Dim512	Dim1024	A1	A2	A3	S1
SetClust	**1.00**	**1.00**	**0.97**	**0.96**	**0.97**	**0.97**
Clustream	**1.00**	**1.00**	0.79	0.82	0.83	0.80
ClusTree	**1.00**	**1.00**	0.75	0.74	0.56	0.80
DenStream	**1.00**	**1.00**	0.70	0.66	0.61	0.73

As showed in the table, the first two datasets were easy for all the algorithms due to its spread nature. The next four datasets were more challenging because of the complex nature of clusters shapes and the addition of some outliers present on them. In those datasets, the proposed algorithm clearly shows superior performance, showing the highest score on all cases. Numerical experiments were conducted using the Python programming language (Python 3.XX) on a 2.50 GHz Intel Core i7-4710HQ with 12 GB of RAM and running Windows 10 version 1809 as operating system. The source code of the SetClust algorithm is available in [4]. For the other algorithms, we used the MOA framework for Big Data stream mining [3].

5   Discussion

The selection of hyperparameters σ_{ini} and c can have a deep interpretation when looking at the structure of the dataset used. The parameter σ_{ini} can be interpreted as a first approximation to the standard deviation that a cluster will have, for that, it might be a good practice to choose its value looking at the "separation degree" of the dataset. The parameter c can be seen similarly: its value can be interpreted as a guess of how spread the clusters will be during the streaming. In the same way, looking at the structure of the dataset can help to make a good choice for its value.

The Clustream and ClusTree algorithms make use of the correct number of clusters to be formed. The DenStream algorithm, despite not needing this information, requires tuning a great number of other hyperparameters. The proposed algorithm has exactly two hyperparameters, which makes it suitable for a streaming scenario with semi-unknown information.

6   Conclusions

In this paper, a new algorithm for variable data streaming clustering was proposed, the SetClust algorithm. The algorithm has a disjoint-set operations background and can be used as a data structure with online query support.

A maximum clustering quality was achieved when the clusters are well spread. This case is an optimal scenario for the SetClust algorithm (as well as for the other algorithms). The experiments also show that, for the last four datasets, the proposed algorithm finds better clusters than the other tested algorithms.

In spite of the theoretical efficient based formulation of the algorithm, there are lots of implementation details that give much freedom when implementing it. As future work, we will focus on adapting better data structures to handle redundant information so as to make a more efficient implementation of the algorithm. Also, we plan to create a more sophisticated version of SetClust incorporating aging to the data. We also plan to perform running time comparisons between the SetClust algorithm and other Data Streaming Clustering algorithms.

References

1. Aggarwal, C.C., Reddy, C.: Data Clustering: Algorithms and Applications, 1st edn. Chapman & Hall/CRC (2013)
2. Aggarwal, C.C., Han, J., Wang, J., Yu, P.S.: A framework for clustering evolving data streams. In: Proceedings of the 29th International Conference on Very Large Data Bases, VLDB 2003, vol. 29, pp. 81–92. VLDB Endowment (2003)
3. Bifet, A., Holmes, G., Kirkby, R., Pfahringer, B.: MOA: massive online analysis. J. Mach. Learn. Res. **11**, 1601–1604 (2010)
4. Campos, I., Leon, J.: Setclust. Zenodo, July 2019. https://doi.org/10.5281/zenodo.3270842
5. Cao, F., Ester, M., Qian, W., Zhou, A.: Density-based clustering over an evolving data stream with noise. In: Conference on Data Mining (SIAM 2006), pp. 328–339 (2006)
6. Cormen, T., Leiserson, C., Rivest, R., Stein, C.: Introduction to Algorithms, 3rd edn. MIT Press, Cambridge (2009)
7. Fränti, P., Sieranoja, S.: K-means properties on six clustering benchmark datasets. Appl. Intell. **48**(12), 4743–4759 (2018). https://doi.org/10.1007/s10489-018-1238-7
8. Fränti, P., Virmajoki, O.: Iterative shrinking method for clustering problems. Pattern Recognit. **39**(5), 761–775 (2006)
9. Galler, B.A., Fisher, M.J.: An improved equivalence algorithm. Commun. ACM **7**(5), 301–303 (1964)
10. Jain, A., Dubes, R.: Algorithms for Clustering Data. Prentice-Hall Inc., Upper Saddle River (1988)
11. Karkkainen, I., Franti, P.: Dynamic local search for clustering with unknown number of clusters. In: Object Recognition Supported by User Interaction for Service, vol. 2, pp. 240–243 (2002)
12. Kranen, P., Assent, I., Baldauf, C., Seidl, T.: Self-adaptive anytime stream clustering. In: 2009 Ninth IEEE International Conference on Data Mining, pp. 249–258 (2009)
13. Muthukrishnan, S.: Data streams: algorithms and applications. Found. Trends Theor. Comput. Sci. **1**(2), 117–236 (2005)
14. Rosenberg, A., Hirschberg, J.: V-measure: a conditional entropy-based external cluster evaluation measure. In: Proceedings of the 2007 Joint Conference on Empirical Methods in Natural Language Processing and Computational Natural Language Learning, pp. 410–420. EMNLP-CoNLL (2007)

Sparse Non-negative Matrix Factorization for Retrieving Genomes Across Metagenomes

Vincent Prost[1,2,3($\boxtimes$)], Stéphane Gazut[1], and Thomas Brüls[2,3]

[1] CEA, LIST, Laboratoire Sciences des Données et de la Décision,
91191 Gif-sur-Yvette, France
{vincent.prost,stephane.gazut}@cea.fr
[2] CEA, DRF, Institut Jacob, Genoscope, 91057 Evry, France
thomas.bruls@cea.fr
[3] CNRS-UMR8030, Université Paris-Saclay, UEVE, 91057 Evry, France

Abstract. The development of massively parallel sequencing technologies enables to sequence DNA at high-throughput and low cost, fueling the rise of metagenomics which is the study of complex microbial communities sequenced in their natural environment. A metagenomic dataset consists of billions of unordered small fragments of genomes (reads), originating from hundreds or thousands of different organisms. The *de novo* reconstruction of individual genomes from metagenomes is practically challenging, both because of the complexity of the problem (sequence assembly is NP-hard) and the large data volumes. The clustering of sequences into biologically meaningful partitions (e.g. strains), known as binning, is a key step with most computational tools performing read assembly as a pre-processing. However, metagenome assembly (and even more cross-assembly) is computationally intensive, requiring terabytes of memory; it is also error-prone (yielding artefacts like chimeric contigs) and discards vast amounts of information in the form of unassembled reads (up to 50% for highly diverse metagenomes). Here we show how online learning methods for sparse non-negative matrix factorization can recover relative abundances of genomes across multiple metagenomes and support assembly-free read binning by using abundance covariation signals derived from the occurrence of unique k-mers (subsequences of size k) across samples. The combinatorial explosion of k-mers is controlled by indexing them using locality sensitive hashing, and sparse coding and dictionary learning techniques are used to decompose the k-mer abundance covariation signal into genome-resolved components in latent space.

Keywords: Non-negative matrix factorization · Sparse coding · Dictionary learning · Online learning · Metagenomics · Clustering

© Springer Nature Switzerland AG 2020
J. A. Lossio-Ventura et al. (Eds.): SIMBig 2019, CCIS 1070, pp. 97–105, 2020.
https://doi.org/10.1007/978-3-030-46140-9_10

1   Introduction

Metagenomics leverages high-throughput sequencing to extract genomic information about microbial communities *in situ*. Metagenomic studies have already
expanded knowledge in various domains, like microbial ecology or human
medicine through the study of human-associated microbiotas. Metagenomic
datasets consist in billions of unordered small genome fragments, typically a
few hundreds base pairs (bp) at best, which is very small compared to the size
of a typical bacterial genome (about 10^6 bp). Sequences are randomly sampled,
i.e. without knowing the genome nor the position in the genome they are derived
from, often leading to highly fragmented assemblies.

Many computational approaches seek to solve an intermediate problem called
binning, that aims at grouping together reads originating from the same genome.
We can broadly distinguish two different binning strategies. The first one relies
on *de novo* assembly [14] as a pre-processing step and performs binning at the
contig level. The main advantage here is a reduction in the number of objects
to be clustered and more robust compositional signals associated with longer
sequences. Performing *de novo* assembly on metagenomic datasets is however
computationally intensive, especially in terms of computer memory. It is also a
source of artefacts and discards significant amounts of raw data.

A second strategy is to perform binning at the (unassembled) read-level,
followed by targeted assemblies of the resulting lower complexity partitions (see
Subsect. 2.2). A larger number of objects need to be dealt with upfront, but this
approach has the potential to avoid important drawbacks of *de novo* assembly,
like biases against low-abundance sequences. We describe here such a "bin-first
assemble-second" method that achieves read-level binning by decomposing the
k-mer abundance covariation signal into latent genomes using online sparse non-
negative matrix factorization.

2   Related Work

2.1   Clustering Unique k-mers

Many binning methods (e.g. [15]) exploit occurrences of unique k-mers (sub-
strings of size k). With sufficiently long k-mers (e.g. $k > 20$), we can assume
that most of them will be genome-specific. Solving the binning problem is therefore equivalent to clustering unique k-mers. The Lander-Waterman model [9]
assumes that random sequencing will lead to Poisson distributed nucleotide coverage, which provides a rationale for binning k-mers from a given mixture of
genomes. Assuming that occurrences of unique k-mers are Poisson distributed
with parameter λ_i proportional to the abundance of the genome it comes from, the
count $n(w_j)$ of a k-mer w_j is Poisson distributed: $P(n(w_j) = c) = Poisson(\lambda_i; c)$
where $Poisson(\lambda_i; c)$ is the probability of a Poisson random variable taking the
value c. The parameters λ_j can be estimated by maximum likelihood using an
Expectation-Maximization (EM) algorithm [3], see for example [15]. Reads are
then partitioned into bins according to their k-mer content and the estimated
parameters.

2.2   Clustering k-mers Across Multiple Samples

Abundance signals were originally used to cluster k-mers and reads within individual samples. To handle experimental setups involving multiple samples, abundance covariation signals can be used to cluster reads from individual taxa across samples, see for example [11] which proceeds by analogy to LSI (Latent Semantic Indexing [5], a classical method for document classification), by projecting each sample into the singular vector space with SVD (singular value decomposition): $X = U \Sigma V^T$ where U and V are orthogonal and Σ is diagonal. k-mers can then be clustered by doing fixed radius k-means on the lines of V [11].

3   Materials and Methods

3.1   Indexing k-mers by Locality Sensitive Hashing

As the number of possible k-mers can be very large (e.g. $k = 30$ gives $4^{30} \approx 10^{18}$ possible k-mers), the computer memory needed for storing the counts of all observed k-mers can become prohibitive. The use of inverted indexes as in [15] will not be tractable for large or multi-samples datasets. Ref [11] proposes to use Locality Sensitive Hashing (LSH), a technique initially used to improve nearest-neighbour searches in high dimensions [6].

Each k-mer w_i is represented in a k-dimensional complex vector space $\mathbb{C}^k$, for example by using a mapping for each letter of the form: $A = 1, C = i, G = -i, T = -1$. Those numbers can further be weighted by a quality score, which informs about base call confidence. d random hyperplanes are then drawn in $\mathbb{C}^k$, e.g. with normal vector $v_j \in \mathbb{C}^k$. Each hyperplane separates the space into two half spaces with the hashing function: $h_j(w_i) = sign(w_i^T v_j) \in \{-1, 1\}$, and therefore defining 2^d subspaces or buckets.

Thus, each k-mer w_i, initially living in a space of cardinal 4^k, can be associated to a binary code $(h_1(w_i), h_2(w_i), .., h_d(w_i)) \in \{-1, 1\}^d$ of size d and be represented in a space of cardinal 2^d. This way the size of the "dictionary" can be controlled via the number of hyperplanes selected.

3.2   Sparse Non-negative Matrix Factorization

The experimental k-mer count data can be viewed as a sparse composition of positive components, hence non-negative matrix factorization (NMF) stands out as a natural analytical paradigm. This technique was originally proposed by Lee and Seung [10]. In NMF, the goal is to approximate the sample by k-mer count matrix $X \in \mathbb{R}^{n \times 2^d}$ by the product of two non-negative matrices $U \in \mathbb{R}^{n \times K}$ and $V \in \mathbb{R}^{2^d \times K}$, usually by finding a solution to the following constrained minimization problem:

$$U, V = \underset{U,V \geq 0}{\operatorname{argmin}} \mathcal{D}(X || UV^T) + J(U, V) \tag{1}$$

where $\mathcal{D}$ is an error function and J a penalty term ensuring sparsity or regularity on U and V. In our model, the values of X are sparse compositions of k-mer counts. If we denote S_{isj} the count of a k-mer specific to genome s appearing in bucket j and sample i, then:

$$X_{ij} = \sum_{s=1}^{K} S_{isj} \tag{2}$$

S_{isj} follows a Poisson distribution of parameter $U_{is}V_{js}$, where U_{is} is proportional to the abundance of genome s in sample i and V_{js} is a sparse coefficient. Due to the additivity of the Poisson distribution, X_{ij} is also Poisson distributed:

$$P(X_{ij} = c) = Poisson\left(\sum_{s=1}^{K} U_{is}V_{js}; c\right) \tag{3}$$

As stated originally in [10] and elaborated in [2], maximizing the likelihood of this model is equivalent to solving (1) when $\mathcal{D}$ is the Kullback-Leibler divergence:

$$KL(X||UV^T) = \sum_{i}\sum_{j} \log \frac{X_{ij}}{[UV^T]_{ij}} - X_{ij} + [UV^T]_{ij} \tag{4}$$

Lee and Seung [10] proposed an iterative algorithm for solving Eq. (1) when $J := 0$. We refer to this algorithm in the experiments as "L&S-KL".

We can expect V to be very sparse, and this sparsity depends on the expected number of k-mers sharing a same bucket. It therefore depends on the number of buckets 2^d compared to the number of distinct k-mers measured, the latter being related to the k-mer size selected and the genome diversity in the metagenomes analyzed. We therefore need to set constraints in the optimization problem to enforce the sparsity of V, by either penalizing the l_0 or l_1 norm of the lines of V: $J(U, V) = \beta \sum_{i=1}^{2^d} \|v_i\|_\gamma, \gamma \in \{0, 1\}$, where v_i is the ith line of V. On the other hand, we will frequently face situations where $n < K$, hence resorting to sparsity constraints in order to find solutions with the fewest number of non zeros among the infinite number of solutions [1].

3.3 Online Dictionary Learning

Iterative methods like [10] require to keep the whole dataset in memory, which is not always tractable when the right matrix V has large dimensions. The convergence speed can also be slow. Following Mairal et al. [12], we use an online dictionary learning method that aims to solve Eq. (1) when $\mathcal{D}(X||UV^T) = \|X - UV^T\|_2^2$, where $\|.\|_2$ is the Frobenius norm. For each new coming input x_t, it proceeds in an online fashion by alternating a sparse coding step (updating v_t):

$$v_t = \underset{v \geq 0}{\operatorname{argmin}} \|x_t - Uv\|_2^2 + \lambda\|v\|_1 \tag{5}$$

and a dictionary update step (updating matrix U):

$$U^{t+1} = \underset{U \in \mathcal{C}}{\operatorname{argmin}} \sum_{i=1}^{t} \|x_i - Uv_i\|_2^2 \tag{6}$$

where x_i denotes the ith column of X, v_i the ith line of V, and $\mathcal{C}$ is a convex set. We evaluated the method from Mairal and colleagues with different sparse coding steps, and refer to it as lasso-DL when the sparse coding step is a lasso regression like Eq. (5) and omp-DL when it is Orthogonal Matching Pursuit, aiming to solve:

$$v_t = \underset{v \geq 0}{\operatorname{argmin}} \|v\|_0 \text{ subject to } \|x_t - Uv\|_2 < \epsilon \tag{7}$$

Ref [13] proposes an algorithm inspired by [12] but aiming to solve problem (1) when $D(.\|.) := KL(.\|.)$ and with sparsity constraints; it will be noted KL-DL in our experiments.

3.4   Data

We analyzed two types of datasets: (i) synthetic datasets simulating k-mer counts in a sparse Poisson factor model, cf. Eq. (2), (ii) semi-synthetic datasets simulating the sequencing of microbial communities by randomly sampling sequences from controlled mixtures of real genomes.

The first dataset was used to evaluate the performance of the different algorithms in the ideal case of the Lander-Waterman model. We have control over the variables of the model and evaluate the ability of the methods to retrieve the underlying abundances. In the second dataset, real genomes are used to simulate a random shotgun sequencing experiment. In this case, we evaluate the final binning results by quantifying the ability of the different algorithms to cluster reads into genome-resolved partitions with precision and recall metrics (P/R).

4   Results

4.1   Synthetic Data

Following [1], we first evaluate the online learning algorithms on synthetic signals, given random underlying abundance parameters $A \in \mathbb{R}^{n \times K}$. At each iteration, T samples $(x_1, x_2, .., x_T)$ are independently drawn following Eq. (8)

$$x_i^{(j)} = \sum_{k=1}^{K} \pi_k s_k^{(j)}, \quad \pi_k \sim Binomial(p, 3), \quad s_k^{(j)} \sim Poisson(A_{j,k}) \tag{8}$$

where $x^{(j)}$ denotes the jth coordinate of vector x. The computed left matrix U was compared against the known abundance parameter A, with the error defined as the sum of quadratic errors between the columns of A and the closest

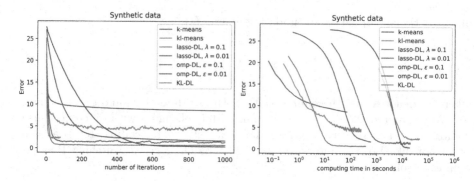

Fig. 1. Left: error as a function of iteration number. Right: error as a function of computation time (on a logarithmic scale).

columns of U : $error = \sum_{k=1}^{K} \min_i \frac{\|A_{.,k}-U_{.,i}\|^2}{\|A_{.,k}\|\|U_{.,i}\|}$. The tests were carried out with parameters $p = 0.05, K = 140, n = 20, T = 1000$. Figure 1 shows the comparison of different online learning algorithms. The curve "k-means" represents the online version of k-means (sequential k-means [4]), while "kl-means" is the same algorithm but with euclidean distance replaced by KL-divergence.

All methods with relaxed sparse constraints performed better than k-means in recovering underlying abundances. Using an OMP sparse coding step tends to slightly improve the estimation at the expense of a higher computing cost. Lasso-DL achieves the best convergence speed both in iteration number and computation time. KL-DL is much slower than other methods and surprisingly fails to improve the final estimation.

4.2   Semi-synthetic Data

We tested the algorithms on artificial metagenomic datasets simulating a cohort of $n = 50$ samples (individuals) [7]. Each sample contains a random subset (of size Genome nb) of (real) bacterial genomes that are randomly sampled to generate shotgun reads (see [7] for details). The number of reads varies from 200,000 (for Genome nb = 20) to 7,5 millions (for Genome nb = 700) per sample.

In the sequence binning process, k-mers are initially segregated, the matrix V is computed and k-mers of bucket i are assigned to cluster k if $k = \text{argmax}_j V_{i,j}$, as in [16]. Following this step, sequences are then assigned to the clusters based on their k-mer content, as in [11]. The sequence data was pre-processed by hashing (cf. Subsect. 3.1) with $d = 27$ (Table 1) and $d = 30$ (Table 2). The number of clusters K was the same for all methods and fixed to $1.5 \times$ Genome nb. Parameters λ and ϵ were set so as to achieve a good compromise between the sparsity of V and the reconstruction error.

It can be seen that the canonical (non regularized) NMF algorithm of Lee and Seung [10] performs best when $n > K$, while the sparse NMF variants outperform the others in the under-determined regime, and that overall the performances decrease with the complexity of the genome mixtures (Table 1).

Table 1. Binning performance on semi-synthetic metagenomic datasets ($d = 27$).

Genome nb	k-means		L&S-KL		omp-DL		lasso-DL		KL-DL		LSA	
	P/R		P/R		P/R		P/R		P/R		P/R	
20	78.5	82.1	83.6	90.0	72.6	71.1	76.9	80.1	78.2	90.7	77.9	77.4
100	80.2	76.0	65.8	66.6	80.5	77.2	80.1	77.0	79.2	80.3	74.9	79.3
200	69.1	67.8	51.7	50.7	70.0	69.9	70.0	68.3	62.3	70.0	56.9	61.4
700	46.6	44.4	30.9	28.7	48.6	50.2	49.1	47.5	–	–	28.8	40.8

Table 2. Binning performance on semi-synthetic metagenomic datasets ($d = 30$).

Genome nb	omp-DL		lasso-DL		LSA	
	P/R		P/R		P/R	
100	93.0	92.1	95.2	92.9	87.3	90.1
200	86.4	90.8	87.2	90.4	70.0	88.4
700	75.2	80.7	76.1	83.3	50.9	78.5

The online dictionary learning methods scale well to large dimensions (Table 2) (neither L&S-KL nor KL-DL could be evaluated for $d = 30$ due to prohibitive computing times) and perform better than the state of the art pre-assembly binning algorithm LSA [11].

5   Conclusion

We have shown that sparse non-negative matrix factorization can be successfully applied to the analysis of metagenomic data. We explored and compared different methods and validated them through experiments on synthetic and semi-synthetic datasets. We have demonstrated that online dictionary learning methods coupled with sparse coding are able to recover underlying parameters in a sparse Poisson factor model and in an under-determined regime that is relevant for the analysis of real-world metagenomic data.

The online dictionary learning method was also applied to a massive real-world metagenomic dataset derived from human gut microbiota, comprising more than 10^{10} reads encompassing 10 terabytes of sequence data. Results from these analyses are described elsewhere [8], and illustrate the ability of the sparse coding method to scale to very large datasets and to recover low-abundance genomes that are typically missed by assembly-based approaches.

Acknowledgments. This work was mainly funded by the office of the High Commissioner of CEA. The authors would like to thank Olexiy Kyrgyzov for sharing some computer code and for the analysis of the real dataset.

References

1. Aharon, M., Elad, M., Bruckstein, A.: K-SVD: an algorithm for designing overcomplete dictionaries for sparse representation. IEEE Trans. Signal Process. **54**(11), 4311–4322 (2006). https://doi.org/10.1109/TSP.2006.881199
2. Cemgil, A.T.: Bayesian inference for non-negative matrix factorisation models. Comput. Intell. Neurosci. **2009**, 4:1–4:17 (2009). https://doi.org/10.1155/2009/785152
3. Dempster, A.P., Laird, N.M., Rubin, D.B.: Maximum likelihood from incomplete data via the EM algorithm. J. Roy. Statis. Soc. Ser. B (Methodological) **39**(1), 1–22 (1977)
4. Duda, R.O.: Pattern recognition for HCI, June 1997. www.cs.princeton.edu/courses/archive/fall08/cos436/Duda/PR_home.htm. Accessed 27 May 2019
5. Dumais, S.T.: Latent semantic analysis. Ann. Rev. Inf. Sci. Technol. **38**(1), 188–230 (2004). https://doi.org/10.1002/aris.1440380105. https://onlinelibrary.wiley.com/doi/abs/10.1002/aris.1440380105
6. Gionis, A., Indyk, P., Motwani, R.: Similarity search in high dimensions via hashing. In: Proceedings of the 25th International Conference on Very Large Data Bases, VLDB 1999, pp. 518–529. Morgan Kaufmann Publishers Inc., San Francisco (1999). http://dl.acm.org/citation.cfm?id=645925.671516
7. Gkanogiannis, A., Gazut, S., Salanoubat, M., Kanj, S., Brüls, T.: A scalable assembly-free variable selection algorithm for biomarker discovery from metagenomes. BMC Bioinform. **17**(1), 311 (2016)
8. Kyrgyzov, O., Prost, V., Gazut, S., Farcy, B., Brüls, T.: Binning unassembled short reads based on k-mer abundance covariance using sparse coding. GigaScience **9**(4), giaa028 (2020). Accessed https://doi.org/10.1093/gigascience/giaa028
9. Lander, E.S., Waterman, M.S.: Genomic mapping by fingerprinting random clones: a mathematical analysis. Genomics **2**(3), 231–239 (1988). https://doi.org/10.1016/0888-7543(88)90007-9. http://www.sciencedirect.com/science/article/pii/0888754388900079
10. Lee, D.D., Seung, H.S.: Algorithms for non-negative matrix factorization. In: Proceedings of the 13th International Conference on Neural Information Processing Systems, NIPS 2000. pp. 535–541. MIT Press, Cambridge (2000). http://dl.acm.org/citation.cfm?id=3008751.3008829
11. Lowman Cleary, B., et al.: Detection of low-abundance bacterial strains in metagenomic datasets by eigengenome partitioning. Nature Biotechnol. **33**, 1053–1060 (2015). https://doi.org/10.1038/nbt.3329
12. Mairal, J., Bach, F., Ponce, J., Sapiro, G.: Online learning for matrix factorization and sparse coding. J. Mach. Learn. Res. **11**, 19–60 (2010). http://dl.acm.org/citation.cfm?id=1756006.1756008
13. Nguyen, D., Ho, T.: Fast parallel randomized algorithm for non-negative matrix factorization with KL divergence for large sparse datasets. Int. J. Mach. Learn. Comput. **6**, 111–116 (2016). https://doi.org/10.18178/ijmlc.2016.6.2.583
14. Zerbino, D.R., Birney, E.: Velvet: algorithms for de novo short read assembly using de Bruijn graphs. Genome Res. **18**, 821–829 (2008). https://doi.org/10.1101/gr.074492.107

15. Wu, Y.W., Ye, Y.: A novel abundance-based algorithm for binning metagenomic sequences using l-tuples. J. Comput. Biol. **18**(3), 523–34 (2011)
16. Xu, W., Liu, X., Gong, Y.: Document clustering based on non-negative matrix factorization. In: Proceedings of the 26th Annual International ACM SIGIR Conference on Research and Development in Information Retrieval, SIGIR 2003, pp. 267–273. ACM, New York (2003). https://doi.org/10.1145/860435.860485. http://doi.acm.org/10.1145/860435.860485

Collect Ethically: Reduce Bias in Twitter Datasets

Lulwah Alkulaib[(✉)], Abdulaziz Alhamadani[(✉)], Taoran Ji, and Chang-Tien Lu

Virginia Tech, Falls Church, VA 22043, USA
{lalkulaib,hamdani,jtr,ctlu}@vt.edu

Abstract. The Twitter platform is appealing to researchers due to the ease of obtaining data and the ability to analyze and produce results rapidly. However, sampling Twitter data for research purposes needs to be regulated to produce unbiased results. In this paper, factors that lead to sampling bias are addressed, case studies that have been encountered are presented, and an approach is proposed to reduce sampling bias and flaws in datasets collected from Twitter. Then, experiments are conducted on two case studies, and a larger dataset is achieved by following the proposed guideline. The results indicate that using multiple Twitter application programming interfaces (APIs) for data collection is the best way to obtain a randomly sampled dataset.

Keywords: Sampling bias · Twitter dataset · Twitter API

1 Introduction

Twitter allows its users to publish 'tweets' up to 280 characters long that are visible to other users in their network. Users that tweet publicly generate a huge amount of data that is available for collection by researchers if needed. Ahmad et al. [8] explain how Twitter is one of the most researched platforms due to data availability, the ease of following conversations, and the ability to use hashtags as a topic-grouping mechanism. However, collecting Twitter data without any considerations will result in a biased dataset. Using the Twitter developer platform, researchers can collect and analyze tweets using one of three application programming interfaces (APIs): Twitter Search API, Twitter Streaming API, or Twitter Firehose. As noted in Table 1, Twitter data access varies depending on the chosen access method. This casts doubt on conclusions drawn from Twitter data samples and impacts the reliability of research findings based on this data.

In research, any trend or deviation from the truth in data collection, analysis, interpretation, or publication is called bias. In our research, the study focuses on sampling bias, which occurs when a sample is collected in such a way that some members of the intended population are not equally represented in the sample, resulting in a non-random sample. If such an error occurs in sampling, the results of the research could be mistakenly attributed to the study phenomenon instead

---

L. Alkulaib and A. Alhamadani — Equally contributed to this work.

© Springer Nature Switzerland AG 2020
J. A. Lossio-Ventura et al. (Eds.): SIMBig 2019, CCIS 1070, pp. 106–114, 2020.
https://doi.org/10.1007/978-3-030-46140-9_11

of the sampling method [2]. This leads us to question the use of Twitter as a data source while considering whether sampling bias has occurred in surveys and its effect on the resulting conclusions. To address this issue, a Twitter data collection guideline is proposed. The main contributions of this paper are as follows:

– Formulating a query expansion guideline consisting of six factors, which when followed, minimizes sampling bias when using Twitter as a data source.
– Using three Twitter APIs (i.e., search, streaming, and firehose) as methods of data collection. The new datasets are collected by following the original query and the expanded query using the proposed guideline. Then, the results of each case study are compared.
– Conducting extensive experiments to validate the proposed guideline's effectiveness and comparing the expanded query results with non-expanded results.

2 Related Work

The availability of Twitter data via APIs has made researchers eager to utilize them in studies. Below, a review of previous studies involving Twitter APIs presented.

Streaming API vs. Firehose: Wang et al. [7] performed a comparative analysis of data samples obtained using Twitter Streaming API and studying the sampling bias that occurs in each sample. They concluded that using the Streaming API does not present a sample as representative as the Firehose API.

Search API vs. Streaming API: Filho et al. cite12filho discussed population sample bias in Twitter data and how it impacts predictive accuracy. They studied the available Twitter data and whether it is comprehensive enough to make user characterizations or predict outcomes. They found that using free Twitter APIs to collect samples is not sufficient to make accurate predictions. **Search API vs. Firehose:** Taking a different approach, Zhang et al. [9] compared three collection methods in event studies: keyword filtering using the Search API, geolocation filtering using the Search API, and random sampling using the Twitter Firehose API. They attributed keyword sampling bias due to outcome selection and proposed geolocated and random sampling as a solution to reduce bias.**Search API vs. Streaming API vs. Random Firehose Sample:** In 2017, Morstatter et al. [3] addressed detecting bias from sampling strategies while comparing datasets with unsampled Twitter Firehose data. They presented multiple strategies to mitigate bias using the Twitter Streaming API. **Hashtag Sampling Bias:** Morstatter et al. [4] measured sampling bias differently. Their work focused on hashtags and their representativeness in the sample in comparison to trends on Twitter. A hashtag is 'biased' if the relative trend is overrepresented or underrepresented to a statistically significant degree when compared to its true trend on Twitter.

Table 1. Twitter API comparison

API	No query	Query			Results		Free
		Keyword	Username	Location	By percentage	By number	
Search API	✗	✓	✓	✗	✗	✓	✓
Streaming API	✗	✓	✓	✓	✓	✗	✓
Firehose	✗	✓	✓	✓	✓	✗	✗

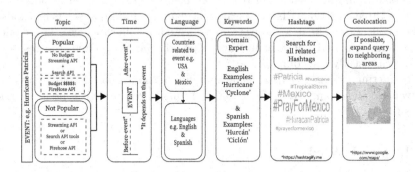

Fig. 1. The flowchart of the proposed data collection approach

To the best of our knowledge, none of the previous studies presented a comparison of the main three Twitter APIs that researchers use as a data collection tool. A new guideline is proposed and applied by collecting and comparing datasets using Twitter Search, Streaming, and Firehose APIs.

3   Proposed Approaches

Data Collection Guideline: The purpose of this work is to build a guideline that will serve as a reference for researchers who collect data from Twitter. The guideline will help minimize sampling bias in Twitter-based research datasets; see (Fig. 1). There are six aspects that researchers should consider since they affect the Twitter APIs' performance.

Topic: Knowing a topic's popularity is essential since the Twitter Streaming API does not capture more than 40% of real-time tweets during popular events [1]. For example, during presidential elections, using the Streaming API alone would lead to a biased dataset. However, if the topic is unpopular (i.e., fewer than six tweets/minute are related to the topic [5]), Twitter Streaming API would be sufficient for data collection.

Time: The key to selecting the data collection period is considering the longest related date range. Collecting data during an event is the most common method. However, events differ in how users tweet about them. Event-related tweets can occur before, during, and after an event or just during and after an event. It is tempting to only collect data during an event, but as shown in our study, a significant number of tweets will be missed when the time factor is not considered. Therefore, collecting Twitter data before and after an event would result in a more inclusive dataset.

Language: When writing an API query, it is crucial to select the language of returned tweets. If the selected event includes different languages, then all languages should be included in the query. For example, in our first case study, Hurricane Patricia traveled through Mexico and the United States (US). Therefore, tweets written in Spanish and English were included in the research.

Keywords: Keyword expansion should be performed by a domain expert. It is important to know what other related words could be used for a certain research topic, and using the expertise of a person with specialized knowledge of the domain will help expand the query correctly.

Hashtags: Expanding the query by utilizing related hashtag topics is essential. For example, when researching Hurricane Patricia, we searched for related hashtags at[1] *(see* Fig. 1 *Hashtags' column).*

Geolocation: Finally, if the location of the initial topic spread is known, expanding the query by location into neighboring areas should also be considered. Using this guideline as a reference when collecting data from Twitter should ensure that there is a standardized method for data collection. It also allows researchers to verify that they avoided factors that could cause sampling bias.

3.1   Methods

In this section, each API's data collection method is described. *Streaming API:* Two datasets collected via the Streaming API and published [10] were chosen. Since published Twitter datasets are only allowed to publish tweet identifications (IDs) to be compliant with Twitter Terms of Service (TOS), the datasets are hydrated [6] using Hydrator[2]. In the dataset description, it is mentioned that the data are collected using the Streaming API and filtered to only capture English results. *Search API:* Twitter's Search API only allows access to data covering the last seven days. Since both datasets covered from 2015 and 2016, a tool called 'GetOldTweets'[3] that bypasses the time limitation of the Search API was used. Then, the datasets were collected using the tool once with the exact query used by Zubiaga and then using the new expanded query after following the data collection guideline. *Firehose:* The Discovery Analytics Center (DAC) at Virginia Tech purchased 10% of the worldwide data on the Twitter Firehose between August 2014 and April 2018. Gnip, an API that allows access to Firehose data and filters it to form a subset of results, was used to access and collect the dataset, following the exact query used by Zubiaga, and then using our expanded query.

---

[1] www.hashtagify.com.

[2] https://github.com/DocNow/hydrator.

[3] https://github.com/Jefferson-Henrique/GetOldTweets-python.

4 Experiments

Two case studies are assumed to have sampling bias due to their collection method. Below, we show how our proposed method is used to reproduce datasets and minimize bias.

Table 2. Chosen datasets.

Datatset	Hurricane Patricia	Egypt Air Hijacking
Date	October 24–December 8, 2015	March 29–30, 2016
Query	hurricane, patricia, #hurricanepatricia, #huracanpatricia	#egyptair, hijacked, plane, cyprus, airport
# of tweets	1, 151, 220	702, 586

Table 3. Query expansion for event "Hurricane Patricia"

Date	2015-10-13 ∼ 2016-01-02
Keywords	#HuracanPatricia, #hurricanepatricia, #huracanpatricia, #globalwarming, #climatechange, #houstonflood, #hurricane, #prayformexico, hurricane, typhoon patricia, cyclone, Tropical storm, hurricane patricia, huracán, ciclon, tormenta tropical, tifon patricia

Table 4. Query expansion for event "Egypt Air Hijacking"

Date	2016-03-28 ∼ 2016-04-30
Keywords	#اختطاف طائرة مصرية#, #الطائرة المصرية, #egyptair, #egyptairhijack, #hijacked, #Αεροπειρατεια, #MS181, #cyprushijack, Egypt Air, Hijack, MS181, Seif AlDin Mustafa, Hijacked, Hijacker, خاطف الطائرة المصرية, الخطوط المصرية, اختطاف الطائرة المصرية, الطياره المصريه, الطائرة المصرية, الطائره المخطوفه, سيف الدين مصطفى, الطيران المصري, الخطوط الجويه المصرية, المختطفة, الظائرة المصرية

4.1 Experiments Setup

Two datasets published by Zubiaga were chosen. The datasets were collected for two events. The datasets are explained in detail in Table 2. The suggested guideline was followed to expand the queries. Both chosen datasets were popular topics, and previous work has shown that using the Streaming API alone will create sampling bias. It was determined that the time buffer for the Hurricane

Patricia dataset should begin with the weather predictions that preceded the hurricane and end with news outlets' last reports about the hurricane's after-effects. However, for the Egypt Air Hijacking dataset, one day prior to the incident was added as a buffer, and it ended with the latest news found about the court proceedings. For Hurricane Patricia, the language was expanded to include Spanish due to the hurricane passing through Mexico and the US, and the language was expanded to include Arabic and Greek for the Egypt Air Hijacking. The hashtags were expanded using co-occurrence and tools that analyzed related hashtags. The keywords were expanded using domain experts in Spanish, Arabic, and Greek and added relevant English keywords using co-occurrence. In the initial datasets, the tweets were not from a significant number of locations, and for this reason, the queries were not expanded by location.

4.2   Data Collection

Streaming API: *Before Hydration:* The initial datasets collected by Zubiaga are described in Table 2. The datasets were downloaded as JSON files containing available matching tweet IDs using Hydrator [10]. *After Hydration:* After hydrating the datasets, 654,965 tweets were retrieved for the Hurricane Patricia event, which was 43% fewer than the number of total tweets. For the second event, 473,210 tweets were retrieved, which was a 33% decrease. The loss is attributed to deleted accounts or deleted tweets.

Search API: *Before Expansion:* GetOldTweets was used to collect data following the same dates and keywords presented in Table 2. The Hurricane Patricia event resulted in 96,671 tweets, whereas the Egypt Air Hijacking event resulted in 129,002 tweets. *After Expansion:* The queries of both events were expanded as shown in (Tables 3 and 4), respectively. The collected data for Hurricane Patricia using GetOldTweets resulted in 1,469,612 tweets, whereas 587,274 tweets were collected for the Egypt Air Hijacking event.

Firehose: *Before Expansion:* To be consistent, the available Firehose was used to collect data for both events following the same criteria presented in Table 2. The Hurricane Patricia event resulted in 658,994 tweets, and there were 100,910 tweets related to the Egypt Air Hijacking event. It is important to note that the low-return of Egypt Air Hijacking data is because the Firehose data in our lab was only 10% of the worldwide Twitter data. *After Expansion:* Following the expanded criteria in (Tables 3 and 4), the data for both events were collected from the available Firehose. The Hurricane Patricia and Egypt Air Hijacking events resulted in 3,462,452 and 151,502 tweets, respectively.

4.3   Results

In this section, the impact of collecting data from multiple Twitter APIs is investigated for each case study.

Hurricane Patricia: As shown in (Fig. 2a), by comparing each API, it can be observed that the Streaming API data decreased 43%, the Search API data increased by more than 1400%, and the Firehose data increased by 425%. *Egypt Air Hijacking:* As depicted in (Fig. 2b), there was a 33% decrease in Streaming

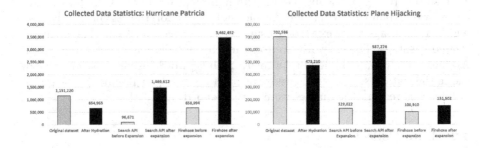

(a) Hurricane Particia.   (b) Egypt Air Hijacking.

Fig. 2. APIs dataset comparison.

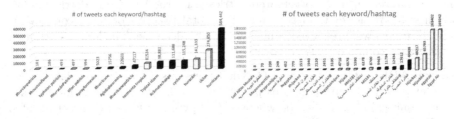

(a) Hurricane Particia.   (b) Egypt Air Hijacking.

Fig. 3. Search API expanded query keywords and hashtags.

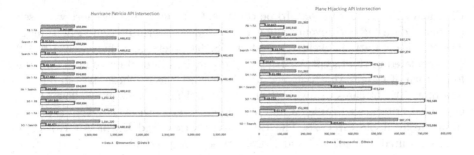

(a) Hurricane Particia.   (b) Egypt Air Hijacking.

Fig. 4. APIs dataset intersection. *Legend: SO: Streaming API Originial; SH: Streaming API after Hydration; Search: Search API after expansion; FB: Firehose before Expansion; FA: Firehose after Expansion*

API-retrieved tweets, while Search API data increased by 355%, and the Fire-hose dataset increased by 50%. These results indicate that within the expanded timeframe, a larger number of relevant tweets were captured, which included some of the keywords, hashtags, or both. (Fig. 3a) and (Fig. 3b) show each key-word and hashtag used in the expanded query, along with their counts in the retrieved tweets. It is apparent that including words from different languages retrieved a lot of missing tweets, which allows the datasets to be representative of the population. In (Fig. 4a) and (Fig. 4b), the intersection between different APIs is investigated to study the number of overlapping tweets. It is evident that in events as popular as Hurricane Patricia, the overlap of data between APIs was minimal. This leads us to conclude that using multiple Twitter APIs retrieves a larger number of relevant tweets, minimizing sampling bias.

4.4 Experiment Discussion

- The experiment finds that the representativeness of data collected from Twit-ter depends on both the query used and the API.
- Twitter Firehose is the only source that provides 100% of the tweets, but it comes at a cost that not all researchers can afford.
- To generate datasets with minimal bias using free Twitter APIs, combining multiple APIs results in a representative dataset. Additionally, expanding the search query could retrieve different tweets when querying multiple APIs.

5 Conclusion

This paper provides an analysis of Twitter data sampling obtained from the Twitter Streaming, Search, and Firehose APIs for two case studies. Comparing datasets collected using the original query and our guideline shows that using a single sampling method could lead to sampling bias. The experiments vali-date the effectiveness of the guideline and demonstrate growth in the resulting datasets when followed.

References

1. Campan, A., Atnafu, T., Truta, T.M., Nolan, J.: Is data collection through Twit-ter streaming API useful for academic research? In: 2018 IEEE International Conference on Big Data (Big Data) (2018). https://doi.org/10.1109/bigdata.2018. 8621898
2. Cortes, C., Mohri, M., Riley, M., Rostamizadeh, A.: Sample selection bias correc-tion theory. In: Freund, Y., Györfi, L., Turán, G., Zeugmann, T. (eds.) ALT 2008. LNCS (LNAI), vol. 5254, pp. 38–53. Springer, Heidelberg (2008). https://doi.org/ 10.1007/978-3-540-87987-9_8
3. Morstatter, F., Liu, H.: Discovering, assessing, and mitigating data bias in social media. Online Soc. Netw. Media 1, 1–13 (2017). https://doi.org/10.1016/j.osnem. 2017.01.001

4. Morstatter, F., Pfeffer, J., Liu, H.: When is it biased? In: Proceedings of the 23rd International Conference on World Wide Web - WWW 14 Companion (2014). https://doi.org/10.1145/2567948.2576952

5. Morstatter, F., Pfeffer, J., Liu, H., Carley, K.M.: Is the sample good enough? Comparing data from Twitter's streaming API with Twitter's firehose (2013)

6. Summers, E., Summers, E.: On forgetting (November 2014). https://medium.com/on-archivy/on-forgetting-e01a2b95272

7. Wang, Y., Callan, J., Zheng, B.: Should we use the sample? Analyzing datasets sampled from Twitter's stream API. ACM Trans. Web 9(3), 1–23 (2015). https://doi.org/10.1145/2746366

8. Woodfield, K., Ahmed, W.: Using Twitter as a data source: an overview of ethical, legal, and methodological challenges. Adv. Res. Ethics Integr. 2, 79–107 (2017). Chapter 4. Emerald

9. Zhang, H., Hill, S., Rothschild, D.: Addressing selection bias in event studies with general-purpose social media panels. J. Data Inf. Qual. 10(1), 1–24 (2018). https://doi.org/10.1145/3185048

10. Zubiaga, A.: A longitudinal assessment of the persistence of Twitter datasets (May 2018). https://onlinelibrary.wiley.com/doi/10.1002/asi.24026

Big Data Recommender System for Encouraging Purchases in New Places Taking into Account Demographics

Hugo Alatrista-Salas[iD], Isaías Hoyos, Ana Luna[(✉)][iD],
and Miguel Nunez-del-Prado[iD]

Universidad del Pacífico, Lima, Peru
{h.alatristas,i.hoyosl,ae.lunaa,m.nunezdelpradoc}@up.edu.pe

Abstract. Recommendation systems have gained popularity in recent years. Among them, the best known are those that select products in stores, movies, videos, music, books, among others. The companies, and in particular, the banking entities are the most interested in implementing these types of techniques to maximize the purchases of potential clients. For this, it is necessary to process a large amount of historical data of the users and convert them into useful information that allows predicting the products of interest for the user and the company. In this article, we analyze two essential problems when using systems, one of which is to suggest products of one commerce to those who have never visited that place, and the second is how to prioritize the order in which users buy certain products or services. To confront these drawbacks, we propose a process that combines two models: latent factor and demographic similarity. To test our proposal, we have used a database with approximately 65 million banking transactions. We validate our methodology, achieving an increase in the average consumption in the selected sample.

Keywords: Recommender system · Latent factor · Consumption patterns · Demographic vector

1 Introduction

Nowadays, there is a large number of products and services that the markets offer. In consequence, many users have difficulties in choosing the items they need in an easy and fast way. This brings a problem for companies that make profits from customers' purchases. Thus, business prioritizes satisfaction to preserve loyalty and close relationship with the clients. Hence, companies face new challenges to elaborate strategies for keeping the client's loyalty. These new strategies need to take into account the buyer's data, commercial activity, preferences, working place, among others. In this context, companies collect large amounts of data from customers to use them as a source of information. They transform data

© Springer Nature Switzerland AG 2020
J. A. Lossio-Ventura et al. (Eds.): SIMBig 2019, CCIS 1070, pp. 115–128, 2020.
https://doi.org/10.1007/978-3-030-46140-9_12

into useful insights that allow customers acquiring products based on their preferences. Therefore recommendation systems help customers to filter information in a personalized and transparent way.

One of the best-known examples of these systems is Netflix. The popular platform for movies and series streaming analyzes large volumes of data, such as what a user watches, at what time, for how long and what device is using. After analyzing the data, the Netflix algorithms recommend the user what to see based on the analyzed data, presenting the recommendations on the home page [11]. The objective of the recommendation algorithms that Netflix uses is to compensate for the low decision power of the human being before a wide range of options [16].

Gallego and Huecas [9] describe another example of a recommendation system in an economic context implemented in Spain. The objective is to recommend commerces taking into account the spatial and temporal dynamics of clients. This system seeks to recommend entities where bank customers can pay with their bank cards. To accomplish this, the bank uses large volumes of customers' data, like the transactions made by clients and the shops they visited. The recommendation looks forward to using the client's credit card and knowing where to use it according to the existing spatial information. But, the main difference in our research approach compared to others is that we add the similarity method that takes into account the demographic characteristics of the clients to prioritize the most similar shops. In this context, the present article describes the process of building an innovative recommendation system. The objective of our proposal is to encourage the use of credit and debit cards from a financial institution having three million users of credit and debit cards in July of 2017.

As a direct consequence of promoting the use of credit and debit cards, the average of the customer's purchase tickets increased. This particular point is one of the motivations of this work. Our aim was to generate a recommendation system that enhances the use of cards in commerces that the clients have never visited before.

The rest of the article is structured as follows. Section 2 describes the state of the art, Sect. 3 introduces the theoretical foundations of our proposal. Then, Sect. 4 describes the experiments and presents the obtained results, while Sect. 5 shows the validation of the results. Finally, Sect. 6 outlines the conclusions and future works.

2   Related Works

There are several studies on recommendation systems, where four approaches are identified and differentiated: *content-based, collaborative filtering, demographic filtering,* and *hybrid.*

The first one considers the profiles of the users and the decisions that they made in the past to recommend a particular item. For this, the similarity between articles is used to suggest those closest to the user's preference [4,17]. The clients' preference description is used to distinguish one article from another [2]. Then, attributes are compared with the user's profile and items with the highest degree of similarity are recommended. Content-based recommendation engine needs existing profiles of users that has information about a user and their taste. So, it works on the basis of item attributes. However, gathering descriptions requires external information that may not be available or that is difficult to collect. Besides, the recommendations tend to overspecialize the products or items. Thus, the obtained recommendations are not novel nor useful. An example of the use of the content-based approach is found in the Genome Musical Project, in which songs based on 400 musical characteristics that capture the musical "identity" of a song are recommended [8]. In this approach, heuristic recommendations were generated using a traditional information retrieval technique known as cosine similarity.

The second approach is *collaborative filtering*, which takes into account the past behavior of the user, namely items valuations or previous acquisitions. This treatment uses the known preferences of the client to predict the unknown ones to make a recommendation. It works finding users in a community that shares appreciations, so they will have similar tastes. Such users build a group or a so-called neighborhood. A user gets recommendations for those items that the user has not rated before but was positively rated by users in his/her neighborhood. So, the collaborative filtering also uses user behavior in addition to product attributes and unlike the content-based recommendation engine, you can recommend articles in other categories that the user never viewed before. There exist two methods in this approach: (1) the *neighborhood method*, based on the similarity between the items and users [1]; and (2) the model of *latent factor*, which consists of representing the users and the items through factors or characteristics [19]. For instance, Koren *et al.* [13], developed a recommendation system for the Netflix competition based on latent factor models, matrix factorization and the use of alternating least squares (ALS). About a couple of years ago, Covington*et al.* [8] described the Youtube recommendation system using deep neural networks and neighborhood methods to process searches. In banking, recommendation systems have been developed with information on customers' use of debit or credit cards, taking into account the clients' spatial and temporal contexts as well as their similarity with other clients when visiting commerces [9].

The third recommendation approach is *demographic filtering*. The main idea behind this approach is that users with similar characteristics and attributes will have similar preferences [4]. Its function is to categorize the user according to his attributes and create recommendations based on demographic variables (such as age and sex, among others) [15]. For example, Al-Shamri [3] proposes five different metrics to measure demographic similarity for recommendation systems. (1) *Mixed Profiling Approach* considers the similarity of each attribute independently and then it aggregates the similarity of each one in a single score. (2) *Categorical Profiling Approach* unifies those attributes that yield a similarity value equal to 1 when their categories are equivalent. (3) *Fuzzy Profiling Approach* exploits the vague nature of the age attribute. Thus, two users with close ages are 100% similar. (4) *Cascaded Profiling Approach* considers age as the only factor for obtaining user similarity in the beginning. Then, the system elects a big set of neighbors relying on age similarity. This more significant set is the input to another system, which takes into account both age and gender attributes. The output of this system is a new smaller set of neighbors. Finally, the system uses age, gender, and occupation attributes. (5) *Single-Attribute Profiling Approach* takes each attribute as a profile. Hence, there is an independent recommender system for each attribute like age, gender, and occupation. To perform experiments, the author used the 100K MovieLens dataset with the Mean Absolute Error, Root Mean Squared Error, Coverage and percentage of the correct predictions metrics for recommendations systems evaluations. He found that the way of outlining users play an essential role in enhancing system performance.

Finally, the literature shows the *hybrid* approach, in which the characteristics of the collaborative filter and the content-based filter are combined, even some authors use recommendation systems based on demographic analysis. Zhao et al. [20] employed demographic information on social media platforms to boost sales. For this purpose, they extracted product and user demographics from online product reviews and social networks built from microblogs for product recommendation.

The authors of the reference [7] investigated and studied the problem that arises in the recommendation systems when the data of the new users are not available. The alternative they propose to minimize this lack of precedents is basing on the user's demographic information.

Additionally, the *hybrid* approaches address the problem of the cold start of the collaborative filter and the over-specialization of content-based techniques. Burke [6] details different methods for linking the existing content-based and collaborative filter approaches by weighting, exchange, mixing, among others. The system needs data to understand the preferences of the users and makes recommendations that express the client's preference towards an item through an explicit or implicit valuation. On the one hand, the explicit valuation indicates the user's choice using a scale, such as assigning 1 to 5 stars to commerce. On the other hand, the implicit valuation is calculated by analyzing the user's behavior in the domain of the system; for example, the amount of time devoted to observing a tab and the amount spent in commerces.

Due to the pros and cons of the methods described above, we propose to combine the factor models and the demographic vector, which allows reordering the recommended shops through the cosine similarity model which is based on linear algebra rather than statistical approach. That model is commonly used to calculate the scores that express how similar users or items are to each other. These scores can then be used as the foundation of user- or item-based recommendation generation.

In this article, the amount of data with which we worked is fixed. However, if the data grows at very high velocity, it is prudent to use complementary methods that can handle such data accurately as well as efficiently in the context of a recommender system. In those cases, Kumar [14] proposes a latent factor model that caters to both accuracy and efficiency by reducing the complexity of the model without compromising on accuracy.

3   Recommendation System Process

Our proposal is divided into six phases, as shown in Fig. 1. First, we obtain a database that contains clients' credit and debit card transactions. Then, online transactions that do not belong to commerce are filtered. After that, remaining transactions are divided according to the area (district) where the commerce belongs. Both data and the filtering process will be described in Sect. 4. Then, using latent factor, alternating matrices factorization, and least squares, the recommender system estimates the unknown valuations of the clients. These techniques are detailed in Subsects. 3.1, 3.2 and 3.3, respectively. Therefore, all the *ratings* of the clients are obtained per commerce. Once ratings are collected, we use demographic characteristics to refine recommended commerces order. Finally, we plotted them in cartography.

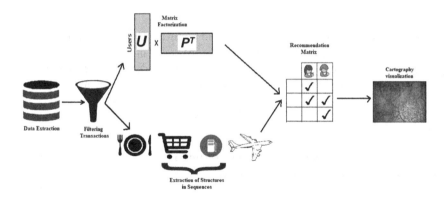

Fig. 1. Operation recommender system scheme.

3.1   Latent Factor Models

The latent factor models characterize the items and the users by factors inferred from the *ratings* to explain items valuations [19]. Matrix factorization techniques are critical to these models, as they find the values of the latent factor to estimate unknown valuations. Each user and each item is modeled with an individual vector of specific features. Using the scalar product of these individual vectors, we would estimate the valuation of a user to an item. In the case of an item, the feature vector indicates its factor as a result of an assigned score. The higher the score is, the better is the item characterized. For example, a movie that has a high rating on the "Drama" feature will be a dramatic genre movie.

3.2 Matrix Factorization

Based on the latent factor models, the matrix factorization represents the inter-actions between users and items as a scalar product to obtain the unknown ratings. This approach is the most accurate when dealing with the sparse data in the valuations matrices [5]. Given $u_i \in U$ and $m_j \in M$, which represent the feature vector of the i-th user and the j-th item, respectively, the internal product $u_i^T m_j$ is the interaction between the respective users and items, where u_i^T is the transpose of u_i. Due to the item-user interaction is given by the user's valuation, the Eq. 1 expresses the i-th user's valuation to the j-th item.

$$r_{ij} = u_i^T m_j \tag{1}$$

To calculate the values for the matrices U and M, the matrix R must be approximated by minimizing the loss function. Thus, given a pair of matrices U and M, the total loss of the model will be the sum of all the losses in all known valuations, which results in the mean square error (MSE, $c.f.$, Eq. 2).

$$f(R, U, M) = \frac{1}{n} \sum_{i,j} (r_{i,j} - u_i^T \times m_j)^2. \tag{2}$$

When valuing the error, one should avoid counting items with no valuations. For this reason, in the Eq. 2, we added a matrix W of weights with the same dimension as the matrix R. If $r_{i,j}$ exists, then $w_{i,j}$ takes the value of 1, and 0 otherwise. Therefore, the loss function can be rewritten as shown in Eq. 3.

$$f(R, W, U, M) = \frac{1}{n} \sum_{i,j} w_{i,j}(r_{i,j} - u_i^T \times m_j)^2. \tag{3}$$

Then, one can formulate the problem of finding the values of U and M that best approximate the matrix R through Eq. 4.

$$(U, M) = \underset{(U,M)}{\arg\min} f(R, W, U, M), \tag{4}$$

3.3 Alternating Least Squares (ALS)

ALS is an optimization method to solve Eq. 3. Since we have a non-convex function, we ignore both the values of U and M. Thus; we must solve Eq. 3 for each unknown variable separately [21]. Besides, we have $(i + j) \times k$ unknown parameters that must be calculated, and an R sparse matrix (since not all users score all trades), and when solving the Eq. 3 can generate data overfitting. Therefore, we add a term in Eq. 3 using the Tikhonov regularization method [10], as observed in Eq. 5.

$$f(R, W, U, M) = \sum_{(i,j)} w_{(i,j)}(r_{(i,j)} - u_i^T \times m_j)^2 +$$

$$\lambda(\sum_i n_{u_i} ||u_i||^2 + \sum_j n_{m_j} ||m_j||^2), \tag{5}$$

Being n_{u_i} and n_{m_j} the number of valuations that the user i has on the item m_j, respectively. Using Eq. 5 as the function to be minimized, the way to proceed using alternating least squares is as follows:

- Initialize M randomly with values between 1 and 0
- Fix M, and derive partially from U
- Fix U, and derive partially from M
- Repeat the 2nd and 3rd step until reaching the pre-established detention criterion.

The detention criterion is set as the square root of the difference between MSE in steps n and $n - 1$. In our case, we used 10^{-4} as the threshold for the stop criterion, as suggested in Zhou *et al.* [21].

3.4   Demographic Rearrangement

The first phase of this stage consisted of generating a commerce demographic vector (d_c) composed of the percentage of males and females who purchased in that specific commerce and the percent of the clients in age ranges from 18–24, 25–30, 31–40, 41–50, 51–60, and 61+. Analogously, we characterized the clients (d_u). It is worth noting that the age ranges were found empirically. Once their demographic vectors describe clients and commerce, it is possible to rearrange the order of the recommendation based on the demographic similarity of the commerce d_c to the client d_u. Therefore, to sort these stores, we use Cosine Similarity, detailed in Eq. 6. This process allows us to measure the demographic correspondence of a user and the recommended shops. Thus, the closer to one is the cosine, the higher the similarity is.

$$cosim(\overrightarrow{d_c}, \overrightarrow{d_u}) = \frac{(\overrightarrow{d_c} \cdot \overrightarrow{d_u})}{\|\overrightarrow{d_c}\| \times \|\overrightarrow{d_u}\|},$$ (6)

4   Experiments and Results

The data used in this work are associated with banking transactions registered for one year, specifically between June 2016 to July 2017. In total, we recorded 65 085 138 transactions; approximately 80% of them correspond to transactions made with a debit card, while the remaining 20% were made with credit cards. Besides, 25 variables provide information about the customer, the card owner, the commerce of the transaction, among others. For our experiments, the variables *CodClient*, *CodCommerce*, *Category*, and *Amount_Rating* were selected. We calculated the latter using the Eq. 7, which is the ratio between the purchase value in certain commerce and the total amount spent by a customer. This variable represents the valuations of the clients towards the commerces.

$$amount\_rating_{i,j} = \frac{amount\_commerce_j}{amount\_total_i}$$ (7)

First of all, we grouped the data by regions (districts) in which the commercial transactions were carried out. For each region, the valuation sparse matrix R is generated. As there are many unknown valuations, the matrix R^* is estimated by matrix factorization, and alternating least squares, finding the values of the user matrix U and the items matrix M. In R^*, the valuation of the client i to the commerce j is represented by r_{ij}.

We used the Python programming language and an instance of Elastic Compute Cloud (EC2) from Amazon Web Services (AWS) to process the data. Once we calculated the matrices, we normalized the rows, and then, the n commerces with the highest valuations are recommended.

The bank classified the commerces to find the user's consumption patterns. To do this, it groups related elements and groups them into different categories. Finally, 22 types of classifications were obtained, each of them coded by a symbol, as shown in Table 1.

Table 1. Categories' Table

NAME_CATEGORÍE	COD	NAME_CATEGORÍE	COD
PRODMARKET	a	RESTBAR	b
HEALTH	c	VEHIDER	d
PRIVSHOP	e	ENTRENT	f
FASHCLOT	g	BEAUTY	h
TELECOMM	i	RENTGOODS	j
FINANC	k	ELECTPROD	l
ARTCULT	m	EDUCATION	n
LOCALPROD	o	TRANSLI	p
DIVPROP	q	CLUBMA	r
HOGOFIC	s	PROFDIV	t
INFORM	u	RETMAN	v

To accomplish our work, we first applied the ALS optimization method in the district of Barranca, located in the province of the same name, in the department of Lima. We showed in Fig. 2 that after 5 iterations, the MSE obtained by minimizing Eq. 5 is 0.0000026. Thus, the R matrix converges to the matrix R^* quickly.

Then, the predicted valuations are in the matrix R^*. Since there are 167 883 clients, 19 949 commerces and more than 3 billion of valuations, Table 2 shows, for example, valuations for three clients to three commerces. From this matrix, the *ratings* are expressed using demographic similarity.

In the next section, we describe the method to validate the results of the recommender system.

5   Recommendation System Validation

For the recommender verification, a preliminary test and validation were performed on samples corresponding to some districts of Lima city.

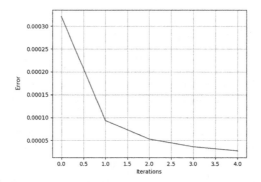

Fig. 2. MSE analyzed in Barranca district

Table 2. Predicted valuations Matrix: district of Barranca

	100070254	100073401	101081734
Bob	0.7935	0.5134	0.2376
Alice	0.8317	0.9205	0.5462
Eve	0.6911	0.4123	0.3433

5.1   Preliminary Test

For the recommendation system test, a survey on the acceptance of the results was conducted with 10 credit and debit cards clients. We computed the recommended commerces by estimating the valuations of 149 362 clients. We divided these commerces into two types: (1) recurring, places that the client had previously visited, and (2) recommended new places for the client. The surveys measured the acceptance of the recommendation by customers for different categories and commerces. In summary, the study was personalized for each user based on their historical consumption and recommendation of new commerces.

Table 3 presents the percentage of recommendations of commerces and categories, both recurrent and novel, in which the client would accept to make some consumption.

Table 3. Test results

	Recurrent	New
Category	77.0%	76.0%
Commerce	84.5%	70.0%

In the case of the commercial category, the acceptance is 77% and 76% for recurring and new commerces, respectively. In the case of merchants *per se*, the acceptance is 84.5% for recurrent commerces and 70% for new commerces (*c.f.*, Table 3). Although the size of the taken sample is small, this allowed us to test the congruence of the recommender in a pilot test. Based on the results, it is possible to see that the recommendation engine is 76% relevant in terms of the new items it suggests, and 70% concerning the new commerces.

This first test was carried out to verify the coherence of the recommendations ratified by the users surveyed. However, for a statistically rigorous validation, the sample size and other factors presented below must be taken into account.

5.2   Validation

For the validation process, we chose four districts of Lima: San Isidro, San Borja, Miraflores, and Independencia, and for each of them, we took a random sample of clients, n = 4500. Due to confidentiality reasons, we can not rebel the exact number of clients by district. However, to give an idea of the order of magnitude of clients, in the Table 4 we see that San Isidro, San Borja, Miraflores, and Independencia represent three, four, five and two times approximately the size of the sample. To verify that the sample is representative of the population, we carried out three different tests. First, we prove that the samples have the same mean as their respective populations using the test *One Sample t Test* [18]. To perform this test, the confidence of 5% (*i.e.*, α=0.05) was taken with 4499 degrees of freedom and a T value of 1.9605 for a two-tailed test. We raised the null hypothesis which was that the samples mean of the consumption and the population are equal $H_0 : \mu_0 - \mu = 0$. The alternative hypothesis is that these

Table 4. Summary of the sample validation results

District	San Isidro	San Borja	Miraflores	Independencia
Sample size	3n	4n	5n	2n
Sample mean	0.0043	0.0071	0.0080	0.004
Sample population	0.0042	0.0072	0.0079	0.003
Test-t	−0.55	0.25	−0.36	1.72
KLD	0.0009	0.001	0.0018	0.0009
Minimum sample size	410	422	415	400

means are different $H_{alt} : \mu_0 - \mu \neq 0$. The calculated values of the *test t* are found in Table 4 and were calculated using Eq. 8.

$$t = \frac{\overline{x} - \mu}{\frac{s}{\sqrt{n}}} \tag{8}$$

Where $\overline{x}$ is the population mean, μ is the sample mean, s is the standard deviation, and n is the size of the sample. As a result of the test, the null hypothesis is accepted, so the mean of the sample and population consumption are equal.

The second method uses the divergence of *Kullback-Leibler* to show that from the distribution of the sample p, we can reconstruct the distribution of the population q [12]. For this, we use Eq. 9. We compared the distributions in Fig. 3.

$$KLD = \sum_{k=1}^{n} p_k \times ln(\frac{(p_k)^2}{q_k}) \tag{9}$$

Thus, Table 4 shows the values obtained for the divergence. Note that the values close to zero mean that there is no divergence, that is, the distributions are equal.

Finally, the size of the sample $(n*)$ necessary to have a statistically significant representation was calculated. Knowing the number of clients in each of the districts, we use the formula of Eq. 10 to calculate the value of $n*$.

$$n* = \frac{N \times (Z)^2 \times p \times q}{(e)^2 \times (N-1) + (Z)^2 \times p \times q} \tag{10}$$

Where N is the size of the population, Z is the deviation from the average value that we accept to achieve the desired level of confidence (95%), in our case $Z = 1.96$, p is the probability of success or proportion that we expect to find (50%), q represents the probability of failure and e is the maximum margin of error that we admit (5%). To preserve the confidentiality of the exact number of clients, Table 4 was obtained, overestimating the sample size values $n*$. In all cases, the results obtained are an order of magnitude lower than the real value taken for each district.

Once it has been demonstrated that the samples taken are statistically representative of their respective populations, we described the results of the recommendation engine. The validation of the engine was carried out using the customers selected as sample, to whom personalized offers were sent in two retail items and restaurants during the first three weeks of March 2018. At the end of that month, the average tickets were compared to the sample and the population without the users in the sample, and it was observed that there was an increase in the average consumer ticket in retailers and restaurants of 10% and 22%, respectively. That meant an increase in expenses from 33.6 USD to 37 USD in retailers and from 27.88 USD to 34.24 USD in restaurants. These results show us the relevance of the recommendation engine and its potential impact on the commerces.

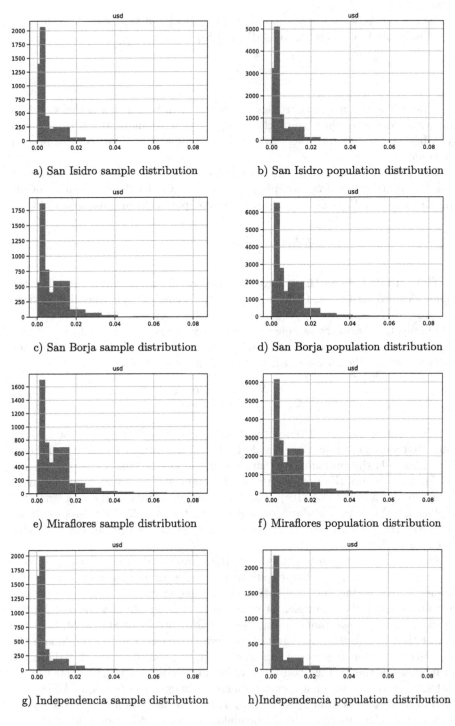

a) San Isidro sample distribution

b) San Isidro population distribution

c) San Borja sample distribution

d) San Borja population distribution

e) Miraflores sample distribution

f) Miraflores population distribution

g) Independencia sample distribution

h) Independencia population distribution

Fig. 3. Samples and populations distributions from different districts.

6   Conclusions and Future Works

In this work, we developed a recommendation system for a financial institution. We noted that the amount spent on trade could be used as an implicit valuation, and reflected the preference of the client for different commerces, so the higher the amount paid by the client, the greater is the probability that the client chooses that kind of stores or restaurants.

We took into account the geographic context of the clients when we generated the grouping by area (district), identifying where they made the transactions. The district's geographic division maintained the recommendations within a coherent geographic framework, avoiding recommending commerces in remote areas or places that were visited only once, for example, during the vacation period. Besides, using the measure of cosine similarity, an order of priority was obtained in the recommended commerces. The recommendations are innovative, although it is not ruled out that previously visited commerces are included in the list of recommended commerces.

In relation to future work, we will explore the study and a more detailed density analysis with all the districts of Lima, in order to improve the visualization. In addition, given the high volume of data that we worked on, we are planning to use the integrated Apache Spark *framework* to implement advanced analysis, such as processing data in parallel and working in a shared environment. This can be executed in *clusters* of Elastic Map Reduce (EMR) using MrJob in Hadoop, PySpark or Scala. Also, the privacy of the users and their data must be taken into consideration, with which the recommendations are executed. Consequently, our idea is to implement an additional layer to the recommendation engine to guarantee a certain level of privacy. Finally, we intend to perform a large-scale pilot with ten thousand users to validate the recommender system and have a better measure of real accuracy and not subjective.

References

1. Abdollahpouri, H., Abdollahpouri, A.: An approach for personalization of banking services in multi-channel environment using memory-based collaborative filtering. In: The 5th Conference on Information and Knowledge Technology, pp. 208–213, May 2013. https://doi.org/10.1109/IKT.2013.6620066
2. Aggarwal, C.C.: Recommender Systems. Springer, Cham (2016). https://doi.org/10.1007/978-3-319-29659-3
3. Al-Shamri, M.Y.H.: User profiling approaches for demographic recommender systems. Knowl. Based Syst. **100**, 175–187 (2016)
4. Bobadilla, J., Ortega, F., Hernando, A., Gutiérrez, A.: Recommender systems survey. Knowl. Based Syst. **46**, 109–132 (2013)
5. Bokde, D., Girase, S., Mukhopadhyay, D.: Matrix factorization model in collaborative filtering algorithms: a survey. Procedia Computer Science, 49(Supplement C), 136–146 (2015). https://doi.org/10.1016/j.procs.2015.04.237, http://www.sciencedirect.com/science/article/pii/S1877050915007462. proceedings of 4th International Conference on Advances in Computing, Communication and Control (ICAC3'15)

6. Burke, R.: Hybrid recommender systems: survey and experiments. User Model. User-Adap. Interact. **12**(4), 331–370 (2002). https://doi.org/10.1023/A:1021240730564
7. Callvik, J., Liu, A.: Using demographic information to reduce the new user problem in recommender systems (2017)
8. Covington, P., Adams, J., Sargin, E.: Deep neural networks for youtube recommendations. In: Proceedings of the 10th ACM Conference on Recommender Systems, pp. 191–198. RecSys 2016, New York (2016). https://doi.org/10.1145/2959100.2959190
9. Gallego, D., Huecas, G.: An empirical case of a context-aware mobile recommender system in a banking environment. In: Proceedings of the 2012 Third FTRA International Conference on Mobile, Ubiquitous, and Intelligent Computing, pp. 13–20. MUSIC 2012, Washington (2012). https://doi.org/10.1109/MUSIC.2012.11
10. Golub, G.H., Hansen, P.C., O'Leary, D.P.: Tikhonov regularization and total least squares. SIAM J. Matrix Anal. Appl. **21**(1), 185–194 (1999)
11. Gomez-Uribe, C.A., Hunt, N.: The netflix recommender system: algorithms, business, value and innovation. ACM Trans. Manage. Inf. Syst. **6**(4), 13:1–13:19 (2015). https://doi.org/10.1145/2843948
12. Joyce, J.M.: Kullback-leibler divergence. International Encyclopedia of Statistical Science, pp. 720–722 (2011)
13. Koren, Y., Bell, R., Volinsky, C.: Matrix factorization techniques for recommender systems. Computer **42**(8), 30–37 (2009). https://doi.org/10.1109/MC.2009.263
14. Kumar, B.: A novel latent factor model for recommender system. JISTEM-J. Inf. Syst. Technol. Manage. **13**(3), 497–514 (2016)
15. Lu, J., Wu, D., Mao, M., Wang, W., Zhang, G.: Recommender system application developments: a survey. Decis. Supp. Syst. **74**, 12–32 (2015)
16. Oulasvirta, A., Hukkinen, J.P., Schwartz, B.: When more is less: the paradox of choice in search engine use. In: Proceedings of the 32nd International ACM SIGIR Conference on Research and Development in Information Retrieval, pp. 516–523. SIGIR 2009, New York (2009). https://doi.org/10.1145/1571941.1572030
17. Pazzani, M.J.: A framework for collaborative, content-based and demographic filtering. Artif. Intell. Rev. **13**(5–6), 393–408 (1999)
18. Ross, A., Willson, V.L.: Basic and Advanced Statistical Tests. Sense Publishers, Rotterdam (2017). https://doi.org/10.1007/978-94-6351-086-8
19. Su, X., Khoshgoftaar, T.M.: A survey of collaborative filtering techniques. Adv. Artif. Intell. **2009**, 4:2 (2009). https://doi.org/10.1155/2009/421425
20. Zhao, W.X., Li, S., He, Y., Wang, L., Wen, J.-R., Li, X.: Exploring demographic information in social media for product recommendation. Knowl. Inf. Syst. **49**(1), 61–89 (2015). https://doi.org/10.1007/s10115-015-0897-5
21. Zhou, Y., Wilkinson, D., Schreiber, R., Pan, R.: Large-scale parallel collaborative filtering for the netflix prize. In: Proceedings of the 4th International Conference on Algorithmic Aspects in Information and Management, pp. 337–348. AAIM 2008 (2008)

Privacy Preservation and Inference with Minimal Mobility Information

Julián Salas^{1,3} and Miguel Nunez-del-Prado$^{2(\boxtimes)}$

^{1} Internet Interdisciplinary Institute (IN3), Universitat Oberta de Catalunya,
Barcelona, Spain
jsalaspi@uoc.edu
^{2} Universidad del Pacífico, Av. Salaverry 2020, Lima, Peru
m.nunezdelpradoc@up.edu.pe
^{3} CYBERCAT-Center for Cybersecurity Research of Catalonia, Barcelona, Spain

Abstract. There is much debate about the challenge to anonymize a large amount of information obtained in big data scenarios. Besides, it is even harder considering inferences from data may be used as additional adversary knowledge. This is the case of geo-located data, where the Points of Interest (POIs) may have additional information that can be used to link them to a user's real identity. However, in most cases, when a model of the raw data is published, this processing protects up to some point the privacy of the data subjects by minimizing the published information. In this paper, we measure the privacy obtained by the minimization of the POIs published when we apply the Mobility Markov Chain (MMC) model, which extracts the most important POIs of an individual. We consider the gender inferences that an adversary may obtain from publishing the MMC model together with additional information such as the gender or age distribution of each POI, or the aggregated gender distribution of all the POIs visited by a data subject. We measure the unicity obtained after applying the MMC model, and the probability that an adversary that knows some POIs in the data before processing may be able to link them with the POIs published after the MMC model. Finally, we measure the anonymity lost when adding the gender attribute to the side knowledge of an adversary that has access to the MMC model. We test our algorithms on a real transaction database.

Keywords: Mobility Markov Chain · Gender inference · Geo-located data privacy · Data protection regulation

1 Introduction

Inferring demographics are useful for targeting, profiling costumers and improve services provided to them by all kind of businesses. Demographic data, together with the mobility profiles of customers, may be used for better understanding their choices and preferences. However, revealing attributes like the home locations or the gender of users in a database may lead to re-identification, and

© Springer Nature Switzerland AG 2020
J. A. Lossio-Ventura et al. (Eds.): SIMBig 2019, CCIS 1070, pp. 129–142, 2020.
https://doi.org/10.1007/978-3-030-46140-9_13

possibly to discrimination. Hence, protecting from such inferences and finding a balance between the amount of data processed and the privacy of the individuals is an important open issue.

In this paper, we study the effects of minimizing the POIs and the data published on privacy protection. Concretely, we apply the MMC model [7], which extracts the most important POIs of an individual and guarantees data minimization, a privacy design strategy [4] that has been suggested by the General Data Protection Regulation (GDPR) from EU for improving protecting privacy in data processing. We study the inference of the gender attribute after applying the MMC model together with minimal additional information, then compare the anonymity (measured as the unicity) obtained by applying the MMC model with the unicity of the data before processing. We measure the anonymity lost when the gender attribute is added as side knowledge of an adversary that uses observed POIs of an individual to try to re-identify him on the dataset.

Finally, we obtain a general formula that relates the number of raw POIs, the published POIs and the adversary's side knowledge of raw POIs, to the probability that he is able to link them to the published POIs. We use it to measure how privacy is improved by minimization of the published POIs.

The present effort is organized as follows: Sect. 2 describes the related works. Then, Sect. 3 introduces the basic concepts, while Sect. 4 presents the results. Finally, Sect. 5 concludes the paper and gives some new research avenues.

2   Related Works

Different kind of datasets have been used to infer demographics. For instance, Hu *et al.* [12] use the browsing behavior to predict them. First, they propagate users age and gender to browsed pages and predict the Web page's gender and age tendency. Then, using a Bayesian framework, they predict the age and gender of users based on the tendency of the Web pages that he or she has browsed. Bi *et al.* [1] show that users' traits may be predicted from search query logs by applying models developed on the Facebook Likes data.

Weinsberg *et al.* [21] show that a recommender system can infer the gender of a user with high accuracy, based uniquely on the ratings to movies provided by users, and a relatively small number of users who share their demographics. They use Movielens and Flixster dataset, in which some users have included their demographic information. Their strategy for gender obfuscation is to add fake movies to a user's record, which are strongly correlated to the opposite gender of the user.

Wang *et al.* [20] use Structured Neural Embedding (SNE) Model to infer age, gender and marital status. They model the possible multi labels as an eight-bit vector. Then, authors compare SNE, Pseudo Outer-Product (POP), Singular Value Decomposition (SVD) Single, SVD-Structured, and Join Neural Embedding (JNE) algorithms for the attributes prediction. They use the BeiRen dataset, which is composed of 49 290 149 transactions over 220 828 items belonging to 1 206 379 users during 2012-2013. The obtained results in terms of weighted precision are ranging from 0.083 to 0.371.

Other works in the literature use mobility traces to infer demographic attributes. For example, Mayer *et al.* [13] studied privacy implications from metadata of mobile users. They used DBSCAN and extract the business that users have visited from telephone metadata, to re-identify the home location of individuals. Other algorithms for home location inference have also been studied in [3, 19] and mechanisms for protection from this inference have been provided in [18].

From the before mentioned works, we observe that home location inference is relatively straightforward when using GPS, check-ins or other real-time location data. Moreover, location data may be used for linking users among different domains [16].

Wang *et al.* [20] use non-negative matrix factorization to deduce demographic attributes based on mobile devices trajectories when connecting to access points. The authors collected data from 51 903 mobile devices for 21 days on two campuses. Authors build a three order tensor composed of mobile phones social networks (u), time (t) and location (V). Then, they associate the rank-one vector to the demographic characteristics of mobile devices users and use it as the input of an SVM and Logistic Regression classification algorithms, obtaining a precision between 69.9% and 72.2%.

Zang *et al.* [23] propose a framework for demographic inference. In detail, they reconstruct a graph representing social ties among individuals of the dataset using a multilabel regression technique. Then, the average of tree-based, linear and kernel-based classification algorithms to infer individuals gender. Authors obtained an accuracy between 69.23% and 92.30%.

Zhong *et al.* [24] propose a location to profile (L2P) framework for inferring demographic attributes of online users. This inference includes both gender and age from location check-ins considering the temporality and spatiality. The former estimates at what times the individuals develop their activities such as transportation or shopping on their POIs. The later guesses where are those activities carried out (location of POIs). Also, they try to know the semantics of the POIs (*i.e.*, category, price, and range of a restaurant), which can be enriched with customer reviews or comments.

Regarding privacy protection, several methods have been developed for trajectory data, cf. [5]. While, others have measured the unicity of mobility and transaction data (even when it is coarsened) for privacy protection [14,15]. However, none of them has assessed the effect of minimizing the published records on the privacy of individuals. We minimize the amount of information collected, infer demographics and test the unicity of the data, to measure the privacy preserved by applying the MMC model from [7]. We also measure the loss in anonymity when considering the additional knowledge of gender or age attributes.

Finally, we give a general formula for measuring the privacy obtained by the minimization of the POIs published. Data minimization is one of the diverse challenges for big data privacy protection [17], and is consistent with recent policy recommendations (e.g., GDPR law from EU) for guaranteeing privacy by design in data collection and publishing [4].

3   Background

In the present section, we introduce the mobility model and the adversary side knowledge used for the inference attacks. We selected the MMC mobility model [7] because it has been used to perform different inference attacks, such as POI extraction [9], next whereabouts prediction [8], and de-anonymization [10].

3.1   Mobility Markov Chain

A *Mobility Markov Chain* (MMC) [7] models the mobility behavior of an individual as a discrete stochastic process in which the probability of moving to a state (*i.e.*, a point of interest) depends only on the previously visited state and the probability distribution on the transitions between states. More precisely, a MMC is composed of:

- A set of states $P = \{p_1, \dots p_n\}$, in which each state is a frequent POI (ranked by decreasing order of importance), with the exception of the last state p_n that corresponds to the set made of all infrequented POIs. POIs are usually learned by running a clustering algorithm on the mobility traces of an individual. These states generally have an intrinsic semantic meaning and therefore semantic labels such as "home" or "work" can often be inferred and attached to them.
- Transitions, such as $t_{i,j}$, represent the probability of moving from state p_i to state p_j. A transition from one state to itself is possible if the individual has a non-null probability from moving from one state to an occasional location before coming back to this state. For instance, an individual can leave home to go to the pharmacy and then come back to his home. In this example, it is likely that the pharmacy will not be extracted as a POI by the clustering algorithm, unless the individual visits this place on a regular basis.

Note that many mobility models relying on a Markov chains have been proposed in the past [7], including the use of hidden Markov models for performing inference attacks [22]. In a nutshell, building a MMC is a two step process. During the first phase, a clustering algorithm is run to extract the POIs from the mobility traces. We use the clustering algorithm called Density Joinable cluster (DJ-Cluster) that was used in the study of Gambs *et al.* [7], however, other clustering algorithms are possible. In the second phase, the transitions between those POIs are computed.

DJ-Cluster takes as input a trail of mobility traces and 3 parameters: the minimal number of points $MinPts$ needed to create a cluster, the maximum radius r of the circle within which the points of a cluster should be contained and a distance d at which neighboring clusters are merged into a single one. DJ Cluster works in three phases. During the first phase, which corresponds to a pre-processing step, all the mobility traces in which the individual is in movement (*i.e.*, whose speed is above some small predefined value), as well as subsequent static redundant traces, are removed. As a result, only static traces are kept. The second step consists in the clustering itself: all remaining traces are processed in order to extract clusters that have at least $MinPts$ points within a radius r of the center of the cluster. Finally, the last phase merges all clusters that have a trace in common or whose centroids are within d distance of each other.

Once the POIs (*i.e.*, the states of the Markov chain) are identified, the probabilities of the transitions between states can be computed. To realize this, the trail of mobility traces is examined by chronological order and each mobility trace is tagged with a label that is either the number identifying a particular state of the MMC or the value "unknown". Finally, when all the mobility traces have been labeled, the transitions between states are counted and normalized by the total number of transitions in order to obtain the probabilities of each transition. The MMC is represented as a transition matrix of size $n \times n$, the rows and columns correspond to states of the MMC while the value of each cell is the probability of the associated transition between the corresponding states.

The *predictability* [8] is a theoretical measure quantifying how predictable is the mobility of an individual based on his MMC model. The predictability *Pred* of a particular user u corresponds to the sum of the product between each element $\pi_{i,u}$ of the stationary vector computed from the MMC of user u:

$$Pred(u) = \sum_{i=1}^{n_u} (\pi_{i,u} \times p_{max\_out}(i, u)), \qquad (1)$$

in which $\pi_{i,u}$ is the probability of being in a particular state (for n_u, the total number of states of the MMC of user u) and $p_{max\_out}(i, u)$ represents the maximum outgoing probability leaving from the ith state.

In general, the *(Shannon) entropy* is a measure of uncertainty regarding the output of a random variable. In the context of mobility, the entropy of a user quantifies the spatial uncertainty about the exact location of a user. Considering a particular user u, we can compute his entropy by applying the following formula:

$$H(u) = -\sum_{i=1}^{n_u} p_{i,u} \log_2 p_{i,u}, \qquad (2)$$

in which p_i, u represents the probability of user u to be located in his i^{th} POI while n_u corresponds to the total number of POIs characterizing his mobility.

In Table 1 we show the information generated using the MMC model from a transactions dataset. As we can see each row shows a Point of Interest (in this case represented by the Business ID), a user identifier (Name), his/her age, gender, home district, user's entropy, user's predictability, and a stationary probability corresponding to that POI.

3.2 Adversary Model

For defining the adversary knowledge, we introduce the four pieces of information an adversary may have for performing the gender inference. First, the *MMC properties* from Table 1.

Table 1. MMC properties example.

User ID	Age	Gender	District	Entropy	Predictability	Business ID	Stat probability
Bob	49	M	SAN ISIDRO	1.53	0.89	10907215	0.33
Bob	49	M	SAN ISIDRO	1.53	0.89	10010695	0.45
Bob	49	M	SAN ISIDRO	1.53	0.89	10012805	0.22

The second piece of information is the *aggregated probability*, which considers the POIs visited by each user and the gender distribution by POI. Then, we aggregate the probabilities of all the POIs that a user has visited to obtain the gender probability for each user. This information is computed based on the aforementioned *MMC properties*. Table 2a shows an example of this information.

Table 2. Adversary knowledge examples.

a) Aggregated probability

User ID	Female probability
Bob	0.35
Alice	0.8
Eve	0.82

b) Male/female count

Business ID	Male	Female
00128826	523	497
00155626	179	234
00112326	139	156

c) Male/female count per age example

Business ID	18-25		25-30		30-40		40-50		50-60		60	
	M	F	M	F	M	F	M	F	M	F	M	F
00136626	35	30	3	7	24	20	14	17	32	37	6	6
00136624	135	230	13	17	32	25	17	19	37	39	16	26
00136628	53	34	31	74	21	20	37	57	23	77	11	34

Finally, the *male/female count* is the gender proportion by POI as shown in Table 2b and the *male/female count per age* is the gender proportion by POI and age range as depicted in Table 2c.

Based on the before mentioned pieces of information, we have built five different scenarios with distinct cases. Each scenario and case denote the use of a combination of one or two pieces of information to represent the scenario attack by the adversary as introduced in Table 3. For instance, in Scenario three the adversary uses the *MMC properties* as well as the *aggregated probability* as prior information to perform the attack.

In the following section, we detail specific cases of these different scenarios to perform the gender inference attack.

Table 3. Adversary *a priori* knowledge. Where *Age* is the male and female count by age.

Scenario	MMC properties	Aggregated prob	M/F count	Age
1	✓	–	–	–
2	✓	–	✓	–
3	✓	✓	–	–
4	✓	–	–	✓
5	–	✓	–	–

4   Results

In the present section, we perform some experiments for inferring the gender of bank users based on their transactions and also carry out unicity tests concerning their POIs.

4.1   Experiments

In the present effort, we use 65 millions of banking transactions dataset, which is composed of (1) pseudonym of the user as ID; (2) age; (3) gender; (4) Merchant Category Code (MCC)[1]; (5) the timestamp of the transaction; (6) the number of monetary units spent; (7) quantity of transactions; and, (8) the district ID of the transaction. The dataset was gathered from June 2016 to May 2017 in Peru.

First of all, we need to find a suitable classification algorithm for implementing the inference attack. In the present work, we use four different classification algorithms, namely Gradient Boosted Regression Trees [6], Extremely Randomized Trees [2], Discrete and Real AdaBoost [11]. Figure 1 shows the precision when inferring the gender using the *MMC properties* as the input of the different classification algorithms per number of estimators, and we observe that Gradient Boosted Regression Trees performs the best with 199 estimators. Therefore, we use this algorithm for further experiments.

Since we have settled the classification algorithm, the adversary performs attacks in different scenarios and cases, as shown in Table 4. We observed seven different scenarios for gender inference. The adversary uses either 10-fold cross-validation or Grid search for the rest. For instance, in Scenario one Case one *S1C1*, the adversary uses Gradient Boosted Regression Trees (*GB*) algorithm over the *MMC properties* to infer gender. We observe a precision of 0.56, which is poor. In *S2C1*, the adversary combines two pieces of information, the *MMC properties* and the *male/female count per business*. Therefore, *GB* takes as input the *MMC properties* for training. Then, when the classifier estimates whether a subject is female if the probability of the prediction is under the threshold (60%), the adversary looks at the supplementary knowledge (*i.e.*, the male/female count) to

---

[1] VISA Merchant Category Classification (MCC) codes directory.

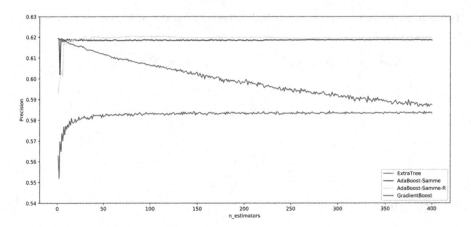

Fig. 1. Evaluation of the Gradient Boosted Regression Trees (*GradientBoost*), Extremely Randomized Trees (*ExtraTree*), Discrete AdaBoost (*AdaBoost Samme*), and Real AdaBoost (*AdaBoost Samme R*) for inferring users' gender.

infer the gender. Thus, the adversary uses a voting system where each POI votes for male or female based on the number of male or female visitors. In the same spirit, scenarios *S2C2* and *S3C1* utilize *GB* taking as input the *MMC properties* for training but they vary for the decision making. In the former, the adversary chooses whether a person is male if the sum of all males visitors in the POIs of his MMC model is bigger than the number of the females' counterparts. The latter follows the same logic, but instead of the *male/female count*, it employs the *aggregated probability* to perform the inference. Therefore, for scenarios *S2C1*, *S2C2*, and *S3C1*, we have obtained 57.65%, 57.8%, and 59.07% as best precisions, respectively. Finally, scenario *S4C1* adopts the same process as scenario *S2C2*, but it uses the *male/female count* by age to decide whether a given user is male if the classification probability is under a threshold of 60% obtaining 59.01%. It is worth noting that thresholds have been chosen empirically.

Concerning the scenarios *S3C2* and *S5C1*, they use Logistic Regression (*LR*) algorithm with Grid Search to fine tune the parameters of the regressor. In scenario *S5C1*, the adversary applies the LR directly over the *aggregated probabilities* information reaching a precision of 62%. While, in scenario *S3C2* the adversary utilizes also LR algorithm over the merge of two pieces of information such as *MMC properties* and *aggregated probabilities* getting the best precision of all (*i.e.*, 63%) (Fig. 2).

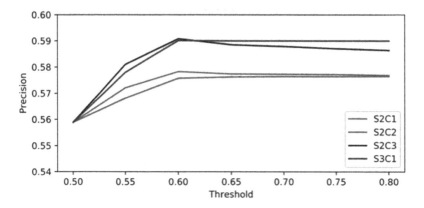

Fig. 2. Precision obtained depending on the threshold.

Table 4. Attack scenarios. Where GB = Gradient Boosted Regression Trees and LR = Logistic Regression.

code	Scenario	Case	Algorithm	Training	Precision	Threshold
S1C1	1	1	GB	10-fold cross validation	0.56	–
S2C1	2	1	GB	10-fold cross validation	0.5765	0.6
S2C2	2	2	GB	10-fold cross validation	0.578	0.6
S3C1	3	1	GB	10-fold cross validation	0.5907	0.6
S3C2	3	2	LR	Grid search	0.63	–
S4C1	4	1	GB	10-fold cross validation	0.5901	0.6
S5C1	5	1	LR	Grid search	0.62	–

4.2 Unicity Tests

In this section, we study the unicity of the transaction records after we apply the MMC model. This information is used in [14] to show that the mobility traces are highly unique even when their time and location are coarsened, and thus, they are susceptible to re-identification.

We will show that publishing the MMC decreases the possibility of finding unique records in published data. First, we test the unicity of the MMC, considering two, three, four, and five random POIs as the adversary knowledge, for each of the records in the MMC. Observe that most of the records have only 2 POIs in the MMC, while in the original database they may have many more, as we can see in Table 5.

We depict the unicity in Fig. 3 by sampling $p \in \{2, 3, 4, 5\}$ random POIs for each user and counting the number of records that contain the same p points. If there is only one user with such p points, it can be uniquely identified by this adversary's knowledge. We compare how the unicity increases if the adversary

Table 5. Statistics of number of POIs per user after MMC.

	Original	MMC
Min.	2	2
1st Qu.	28	2
Median	51	2
Mean	67.1	2.4
3st Qu.	89	3
Max.	674	13

knows also the gender attribute. For example, the unicity increases from 23.8% to 35.7% for an adversary that knows 2 POIs and learns the gender attribute.

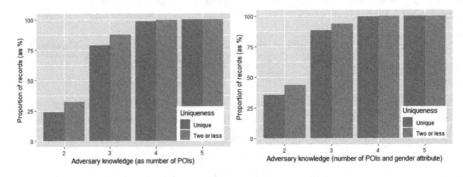

Fig. 3. Unicity of records after obtaining MMC, depending on the number of POIs that an adversary knows and gender attribute.

Privacy Obtained by Minimization. As we have previously explained, the MMC model does not publish all the POIs of an individual but only a few of the most relevant. So, we would like to measure how much privacy is gained by publishing less POIs than the original POIs for each individual.

For this, we consider an adversary that knows x random POIs of the original data of a user and tries to link them to his published data on the MMC.

First, we calculate the probability that x random POIs of adversary knowledge in the original data contain two specific POIs of the MMC of a given user.

Then, we consider how many POIs an adversary must know to have the certainty (with probabilities 0.25, 0.5, 0.75, 0.95 and 1) that such two POIs are published in the MMC. This is depicted in Fig. 4.

We can see that in average an adversary has to know 34.38 POIs to have the certainty up to 25% that such side knowledge of a user will contain the two POIs of the user published in the MMC. If the adversary wants to have a certainty of 50% he must have 48.2 POIs of side knowledge. For 75% he needs 58.81 POIs, for 95% needs 66.06 POIs, and for 100% certainty needs to know all the POIs that in average are 67.27, see Fig. 4.

Another way of interpreting these results is that if an adversary knows 34 POIs of a user which has 2 POIs in the MMC model, he may be able to uniquely identify such user in the data with a probability $0.057 = 0.25 * 0.23$, which is the probability that the 34 POIs contain that user's 2 POIs published in the MMC and that such 2 POIs are unique. Thus, we can see that the minimization of the published POIs in the MMC is effective for privacy protection.

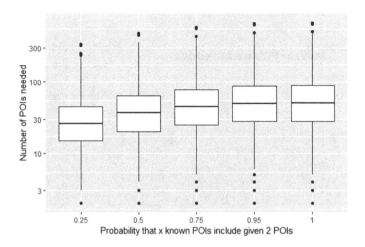

Fig. 4. Probability that given user with x POIs in the original data, contain 2 specific POIs of the MMC of a given user.

Generalization. We consider that an individual has n POIs, there have only been published $m \geq 2$ and the adversary knows r of the original n POIs. We give a closed formula for the probability (denoted by $Pr(Y = p)$) that an adversary who knows r of the original POIs has exactly p of them among the published POIs.

Therefore, we consider that $m < n$ data points have been published and the adversary knows $r \leq n$ of the original POIs.

We know that all the possible subsets with r points are $\binom{n}{r}$. If we assume that there are exactly p of the r POIs of the adversary that are part of the published POIs, then there are $r - p$ adversary POIs in the remaining $n - m$ not published POIs. Hence, there are $\binom{m}{p}$ ways in which their p adversary POIs belong to the published POIs and $\binom{n-m}{r-p}$ possible ways in which the remaining adversary POIs are distributed among the non-published POIs.

Therefore, in general, the probability that an adversary who knows r real POIs, gets to know precisely p of the m published POIs is:

$$Pr(Y = p) = \frac{\binom{m}{p} * \binom{n-m}{r-p}}{\binom{n}{r}} \tag{3}$$

We make an example, considering a user from our dataset with 67 POIs (average number of POIS in our dataset), and assume that we have published only seven of them. In Fig. 5, we use Eq. (3) to calculate the different probabilities that an adversary knows at least two, three, four, five, six or all the published POIs, depending on the number of POIs that he might have as auxiliary (previous) knowledge.

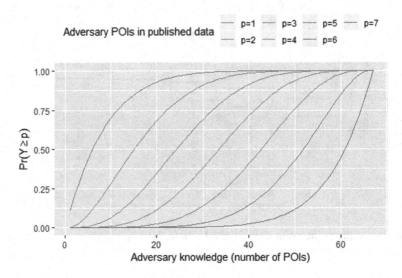

Fig. 5. Example of user with 7 published POIs and 67 POIs before publishing.

It is worth noting that an adversary needs more data points r to know at least p POIs.

5   Conclusions

In this paper, we have studied the effect that minimization has on the privacy of the data published after applying the MMC model. We considered the gender inference that can be carried out using the MMC model, gender and age distributions by POI. We have used a banking transactions dataset processed with the MMC model, together with the Male/Female and age distributions by POI to make inferences with Gradient Boosted Regression Trees, Extremely Randomized Trees and Logistic Regression.

We have investigated which are the best algorithms for inference and made comparisons of the different combinations of side knowledge to infer the gender attribute. We obtained that the Logistic Regression with the aggregated knowledge of the gender distributions of all the POIs visited by an individual gives the best precision (63%).

We have calculated the unicity of records published with the MMC and measured how it decreases if an adversary also infers the gender attribute. In the worst case, knowing the gender attribute besides 2 POIs would allow him to identify 11.9% more records uniquely. Finally, we have measured the capability of an adversary to link several POIs of side knowledge from raw data to a record after applying the MMC. We have shown that an adversary must know several points, to have a reasonable probability of linking his knowledge to a unique record, for example, an adversary must know in average half of the raw POIs of an individual to link this knowledge to the two corresponding POIs published after the MMC model with 0.25 certainty.

Hence, in that case, the probability of finding a unique record in the MMC model data is 0.05. This shows the effectivity of data minimization for protecting privacy obtained from the MMC model.

Possible future work is to repeat our study with Call Detail Record (CDR) data, to obtain a general formula for the probability of linking the raw data points to any given amount of POIs published and to test the effects of minimization of data publishing on the inference of other attributes.

Acknowledgement. This work was supported by the Spanish Government, in part under Grant RTI2018-095094-B-C22 "CONSENT", and in part under Grant TIN2014-57364-C2-2-R "SMARTGLACIS."

References

1. Bi, B., Shokouhi, M., Kosinski, M., Graepel, T.: Inferring the demographics of search users: social data meets search queries. In: Proceedings of the 22nd International Conference on World Wide Web, WWW 2013, pp. 131–140. New York (2013)
2. Breiman, L.: Random forests. Mach. Learn. **45**(1), 5–32 (2001). https://doi.org/10.1023/A:1010933404324
3. Cho, E., Myers, S.A., Leskovec, J.: Friendship and mobility: user movement in location-based social networks. In: Proceedings of the 17th ACM SIGKDD International Conference on Knowledge Discovery and Data Mining, KDD 2011, pp. 1082–1090. New York (2011)
4. Danezis, G., et al.: Privacy and data protection by design - from policy to engineering. Technical report, ENISA (2015)
5. Fiore, M., et al.: Privacy of trajectory micro-data: a survey. CoRR abs/1903.12211 (2019)
6. Friedman, J.H.: Greedy function approximation: a gradient boosting machine. Ann. Stat. **29**, 1189–1232 (2001)
7. Gambs, S., Killijian, M.O., del Prado Cortez, M.N.: Show me how you move and I will tell you who you are. Trans. Data Priv. **4**(2), 103–126 (2011)
8. Gambs, S., Killijian, M.O., Núñez del Prado Cortez, M.: Next place prediction using mobility Markov chains. In: Proceedings of the First Workshop on Measurement, Privacy, and Mobilit, Bern, Switzerland, vol. 3, pp. 1–6, April 2012

9. Gambs, S., Killijian, M.O., Núñez del Prado Cortez, M.: GEPETO: a geoprivacy-enhancing toolkit. In: 2010 IEEE 24th International Conference on Advanced Information Networking and Applications Workshops, pp. 1071–1076. IEEE (2010)

10. Gambs, S., Killijian, M.O., del Prado Cortez, M.N.: De-anonymization attack on geolocated data. J. Comput. Syst. Sci. **80**(8), 1597–1614 (2014)

11. Hastie, T., Rosset, S., Zhu, J., Zou, H.: Multi-class AdaBoost. Stat. Interface **2**(3), 349–360 (2009)

12. Hu, J., Zeng, H.J., Li, H., Niu, C., Chen, Z.: Demographic prediction based on user's browsing behavior. In: Proceedings of the 16th International Conference on World Wide Web, WWW 2007, pp. 151–160. ACM, New York (2007)

13. Mayer, J., Mutchler, P., Mitchell, J.C.: Evaluating the privacy properties of telephone metadata. Proc. Nat. Acad. Sci. **113**(20), 5536–5541 (2016)

14. de Montjoye, Y.A., Hidalgo, C.A., Verleysen, M., Blondel, V.D.: Unique in the crowd: the privacy bounds of human mobility. Sci. Rep. **3**, 1376 (2013)

15. de Montjoye, Y.A., Radaelli, L., Singh, V.K., Pentland, A.S.: Unique in the shopping mall: On the reidentifiability of credit card metadata. Science **347**(6221), 536–539 (2015). https://doi.org/10.1126/science.1256297

16. Riederer, C., Kim, Y., Chaintreau, A., Korula, N., Lattanzi, S.: Linking users across domains with location data: theory and validation. In: Proceedings of the 25th International Conference on World Wide Web, WWW 2016, pp. 707–719, International World Wide Web Conferences Steering Committee, Republic and Canton of Geneva, Switzerland (2016)

17. Salas, J., Domingo-Ferrer, J.: Some basics on privacy techniques, anonymization and their big data challenges. Math. Comput. Sci. **12**(3), 263–274 (2018). https://doi.org/10.1007/s11786-018-0344-6

18. Salas, J., Megías, D., Torra, V.: SwapMob: swapping trajectories for mobility anonymization. In: Domingo-Ferrer, J., Montes, F. (eds.) PSD 2018. LNCS, vol. 11126, pp. 331–346. Springer, Cham (2018). https://doi.org/10.1007/978-3-319-99771-1_22

19. Scellato, S., Noulas, A., Lambiotte, R., Mascolo, C.: Socio-spatial properties of online location-based social networks. In: Proceedings of the Fifth International Conference on Weblogs and Social Media, Barcelona, Catalonia, Spain, 17–21 July 2011 (2011)

20. Wang, P., Guo, J., Lan, Y., Xu, J., Cheng, X.: Your cart tells you: inferring demographic attributes from purchase data. In: Proceedings of the Ninth ACM International Conference on Web Search and Data Mining, pp. 173–182. ACM (2016)

21. Weinsberg, U., Bhagat, S., Ioannidis, S., Taft, N.: BlurMe: inferring and obfuscating user gender based on ratings. In: Proceedings of the Sixth ACM Conference on Recommender Systems, RecSys 2012, pp. 195–202. New York (2012)

22. Yan, Z., Chakraborty, D., Parent, C., Spaccapietra, S., Aberer, K.: SeMiTri: a framework for semantic annotation of heterogeneous trajectories. In: Proceedings of the 14th International Conference on Extending Database Technology, EDBT/ICDT 2011, pp. 259–270. ACM, New York (2011)

23. Zhong, E., Tan, B., Mo, K., Yang, Q.: User demographics prediction based on mobile data. Pervasive Mob. Comput. **9**(6), 823–837 (2013)

24. Zhong, Y., Yuan, N.J., Zhong, W., Zhang, F., Xie, X.: You are where you go: inferring demographic attributes from location check-ins. In: Proceedings of the Eighth ACM International Conference on Web Search and Data Mining, WSDM 2015, pp. 295–304. ACM, New York (2015)

Development of a Hand Gesture Based Control Interface Using Deep Learning

Dennis Núñez-Fernández$^{(\boxtimes)}$

Universidad Nacional de Ingeniería, Lima, Peru
dnunezf@uni.pe

Abstract. This paper describes the implementation of a control system based on ten different hand gestures, providing a useful approach for the implementation of better user-friendly human-machine interfaces. Hand detection is achieved using fast detection and tracking algorithms, and classification by a light convolutional neural network. The experimental results show a real-time response with an accuracy of 95.09%, and making use of low power consumption. These results demonstrate that the proposed system could be applied in a large range of applications such as virtual reality, robotics, autonomous driving systems, human-machine interfaces, augmented reality among others.

Keywords: Gesture recognition · Human-machine interface · Deep learning · Real-time · Hand poses

1 Introduction

Hand gesture recognition is an important way to build user-friendly human-machine interfaces. In a near future, hand posture recognition technology would allow for the operation of complex machines and smart devices through only series of hand postures, finger and hand movements, eliminating the need for physical contact between user and machine. However, hand poses recognition on images from single camera is a difficult task due occlusion, variations of posture, appearance and differences in hand shapes. Despite these problems, several approaches to gesture recognition on images has been proposed [1].

During the last years, Convolutional Neural Networks (CNNs) have become the state-of-the-art for object recognition tasks [2–4]. However, only few papers report successful results [1,5]. Some obstacles to wider and more efficient use of CNNs in hand pose classification problem are lack of sufficiently large datasets, high computational costs, as well as lack of hand detectors suitable for CNN-based classifiers. In [6], a CNN has been used for classification of 6 hand poses to control robots via colored gloves, but the use of such additional hardware makes of the system difficult to employ for touchless applications. A more recent work [7], a multichannel CNN for the Nao humanoid robot was implemented, it employs the JTD dataset and make use of three channels, they obtained an F1 score of 92%. In another recent work [8], a CNN was trained on one million of

© Springer Nature Switzerland AG 2020
J. A. Lossio-Ventura et al. (Eds.): SIMBig 2019, CCIS 1070, pp. 143–150, 2020.
https://doi.org/10.1007/978-3-030-46140-9_14

images, however only a portion of the dataset with 3361 manually labeled frames in 45 classes of sign language is publicly available, it makes of such work difficult to reproduce. In addition, state-of-the-art works [9] obtain a high accuracy rate but use depth cameras and large CNNs, which make difficult to use in human-machine interfaces that demand a real-time response.

In this work we developed a system for hand pose recognition to work on embedded computers with limited computational resources. In order to accomplish the targets, we employ low-processing algorithms and a light CNN, which was optimized to balance high accuracy, high response time and low power and computational consumption.

2 Proposed Method

2.1 Overview

The proposed system works with images captured from a standard camera and executed on a regular computer with low computational resources without GPU support. Therefore, the main objectives are as follows: high accuracy rate, fast time response, low power consumption and low computational costs.

The system is composed of three main steps: hand detection, hand region tracking and hand gesture recognition (see Fig. 1). In the first step the Haar cascades classifier detects a basic hand shape in order to have a good hand detection. Then, this hand region is tracked using the MOSSE (Minimum Output Sum of Squared Error) tracking algorithm. Finally, hand gesture recognition is performed based on a trained Convolutional Neural Network. Since the steps described before are designed to consume few computational resources, the whole system will be implemented on a personal computer without GPU support.

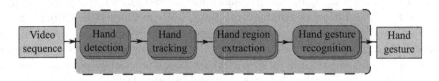

Fig. 1. Diagram for the proposed recognition system

2.2 Hand Detection and Tracking

Haar cascade classifier allows better detection of objects with static features such as balloons, boxes, faces, eyes, mounts, noise, etc. But a hand in motion has few static features because its shape and fingers can change as well as its orientations. So, Haar cascade classifier allows detection of only basic hand poses, which are not suitable to recognize a hand in motion with a long mount of different poses.

Since hand detection using Haar cascades in not a robust method, this deficiency is compensated with a hand tracker based on wrist region. This hand region is proposed for tracking due this region have both invariant and static features when hand changes to different poses, shapes and orientations.

In addition to this, hand tracking allows the reduction of the processing time since tracking requires less computational resources than hand detection (whole image evaluation versus local evaluation). Figure 2 shows the different hand regions used for detection and tracking, as image shows the hand region for tracking (blue box) encloses the hand in different shapes and poses. Therefore, the hand region inside the blue box will be used by the CNN to perform gesture recognition.

Fig. 2. Wrist region for detection (red) and hand region for tracking (blue) (Color figure online)

In this project, the MOSSE tracking (Minimum Output Sum of Squared Error) algorithm is used for hand tracking. The MOSSE tracker uses adaptive correlation for object tracking which produces stable correlation filters when initialized using a single frame [10]. MOSSE tracker is robust to variations in lighting, scale, pose, and non-rigid deformations. It also detects occlusion based upon the peak-to-sidelobe ratio, which enables the tracker to pause and resume where it left off when the object reappears. MOSSE tracker also operates at a higher fps (450 fps and even more). In addition, the proposed tracking algorithm consumes less memory and computational resources than the Haar cascade classifier.

2.3 Skin Detection

Skin color is a potent characteristic for fast hand region detection. Essentially, all skin color-based methodologies try to learn a skin color distribution, and then use it to extract the hand region. In this project the hand region has been obtained on the basis of statistical color models [11]. In this way, a model in RGB-H-CbCr color spaces were constructed on the basis of a training set. Later, the hand probability image was threshold. Finally, after morphological closing, a connected components labeling was used to extract the gravity center of the hand region, the coordinates of the most top pixel as well as coordinates of the most left pixel of the hand region.

2.4 Hand Poses Dataset

The dataset for hand gesture classification was obtained from a publicly available database of the AGH University of Science and Technology. It is composed of 73,124 grayscale images of size 48×48 pixels divided into 10 different hand poses, captured from different persons of various nationalities. This dataset was divided in 80% (42,027 images) for training and 20% (14,667 images) for testing. Figure 3 shows samples of each hand gesture, also called class. The principal benefit of this dataset is that in each class the wrists are approximately located at the same position. Furthermore, thanks to such an approach the recognition of hand poses at acceptable frame rates can be succeeded with a simple convolutional neural network and at a lower computational cost.

Fig. 3. Hand gestures poses

2.5 Convolutional Neural Network

For the CNN we use binary images of 48×48 pixels, and a small CNN with fewer layers and learnable parameters. The proposed CNN consists of two convolutional layers with kernels of 5×5 size each one, a non linearity (ReLU) activation function and a max-pooling layer after every convolutional layer, and two full-connected (FC) layers of 150 neurons length followed by a final 10-way softmax (see Fig. 4). Additionally, the posposed CNN has only 60 K learnable parameters. This number of parameters are significantly less than the AlexNet network (60 M learnable parameters) [2] and the GoogleNet (6.8 M learnable parameters) [12].

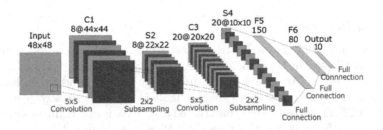

Fig. 4. Architecture of the proposed CNN

3   Experimental Results

3.1   Experimental Results of the Model

The performance of the CNN for hand poses classification was evaluated using different metrics such as the accuracy and the confusion matrix. This matrix presents a visualization of the misclassified classes and helps to add more training images in order to improve the model. The confusion matrix of our model is shown in Fig. 5 and discloses which hand poses are misclassified. These errors happen because of similarities between the classes. Furthermore, our architecture shows an outstanding accuracy of 95.09% and a F1 score of 95.12%.

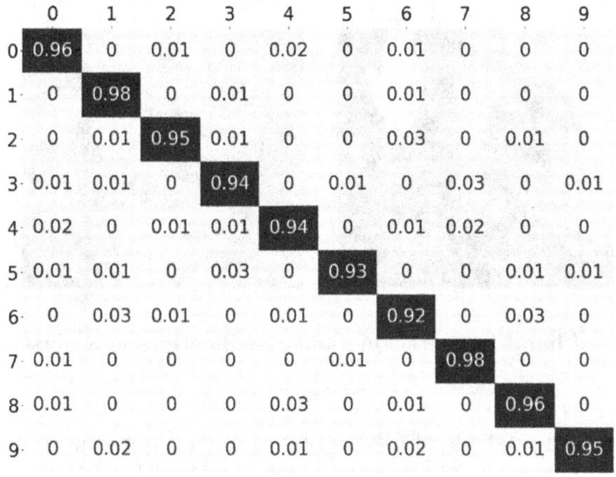

	0	1	2	3	4	5	6	7	8	9
0	0.96	0	0.01	0	0.02	0	0.01	0	0	0
1	0	0.98	0	0.01	0	0	0.01	0	0	0
2	0	0.01	0.95	0.01	0	0	0.03	0	0.01	0
3	0.01	0.01	0	0.94	0	0.01	0	0.03	0	0.01
4	0.02	0	0.01	0.01	0.94	0	0.01	0.02	0	0
5	0.01	0.01	0	0.03	0	0.93	0	0	0.01	0.01
6	0	0.03	0.01	0	0.01	0	0.92	0	0.03	0
7	0.01	0	0	0	0	0.01	0	0.98	0	0
8	0.01	0	0	0	0.03	0	0.01	0	0.96	0
9	0	0.02	0	0	0.01	0	0.02	0	0.01	0.95

Fig. 5. Confusion matrix

3.2   Experimental Results of Inference

The implementation of the proposed recognition system on a personal computer with GPU support has no issues due to its high computational resources. However, when a recognition system is implemented on standard computers with no GPU support we have two major obstacles working against us: limited RAM memory and restricted processor speed. In order to obtain a better computation performance, the system was implemented using C++ language. In spite of the processing and memory limitations mentioned above, our real-time recognition system shows promising results during the evaluation step. Figure 6 depicts its performance under real conditions. As you can see, the system correctly recognizes different hand poses, despite different shifted positions, shape distortions, low light conditions, different sizes, and even when the recognition is done on images taken by a different camera. In addition, we obtain a fast response time of about 55.1 ms (average of 100 iterations) to detect and classify a single hand pose (Fig. 7).

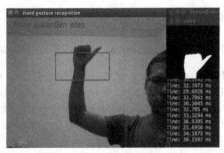

Fig. 6. Results of hand pose detection on a personal computer

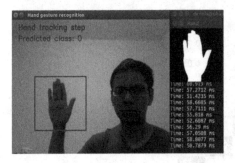
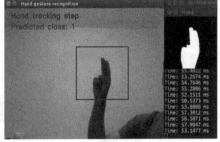

Fig. 7. Results of hand pose tracking and classification on a personal computer

Table 1 shows some details of CNNs tested on the personal computer without GPU support. As the table shows, the proposed CNN achieves a fast response time of around 60 ms and a low power consumption of 0.47 Joules per image. These results were expected due to their simple but efficient design explained in the previous sections. Furthermore, compared with state-of-the-art CNN models for similar recognition tasks and tested on an identical computer without GPU support, the proposed architecture achieves the highest response time and the lowest power consumption.

Table 1. Response time and power consumption for evaluation of different CNN models on a personal computer without GPU support using Caffe framework

Model	Proposed CNN	AlexNet v2 [13]	OverFeat [13]	VGG_A [13]	GoogleNet [13]
Layers	8	11	11	16	22
Power (J./img.)	0.47	0.75	2.00	5.00	3.50
Time (s.)	0.06	0.35	0.88	2.35	1.87

4   Conclusions

This paper introduced the implementation of a hand gesture recognition system for a touchless control interface based on images acquired by a single color camera. In order to obtain the fastest response time and a low power consumption, we employed fast computer vision algorithms and a light convolutional neural network. In this way, the proposed recognition system shows promising results, achieving an accuracy of 95.09% for the classification of 10 different hand poses. Furthermore, the evaluation of the hand gesture system in a personal computer with a single image gives an average processing time of about 55.1 ms, and a low energy consumption of 0.47 J. per image. The results mentioned above demonstrate that the proposed recognition system can be used in a large range of applications, from robotics to entertainment.

References

1. Oyedotun, O.K., Khashman, A.: Deep learning in vision-based static hand gesture recognition. Neural Comput. Appl. **28**(12), 3941–3951 (2016). https://doi.org/10.1007/s00521-016-2294-8
2. Krizhevsky, A., Sutskever, I., Hinton, G.E.: ImageNet classification with deep convolutional neural networks. In: NIPS, pp. 1097–1105 (2012)
3. Kwolek, B.: Face detection using convolutional neural networks and gabor filters. In: Duch, W., Kacprzyk, J., Oja, E., Zadrożny, S. (eds.) ICANN 2005. LNCS, vol. 3696, pp. 551–556. Springer, Heidelberg (2005). https://doi.org/10.1007/11550822_86
4. Arel, I., Rose, D., Karnowski, T.: Research frontier: deep machine learning-a new frontier in artificial intelligence research. Comp. Intell. Mag. **5**(4), 13–18 (2010)
5. Tompson, J., Stein, M., Lecun, Y., Perlin, K.: Real-time continuous pose recovery of human hands using convolutional networks. ACM Trans. Graph. **33**(5), 1–10 (2014)
6. Nagi, J., Ducatelle, F., et al.: Max-pooling convolutional neural networks for vision-based hand gesture recognition. In: IEEE ICSIP, pp. 342–347 (2011)
7. Barros, P., Magg, S., Weber, C., Wermter, S.: A multichannel convolutional neural network for hand posture recognition. In: Wermter, S., Weber, C., Duch, W., Honkela, T., Koprinkova-Hristova, P., Magg, S., Palm, G., Villa, A.E.P. (eds.) ICANN 2014. LNCS, vol. 8681, pp. 403–410. Springer, Cham (2014). https://doi.org/10.1007/978-3-319-11179-7_51
8. Koller, O., Ney, H., Bowden, R.: Deep hand: How to train a CNN on 1 million hand images when your data is continuous and weakly labelled. In: IEEE Conference on Computer Vision and Pattern Recognition, pp. 3793–3802 (2016)
9. Yuan, S., Ye, Q., Stenger, B., Jain, S., Kim, T.: BigHand2.2M benchmark: hand pose dataset and state of the art analysis. In: 2017 IEEE Conference on Computer Vision and Pattern Recognition (CVPR), Honolulu, HI, pp. 2605–2613 (2017)
10. Bolme, D.S., Beveridge, J.R., Draper, B.A., Lui, Y.M.: Visual object tracking using adaptive correlation filters. In: 2010 IEEE Computer Society Conference on Computer Vision and Pattern Recognition, San Francisco, CA, pp. 2544–2550 (2010)

11. Jones, M.J., Rehg, J.M.: Statistical color models with application to skin detection. Int. J. Comput. Vision **46**(1), 81–96 (2002)
12. Szegedy, C., et al.: Going deeper with convolutions. In: 2015 IEEE Conference on Computer Vision and Pattern Recognition (CVPR), Boston, MA (2015)
13. Li, D., Chen, X., Becchi, M., Zong, Z.: Evaluating the energy efficiency of deep convolutional neural networks on CPUs and GPUs. In: 2016 IEEE International Conferences on Big Data and Cloud Computing (BDCloud), Social Computing and Networking (SocialCom), Sustainable Computing and Communications (SustainCom) (BDCloud-SocialCom-SustainCom), Atlanta, GA, pp. 477–484 (2016)

A Progressive Formalization of Tacit Knowledge to Improve Semantic Expressiveness of Biodiversity Data

Andréa Corrêa Flôres Albuquerque[✉] and José Laurindo Campos dos Santos

Laboratório de Interoperabilidade Semântica – LIS, Instituto Nacional de Pesquisas da Amazônia – INPA, Av. André Araújo 2936, Manaus, AM, Brazil
andreaalb.1993@gmail.com, laurindo.campos@inpa.gov.br

Abstract. The majority of biodiversity data available on the Web are structured, lacking unstructured features such as tacit knowledge, images, audios, text documents, among others. Tacit knowledge can be used to add more expressiveness to ontologies. To achieve that, the knowledge needs to be elicited and formalized and further incorporated into an ontology. This paper aims to present a Progressive Formalization Schema (PFS) to formalize tacit knowledge into different levels of granularity.

Keywords: Knowledge · Formalization · Semantic · Ontology · Biodiversity data

1 Introduction

There is lack of unstructured biodiversity data, e.g., legacy knowledge of the researchers, the bushmen, fishermen, local guides, etc., and therefore there is unexplored potential to add value to data currently available. These data are found in expert's[1] mental models[2] (EMMs) or field notes and tend to be lost in the process of information transfer. EMMs are not expressed in traditional databases, since this knowledge is rarely represented/formalized and was learned and documented through years of the expert's experience, but it can consist of important and also relevant information that can help to guide future actions.

Based on the above facts, it is imperative the need of tacit knowledge formalization to improve semantic expressiveness of biodiversity data, together with, biodiversity ontologies.

---

[1] An expert can be understood as an individual who has valuable knowledge that can be used by someone or an organization (Kendal and Creen 2016).

[2] According to Carey and Spelke (1994), "It represents a person's thought process for how something works (i.e. the understanding of the world around). Based on incomplete facts, past experiences and even intuitive perceptions. They help to define actions and behaviors, influence what will be considered most relevant in complex situations and define how individuals confront and solve problems."

© Springer Nature Switzerland AG 2020
J. A. Lossio-Ventura et al. (Eds.): SIMBig 2019, CCIS 1070, pp. 151–164, 2020.
https://doi.org/10.1007/978-3-030-46140-9_15

Knowledge formalization in this context, refers to making knowledge processable or understandable by computers. The knowledge may be presented at different levels of formalization, for example, from text documents to explicit rules (Baumeister et al. 2011).

A simple inference of a fishman experience, such as, *"the presence of swamp rice grass (Leersia hexandra) in the river, indicates the likely occurrence of malaria in the region, since this vegetation provides suitable conditions for the proliferation of Anopheles darlingi, the malaria vector"* can generates new knowledge or guides new knowledge acquisition (Albuquerque 2016). Additionally, this tacit knowledge could be used to infer structured data organized in structuring instruments of knowledge, such as ontologies or databases.

This paper presents a method named Progressive Formalization Schema (PFS), that allows to navigate the elicited and formalized knowledge for further use (to improve the degree of formalization or to recover semantic lost). Also, it allows access to knowledge at different levels of granularity and minimizes the semantic losses that may occur in the process of Knowledge Representation (KR).

In this research, the addition of tacit knowledge of an expert into formal ontologies (Guizzardi 2005) was performed. The tacit knowledge considered is the scientific, according to Collins (2001), which is not necessarily formalizable, but must be, in some way, capable of systematization; and in agreement with the fundamental conceptual structure of the domain. Tacit knowledge into ontological schemas is innovative and has the purpose of increasing the expressiveness of ontologies.

This paper is organized as follows: in Sect. 2, a characterization of the research context is presented; the related works to this research are described briefly at Sect. 3; PFS is presented in Sect. 4; an EMM's formalization describing each step of the PFS for OntoBio is presented in Sect. 5, followed by the conclusions of this work at Sect. 6.

2 Characterization of the Research Context

The knowledge acquisition process is not always organized or systematically explainable. Some knowledge is acquired, and the entire process cannot be fully comprehended. This happens because part of the knowledge is considered tacit. In this research, we consider the tacit scientific knowledge, that refers to the knowledge or skill that can be passed among experts by interactions, but difficult to be expressed or described in formulas, diagrams, verbal descriptions or instructions for action (Collins 2001). In this sense, it is knowledge based on scientific information, however it is related to the experience and competence of the expert, therefore difficult to systematize and represent. It concerns the knowledge that is better transferred and assimilated informally. By its subjective nature, it is difficult to formalize tacit scientific knowledge, since it is dynamic and can only be accessed through direct collaboration and communication with people who have knowledge in the same domain. This is what makes the process of transferring this type of knowledge so difficult, costly and uncertain, because it is experts dependent. If it is well explored and these experiences can be transmitted to others, this type of knowledge can become a differential for semantic richness. Only part of scientific tacit knowledge can be formalized since it makes use of informal communication (Albuquerque 2016; Leite 2006).

From the interaction between explicit scientific knowledge - registered scientific knowledge, scientific literature - and tacit scientific knowledge - what specialists know, learned and are communicated through interactions and unstructured means -, it becomes feasible to create a new scientific knowledge (Nonaka and Takeuchi 1995).

Knowledge formalization, also referred to, as KR, which is an area in Artificial Intelligence concentrated in formalizing knowledge to be computable. It represents knowledge to facilitate inference (Romanov 2005).

Humans have been developing many formalisms for KR. These formalisms can range from a purely textual formalism to graphical representations (conceptual maps) (Novak and Gowin 1984).

However, the most powerful formalisms use more complex techniques (logic, semantic networks, frames, scripts, production rules, ontologies, among others) (Sowa 2000). They are mostly based on mathematics, philosophy and cognitive science. These disciplines provide basic ideas of how the world is perceived and modeled.

Mathematics provides a compact set of principles widely shared in society. These shared principles allow for the construction of powerful expressions.

Philosophy studies the nature of knowledge and how to create and manage it, and to do so, some mathematical tools are designed and used. For example, ontology and logic are two building blocks of KR. Therefore, KR can be defined as the application of logic and ontology to the task of developing computable models of some domain (Sowa 2000). Logic and ontology provide the formal mechanisms required to make significant models easily shareable and usable by computers (Lofting 2015). Ontologies are of particular interest in this research to organize, structure and thus represent knowledge (Albuquerque 2016).

In this work, KR considers the knowledge found in the mental models of biodiversity experts (EMMs) and becomes explicit through an PFS. Despite all the formalisms possibilities for representing knowledge, it is important to emphasize that tacit knowledge is richer than any description of it, and eventually loss of semantics is expected during the process of formalization.

3 Related Work

The concepts presented in knowledge PFS are referenced in the literature in a broader context. McGuinness (2003) presents ontologies and provides criteria necessary, prototypical, and desirable for developing simple and complex ontologies, focusing on the ontology languages and environment.

Uschold and Gruninger (2004) presents different types of ontologies, from terms to the general logic. The main difference between them is the manner of specifying the meaning of terms. This is a continuum of kinds of ontologies. Moving along the continuum increases the amount of meaning specified and the degree of formality. Although they do not propose transitions between particular types or propose to use them together in the development of intelligent systems.

Millard et al. (2005) present an approach that consists of a vector-based model of the formality of semantics in hypertext systems, where the vectors represent the translation of semantics from author to system and from system to reader, foreseeing semantic loss (intermediation). Its scale defines a subset of KR instruments ranging from simple text to RDF data.

Furthermore, Schaffert et al. (2006) understand that knowledge can be represented on many different levels of formality and in a wide variety of formalisms (similar to PFS). They classify ontologies using three properties: model scope, acceptance of the model and the level of expressiveness, where the latter defines a subspace of knowledge PFS. The level of expressiveness ranging from lightweight ontologies, with lists of terms as the least significant representative, to heavy-weight ontologies with very significant restrictions as the most significant.

Gruber (2008) correlates the degree of knowledge formalization with the depth of inference and discusses the exchange cost/benefit of the captured knowledge.

Baumeister et al. (2011) describe a knowledge formalization continuum to help domain specialists during the knowledge acquisition phase. To make use of the knowledge formalization continuum, the agile use of KR within a knowledge engineering project is proposed, as well as transitions between the different representations, when required.

Nalepa et al. (2011) discuss a new formalized KR for rule-based systems called XTT2, a hybrid KR that combines decision diagrams with extended decision tables. The structure of XTT2 constitutes a hierarchical KR consisting of lower level knowledge components, where specification is provided by a set of rules working in the same context, and at the higher level, where the decision diagram defines the overall structure of the knowledge base.

Klein et al. (2015) identify a need for a framework-independent solution to formalize design knowledge and derives corresponding objectives to be fulfilled by this solution.

4 Progressive Formalization Schema (PFS): An Overview

In this research, it is adopted a PFS to assist knowledge acquisition and to formalize the knowledge elicited.

The PFS provides to the knowledge engineer flexibility in KR of the EMM. This formalization schema emphasizes that the usable knowledge ranges from very informal (such as text and images) to very explicit representations (such as logical formulas or ontologies). Also, PFS allows knowledge engineers to focus on a certain degree of knowledge formalization and offers a versatile understanding of the process of formalization, since it supports the representation of knowledge at various levels of granularity.

In a PFS, the same knowledge of a domain can be presented in several forms of representations, where adjacent representations are similar to each other, for example, tabular data and XML. However, the most extreme representations are quite different, e.g., text versus logical rules. Gradual transitions in the degree of formalization of the same knowledge are possible, but the knowledge to be modeled is not subjected to sudden changes or discontinuities. Although the PFS can be considered as a schema that involves several levels of granularity of formalized knowledge, the represented domain knowledge remains the same. The PFS also emphasizes that knowledge is subject to changes, a continuous development in which a change can also result in a new representation. The PFS helps domain experts and knowledge engineers to visualize the data, even simple as text and multimedia, as more formal knowledge that can be transformed by gradual transitions when requested. The data provided by textual documents represent one of the simplest formal possibilities and functional models concentrated knowledge in a formal level.

Figure 1 illustrates techniques for KR in a PFS. This list of representations does not intend to be exhaustive, and nor the described order of representations of data and knowledge intended to be explicit. In fact, it does not seem possible to define the total order of representations in general. The order described was motivated by the possible level of expressivity related to built systems reasoning capacity using a particular representation. For example, text can be used for retrieval and conventional search based on keywords, while texts with semantic annotation enables semantic queries and browsing. At the IV Quadrant, the rules-based knowledge supports more complex reasoning capacity.

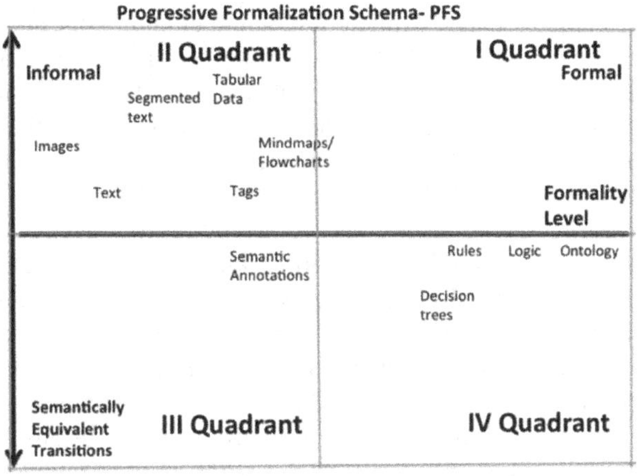

Fig. 1. Possible KR of PFS. Adapted from (Baumeister et al. 2011)

Each level of formalization has its advantages and disadvantages. For example, textual knowledge is easier to be elicited (when explicit) and is often already available in the domain. But the automated reasoning using the textual knowledge is not possible with current methods; and knowledge can be recovered only through strings matching methods but not by applying semantic queries. Logical rules or models are suitable for automated reasoning, and queries can be processed at the semantic level. In contrast to textual knowledge, the acquisition of rules and models is typically a complex and time-consuming task. Authors of rules need to be trained before constructing knowledge bases on the explicit level with regard to the principles of knowledge engineering and modeling tools. For this research's purposes, the conceptual framework requires the adoption of an ontology object of study to guide the formalization process, mainly in the IV Quadrant of Fig. 1, rules, logic and ontology. We used OntoBio, a formal ontology applied to biodiversity data, developed in a research initiative involving the Institute of Computing at the Federal University of Amazonas and INPA's Biological Collection

Program (Albuquerque 2015). OntoBio was modeled conceptually through OntoUML language (Guizzardi 2005).

For a given knowledge base, which is formalized using a particular KR, there is often semantically equivalent transitions (indicated by the Formality Level axis in Fig. 1). The knowledge is often taken to a semantically equivalent representation to allow extensions for the domain knowledge.

Between the two extremes (text versus logic) there is a wide range of KR formats in different degrees of formalization. Any instance of the formality level can be the most useful representation for a specific application design.

For a given formalization project, it is important to select the most suitable level of formalization as representation target. Since knowledge (or its fragments) is generally available in textual or tabular form, the development process is centered on bringing the existing forms to an appropriate level. Usually, it is necessary to fill in the missing pieces of knowledge, but its original nature remains. Thus, the choice of a more formal representation may require a more explicit description of knowledge and can enrich the resulting knowledge with additional semantics. Each transition is a separate operation that modifies the KR. However, the mental model of knowledge remains the same. It can be observed that in each transition of the level of formalization, there may be loss of semantics expressiveness as the resource for KR used in each level of formalization (e.g., conceptual maps, first-order logic, ontologies) cannot be able to represent certain aspects of knowledge.

Transitions between different levels of formalization, for example, text to semantic annotations can be made manually and sometimes in semi-automated manner.

The direction of the transition to a less formal KR is required, for example, to analyze/evaluate the developed knowledge bases, or, to retrieve knowledge that has become hidden between the different levels of KR. Thus, it enables a backtracking, from the more formal knowledge level to a least formally, enabling revisits and knowledge recovery on different levels of granularity. At this point, a visualization of a less formal knowledge base, however precise, helps to understand the semantics of implemented knowledge.

From a more informal to a more formal KR, we have a representation of knowledge as ontology to be compared with OntoBio. The typical direction in knowledge engineering is the transition from barely structured/unstructured data to a more explicit representation. It is possible to backtrack (from the more formal knowledge level to the least formal) with the purpose of identifying tracks of lost knowledge in the process of formalization and which may be used in the acquisition of new knowledge.

The PFS considers that knowledge is usually represented at different levels of formality. The schema supports the use of knowledge engineering in an arbitrary level of formality and offers possible knowledge transitions to a level where the cost/benefit principle (Lidwell et al. 2003) is the best.

The PFS does not require the formalization of the whole knowledge collection (in this study, EMM), but the performance of transitions in parts of the collection when it is possible and recommended. Consider the fact that sometimes not all parts of a domain can be formalized at a specific level or that the formalization of the whole domain of knowledge is too complex.

Even considering the cost/benefit, there is a need to transform pieces of knowledge into a formal level where costs (knowledge engineering) are minimized and the benefits of using are maximized. Therefore, the PFS must not only support transitions of particular pieces of knowledge but must also be able to maintain references amongst parts less and more formalized of the entire collection of knowledge.

5 EMM's Formalization

This work deals with knowledge expressed in biodiversity EMMs, specifically ichthyologists. During the knowledge formalization schema through a PFS, based on OntoBio, the following KR are adopted, as presented in Fig. 2.

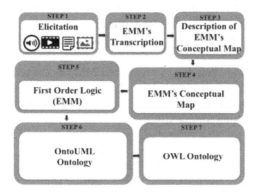

Fig. 2. PFS model.

Steps 1 and 2 are represented with the media of the interview used to elicit knowledge and its transcription, respectively. A record of the knowledge elicitation media and its transcription must be kept for further use. Step 3 is the description of the conceptual map according to the analyst view. Step 4 represents the conceptual map designed by the analyst (ontology engineer); that is the analyst view of what was elicited. Step 5 represents the conceptual map description in First-Order Logic, FOL; 6 represents conceptual map description on a foundation ontology and 7 represents the conceptual map description in Ontology Web Language (OWL). Steps 1 and 2 deals with knowledge elicitation and were discussed in detail in (Albuquerque et al. 2016). Steps 3, 4, 5, 6 and 7 are briefly presented in the following sections.

5.1 Conceptual Map Description: An Analyst View of EMM

This description is subjected to the analyst understanding of the EMM and decision of which knowledge and how it is going to be modelled. During the transition between the transcription of interview and the description of an EMM, semantic losses may occur.

For illustration, the following conceptual map description elicited during an interview with ichthyology experts is used:

EMM – To fish jatuarana (*Brycon* genus) use jauari seed (*Astrocarium* genus).

This EMM can be understood in two ways: (a) jauari seed can be used as a bait to fish jatuarana (most ever it is understood that jauari can be used as bait, but in fact, it is jauari's seed); or (b) jauari can be used as food to jatuarana and food is important in the food chain to attract other species.

5.2   Conceptual Map Tool for EMM's Representation

Some computational tools are used to help the process of knowledge elicitation such as xLine, IThought, and SimpleMind, among others (Clark 2011). These tools produce conceptual maps used to organize and represent knowledge. Special attention is devoted to some tools influenced by the Semantic Web and ontology. Recent versions of PCPACK support the export of RDF, while plug-ins for knowledge elicitation in Protégé (Noy et al. 2001) interoperate with the Protégé-OWL plug-in (Wang et al. 2006). There are also CmapTools extending initiatives to provide support for viewing and editing OWL ontologies.

Any of these tools are suitable to represent EMMs as conceptual maps, since no semantic support is demanded at this phase of the research and they are only used as a graphical source to view the EMMs. Figure 3 presents the conceptual map of the EMM described in Sect. 5.1 using SimpleMind.

Fig. 3.   MME represented as a conceptual map.

5.3   Representing EMM in First Order Logic (FOL)

The reason why logic is relevant to KR and reasoning is that logic is the study of relationships-language linking, truth conditions and rules of inference (Brachman and Levesque 2004). Specifically, it will be used at this stage of the research FOL or First Order Predicate Calculus (FOPC), which is only a starting point, a simple logic to formalize knowledge (Brachman and Levesque 2004).

The language of FOL is built around objects and relationships. FOL has been important for mathematics, philosophy and artificial intelligence, because in these fields of knowledge, much of everyday human life, can be thought of as objects and the relationships between them. FOL can also express facts about objects. This allows to represent general laws or general rules (Russel and Norvig 2010). Following, is the elicited EMM, now expressed in FOL.

```
EMMa - ∀ Jauari ⇒ ∃ Jatuarana | [MaterialEntity (Jatuarana) •
CollectionMethod (Bait(Jauari)) • Has((Bait(Jauari), Jatuarana)]
```

Or,

```
EMMb - ∀ Jauari ⇒ ∃ Jatuarana | [MaterialEntity (Jatuarana) •
BioticEntity (Jauari) • Eats(Jauari, Jatuarana)]
```

Such representations drive us to some considerations:

- The formalization of knowledge in steps 5, 6 and 7 of PFS must use a domain ontology to guide the process. At these steps, the knowledge engineer can already identify similar concepts and relationships as well as those that do not exist in the domain ontology;
- The representation of EMM in FOL may present semantic loss in consequence of limitation of the KR feature.

5.4 Representing EMM in OntoUML: Level of Analysis

The OntoUML ontological schema of EMM is designed similarly to OntoBio's schema.

Guizzardi proposed a conceptual modeling language that includes as a modeling primitive, ontological distinctions proposed by UFO-A (Guizzardi 2005). This language (now called OntoUML) was built following a process in which: (i) the metamodel of the original language (in this case, the UML 2.0) is fixed to ensure an isomorphism in its mapping to the structure defined by the reference ontology (in this case, UFO-A); (ii) secondly, the axiomatization of the foundational ontology is transferred to the language metamodel through formal restrictions built into this metamodel. The purpose was to ensure that the language only accept as grammatically valid models those models that satisfy (in the logical point of view) the axiomatization of UFO, that is, those models that are considered valid according to this theory. In addition, Guizzardi (2005) proposed a set of methodological guidelines for the creation of ontologies using OntoUML language. The use of OntoUML is justified because it is an ontology conceptual modeling language based on foundational ontologies.

Both UFO foundational ontology and OntoUML language has been used in several case studies for building domain ontologies, and the development of applications based on these ontologies. Examples of areas covered include electrocardiology (Gonçalves et al. 2009), exploration and production of oil (Guizzardi 2009), biodiversity (Albuquerque et al. 2015), among others.

The ontological schema should be designed using a tool with UML graphical support. The tool used in this step of the PFS was Enterprise Architect. Once the ontological schema is completed, it must be exported as XMI file and then imported by the OntoUML LightWeight Editor (OLED) tool (now called Menthor), where an OWL file can be generated.

OLED is an environment for the development, evaluation and implementation of domain ontologies, using OntoUML based on UFO. OLED supports the Sparx Enterprise System Architect models. Figure 4 and 5 present the OntoUML schema for EMMa and EMMb respectively.

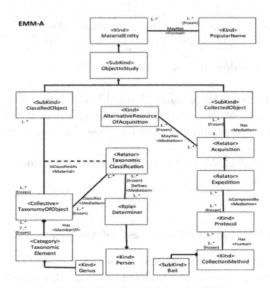

Fig. 4. The OntoUML schema for EMMa.

5.5 Representing EMM in OWL: Level of Application

W3C recommends the use of OWL for developing ontologies in application level (McGuinness and Harmelen 2004). Protégé (Wang et al. 2006) is the OWL editor used in the PFS. It is a tool developed in Java language, which supports plugins to extend its functionality and also provide a flexible basis for the development of prototypes and applications efficiently. One of the main features of this tool is to support two ways of modeling and implementing ontologies: based on frames and on OWL language.

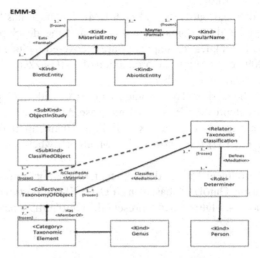

Fig. 5. The OntoUML schema for EMMb.

Although OLED allows the automatic generation of OWL code of the ontological schema designed, it is important to remember that a language in the level of analysis for ontologies as OntoUML has greater power of expressiveness than a language for ontologies in the level of implementation, such as OWL. Thus, a code generated automatically in OWL may not reflect the reality modeled, requiring adjustments to maintain the integrity of which has been modeled, thus justifying the use of Protégé for this. This is a recurrent issue in the development of ontologies that still requires research and solution.

Figure 6 illustrates a part of the PFS related to the EMM presented in this paper. Others EMMs used in our experiments, together with OntoUML schemas and OWL codes can be found at https://andreaalb1993.wixsite.com/ontobio.

There is more than one way to understand the knowledge and, consequently, more than a way to formalize it. This implies that the same EMM can have more than one PFS associated to it. The knowledge engineer should select a PFS according to the need of a specific application within the domain.

In Fig. 6, jauari is understood as a kind of bait. Bait is a specialization of the collection method adopted to capture a living organism (EMM-A). If jauari is understood to be in the food chain of jatuarana, the associated PFS presents another configuration as shown in Fig. 7.

Figures 6 and 7, show the semantics loss in the several levels of KR used in the PFS. For example, the fact that the part of jauari that attracts jatuarana is the seed (and not the bark of the trunk, or the fruit, or leaves, or fruit pulp). However, it is possible to visualize from the original flow of formalization, that the simplest level of KR (illustrated here by the management of the medias that store elicited knowledge and can make use of tags to facilitate the management process, STEP 1) to the currently considered more formal (ontology, STEP 7), the loss existed in the transition from one form of representation to another, but the knowledge is still the same and can be recovered when change the direction of the flow of the different formalizations presented (light gray arrows, backtracking).

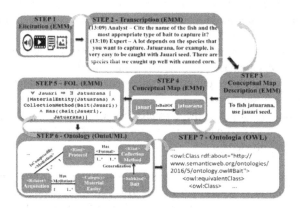

Fig. 6. PFS from EMM. Jauari as bait.

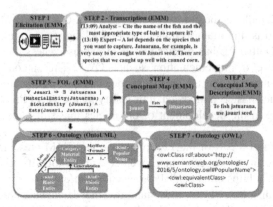

Fig. 7. PFS from EMM. Jauari as food.

6 Conclusions

This work presented contributions in the field of knowledge management which comprise: a new method to formalize scientific tacit knowledge, PFS, and; its use with automatic tools that are able to structure knowledge, such as, database, ontologies, semantic networks, intelligent heuristics mechanisms, etc.

The use of the PFS provides technological advancements, bringing a range of research possibilities, which include: (a) generation of new knowledge; (b) identification and classification of parameters and processes outputs for decision-making; (c) development of mechanisms for data preservation and organizational memory; and (d) data enrichment for use in the process of analysis and synthesis.

There are still limitations regarding semantic expressiveness in the PFS, due to various levels of granularity of knowledge, imposing loss of expressiveness in the transition between the different levels of formalization. To solve that, it is necessary to develop a method to measure the threshold for semantic acceptable loss that does not compromise the quality of the formalization.

An important issue for knowledge formalization in our scenario is that, since the transcription of EMM's are based on informal communication, the EMM's comprehension is subject to the knowledge engineer's interpretation. It means that the same EMM can be formalized in different ways.

The PFS permits to navigate the formalized knowledge in its different levels of granularity to retrieve missed parts of it or even use the PFS in another moment when acquiring additional knowledge.

Acknowledgements. This research was partially supported by FAPEAM (Foundation for the State of Amazonas Research) - Grant Number. 062.01502/2018 – FIXAM program. Thanks, are also due to INPA/LIS, and researchers of INPA's Ichthyology Group for their support.

References

Albuquerque, A.C.F., dos Santos, J.L.C., de Castro Júnior, A.N.: Elicitation taxonomy for acquiring biodiversity knowledge. In: Ngonga Ngomo, A.-C., Křemen, P. (eds.) KESW 2016. CCIS, vol. 649, pp. 157–172. Springer, Cham (2016). https://doi.org/10.1007/978-3-319-45880-9_13

Albuquerque, A.C.F.: Um Framework Conceitual para Integrar Conhecimento Tácito Científico. Tese (Doutorado em Informática) – Universidade Federal do Amazonas (2016)

Albuquerque, A.C.F., Santos, J.L.C., Castro Jr., A.N.: OntoBio: a biodiversity domain ontology for amazonian. In: Proceedings of 48th Hawaii International Conference on System Sciences HICSS 2015, Kauai, Hawaii, 5–8 January (2015). ISBN 978-1-4799-7367-5

Baumeister, J., Reutelshoefer, J., Puppe, F.: Engineering intelligent systems on the knowledge formalization continuum. Int. J. Appl. Math. Comput. Sci. 21(1), 27–39 (2011). https://doi.org/10.2478/v10006-011-0002-5. No. 1

Brachman, R.J., Levesque, H.J.: Knowledge Representation and Reasoning. Morgan Kaufmann Publishers Inc., San Francisco, Elsevier, San Diego (2004). ISBN 1558609326

Carey, S., Spelke, E.: Domain-specific knowledge and conceptual change. In: Hirschfeld, L.A., Gelman, S.A. (eds.) Mapping the Mind, pp. 169–200. Cambridge University Press, Cambridge (1994)

Clark, C.: Ten Popular Concept Mapping Tools. NspireD2, Kaneb Center, University of Notre Dame (2011). https://ltlatnd.wordpress.com/2011/05/11/ten-popular-concept-mapping-tools/. Accessed Mar 2019

Collins, H.M.: Tacit knowledge, trust and the Q of sapphire. Soc. Stud. Sci. 31(1), 71–85 (2001)

Gonçalves, B., Zamborlini, V., Guizzardi, G.: An ontological analysis of the electrocardiogram. RECIIS Electron. J. Commun. Inf. Innov. Health (English edition. Online) 3, 45–59 (2009)

Gruber, T.: Collective knowledge systems: where the social web meets the semantic web. Web Semant. 6(1), 4–13 (2008)

Guizzardi, G.: Ontological foundations for structural conceptual models. Ph.D. thesis (CUM LAUDE), University of Twente, The Netherlands. Published as the same name book in Telematica Institute Fundamental Research. Series no. 15, ISBN 90-75176-81-3, ISSN 1388-1795, no. 015. CTIT Ph.D. thesis. ISSN 1381-3617, no. 05–74, Holanda (2005)

Guizzardi, G.: The problem of transitivity of part-whole relations in conceptual modeling revisited. In: van Eck, P., Gordijn, J., Wieringa, R. (eds.) CAiSE 2009. LNCS, vol. 5565, pp. 94–109. Springer, Heidelberg (2009). https://doi.org/10.1007/978-3-642-02144-2_12

Kendal, S., Creen, M.: An Introduction to Knowledge Engineering. Springer, London (2007). https://doi.org/10.1007/978-1-84628-667-4

Klein, P., Luetzenberger, J., Thoben, K.-D.: A proposal for knowledge formalization in product development processes. In: Proceedings of the 20th International Conference on Engineering Design (ICED 2015), Milan, Italy, vol. 10: Design Information and Knowledge Management, pp. 261–272 (2015). ISBN 978-1-904670-73-5

Leite, F.C.L.: Gestão do Conhecimento Científico no Contexto Acadêmico: Proposta de um Modelo Conceitual. 240 f. Dissertação (Mestrado em Ciência da Informação)– Programa de Pós-Graduação em Ciência da Informação, Universidade de Brasília, Brasília (2006)

Lidwell, W., Holden, K., Butler, J.: Universal Principles of Design. Rockport Publishers, Minnespolis (2003)

Lofting, C.J.: The Neuro-Cognitive and Emotional Roots of Mathematics (2015). http://pages.prodigy.net/lofting/NeuroMaths3.htm. Accessed Apr 2019

McGuiness, D.L.: Ontologies come of age. In: Fensel, D., Hendler, J.A., Lieberman, H., Wahlster, W. (eds.) Spining the Semantic Web, pp. 171–194. MIT Press, Cambridge (2003)

McGuiness, D.L., Harmelen, F.V.: OWL Ontology Language Overview. W3C Recommendation (2004). https://www.w3.org/TR/owl-features/. Accessed Mar 2019

Millard, D.E., Gibbins, N.M., Michaelides, D.T., Weal, M.J.: Mind the semantic gap. In: HYPER-TEXT 2005: Proceedings of the 16th ACM Conference on Hypertext and Hypermedia, Salzburg, Austria, pp. 54–62 (2005)

Nalepa, G.J., Ligęza, A., Kaczor, K.: Overview of knowledge formalization with XTT2 rules. In: Bassiliades, N., Governatori, G., Paschke, A. (eds.) RuleML 2011. LNCS, vol. 6826, pp. 329–336. Springer, Heidelberg (2011). https://doi.org/10.1007/978-3-642-22546-8_26

Nonaka, I., Takeuchi, H.: The Knowledge-Creating Company: How Japanese Companies Create the Dynamics of Innovation. Oxford University Press, New York (1995)

Novak, J.D., Gowin, D.B.: Learning How to Learn. Cambridge University Press, Cornell University, New York (1984). ISBN 9780521319263

Noy, N., Sintek, M., Decker, S., Crubézy, M., Musen, M.: Creating semantic web contents with protege-2000. IEEE Intell. Syst. 16(2), 60–71 (2001)

Romanov, L.: Notes re: personal knowledge formalization and modeling. J. Knowl. Manag. Pract. 6 (2005). In The Knowledge Garden. ISSN 1705-9232

Russel, S., Norvig, P.: Artificial Intelligence - A Modern Approach. Prentice Hall Series in AI, Englewood Cliffs (2010)

Schaffert, S., Gruber, A., Westenthaler, R.: A semantic wiki for collaborative knowledge formation. In: Proceedings of the SEMANTICS 2005 Conference, Vienna, Austria (2006)

Sowa, J.F.: Knowledge Representation: Logical, Philosophical and Computational Foundations. Brooks Cole Publishing Co., Pacific Grove (2000). Pgs 10, 22, 159. ISBN 0-534-94965-7

Uschold, M., Gruninger, M.: Ontologies and semantics for seamless connectivity. SIGMOD Rec. 33(4), 58–64 (2004)

Wang, Y., Sure, Y., Stevens, R., Rector, A.: Knowledge elicitation plug-in for Protégé: card sorting and laddering. In: Mizoguchi, R., Shi, Z., Giunchiglia, F. (eds.) ASWC 2006. LNCS, vol. 4185, pp. 552–565. Springer, Heidelberg (2006). https://doi.org/10.1007/11836025_53

Peruvian Sign Language Recognition Using a Hybrid Deep Neural Network

Yuri Vladimir Huallpa Vargas$^{(\boxtimes)}$ ⓘ, Naysha Naydu Diaz Ccasa ⓘ,
and Lauro Enciso Rodas ⓘ

Universidad Nacional de San Antonio Abad del Cusco,
Av. de La Cultura 773, Cusco, Peru
yurihuallpavargas@gmail.com
http://in.unsaac.edu.pe/home/

Abstract. Hearing impaired people have the ability to communicate with their hands and interpret sign language (SL), but this builds a communication gap with normal people. There are models for SL recognition that have images sequence RGB as input; however, the movements of the body in 3D space is necessary to consider due to the complexity of the gestures. We built a model for Peruvian sign language recognition (PSL) to Spanish composed by 4 phases; first, the preprocessing phase in charge to process RGB, depth and skeleton streams obtained through the Kinect sensor v.1; second, the feature extraction which learn spatial information through 3 types of convolutional neural network (CNN); third, the bidirectional long short term memory (BLSTM) with residual connections in charge to reduced and encode the information. Finally, a decoder with attention mechanism and maxout network which learn the temporal information. Our proposed model is evaluated in LSA64 and ourself-built dataset. The experimental results show significant improvement compared to other models evaluated in these dataset.

Keywords: Sign language recognition · Recurrent Neural Network · Long short term memory · Convolution Neural Network

1 Introduction

Currently, people don't have the need to learn SL that is unique to each community and designed by themselves, i.e. the spanish SL is not completely similar as peruvian although them speak spanish. There are models that use CNN, Recurrent Neural Network (RNN) and Bidirectional Recurrent Neural Network (BRNN) that get good results for their SLs; however, they lose useful information by capturing only one type of data. Create a specific dataset for a SL is complicated because they have their own large dictionary; therefore, it is not possible to apply the same models and dataset for peruvian context. For developing an architecture that achieves an acceptable success rate, it is necessary to identify techniques as DNN (Deep Neural Network) and Natural Language

ⓒ Springer Nature Switzerland AG 2020
J. A. Lossio-Ventura et al. (Eds.): SIMBig 2019, CCIS 1070, pp. 165–172, 2020.
https://doi.org/10.1007/978-3-030-46140-9_16

Processing (NLP), for build our model with CNN along with RNN we used techniques as early stoping (ES), transfer learning (TL) and dropout; in addition to, our dictionary is done with expressions rather than just using simple words, to have better accuracy we use three types of stream: rgb, detph and skeleton which provide more signal information regarding distance and position of the gesture.

2   Related Works

In the last decades a lot of research focused on the actions recognition that emulate the human capacity to interpret the outside world, they have generated different contributions for translating SL based on images. In [22] applies 3D convolution network in a sequence of videos in order to maintain temporal information unlike 2D CNN that losing temporal information. Another research [13] makes use RGB and 3D skeleton stream as input, uses VGG-16 CNN to extract features for each frame from RGB then both data are passed to different encoder-decoder with LSTM, their outputs are merged using a combination probability to improve accuracy. In [4] perform activity recognition and image tagging with VGG then it feed to LSTM to learn spatial-temporal information, the training and testing were performed at UCF101 dataset and verified that a recurrent neural network (RNN) with two layers achieves better results than single layer. [19] use a Time of Flight (TOF) sensor, the least relevant depth data were removed using principal component analysis (PCA) and persistent feature histogram [18] was used to feed a LSTM with softmax. In [16] propose an attention model with a LReLU activation function that only depends on the output hidden state of the LSTM, the LSTM have TanH and LRelU activation functions which accelerates the convergence; the disadvantage of this model is unable to distinguish the order of a sequence. [12] proposes two models of attention; global and local attention, which differ in data dependency of the input, global attention considers all hidden states of the encoder as long as local attention processes the hidden states through slide window while the inputs are processed. Finally, in [14] propose two approaches to infer gestures from dataset LSA64 [17]; first approach called Prediction Approach represents each video by a sequence of predictions made by an inception network and then passed to an RNN and the second model called Pool layer represents each video by a feature vector of size 2048 made by the last pooling layer and then it passed to the RNN.

3   Propose Method

In this section we describe the model. First, we preprocess each frame from depth and skeleton stream since they have different distribution respect to necessary input for ResNet50 [8]; however, each frame from RGB stream is only resized. Second, we have 3 CNN (rgbResNet50, depthResNet50 and skeleton-ResNet50) which are fed by each frames from streams had already preprocessed, then extract the main features and joined them. Third, the joined features feed to encoder for reducing the dimensionality. Fourth, all output sequence from encoder feed to attention mechanism from decoder and for each time step t the attention pass context ctx towards LSTM from decoder to produce one output $\hat{y}_t$. At the end $\hat{y}_t$ is analized to interpret what SL is it, see Fig. 1.

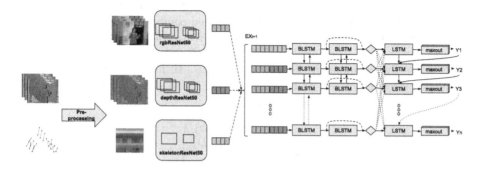

Fig. 1. Flow of the proposed method for Peruvian SL Recognition.

3.1 Preprocessing

We perform the preprocessing for our 3 data types and them are resized by area interpolation. First, RGB streams are only resized to $244 \times 244 \times 3$ so that have similar distribution as needed input to ResNet50. To depth stream, let $D = (a_{ij})_{480 \times 640}, \forall a_{ij} \in \mathbb{R}^2$ a matrix that represents a depth frame, for each position (a_{ij}) kinect return k, $\forall k \in \mathbb{N}$; k is transformed into a binary number of 16 bits with 3-bits shifted to the right to obtain the distance in millimeters and it is scaled to values between 0 to 1 by the Equation (1). Where D' is the scaled matrix, $\min(D)$ and $\max(D)$ is the minimum and maximum value respectively; then viridis [15] is used to map each position (a_{ij}) from D' in one RGB color, where purple indicates the closest pixel to the kinect sensor and yellow is the farthest. Finally, the result of size $480 \times 640 \times 3$ is resized to $244 \times 244 \times 3$.

$$D'(a_{ij}) = \frac{D(a_{ij}) - \min(D)}{\max(D) - \min(D)} \tag{1}$$

Each frame from skeleton stream consists of 20 (x, y, z) coordinates, we only consider 10 coordinates for upper body. To preprocess the skeleton stream a methodology similar to [11] is followed where the (x, y, z) coordinates are mapped into X, Y and Z matrix, before to stack $[X; Y; Z]$ to get one image $S = (a_{ijk})_{10 \times F \times 3}$ where F is the number of frames in one stream, we apply the Equation (1); After, let $I_r = \lceil \frac{244}{10} \rceil$, $I_c = \lceil \frac{244}{F} \rceil$ where I_r and $I_c \in \mathbb{N}$, each row and column of S are repeated I_r and I_c times respectively to get a new $S = (a_{ijk})_{(I_r \times 10) \times (I_c \times F) \times (3)}$; at the end S is resized to $244 \times 244 \times 3$.

3.2 Features Extraction

The CNN are used in many researches [3,10,24] that show a satisfactory efficiency in the classification. We used pretrained ResNet50 as a basis to build our components (rgbResNet50, depthResNet50 and skeletonResNet50), removed the last fully conected layer (FC) of 1000 neurons, for depthResNet50 and skeleton-ResNet50 we added dropout with a keep-prop of 0.8, FC layer with 14 and 21 neurons to classify depth and skeleton images in our dataset; and them are retrained by applying transfer learning [1]. After training, the last average pooling layer of $7 \times 7 \times 2048$ are taken from the aforementioned components and applied max pooling with a kernel of 7×7 which returns a vector of 1×2048 considered as features vectors. Let $R_i = \nu(rgb_i)$, $D_i = \rho(depth_i)$ and $S_1 = \delta(skeleton_1)$ where ν, ρ y δ are the components, R_i and D_i are the i-th feature vector from RGB and depth stream, where $i = 1, \cdots, F$ and S_1 is the skeleton's feature vector. The feature vectors are combined by the Eq. 2.

$$X_{F+1\times4096} = Concat \begin{pmatrix} S_1 & S_1 \\ R_1 & D_1 \\ \vdots & \vdots \\ R_F & D_F \end{pmatrix}_{F+1\times4096} \tag{2}$$

3.3 Encoder Multilayer Bidirectional LSTM with Residual Connections

LSTM [9] is a variation of RNN useful for dealing the problem of vanishing gradient, Eq. 3. LSTM use the past context h_{t-1} to produce the output h_t, but for SL is necessary to know past and future context; hence, we used BRNN that can perform the aforementioned process by exploring the past and future context, its output is $h_t = [\overrightarrow{h}_t; \overleftarrow{h}_t]$. [8] shows that adding skip connections between adjacent layers can accelerate training and achieve better results, see Fig. 2. Where x_t^i is input, h_t^i is hidden state, H_i is the BLSTM function associated with the i-th layer ($i = 1, \cdots, L$), L is number of layers and x_t^{i+1} is the element-wise added between x_t^i and h_t^i. According [3,7,21] the RNN with multiple layers stacking tends to achieve higher performance than shallower RNNs. Our encoder consists of 2 BLSTM and the last layer is a residual layer.

$$\begin{aligned} i_t &= \Theta\left(x_t W_i + h_{t-1} U_i + b_i\right) \\ f_t &= \Theta\left(x_t W_f + h_{t-1} U_f + b_f\right) \\ o_t &= \Theta\left(x_t W_o + h_{t-1} U_o + b_o\right) \\ \hat{c}_t &= tanh\left(x_t W_c + h_{t-1} U_c + b_c\right) \\ c_t &= f_t \odot c_{t-1} + i_t \odot \hat{c}_t \\ h_t &= o_t \odot c_t \end{aligned} \tag{3}$$

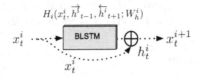

Fig. 2. Bidirectional LSTM with residual connection.

3.4   Attention Decoder with Maxout Network

Attention mechanisms has been used in many researches [12,16] since it generates a behavior similar to how a human interprets the outside world, focusing only on the relevant information. So our decoder incorporate attention mechanism [2] that return a context vector ctx_t witch depend on sequence output of encoder h_t and previous hidden state of decoder s_{t-1}, for each time step encoder return hidden state $s_t = LSTM(\hat{y}_{t-1}, s_{t-1}, [ctx_t, s_{t-1}])$, then each s_t pass to feed-forward maxout network [6] defined by the following equation:

$$\alpha_t(s) = \max_{j \in [1,k]} z_{tj}$$
$$z_{tj} = s^T W_{...tj} + b_{tj} \tag{4}$$

$W \in \mathbb{R}^{d \times m \times k}$ y $b \in \mathbb{R}^{m \times k}$ are trainable weight, k is the number of linear neuron that compose a one hidden unit of maxout. Maxout network is quite robust to handle the problem of vanishing gradient however it is prone to overfitting; but dropout can be applied to control this problem and get better performance [20], we infer $\hat{y}_t = softmax(\alpha_t)$ by applying softmax clasifier on the output of maxout.

4   Experiments

In this section we perform a series of tests on the proposed model in ourself-built dataset VideoLSP10 [23] and LSA64 [17]; dataset was divided through hold-out. We trained the model in train set and evaluated the performance with four evaluation metrics in validation set, VideoLSP10 is made up of 3 dataset. First, depthLSP contains 2045 depth data divided into 14 classes to train the component depthResNet50 and is divided in the following way: 96% for training and 4% for validation. Second, skeletonLSP contains 1701 skeleton movements which was divided into 21 classes, each frame of a movement is composed by 10 coordinates (x, y, z), we used it for training the component skeletonResNet50 and is divided in the following way: 90% for training and 10% for validation. Finally, LSP10 contains rgb, depth and skeleton data, see Fig. 3; it consists of 600 videos divided in 10 classes of peruvian phrases and is divided in the following way: 84% for training and 16% for validation.

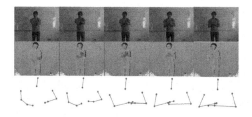

Fig. 3. RGB, Depth and Skeleton stream from LSP10.

4.1 Hyperparameters

We use stochastic gradient descent (SGD) with a learning rate $\alpha = 0.001$ and momentum $\beta = 0.9$ for retraining depthResNet50 and skeletonResNet50.

Our proposed RNN have 2 BLSTM layers with 500 units in the encoder, the last layer contains residual connections; the decoder have attention mechanism with 64 units, one layer LSTM with 900 units, maxout network with 90 units where each linear units have 5 neurons and the output is softmax classifier. We applied dropout and recurrent dropout [5] $keepProp = 0.5$ in encoder, dropout with $keepProp = 0.7$ in maxout network. Finally, the parameters are optimized using Root Mean Square Propagation (RMSprop) with a learning rate $\alpha = 0.045$, $\rho = 0.94$, $\epsilon = 1$ and learning decay= 0.00. Our rgbResNet50 linked to RNN is compared with the approaches [14], the parameters are optimized using Adam optimization with a learning rate $\alpha = 0.001$, $\beta_1 = 0.9$, $\beta_2 = 0.999$ and learning decay= 0.1. For each training are used mini-bach of 4 streams using the categorical-cross-entropy loss function and to prevent overfitting early stopping is used.

5 Results

Based on the experimentation, we obtain the results of the components and models evaluated in the validation set, see Table 1. DepthResNet50 trained in depthLSP dataset achieve 97.67 % of accuracy, for skeletonhResNet50 trained in skeletonLSP achieve 95.24% of accuracy. However, rgbResNet50 has no results since ResNet50 is used as FE; subsequently, the FE components were added to RNN (encoder linked to decoder). The result of rgbResNet50 linked to RNN in $LSP10_{rgb}$ achieved 88.6% of accuracy, depthResNet50 linked to RNN in $LSP10_{depth}$ achieved 85.3%. Finally, joining the 3 FEs to the RNN using the LSP10 data set achieved 99.2 % accuracy.

Our model rgbResNet50 linked with RNN has been compared with proposed models in [14]: Prediction Approach and Pool Layer Approach using the LSA64

Table 1. Results in the validation set for FE components and models, using the VideoLSP10 dataset.

Components		Dataset	% Accuracy	Precision	Recall	F1 Score
FE	rgbResNet50	-	-	-	-	-
	depthResNet50	depthLSP	97.67	1	94.8	97.1
	skeletonResNet50	skeletonLSP	95.24	98.9	92.7	94.8
Models						
rgbResNet50+RNN		$LSP10_{rgb}$	88.6	88.8	84.0	85.8
depthResNet50+RNN		$LSP10_{depth}$	85.3	84.2	81.4	81.7
FE+RNN		LSP10	**99.2**	**99.0**	**99.5**	**99.2**

dataset, Our model achieved **98.44** % of accuracy, Pool Layer Aproach achieved 95.21 % of accuracy and Prediction Approach achieved 80.87 % of accuracy.

6 Conclusions

We propose a hybrid model based on CNN and RNN which incorporates advanced models such as maxout, attention mechanisms and residual connections. The model is composed of four parts. Firstly, the preprocessing phase of RGB, depth and skeleton. Secondly, feature extraction phase that use CNN based in ResNet50. Thirdly, encoder phase that reduce the inputs dimensionality. Finally, a decoder to relate the temporal information and infer what sign it is. The model is able to translate a phrase from the VideoLSP10 dataset achieving 99.2% of accuracy and in LSA our model achieve an accuracy of 98.44% only using RGD data. Hence, our model can be used for any sign language since in both dataset an acceptable accuracy are achieved and also VideoLSP10 is challenger than LSA64. Eventually future researches may improve the model and apply it to a larger dataset.

References

1. Akilan, T., Wu, Q.M.J., Yang, Y., Safaei, A.: Fusion of transfer learning features and its application in image classification. In: 2017 IEEE 30th Canadian Conference on Electrical and Computer Engineering (CCECE), pp. 1–5, April 2017. https://doi.org/10.1109/CCECE.2017.7946733
2. Bahdanau, D., Cho, K., Bengio, Y.: Neural machine translation by jointly learning to align and translate. arXiv e-prints abs/1409.0473, September 2014. https://arxiv.org/abs/1409.0473
3. Cai, M., Liu, J.: Maxout neurons for deep convolutional and LSTM neural networks in speech recognition. Speech Commun. **77**, December 2015. https://doi.org/10.1016/j.specom.2015.12.003
4. Donahue, J., Hendricks, L.A., Guadarrama, S., Rohrbach, M., Venugopalan, S., Saenko, K., Darrell, T.: Long-term recurrent convolutional networks for visual recognition and description. CoRR abs/1411.4389 (2014). http://arxiv.org/abs/1411.4389
5. Gal, Y., Ghahramani, Z.: A theoretically grounded application of dropout in recurrent neural networks. In: Lee, D.D., Sugiyama, M., Luxburg, U.V., Guyon, I., Garnett, R. (eds.) Advances in Neural Information Processing Systems 29, pp. 1019–1027. Curran Associates, Inc. (2016). http://papers.nips.cc/paper/6241-a-theoretically-grounded-application-of-dropout-in-recurrent-neural-networks.pdf
6. Goodfellow, I., Warde-Farley, D., Mirza, M., Courville, A., Bengio, Y.: Maxout networks. In: Dasgupta, S., McAllester, D. (eds.) Proceedings of the 30th International Conference on Machine Learning, No. 3 in Proceedings of Machine Learning Research, PMLR, Atlanta, Georgia, USA, pp. 1319–1327, 17–19 June 2013. http://proceedings.mlr.press/v28/goodfellow13.html
7. Graves, A., Mohamed, A., Hinton, G.E.: Speech recognition with deep recurrent neural networks. CoRR abs/1303.5778 (2013). http://arxiv.org/abs/1303.5778

8. He, K., Zhang, X., Ren, S., Sun, J.: Deep residual learning for image recognition. CoRR abs/1512.03385 (2015). http://arxiv.org/abs/1512.03385

9. Hochreiter, S., Schmidhuber, J.: Long short-term memory. Neural Comput. **9**, 1735–80 (1997). https://doi.org/10.1162/neco.1997.9.8.1735

10. Huang, S., Mao, C., Tao, J., Ye, Z.: A novel chinese sign language recognition method based on keyframe-centered clips. IEEE Signal Process. Lett. **25**(3), 442–446 (2018). https://doi.org/10.1109/LSP.2018.2797228

11. Laraba, S., Brahimi, M., Tilmanne, J., Dutoit, T.: 3D skeleton-based action recognition by representing motion capture sequences as 2D-RGB images. Comput. Animat. Virtual Worlds **28**, May 2017. https://doi.org/10.1002/cav.1782

12. Luong, M., Pham, H., Manning, C.D.: Effective approaches to attention-based neural machine translation. CoRR abs/1508.04025 (2015). http://arxiv.org/abs/1508.04025

13. Mao, C., Huang, S., Li, X., Ye, Z.: Chinese sign language recognition with sequence to sequence learning. In: Yang, J., Hu, Q., Cheng, M.-M., Wang, L., Liu, Q., Bai, X., Meng, D. (eds.) CCCV 2017, Part I. CCIS, vol. 771, pp. 180–191. Springer, Singapore (2017). https://doi.org/10.1007/978-981-10-7299-4_15

14. Masood, S., Srivastava, A., Thuwal, H.C., Ahmad, M.: Real-time sign language gesture (word) recognition from video sequences using CNN and RNN. In: Bhateja, V., Coello Coello, C.A., Satapathy, S.C., Pattnaik, P.K. (eds.) Intelligent Engineering Informatics. AISC, vol. 695, pp. 623–632. Springer, Singapore (2018). https://doi.org/10.1007/978-981-10-7566-7_63

15. Smith, N., Van der Walt, S.: MPL Colormaps (2015). https://bids.github.io/colormap/

16. Raffel, C., Ellis, D.P.W.: Feed-forward networks with attention can solve some long-term memory problems. CoRR abs/1512.08756 (2015). http://arxiv.org/abs/1512.08756

17. Ronchetti, F., Quiroga, F., Estrebou, C., Lanzarini, L., Rosete, A.: Lsa64: A dataset of argentinian sign language. In: XX II Congreso Argentino de Ciencias de la Computación (CACIC) (2016)

18. Rusu, R.B., Blodow, N., Marton, Z.C., Beetz, M.: Aligning point cloud views using persistent feature histograms. In: 2008 IEEE/RSJ International Conference on Intelligent Robots and Systems, pp. 3384–3391, September 2008. https://doi.org/10.1109/IROS.2008.4650967

19. Sarkar, A., Gepperth, A., Handmann, U., Kopinski, T.: Dynamic hand gesture recognition for mobile systems using deep LSTM. In: Horain, P., Achard, C., Mallem, M. (eds.) IHCI 2017. LNCS, vol. 10688, pp. 19–31. Springer, Cham (2017). https://doi.org/10.1007/978-3-319-72038-8_3

20. Srivastava, N., Hinton, G., Krizhevsky, A., Sutskever, I., Salakhutdinov, R.: Dropout: a simple way to prevent neural networks from overfitting. J. Machi. Learn. Rese. **15**, 1929–1958 (2014). http://jmlr.org/papers/v15/srivastava14a.html

21. Su, P., Ding, X., Zhang, Y., Miao, F., Zhao, N.: Learning to predict blood pressure with deep bidirectional LSTM network. CoRR abs/1705.04524 (2017). http://arxiv.org/abs/1705.04524

22. Tran, D., Bourdev, L.D., Fergus, R., Torresani, L., Paluri, M.: C3D: generic features for video analysis. CoRR abs/1412.0767 (2014). http://arxiv.org/abs/1412.0767

23. Vargas, Y.V.H.: Peruvian sign language videolsp10 (2019). https://github.com/videoLSP/VideoLSP10

24. Xu, K., et al.: Show, attend and tell: Neural image caption generation with visual attention. CoRR abs/1502.03044 (2015). http://arxiv.org/abs/1502.03044

Chronic Pain Estimation Through Deep Facial Descriptors Analysis

Antoni Mauricio[1,2]([⊠]) [iD], Jonathan Peña[2], Erwin Dianderas[3],
Leonidas Mauricio[2], Jose Díaz[2][iD], and Antonio Morán[2]

[1] Department of Computer Science, Universidad Católica San Pablo, Arequipa, Peru
manasses.mauricio@ucsp.edu.pe
[2] Universidad Nacional de Ingeniería, Lima, Peru
jonathan.pena.a@uni.pe, jcdiazrosado@uni.edu.pe, amoran@ieee.org
[3] Instituto De Investigaciones De La Amazonía Peruana, Iquitos, Peru
erwin.dianderasc@ciplima.org.pe

Abstract. Worldwide, chronic pain has established as one of the foremost medical issues due to its 35% of comorbidity with depression and many other psychological problems. Traditionally, self-report (VAS scale) or physicist inspection (OPI scale) perform the pain assessment; nonetheless, both methods do not usually coincide [14]. Regarding self-assessment, several patients are not able to complete it objectively, like young children or patients with limited expression abilities. The lack of objectivity in the metrics draws the main problem of the clinical analysis of pain. In response, various efforts have tried concerning the inclusion of objective metrics, among which stand out the Prkachin and Solomon Pain Intensity (PSPI) metric defined by face appearance [5]. This work presents an in-depth learning approach to pain recognition considering deep facial representations and sequence analysis. Contrasting current state-of-the-art deep learning techniques, we correct rigid deformations caught since registration. A preprocessing stage is applied, which includes facial frontalization to untangle facial representations from non-affine transformations, perspective deformations, and outside noises passed since registration. After dealing with unbalanced data, we fine-tune a CNN from a pre-trained model to extract facial features, and then a multilayer RNN exploits temporal relation between video frames. As a result, we overcome state-of-the-art in terms of average accuracy at frames level (80.44%) and sequence level (84.54%) in the UNBC-McMaster Shoulder Pain Expression Archive Database.

Keywords: CNN-RNN hybrid architecture · Pain recognition · Deep facial representations

The present work was supported by grant 234-2015-FONDECYT (Master Program) from Cienciactiva of the National Council for Science, Technology and Technological Innovation (CONCYTEC-PERU) and the Vicerrectorate for Research of Universidad Nacional de Ingeniería (VRI - UNI).

© Springer Nature Switzerland AG 2020
J. A. Lossio-Ventura et al. (Eds.): SIMBig 2019, CCIS 1070, pp. 173–185, 2020.
https://doi.org/10.1007/978-3-030-46140-9_17

1   Introduction

According to Raffaeli et al. [9], chronic pain is one of the most complex medical ills, treated in multiple ways depending on its severity. In 2011, 20% of adults worldwide suffered at least one kind of pain, and some estimations point that around 10% of adults would be diagnosed with chronic pain each year. In 2017, Souza et al. [12] documented that patients diagnosed with chronic pain rose to 50%, although distribution varies per region due to many factors, including life quality and stress. Pain feeling is a personal experience, which can be expressed to the medics using a Visual-Analogue-Scale (VAS) or estimated by a standardized Observed Pain Intensity Scale (OPI). Nevertheless, both metrics tend not to coincide because patients could misexpress the pain or misinterpret by medics [14].

In the computational field, automatic pain recognition has received increased attention since Lucey et al. [4] published the UNBC-McMaster Shoulder Pain Expression Archive Database. The problem has been intensely explored either for computer vision classical methods [2,3,8,10,15] or brand-new deep learning approaches [6,11,16]. The UNBC-McMaster database consists of 200 video clip sequences taken from 25 patients who were suffering from shoulder pain. It is labeled both at frames (PSPI on a range of [0–15]) and sequences level (VAS on a scale of [0–10] and OPI on a range of [0–5]). Classic proposals have shown outstanding results through geometrical analysis but almost limited to the frame level analysis. However, even though temporal analysis allows us to explore the problem deeply, it does not present such remarkable results. This result seems to be caused by the vanishing gradient problem, which is proportional to the sequence size [13].

In this paper, we aim to solve two issues: (1) untangle the facial representations between aspects and facial pain expression; and, (2) prevent the vanishing gradient problem in temporal analysis. To accomplish them, we propose two procedures. First, a preprocessing stage that considers facial landmarks for masking and frontalization. Second, a CNN-RNN hybrid model which is designed to surpass the vanishing gradient problem by using low-processing sequential units. The upcoming sections go as follows: Sect. 2 covers the current state-of-the-art related to pain analysis. Section 3 exposes the detail of our proposals. Section 4 includes the most relevant experiments and their respective results contrasted with literature. Finally, we discuss our findings and conclusions in Sect. 5, including future improvements.

2   Related Work

Like most current computer vision applications, research papers can be grouped based on its features extraction approach. Table 1 presents a summary of multi-class classification research works, including their metrics and results. Florea et al. [2] propose to transfer the pivotal face features extracted from the Cohn-Kanade (CK+) dataset using a Histogram of Topographical Features

(HoT) to a two-levels-of-classification model based on Support Vector Regressors (SVR). Rathee et al. [10] define the facial deformations using rigid and nonrigid parameters by Thin-Plate Spline (TPS) mapping. Moreover, they mapped the deformation parameters to higher discriminative space using the Distance Metric Learning (DML) method and use an SVM to carry out the 16-classes classification.

Table 1. Metrics comparison of the-state-of-the-art. The table includes the classifier description, features selection, implementation details, metrics, and score. The implementation details are "x" if the paper considers a balancing algorithm (**Ba**) and/or a preprocessing schedule (**Pp**).

	Classifier	Features	Details		Pain levels	Metric	Score
			Ba	Pp			
Zhao et al. [15]	OSVR-L2	LBP + Gabor	x	x	[0–5]	PCC	0.60
						MAE	0.81
						ICC	0.56
Kaltwang et al. [3]	RVM	DCT + LBP	–	–	[0–15]	MSE	1.39
						PCC	0.59
						ICC	0.50
Florea et al. [2]	SVR	HoT	–	–	[0–15]	MSE	1.18
						PCC	0.55
Rathee et al. [10]	SVM	TPS + DML	x	–	16	ACC	0.96
Zhou et al. [16]	RCNN	–	x	x	16	MSE	1.54
						PCC	0.65
Bellantonio et al. [6]	CNN-LSTM	–	–	x	14	ACC	0.619
Rodriguez et al. [11]	CNN-LSTM	–	x	x	5	MAE	0.5
						MSE	0.74
						PCC	0.78
						ICC	0.45

Kaltwang et al. [3] propose a continuous pain estimation adopting Local Binary Patterns (LBP) and the Discrete Cosine Transform (DCT) as features. Then, 2-levels of Relevance Vector Machines (RVM) perform the prediction. The first one estimates the pain intensity for each element independently, while, the second calculates the pain intensity, considering the previous layer results. Zhao et al. [15] propose an Ordinal Support Vector Regression (OSVR) based on an SVR and an Ordinal Regression (OR). As a result, the OR establishes the temporal order while the SVR computes the intensity value. Each frame splits into five regions to extract two features per each: LBP and Gabor wavelet coefficients. Subsequently, a PCA is used to couple the feature vector of each area. For regression, they use linear kernel (L1) and quadratic kernel (L2) alongside the OSVR.

The majority of deep-learning approaches consider temporal rather than spatial analysis. Zhou et al. [16] propose a recurrent CNN (RCNN) to achieve a continuous pain estimation. To do so, they develop a preprocessing scheme, which includes: histogram equalization, face masking, and framing using facial landmarks and eye patches as references. Face images are flattened into 1D vectors and merge into a matrix, which is processed by the RCNN considering the last frame's label as output. Bellantonio et al. [6] use a CNN-LSTM architecture to perform a 14-levels pain classification. They introduce a data balancing module by resolution variations over the less numerous classes. Then, a pre-trained VGG-16 architecture is fine-tuned to use it as a feature extractor. Finally, one LSTM layer performs the temporal analysis using the last frame's label as the sequence's label.

Rodriguez et al. [11] follow the same steps proposed by [6] but adding a preprocessing scheme like Zhou et al. [16]. Also, they prioritize the frontalization problem and develop a data augmentation module by landmark-based random deformations and vertical flipping. Frontalization attempts to solve the camera perspective error by estimating the projection matrix [1]. Data augmentation supports the less represented data and increases the training data. Finally, there are two considerations to make a fair comparison. First, the number of pain levels are proportional to the estimation accuracy. Second, the temporal analysis is much more complex, but it has greater medical acceptance than the stationary report.

3   Methodology

We use a standard pipeline for spatiotemporal analysis. First, we propose a preprocessing scheme that depends on the dataset conditions and the CNN requirements. Second, we do data balancing and data augmentation policies to offset unbalance. Regarding the architecture, we provide the implementation details alongside their explanations at each stage. Figure 1 illustrates our proposal overview.

3.1   Image Preprocessing

We consider three stages for pre-processing: (1) light normalization; (2) masking; and, (3) frontalization. Normalization bypasses the illumination problem and standardizes the input values. For masking, we use the convex hull algorithm over the facial landmarks given in the dataset. The frontalization matches the original landmarks with the frontal-view landmarks of a 3D-model[1] by computing the camera matrix and the projection matrix during the camera calibration. Thereupon, the projection matrix maps the original image to estimate the frontalized frame. Finally, the frontalized face undergoes a smooth symmetry process that fills the occluded parts using the opposite half of the face. Nonetheless, frontalization modifies and introduces new information or noises that could

---

[1] https://github.com/dougsouza/face-frontalization.

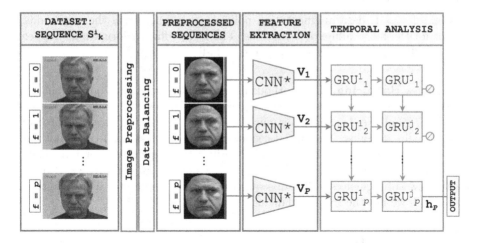

Fig. 1. Overview of our proposal. Given a sequence S_k, we extract the faces from each frame f that belongs to S_k. Then, a pre-trained CNN obtains the feature vector V_f from each face. Latter, an RNN establish the temporal correspondence between the feature vectors and the pain level. The RNN is composed of j layers of GRU layers units (GRU_p^j). The last frame's label (h_p) is the output of the whole sequence instead of its offline value.

interfere with the faces representation inside the model [1]. To surmount this problem, we define critical landmarks based-on the PSPI metric to compute the frontalization; these are the ones from the chin and cheeks contours; and, in the extremes of eyes, mouth, and eyebrows.

3.2   Data Balancing

The UNBC-McMaster Shoulder Pain database has a notorious unbalance at frames and patient distributions. For the temporal analysis, each patient has different amounts of videos, and each video has different sizes. To deal with the imbalance at frames and sequence level, we consider similar strategies to those raised by Bellantonio et al. [6] and Rathee et al. [10]. Data augmentation includes rotations ($3°, 6°$ and $9°$), flipping and facial affine deformations. Finally, we introduce two sequential data generation policies: (1) sequences fragmentation; and, (2) overlapping.

Frames Balancing. The frames balancing includes (1) downsampling the most represented classes; and, (2) a data augmentation policy for the least represented. The distribution matrix $M_{[p,l]}$ represents the data distribution for the patients $p \in \mathbb{P}$ and pain levels $l \in \mathbb{L}$. Then, we compute the scaling matrix $T_{[p,l]}$ which is formed by the scale factor τ of each element of $M_{[p,l]}$ concerning an established number of samples. The scale factor defines the policies to carry out and belongs to the $[0, \tau_{max}]$ range. So, if $\tau < 1$, downsampling is done with a probability of

τ, while if $\tau > 1$, data augmentation policies are applied with the same odds, except for the facial affine deformations. The facial affine deformations happen between 20% and 30% over the samples, including the generated ones.

Sequences Balancing. The methods presented also work for sequence balancing by applying them to every frame of a sequence. However, these sequences are not the original ones because they must have the same size and have to represent a single pain stimulus. The initial sequences have painless dead-times both at the beginning and the end of the videos. First, the sequences split into 'pain' sections and 'painless' sections. Thereupon, a window runs along each section to create new subsequences. The subsequences obtained generates a distribution, over which we use the frame balancing reasoning.

3.3   Feature Extraction

Feature extraction is the core of convolutional neural networks (CNN). Convolutional layers learn the main features of a dataset, then, fully connected layers correlate feature vectors with the outputs. For our case, we made a transfer learning procedure from VGG_faces[2] [7] to our VGG16 architecture. Figure 2 shows the VGG_faces model while Table 2 presents the model configuration. We apply a categorical cross-entropy loss to maximize the separation between classes; 50% of dropout probability; and, SGD optimization with a learning rate equal to 0.001 and momentum equal to 0.9. After evaluating the feature vectors, we opt to use the ttfc6 layer for the temporal analysis.

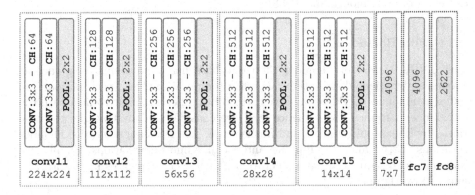

Fig. 2. Architecture VGG_faces raised by [7]. It is composed of 13 convolutional layers, five pooling layers and three fully connected layers. CONV and POOL are convolutional and max-pooling kernel sizes, respectively, while CH is the number of output channels. fc layers correlate the feature vectors to face classification tasks. fc8 has 2622 output classes.

---

[2] http://www.robots.ox.ac.uk/~vgg/software/vgg_face/.

Table 2. VGG_faces configuration. From left to right: (1) layers description; (2) number of filters; (3) input size; (4) kernel size; (5) stride value Str; (6) padding value Pad; and, (7) activation function.

Layers		Number of filters	Input size	Kernel size	Str	Pad	Activation function
Input	Image	1	$224 \times 224 \times 3$	–	–	–	ReLU
1	$2 \times$ conv1	64	$224 \times 224 \times 64$	3×3	$(1, 1)$	$(1, 1)$	ReLU
	MaxPool	64	$112 \times 112 \times 64$	2×2	$(2, 2)$	$(0, 0)$	ReLU
3	$2 \times$ conv1	128	$112 \times 112 \times 128$	3×3	$(1, 1)$	$(1, 1)$	ReLU
	MaxPool	128	$56 \times 56 \times 128$	2×2	$(2, 2)$	$(0, 0)$	ReLU
5	$3 \times$ conv1	256	$56 \times 56 \times 256$	3×3	$(1, 1)$	$(1, 1)$	ReLU
	MaxPool	256	$28 \times 28 \times 256$	2×2	$(2, 2)$	$(0, 0)$	ReLU
8	$3 \times$ conv1	512	$28 \times 28 \times 512$	3×3	$(1, 1)$	$(1, 1)$	ReLU
	MaxPool	512	$14 \times 14 \times 512$	2×2	$(2, 2)$	$(0, 0)$	ReLU
11	$3 \times$ conv1	512	$14 \times 14 \times 512$	3×3	$(1, 1)$	$(1, 1)$	ReLU
	MaxPool	512	$7 \times 7 \times 512$	2×2	$(2, 2)$	$(0, 0)$	ReLU
14	fc6	4096	512	7×7	$(1, 1)$	$(0, 0)$	ReLU
15	fc7	4096	4096	1×1	$(1, 1)$	$(0, 0)$	ReLU
16	fc8	2622	4096	1×1	$(1, 1)$	$(0, 0)$	ReLU
Output	Prediction	2622	2622	1×1	$(1, 1)$	$(0, 0)$	*Softmax*

3.4   Temporal Analysis

The temporal analysis is a complex problem which allows establishing correlations between the features from different states in a time series. For our case, pain estimation in a sequence depends on the pain expressed in each of its frames. Then, each sequence records to the pain stimulus effect fade in timespans. Based on this assumption, offline metrics were developed to evaluate each series as a whole. Nonetheless, the offline metrics are subjective, unlike the PSPI metric, which is physiognomic. To overcome this problem, we design the subsequence generation algorithm considering the last frame's label as the sequence's label. Thereby, the PSPI metric is used to label the new series.

GRUs are an alternative method to LSTMs to buffer the gradient vanishing problem. Similar to LSTMs, GRUs use gates to control its internal memory (h') and shared memory (h) along with each unit. These gates are the update gate (z_k) and the reset gate (r_k). Vizcarra et al. [13] argue that sequential-processing efficiency depends on its size. Thus, GRU simplicity reduces training time and favor short sequences processing. Figure 3 shows GRU schema in detail. Update gate z_k controls the influence of the previous state h_{k-1} and the current entry x_k over h_k and h'_k (Eq. 1). Restart gate r_k defines the information must be reinforced from h_{k-1} and x_k in the unit memory h'_k (Eq. 2). Equation 3 shows

h'_k after r_k. $1 - z_k$ is used as an add-on to update h_{k-1} because z_k is close to 1. Finally, to compensate $1 - z_k$, z_k updates h'_k which adds new information to h_k (Eq. 4).

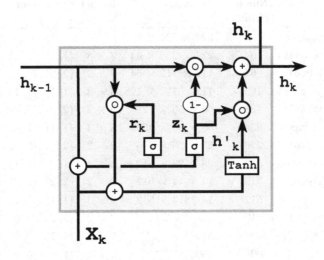

Fig. 3. Outline of a GRU. X_k and h_k are input and output of unit k, respectively. h_k is the shared memory that passes through all groups; h'_k is the internal memory; and, z_k and r_k are the update and reset gates, respectively. σ_g represents a sigmoid activation function while $tanh$ is a hyperbolic tangent; and, $\odot$ represents the Hadamard product.

$$z_k = \sigma_g(W_z X_k + U_z h_{k-1} + b_z) \tag{1}$$

$$r_k = \sigma_g(W_r X_k + U_r h_{k-1} + b_r) \tag{2}$$

$$h'_k = tanh(W_h X_k + U_h(h_{k-1} \odot r_k) + b_h) \tag{3}$$

$$h_k = h_{k-1} \odot (1 - z_k) + h'_k \odot z_k \tag{4}$$

4   Experiments and Results

In this section, we present the results of each stage; also, the dataset description. To run experiments, we use a PC with the following settings: 3,6 GHz Intel Core i7 processor, 16 GB 3000 MHz DDR4 memory and NVIDIA GTX 1080ti. For training and testing, we use the Pytorch framework.

4.1   Dataset Description

The dataset has nearly 200 videos from 129 participants, 63 men, and 66 women, self-identified with chronic shoulder pain. Healthy arm moves are labeled as painless while the facial expressions obtained with the damaged arm are quantified using the Facial Action Coding System (FACS) of pain. The PSPI metric measures pain intensity at frame level by a linear combination of most relevant AUs. Figure 4 shows some samples from the UNBC-McMaster database, while Table 3 presents the original data distribution per level. Besides, the dataset contains 66 facial landmarks per frame, which are calculated by an Active Appearance Model (AAM).

Table 3. Data distributions before and after balancing at both levels. The proposed policy for sequence balancing generates less data than frames balancing.

	PSPI score															
	0	1	2	3	4	5	6	7	8	9	10	11	12	13	14	15
Original samples	40029	2909	2351	1412	802	242	270	53	79	32	67	76	48	22	1	5
Total	48398															
Balanced frames	500	500	500	500	500	500	500	500	500	500	500	500	500	380	16	80
Total	6976															
Balanced sequences	300	300	300	300	300	300	300	300	300	300	300	300	300	300	16	80
Total	6976															

4.2   Analysis at Frames Level

For the frame-by-frame analysis, we fine-tune a pre-trained CNN due to pain classification is an end-to-end problem. The data split randomly into 80% as the training set and 20% as the testing set. Also, we use the one-subject-out strategy to measure the performance. Figure 5 presents the confusion matrix for the testing set, which is almost a diagonal matrix, although it has blocked at all levels. The best results are obtained in the best-represented levels, albeit data augmentation cushions this effect effectively. Table 4 summarizes all experiments carried out for pain recognition at frames level. The preprocessing and data augmentation stages have a highly significant contribution to the final results.

The results improve according to the processing complexity used; however, some levels show particular details, such as class 14, that has the least amount of data, so its representation is almost trivial. The camera perspective affects the sample representation due to the frontalization error increases between more occlusions exist. Table 5 shows the comparison of the result with the state-of-the-art in handcrafted features because most of those methods perform a frame-by-frame analysis.

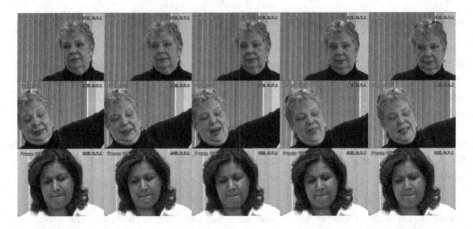

Fig. 4. Examples of some sequences cuts from the UNBC-McMaster Pain Shoulder Archive. First row: the painless patient. Second row: each frame has a PSPI = 2. Third row: each frame has a PSPI = 3. Face deviations, as well as perspective deformation, can be seen.

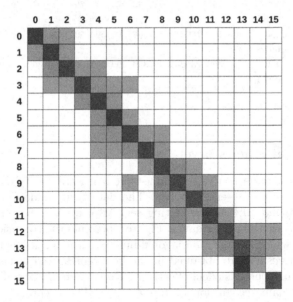

Fig. 5. Confusion matrix for 16-classes at frames level. The trend is mainly diagonal, which shows high precision.

4.3 Analysis at Sequences Level

Sequential analysis is a seq-to-end problem and has three key hyperparameters to tune: sequences resampling rate rr; sequences size ss; and, the number of recurrent layers nl. We can use the feature vectors from any of the fully-connected layers, although the fc6 layer has a higher dimension and implies a better facial representation. Feature vectors feed each GRU unit as inputs, and the last frame's label defines the sequence's label. Table 6 shows some results of pain recognition at sequence level considering the following set of hyperparameters: $rr = 3$, $ss = 15$ and $nl = 2$. Data augmentation enables some levels to overcome the lack of data while decreasing the precision gap between classes. Table 7 shows the state-of-the-art comparison including our results.

Table 4. The comparison of result for different processing stages during the frame-by-frame analysis. We test our model using downsampled data (Down), preprocessed data (Prep) and preprocessed augmented data (Prep-Aug).

	Frames level															
	0	1	2	3	4	5	6	7	8	9	10	11	12	13	14	15
Down	62.5	56.5	48.8	56.3	50.3	55.2	48.1	41.4	45.4	45.7	52.7	48.4	45.2	51.8	0	80
Average accuracy: 55.86%																
Prep	87.3	74.8	69.2	68.2	72.0	69.1	63.8	68.1	54.6	58.3	63.4	49.1	45.0	57.1	0	100
Average accuracy: 78.17%																
Prep Aug	91.2	85.6	78.6	83.1	82.5	85.1	83.2	81.1	78.4	73.9	72.4	84.1	74.3	69.9	**13.3**	76.2
Average accuracy: 80.44%																

Table 5. Comparison of metrics at frames level

	Metrics				
	MAE	MSE	PCC	ICC	ACC
Zhao et al. [15]	0.81	–	0.60	**0.56**	–
Florea et al. [2]	–	1.18	0.55	–	–
Kaltwang et al. [3]	–	1.39	0.59	0.50	–
Rathee et al. [10]	–	–	–	–	**0.96**
Our	**0.475**	**0.592**	**0.723**	0.52	0.80

Table 6. The comparison of results for different processing stages during the sequential analysis. We test our model using downsampled data (Down), preprocessed data (Prep) and preprocessed augmented data (Prep-Aug).

	Sequential level															
	0	1	2	3	4	5	6	7	8	9	10	11	12	13	14	15
Down	71.9	63.9	66.9	64.9	66.6	74.1	64.7	36.8	81.8	–	80.0	78.6	74.1	–	–	–
Average accuracy: 69.73%																
Prep	85.1	78.2	75.6	69.9	74.9	88.2	74.1	61.7	86.8	–	84.4	78.2	77.3	–	–	–
Average accuracy: 78.27%																
Prep Aug	94.0	86.8	75.1	83.4	86.7	89.3	88.2	87.1	85.4	70.2	82.2	79.2	80.3	72.3	62.8	87.2
Average accuracy: 84.54%																

Table 7. Comparison of metrics at sequences level

	Metrics				
	MAE	MSE	PCC	ICC	ACC
Zhou et al. [16]	–	1.54	0.65	–	–
Bellantonio et al. [6]	–	–	–	-	0.619
Rodriguez et al. [11]	0.5	0.74	**0.78**	0.45	–
Our	**0.487**	**0.615**	0.697	**0.60**	**0.84**

5 Conclusions and Future Works

The pain analysis is very different at frames level that in sequence level, both at the application and processing. The frame-by-frame analysis of pain is done using only the spatial information, instead of considering the temporal correlation. The number of pain levels and its distribution affects the results significantly. Hence, the more degrees of pain, the higher the difficulty in classification. However, most confusions occur in very-close levels because of the closeness of their facial descriptors; as a result of this, the confusion matrix is block-diagonal.

The results show that the preprocessing stages achieved to separate the facial features of pain from the spatial and identity elements, but they can still be improved, especially the frontalization step. Data augmentation allows weight each level result; hence, the average accuracy goes up. Finally, we overcome the-state-of-the-art metrics (accuracy, MAE, MSE, PCC, ICC) at both levels. In the future, we will analyze attention models to focus the learning process on the action units alongside visual interpretability tools.

References

1. Banerjee, S., et al.: To frontalize or not to frontalize: do we really need elaborate pre-processing to improve face recognition? In: 2018 IEEE Winter Conference on Applications of Computer Vision (WACV), pp. 20–29. IEEE (2018)
2. Florea, C., Florea, L., Vertan, C.: Learning pain from emotion: transferred hot data representation for pain intensity estimation. In: Agapito, L., Bronstein, M.M., Rother, C. (eds.) ECCV 2014. LNCS, vol. 8927, pp. 778–790. Springer, Cham (2015). https://doi.org/10.1007/978-3-319-16199-0_54
3. Kaltwang, S., Rudovic, O., Pantic, M.: Continuous pain intensity estimation from facial expressions. In: Bebis, G., et al. (eds.) ISVC 2012. LNCS, vol. 7432, pp. 368–377. Springer, Heidelberg (2012). https://doi.org/10.1007/978-3-642-33191-6_36
4. Lucey, P., et al.: Automatically detecting pain in video through facial action units. IEEE Trans. Syst. Man Cybern. Part B (Cybern.) 41(3), 664–674 (2011)
5. Lucey, P., Cohn, J.F., Prkachin, K.M., Solomon, P.E., Matthews, I.: Painful data: the UNBC-MCMaster shoulder pain expression archive database. In: 2011 IEEE International Conference on Automatic Face & Gesture Recognition and Workshops (FG 2011), pp. 57–64. IEEE (2011)

6. Bellantonio, M., et al.: Spatio-temporal pain recognition in CNN-based super-resolved facial images. In: Nasrollahi, K., et al. (eds.) FFER/VAAM 2016. LNCS, vol. 10165, pp. 151–162. Springer, Cham (2017). https://doi.org/10.1007/978-3-319-56687-0_13

7. Parkhi, O.M., Vedaldi, A., Zisserman, A., et al.: Deep face recognition. In: BMVC, vol. 1, p. 6 (2015)

8. Pedersen, H.: Learning appearance features for pain detection using the UNBC-McMaster shoulder pain expression archive database. In: Nalpantidis, L., Krüger, V., Eklundh, J.-O., Gasteratos, A. (eds.) ICVS 2015. LNCS, vol. 9163, pp. 128–136. Springer, Cham (2015). https://doi.org/10.1007/978-3-319-20904-3_12

9. Raffaeli, W., Arnaudo, E.: Pain as a disease: an overview. J. Pain Res. **10**, 2003 (2017)

10. Rathee, N., Ganotra, D.: A novel approach for pain intensity detection based on facial feature deformations. J. Vis. Commun. Image Represent. **33**, 247–254 (2015)

11. Rodriguez, P., et al.: Deep pain: exploiting long short-term memory networks for facial expression classification. IEEE Trans. Cybern. **99**, 1–11 (2017)

12. Souza, J.B.d., Grossmann, E., Perissinotti, D.M.N., Oliveira Junior, J.O.d., Fonseca, P.R.B.d., Posso, I.d.P.: Prevalence of chronic pain, treatments, perception, and interference on life activities: Brazilian population-based survey. Pain Res. Manage. **2017**, 1–9 (2017)

13. Vizcarra, G., Mauricio, A., Mauricio, L.: A deep learning approach for sentiment analysis in Spanish tweets. In: Kůrková, V., Manolopoulos, Y., Hammer, B., Iliadis, L., Maglogiannis, I. (eds.) ICANN 2018. LNCS, vol. 11141, pp. 622–629. Springer, Cham (2018). https://doi.org/10.1007/978-3-030-01424-7_61

14. Williamson, A., Hoggart, B.: Pain: a review of three commonly used pain rating scales. J. Clin. Nurs. **14**(7), 798–804 (2005)

15. Zhao, R., Gan, Q., Wang, S., Ji, Q.: Facial expression intensity estimation using ordinal information. In: Proceedings of the IEEE Conference on Computer Vision and Pattern Recognition, pp. 3466–3474 (2016)

16. Zhou, J., Hong, X., Su, F., Zhao, G.: Recurrent convolutional neural network regression for continuous pain intensity estimation in video. In: Proceedings of the IEEE Conference on Computer Vision and Pattern Recognition Workshops, pp. 84–92 (2016)

Detection of Non-small Cell Lung Cancer Adenocarcinoma Using Supervised Learning Algorithms Applied to Metabolomic Profiles

Diego Rondon-Soto[✉] and Paulo Vela-Anton[✉]

Department of Biomedical Informatics, Peruvian University Cayetano Heredia,
Lima, Peru
{diego.rondon,paulo.vela}@upch.pe

Abstract. Lung cancer is the most frequent and mortal of all types of cancer for both genders. Approximately 80% of the newly diagnosed lung cancers are non-small cell lung cancers. Early diagnosis improves the chances of survival. Machine learning allows us to process a considerable number of variables involved in this disease. Using metabolites as attributes for the analysis, we can discern lung cancer patients from healthy patients. In addition, machine learning algorithms reveal us which metabolites has a determining contribution in the classification. The objective of this study is to demonstrate the accuracy, sensitivity and specificity of a supervised learning algorithm to classify and predict non-small cell lung cancer, using concentration values found in the serum and plasma metabolome of afflicted and healthy humans. We obtained the dataset from the Metabolomics Work-bench repository, which contains 335 samples and 139 known metabolites detected. Of all the models applied, Random Forest Classifier obtained the highest accuracy. It can classify participants according to diagnosis with >75% accuracy in serum samples. Important serum metabolites for the classification included aspartic acid, fructose, and tocopherol alpha. Cystine, pyruvic acid and tocopherol alpha for plasma. The specified metabolites are strongly associated with this condition, and are potential biomarkers for the disease. By giving clues for an earlier diagnosis, this study remarkably contributes in the field of personalized medicine, and the appreciation of the biological processes of lung cancer.

Keywords: Lung cancer · Metabolomics · Machine-learning

1 Introduction

Lung cancer is the most common type of cancer in the world. During the 2018, it had the highest indicators for incidence and mortality (11.6% and 18.4% respectively) for both genders [1]. However, Non-Small Cell Lung Cancer (NSCLC), a type of epithelial lung cancer, is more dangerous and frequent in males than

© Springer Nature Switzerland AG 2020
J. A. Lossio-Ventura et al. (Eds.): SIMBig 2019, CCIS 1070, pp. 186–193, 2020.
https://doi.org/10.1007/978-3-030-46140-9_18

females [1]. For the year 2040, it is expected an increase in the incidence of 71.38% for both genders [1]. There are several methods for the diagnosis of lung cancer, such as X-rays. If this test does not clearly reveal an abnormal mass or nodule, clinicians may do an additional computed tomography (CT) [2]. Sputum cytology helps to detect tumor cells in the phlegm [3]. Biopsy is the gold-standard test for the detection of different types of cancers [4–6]. Depending on the method of tissue extraction, physicians may do a bronchoscopy, the introduction of tubular camera through the trachea into the lungs [7], or a mediatinoscopy, which needs a surgical incision at the base of the neck to extract sample of the lymph nodes [8]. Another method is needle biopsy, which consist of a needle through the chest cavity into the lungs guided by a clinician [9]. These diagnostic methods are effective, however, they require expensive instruments and specialized personnel. Metabolomics is the science that identifies and quantifies the total metabolites on the cell and extracellular environment. The metabolites are substances produced during the metabolism that give a functional reading of the physiological state of the body [10]. Consequently, we can elucidate what is happening in the organism along the tumorigenesis. The human metabolome is influenced by exogenous factors such as diet, drugs, physical activity and other environmental aspects [11,12], and by endogenous factors such as age, gender, IBM and disease [13,14]. Therefore, a metabolomics' approach is an efficient way for the early detection of certain types of diseases like osteoarthritis [15] and gestational diabetes [16]. Many studies about several types of cancer apply metabolomics to find potential biomarkers [17]. Computer science advances at hectic pace in our times; computers facilitate the collection and interpretation of data and results. During the last decades, computational tools have improved their skills to learn and predict. In the field of artificial intelligence, machine learning (ML) allows the computer to "learn" given patterns and then be able to recognize them. In this study, we test the capacity of prediction of different models of ML: Decision tree classifier (DTC), support vector machine (SVM), random forest classifier (RFC), K-nearest neighbors (KNN), and logistic regression (LR) [18–21]. Our purpose is to train an algorithm to discern lung cancer patients from healthy patients using their metabolomic profiles.

2   Data Collection

We collect the data from the Metabolomics Workbench Repository, a free access metabolomic databank [22]. The identification code of the project in the databank is PR000293. ST000368 and ST000369 are two independent case-control studies that build the whole information of the project. Both studies investigated NSCLC adenocarcinoma by the untargeted metabolomics approach using gas chromatography time-of-flight mass spectrometry to analyse the metabolome of serum and plasma samples. We use the data obtained from the serum and plasma results. The analysis included only the known metabolites from both groups. We selected only 139 metabolites as attributes. The data consist of 166 samples, 92 with cancer diagnosis and 74 controls in the serum group.

169 samples divided in 95 with cancer diagnosis and 74 controls in the plasma group. Figure 1 shows the workflow to collect and preprocess the raw data obtained.

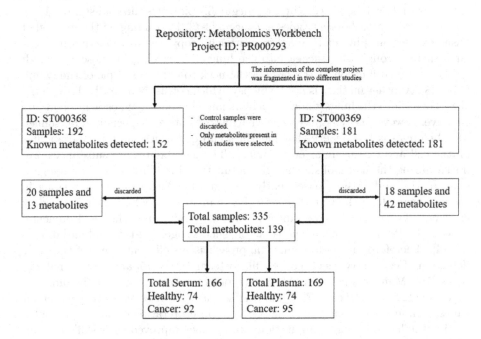

Fig. 1. Data extraction flow chart.

3   Method

The data was preprocessed as follows: non-existent values were replaced by the median of the pertinent input variable. The entire data set was normalized and 60 cancer patients and 60 healthy patients were chosen from each dataset to train the algorithm. The remaining samples were used for validation. Since this is a binary classification, we applied several supervised learning algorithms to find which had the best performance. RFC is a supervised classifier that assembles prediction results of a number of classification and regression trees, and it is commonly used in high variance data. In parallel to RFC analysis, we performed LR, SVM, KNN and DTC on the same datasets. All of them were performed with packages from Orange (Version 3.21). Parameters used in each method and platform are shown in Table 1.

For all the methods, the classification performance was evaluated by 5-fold cross validation, where 80% of the data were used for feature selection and model construction, and the area under the Receiver Operation Characteristic curve (AUROC), Classification Accuracy, Precision, Recall and F1 Score of the model

Table 1. Parameters used for each method in Orange platform.

Method	Parameters
Random Forest	Number of trees: 150 Maximal number of considered features: 5 Fixed random seed: 42 tree depth: unlimited Stop splitting nodes with maximum instances: 5
Logistic Regression	Regularization: Lasso (L1), $C = 1$
SVM	SVM type: SVM, $C = 1.0$, $\epsilon = 0.1$ Kernel: RBF, Numerical tolerance: 0.001 Iteration limit: 100
kNN	Number of neighbors: 5 Metric: Euclidean Weight: Uniform
Decision Tree	Pruning: at least two instances in leaves, at least five instances in internal nodes, maximum depth 100 Splitting: Stop splitting when majority reaches 95% (classification only) Binary trees: Yes
Ensemble Bagging	DecisionTreeRegressor(), n_estimators = 500, bootstrap = True, oob_score = True, random_state = 1, base estimator = Decision TreeRegressor

were evaluated based on the hold-off one fifth data. From the RFC we selected the features with the highest importance, representing the important metabolites associated with the diagnosis. For all the models, the 5-fold cross validation was replicated 300 times, to obtain a report of the average AUROC, Classification Accuracy, Precision, Recall and F1. We made a confusion matrix, and calculated true positive rate (TPR), true negative rate (TNR), kappa measures and Mathews correlation coefficient (MCC) only for RFC.

4   Results

Table 2 presents values of area under the curve (AUC), Classification accuracy (CA), F1 score (F1), precision (Pr) and Recall (Re). The method with the best performance appears in bold. Table 3 displays relevant values after validation with the test sets.

We obtained the highest values for CA and AUC by using the RFC algorithm (0.80 and 0.91 respectively), in comparison with other methods. RFC was the best method to diagnose cancer; it is not affected by outliers and missing values. The model also provides us which metabolites are the most relevant to separate cancer patients from controls. Fig. 2 and Fig. 3 show the concentration intervals of the pertinent metabolites from serum and plasma samples. In respect to serum, fructose indicated low concentration in a greater number of profiles with NSCLC adenocarcinoma in comparison with healthy profiles. Aspartic acid and tocopherol alpha registered more samples of all concentration. In plasma, cystine demonstrated low concentrations in cancer cases and high concentrations in healthy subjects. Pyruvic acid presents medium to high concentrations in cancer patients. Tocopherol alpha has an alternating behavior in relation to the concentration intervals and the state of the individual.

Table 2. Values of AUC, CA, F1, Pr and Re obtained by each method in Orange 3.21 platform.

Method	Serum					Plasma				
	AUC	CA	F1	Pr	Re	AUC	CA	F1	Pr	Re
RFC	**0.919**	**0.807**	**0.798**	**0.797**	**0.807**	**0.638**	**0.584**	**0.576**	**0.577**	**0.584**
LR	0.804	0.771	0.776	0.782	0.771	0.555	0.538	0.54	0.542	0.538
SVM	0.841	0.753	0.727	0.725	0.759	0.544	0.541	0.525	0.528	0.541
KNN	0.845	0.759	0.753	0.749	0.759	0.553	0.55	0.55	0.549	0.55
DTC	0.723	0.765	0.762	0.76	0.765	0.563	0.571	0.571	0.571	0.571
Ensemble Bagging	0.747	0.725	0.725	0.72	0.721	0.731	0.722	0.722	0.717	0.722

Table 3. TPR, TNR, MCC and Kappa Value for Random Forest Classifier.

Measure	Random Forest Classifier	
	Serum	Plasma
TPR	0.65	0.7
TNR	0.67	0.43
K Value	0.43	0.37
MCC	0.54	0.22

5   Discussion

In this study, we went through the best model to diagnose lung cancer in two datasets with metabolomic profiles from different tissue, conformed by 139 attributes each one. RFC proved to be the best method to discern between individuals with cancer and healthy in serum and plasma. The precision to separate afflicted patients from controls was higher in the serum group. The metabolites used for the classification differ between groups. In the case of serum samples, the algorithm found that fructose, tocopherol alpha, aspartic acid, acetophenone, beta alanine and citrulline were decisive components for the prediction. In the plasma group, the algorithm showed that cystine, pyruvic acid, alpha tocopherol, arabinose and lactamide are useful metabolites to detect NSCLC adenocarcinoma. Metabolites used by the algorithm have a biological relationship with the development of cancer and its proliferation. Previous studies shown that the increase in concentration of aspartic acid, citrulline and β-alanine in serum are important characteristics of NSCLC [23]. Fructose promotes lung adenocarcinoma, cell survival and metastasis through GLUT5 [24]. The administration of cystine in tumors in vivo increases the use of glutamine by the cancer cells [25]. Nishith K. et al propose lactamide as a biomarker found in plasma for lung cancer [26]. The algorithm identified alpha-tocopherol as an important metabolite for detection of NSCLC adenocarcinoma. Several studies observed an association between low concentrations of alpha tocopherol and risk of lung cancer [27]. This metabolite acts as an anti-oxidant, preventing DNA damage by free radicals. The results are significant for the treatments of patients due to its value in

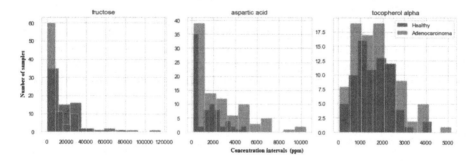

Fig. 2. Number of samples per concentration interval of the three principal metabolites found in the serum samples: fructose, aspartic acid and tocopherol alpha.

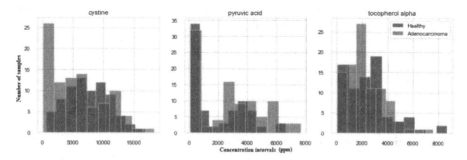

Fig. 3. Number of samples per concentration interval of the three principal metabolites found in the plasma samples: cysteine, pyruvic acid and tocopherol alpha.

a better understanding of the metabolic pathways and the physiopathology of NSCLC adenocarcinoma. The metabolites found are potential biomarkers that could help in the early diagnosis of this cancer in order to improve the survival rate of cancer patients. The first limitation we found was the collinearity of the data when training the models without preprocessing. An explanation for collinearity is that a metabolic pathway involves several metabolites. In this degree, the sub production or overproduction of one can affect the production of another, maintaining a direct proportionality between them [28]. Another drawback was the unbalanced datasets. It is common to find this characteristic in the biomedical field. It affected the recognition of patterns for the minority class, in this case, the healthy patients. It is necessary to increase the size of the datasets found in the metabolomics databases, in order to make a better analysis from a broader number of samples in this studies [29].

6   Conclusion

The RFC proved to be the errorless method to detect NSCLC adenocarcinoma when applied to the metabolomic profiles of serum and plasma. Detection accuracy was higher in serum (approximately 80%) compared to plasma (around 60%). We found that multiple metabolites are strongly associated with the detection of NSCLC adenocarcinoma. Fructose, alpha-tocopherol and aspartic acid were decisive attributes for detection in serum profiles, while cystine, pyruvic acid and alpha-tocopherol were relevant in plasma profiles. We recommend including variables such as age, sex and smokers condition to have a more reliable prediction.

References

1. Bray, F.: Global cancer statistics 2018. GLOBOCAN estimates of incidence and mortality worldwide for 36 cancers in 185 countries. CA Cancer J. Clin. **68**, 394–424 (2018)
2. Patil, S.A.: Chest X-ray features extraction for lung cancer classification. J. Sci. Ind. Res. (India) **69**(4), 271–277 (2010)
3. Ammanagi, A.: Sputum cytology in suspected cases of carcinoma of lung (Sputum cytology a poor mans bronchoscopy!). Lung India **29**(1), 19 (2012)
4. Salomon, L.: Prostate Biopsy in the staging of prostate cancer. Prostate Cancer Prostatic Dis **1**(2), 54–58 (1997)
5. Afyon, M.: Liver Biopsy is the gold standard at present, how about tomorrow? Viral Hepatitis J. **22**(2), 67–68 (2016)
6. This American Society of Breast Surgeons: Performance and Practice Guidelines for Excisional Breast Biopsy. American Society of Breast Surgeons, pp. 1–3 (2014)
7. Manthous, C.: Flexible bronchoscopy (Airway Endoscopy). Am. J. Respir. Crit. Care Med. **191**(9), P7 (2015)
8. Hoeijmakers, F.: Mediastinoscopy for staging of non-small cell lung cancer: surgical performance in The Netherlands. Ann. Thorac. Surg. **107**(4), 1024–1031 (2019)
9. Chojniak, R.: Computed tomography-guided transthoracic needle biopsy of pulmonary nodules. Radiología Brasileira **44**(3), 99–106 (2007)
10. Roessner, U.: What is metabolomics all about? Biotechniques **46**(5), 363–365 (2009)
11. Menni, C.: Targeted metabolomics profiles are strongly correlated with nutritional patterns in women. Metabolomics **9**(2), 506–514 (2013)
12. Floegel, A.: Linking diet, physical activity, cardiorespiratory fitness and obesity to serum metabolite networks: findings from a population-based study. Int. J. Obes. **38**(11), 1388–1396 (2014)
13. Auro, K.: A metabolic view on menopause and ageing. Nat. Commun. **5**, 1–11 (2014)
14. Kochhar, S.: Probing gender-specific metabolism differences in humans by nuclear magnetic resonance-based metabonomics. Anal. Biochem. **352**(2), 274–281 (2006)
15. de Sousa, E.B.: Metabolomics as a promising tool for early osteoarthritis diagnosis. Braz. J. Med. Biol. Res. **50**(11), 1–7 (2017)
16. Mao, X.: Metabolomics in gestational diabetes. Clin. Chim. Acta **475**, 116–127 (2017)
17. Palmnas, M.S.A.: The future of NMR Metabolomics in cancer therapy: towards personalizing treatment and developing targeted drugs? Metabolites **3**(2), 373–396 (2013)
18. Scholkopf, B., Smola, A.: Learning with Kernels: Support Vector Machines, Regularization, Optimization, and Beyond, 1st edn. MIT Press, Cambridge (2001)

19. Witten, I., Frank, E.: Data Mining: Practical Machine Learning Tools and Techniques, 4th edn. Morgan Kaufmann, Burlington (2016)
20. Cuperlovic-Culf, M.: Machine learning methods for analysis of metabolic data and metabolic pathway modeling. Metabolites **8**, 4 (2018)
21. McCullough, B.: On the accuracy of linear regression routines in some data mining packages. WIREs Data Min. Knowl. Discov. **9**, e1279 (2019)
22. Sud, M.: Metabolomics workbench: an international repository for metabolomics data and metadata, metabolite standards, protocols, tutorials and training, and analysis tools. Nucleic Acids Res. **44**(D1), D463–D470 (2015)
23. Klupczynska, A.: Evaluation of serum amino acid profiles utility in non-small cell lung cancer detection in Polish population. Lung Cancer **100**, 71–76 (2016)
24. Yuanyuan, W.: Fructose fuels lung adenocarcinoma through GLUT5. Cell Death Dis. **9**, 557 (2018)
25. Alexander, M.: Environmental cystine drives glutamine anaplerosis and sensitizes cancer cells to glutaminase inhibition. eLife **6**, e27713 (2017)
26. Nishith, K.: Serum and plasma metabolomic biomarkers for lung cancer. Bioinformation **13**(6), 202–208 (2017)
27. The ATBC Cancer Prevention Study Group: The alpha-tocopherol, beta-carotene lung cancer prevention study: design, methods, participant characteristics, and compliance. Ann Epidemiol **4**(1), 1–10 (1994)
28. Fani, R.: Origin and evolution of metabolic pathways. Phys. Life Rev. **6**(1), 23–52 (2009)
29. Calabrese, F.: Are there new biomarkers in tissue and liquid biopsies for the early detection of non-small cell lung cancer? J. Clin. Med. **8**, 414 (2019)

SCUT Sampling and Classification Algorithms to Identify Levels of Child Malnutrition

Juan Baraybar-Huambo and Juan Gutiérrez-Cárdenas[✉]

Universidad de Lima, Lima, Peru
jfbaraybar@outlook.com, jmgutier@ulima.edu.pe

Abstract. Child malnutrition results in millions of deaths every year. This condition is a potential problem in Peruvian society, especially in the rural parts of the country. The consequences of malnutrition range from physical limitations to declining mental performance and productivity for the individual. Government initiatives contribute to decreasing the causes of this disorder; however, these efforts are focused on long term solutions. The need for a fast and reliable way to detect these cases early on still exists. This paper compares classification techniques to determine which one is the most appropriate to classify cases of malnutrition. Neural networks and decision trees are used in combination with different sampling techniques, such as SCUT, SMOTE, random oversampling, random undersampling, and Tomek links. The models produced using oversampling techniques achieved high accuracies. Further, the models produced by the SCUT algorithm achieved high accuracies, preserved the behavior of the data and allowed for better representations of minority classes. The multilayer perceptron model that used the SCUT sampling techniques was chosen as the best model.

Keywords: Child malnutrition · Neural networks · Decision trees · Random forest · Sampling techniques

1 Introduction

Approximately 7.6 million children under five years old die every year. A third of these deaths are related to malnutrition [24]. In 2018, these deaths represented 45% of the total deaths and were mostly registered in low-income countries [25]. Some of the most common causes of this disease are nutritional deficiencies, low birth weights, the social and economic infrastructure, health, and sanitation services [17]. Malnutrition classification in children regards the detection and recognition of malnutrition, which could be directly related to diseases or illnesses with different causes. Malnutrition can result in deteriorated physical and mental conditions or even mortality. Malnutrition caused by illnesses can also be a recurrent factor in hospitalized children, but it could go undetected [16]. The consequences

© Springer Nature Switzerland AG 2020
J. A. Lossio-Ventura et al. (Eds.): SIMBig 2019, CCIS 1070, pp. 194–206, 2020.
https://doi.org/10.1007/978-3-030-46140-9_19

can be severe, including reduced physical and intellectual capacities, chronic diseases, infections, and higher mortality rates [11]. In 2017, malnutrition affected 12.9% of the children less than five years old [13]. As seen, in the last couple of decades, this number has decreased significantly. Public policies implemented by governments have reduced this percentage; however, the results are seen in the long term [12].

This paper proposes the use of classification algorithms in combination with sampling techniques to predict malnutrition in children less than 5 years old in Lima, Peru. Since we faced unbalanced data, we decided to use sampling techniques such as SCUT [1], SMOTE [7] and Tomek links [23], before applying our classification techniques, which include the following: neural networks, decision trees and random forests. We noticed that by using sampling techniques, our classification accuracies are equal to or greater than those in the reviewed literature at the moment of this present research. For example, for the case of SCUT with a multilayer perceptron, we obtained an accuracy of 97.03% compared with the 77% in the literature (young to older women dataset).

2 Related Work

2.1 Factors Associated with Malnutrition

Mariños-Anticona et al. [14] determined that some of the most important factors at the national level were extreme poverty, low birth weights, and mothers' education levels. Additionally, lacking access to sanitation services and anemia were most relevant at the regional level. Sobrino et al. [21] analyzed the trends of malnutrition and anemia in children less than five years old from 2000 to 2011. The most dominant factors were the education level of the mother, living in rural areas, poverty, and having two or more kids. Chinchay [8] classified the different factors using macrocategories and determined that education, the lack of alimentary policies, the nutritional status of the mother, lactation period duration, and access to sanitation services were the most important. Bullón and Astete [5] determined that the most relevant factors for malnutrition in children less than three years old were the mother's education and the growth and development controls. Additionally, most of the malnourished children were from rural areas of the country, while the minority came from the capital.

2.2 Use of Classification Algorithms to Predict Malnutrition

Thangamani and Sudha [22] used supervised learning techniques to classify family health data and predict malnutrition. The data of 254 children were used, and the multilayer perceptron and random forest models provided the same accuracy (77.17%). Yu et al. [28] used a neural network to predict anemia in patients and determine the number of red blood cell packages that were needed for blood transfusions. Their neural network obtained an accuracy of 77%. Yılmaz and Bozkurt [27] developed an application to diagnose iron deficiency anemia in women using neural networks. They used 2,660 blood samples and obtained good results with the implemented model (99.16% accuracy). Azarkhish et al. [3] implemented a neural network and an adaptive neuro-fuzzy inference system (ANFIS) to predict iron deficiency anemia in women. They used a sample of 203 registries, and the best results were obtained by the neural network (96.29% accuracy), which was followed by the ANFIS (90.74%) and a logistic regression model (62.96%). Çarkli Yavuz et al. [6] used the CSA-kNN, CSA-Gini, FNN, and PNN algorithms to determine anemia. They used 2,600 blood samples from women, and the results were as follows. CSA-Gini achieved the highest accuracy (98.73%), and it was followed by the FFN (98.5%), the PNN (97.48%), and, finally, the CSA-kNN (96%). Aruna and Sudha [2] proposed a decision tree to predict malnutrition in women between 18 to 50 years old. The tree with the best performance was the logical decision tree (accuracy of 92.6%), which was followed by the multilayer perceptron (77.17%), random forest (77.17%) and ID3 (68.5%). Park et al. [18] designed a model based on decision trees to detect the risk of malnutrition in the elderly. They used a dataset of 15,146 registries. The model with the best performance in the training phase was C5.0; however, CART had the best overall performance (78.1% training accuracy and 80.95% testing). Ye et al. [26] used decision tree analysis to determine the risk factors in a Chinese metropolis and compared the results to those of logistic regression models. They used data of 1091 children from six to twelve months old. They found that the classifier based on the decision tree was more accurate (88.8%) compared to logistic regression models (87.2%). Dalvi and Vernekar [9] used 500 images of red blood cells to compare the performance of different aggregation methods and classifiers in order to predict anemia. The stacking method that used a combination of the kNN and decision trees with naive Bayes was the best method (92.12% accuracy). Sanap et al. [20] compared a J48 decision tree, a C4.5 one, and a support vector machine based on SMO. In the analysis, 514 blood samples were used. The results showed that the decision tree achieved an accuracy of 97.67% in the validation stage and was better than the support vector machine (87.35%). Markos et al. [15] applied data mining techniques to extract hidden patterns that allowed for the prediction of the nutritional status of children less than 5 years old in Ethiopia. The classifier based on the PART pruned rule induction obtained the best result (accuracy of 97.8%) and was followed by naive Bayes (97.6%) and J48 (97.3%).

3   Background

3.1   The SCUT Sampling Technique

The SCUT sampling technique was proposed by Agrawal et al. [1] to solve imbalanced datasets that are used for classification. There have been multiple studies on improving classification performance for binary class datasets, but little research has been conducted on multiclass balancing.

This technique preserves the structure of the data without converting it, like other approaches tend to do (one versus one and one versus all). The technique uses the SMOTE sampling technique combined with clustered undersampling to address between-class and within-class imbalances. Additionally, the expectation maximization (EM) algorithm was used. This algorithm replaces dense clusters using a Gaussian probability distribution. The SCUT algorithm proceeds as follows. The dataset is split into n parts, where n is the number of classes. The mean m of the number of instances of all classes is calculated. For all the classes that have several instances less than m, oversampling is performed via SMOTE, thereby generating the necessary instances for the number of classes to be equal to m. However, if the number of instances of the class is greater than m, undersampling is performed using the EM technique to find the clusters and extract the same amount of instances of each. As a result, the behavior of these data is not lost, and the number of instances of the class is equal to m. Finally, all the classes are merged in order to obtain a new dataset, and all classes have m instances. The algorithm proposed by Agrawal et al. [1] is shown next:

Algorithm : SCUT
Input : Dataset D with n classes
Output : Dataset D' with all classes having m instances ,
where m is the mean number of instances of all classes .

Undersampling :

```
For each  D_i , i = 1, 2 ,. . ., n; where number of instances > m
        Cluster  D_i  using EM algorithm
            For each cluster  C_i , i = 1, 2 ,. . ., k
                    Randomly select instances from  C_i
                    Add selected instances to  C_i'
            End For
        C = φ
        For i = 1, 2 ,. . ., k
                C = C ∪ C_i'
        End For
        D_i' = C
End For
```

Oversampling :

```
For each  D_i , i = 1, 2 ,. . ., n; where number of instances < m
            Apply SMOTE on Di to get  D_i'
End For
For each Di , i = 1, 2 ,. . ., n; where number of instances = m
        D_i' = D_i
End For
D' = φ
```

For i = 1, 2, . . ., k
$$D = D' \cup D_i'$$
End For
Return D_i

4 Methodology

We used the information from a survey that was conducted by the National Institute of Informatics and Statistics in Lima, Peru named The Demographic and Family Health Survey 2017 (http://iinei.inei.gob.pe/microdatos/index.htm). Approximately 20.355 registries were selected with information about children less than five years old. The variables that were used to build the models were the weight, height, sex, and anemia level of the children and the educational level of the mother. Based on the growth curves that were defined by WHO (www.who.int/child-growth/standards), the nutritional status of children was defined. Additionally, the Body-Mass-Index (BMI = of every patient was calculated). The implementation was done using Python, the scikit-learn, and imbalanced learning libraries. We must mention that the WEKA data mining tool was used to visualize information about the dataset. Feature encoding and normalization were applied when necessary, and multiple sampling techniques were used. The algorithms that were used were SCUT, random oversampling, SMOTE, random undersampling, and Tomek links. To classify the data, we generated models based on the multilayer perceptron, classification and regression tree (CART) and random forest models. The accuracy, sensitivity, specificity, and precision were used to measure the performance of the developed models. A cross-validation test was performed to ensure the reliability of the results of the given models. It is valuable to mention that when we loaded our model in WEKA, we found that the dataset was heavily unbalanced, presenting with three classes (Cronica = chronic, no tiene = absent, and aguda/moderada = acute/moderate) with different numbers of instances, as shown in Fig. 1 and Fig. 2.

To solve these problems, we applied data preprocessing techniques. First, data normalization was applied to continuous features such as weight and height. After that, categorical variables were encoded to be used for the future implementation of the models. Finally, to solve the unbalanced classes, the SCUT algorithm was applied. We found three main classes: chronic malnutrition (15,448 patients), no malnutrition or absent (4,185 patients), and moderate malnutrition (772 patients). The means were calculated for the 6,785 registries for each class. SMOTE was applied for the minority classes. In the case of the majority class, the EM algorithm was applied. When we used the elbow method, we found that the optimal amount of clusters inside the majority class was nine, as shown in Fig. 3. The number of instances that were randomly extracted from each cluster was 1,746. Once all classes were under or oversampled, they were united to form the new dataset that was going to be used for the implementation of the models. After the pre-processing stage, for example, the same weight data that we used before were transformed, as shown in Fig. 4.

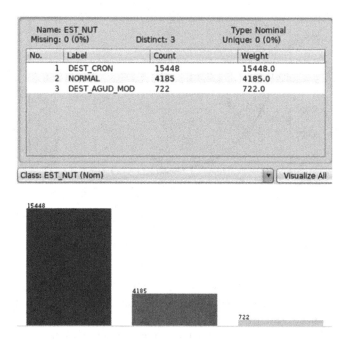

Fig. 1. Nutritional status imbalance.

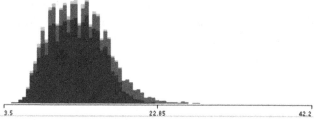

Fig. 2. Weight distribution.

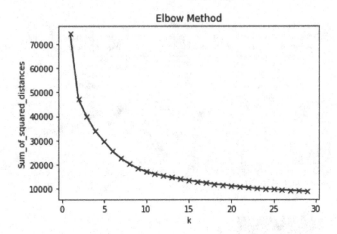

Fig. 3. Elbow method.

After the application of the SCUT algorithm, our balanced data classes are now as shown in Fig. 5. Additionally, after the application of SCUT, the dataset is entirely balanced and avoids under or overfitting problems. After that, we implemented classifiers based on multilayer perceptron (MLP), CART, and random forest. The hyper parameters for the MLP were a learning rate of 0.01, a hidden layer composed of 8 neurons, and a sigmoid activation function. The number of epochs was determined based on the decrease in the loss function. The optimal number of epochs was 250, as shown in Fig. 6. Iterations were performed to tune the hyperparameters from the different tree based-models for a set of various parameters. After that, we analyze the training and test set differences that were present and consider the accuracy of each model. Both the CART and random forest models used the entropy criterion for split selection. Additionally, the random forest model used 64 estimators.

5   Results

Based on the results shown in Table 1, the best combination is provided by the random oversampling technique and the Random forest or the CART algorithm. It is important to say that the undersampling techniques that were used did not converge for the MLP model with the given parameters. To validate our results, we used ten-fold cross-validation. The accuracies and standard deviations are shown in Table 2.

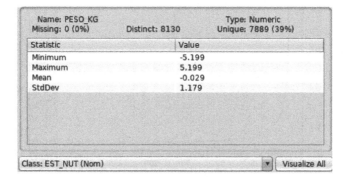

Fig. 4. Weight distribution after preprocessing.

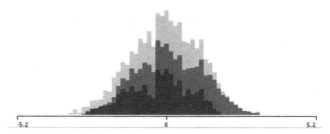

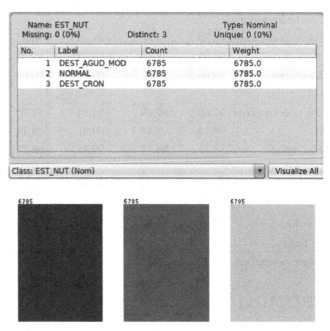

Fig. 5. Balanced classes after application.

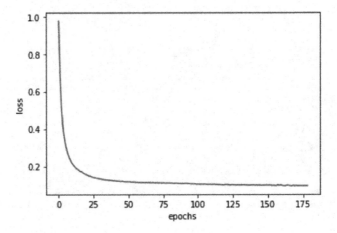

Fig. 6. Decrease in loss function by number of epochs.

Table 1. Performance of the classification algorithms using different sampling techniques in the testing phase.

SCUT				
	Accuracy	Sensitivity	Specificity	Precision
Multilayer perceptron	97.03	97.03	98.52	97.02
CART	95.62	95.61	97.81	95.62
Random forest	96.84	96.82	98.42	96.85
Random oversampling				
Multilayer perceptron	96.80	96.80	98.40	96.83
CART	99.05	99.05	99.53	99.06
Random forest	99.05	99.05	99.53	99.06
SMOTE				
Multilayer perceptron	97.69	97.69	98.84	97.71
CART	98.14	98.14	99.07	98.14
Random forest	98.77	98.77	99.38	98.77
Random subsampling				
Multilayer perceptron	94.10	94.00	97.05	94.16
CART	84.69	84.61	92.36	84.60
Random forest	85.98	85.85	92.96	86.44
Tomek links				
Multilayer perceptron	98.42	95.59	98.95	92.85
CART	96.99	89.52	97.56	90.59
Random forest	96.36	82.01	95.73	96.44

Table 2. Ten-fold cross-validation results

SCUT		
	Accuracy	Standard deviation
Multilayer perceptron	96.12	1.71
CART	95.22	4.66
Random forest	93.56	12.17
Random oversampling		
Multilayer perceptron	97.46	0.48
CART	99.39	0.22
Random forest	99.20	0.29
SMOTE		
Multilayer perceptron	97.54	0.73
CART	98.41	2.36
Random forest	98.62	1.94
Random subsampling		
Multilayer perceptron	94.73	3.38
CART	86.42	4.01
Random forest	88.27	3.68
Tomek links		
Multilayer perceptron	98.32	0.58
CART	97.17	0.73
Random forest	96.28	1.08

6 Discussion

As we can observe in Table 2, the Random forest algorithm or the CART decision tree, in combination with random oversampling, provided surprisingly high
results. However, we believe that these models may be overfitted because a
large number of instances were randomly generated by the sampling techniques
that were used. With respect to this overfitting, there is an agreement among
researchers that the technique that is mentioned above is prone to this behavior
due to the copying of the minority class samples [4]. The same deduction could
be applied to the results that are generated by the SMOTE algorithm. This is
because according to Agrawal et al.[1], SMOTE, even though can avoid overfitting, it could generate this phenomenon in the presence of a highly imbalanced
dataset [4].

However, the SCUT algorithm ensures the balance of the dataset and preserves the behavior of the original data. Methods such as SCUT are not prone
to overfitting, so it is safe to use in the presence of imbalanced data [4,29]. For
the above reasons, when using the SCUT algorithm, the best chosen model
to detect malnutrition was found to be the one that was generated by the

multilayer perceptron, achieving an accuracy of 96.12% with a low standard deviation (±1.71).

As a final test, we decided to compare our classification models by using the 5x2cv paired t-test proposed by Dietterich [10]. For this analysis, we select a threshold of $\alpha = 0.05$, and a null hypothesis that states that both classifiers compared perform equally well. According to the results shown in Table 3, we can reject the null hypothesis in the comparisons of MLP and CART, and MLP and Random forest; meaning that choosing the MLP as a leading model would be suitable for this problem.

Table 3. 5x2cv paired t-test results

	MLP/Decision tree	MLP/Random forest	Decision tree/Random forest
t-statistics	6.93373	5.31515	−1.94913
p-value	0.0009	0.0031	0.10879

Future work could be completed to test known combinations of techniques, such as SMOTE with Tomek links, that could perform well in the presence of skewed data [19] and to test the presented classifiers.

7   Conclusions

This research work explored the use of neural networks and decision trees combined with different sampling techniques to detect malnutrition in children from Lima, Peru. During the testing phase, the best result was from the random forest classifier and the random oversampling technique. A cross-validation test was performed, revealing that the SCUT algorithm as the best sampling technique overall, and the multilayer perceptron was one of the best classifiers. Future work could explore the use of other classification techniques, such as the naive Bayes and logistic regressions, to compare the overall performance of the presented classifiers and determine the best approach for detecting malnutrition in children less than five years old.

References

1. Agrawal, A., Viktor, H.L., Paquet, E.: SCUT: multi-class imbalanced data classification using SMOTE and cluster-based undersampling. In: Proceedings of the 7th International Joint Conference on Knowledge Discovery, Knowledge Engineering and Knowledge Management (IC3K), Lisbon, Portugal, vol. 1, pp. 226–234 (2015). https://doi.org/10.5220/0005595502260234
2. Aruna, S., Sudha, P.: An efficient identification of malnutrition with unsupervised classification using logical decision tree algorithm. Res. J. Pharm. Biol. Chem. Sci. 4(2), 365–373 (2016)

3. Azarkhish, I., Raoufy, M.R., Gharibzadeh, S.: Artificial intelligence models for predicting iron deficiency anemia and iron serum level based on accessible laboratory data. J. Med. Syst. **36**(3), 2057–2061 (2012). https://doi.org/10.1007/s10916-011-9668-3
4. Batista, G., Prati, R., Monard, C.: A study of the behavior of several methods for balancing machine learning training data. ACM SIGKDD Explor. Newsl. **6**(1), 20–29 (2004)
5. Bullón, C., Astete, R.: Determinantes de la Desnutrición Crónica de los Menores de Tres Años en las Regiones del Perú: Sub-Análisis de la Encuesta Endes 2000. Anales Científicos **77**(2), 249 (2016). https://doi.org/10.21704/ac.v77i2.636
6. Çarkli Yavuz, B., Karagül Yildiz, T., Yurtay, N., Pamuk, Z.: Comparison of K nearest neighbours and regression tree classifiers used with clonal selection algorithm to diagnose haematological diseases. AJIT-e Online Acad. J. Inf. Technol. **5**(16), 7 (2014)
7. Chawla, N.V., Bowyer, K.W., Hall, L.O., Kegelmeyer, W.P.: SMOTE: synthetic minority over-sampling technique. J. Artif. Intell. Res. JAIR **16**, 321–357 (2002)
8. Chinchay, K.: Costos Económicos en Salud de la Prevalencia de Desnutrición Crónica en Niños Menores de 5 Años en el Perú en el Período 2007–2013, Lima (2015)
9. Dalvi, P.T., Vernekar, N.: Anemia detection using ensemble learning techniques and statistical models. In: 2016 IEEE International Conference on Recent Trends in Electronics, Information & Communication Technology (RTEICT), pp. 1747–1751. IEEE (2016)
10. Dietterich, T.G.: Approximate statistical tests for comparing supervised classification learning algorithms. Neural Comput. **10**(7), 1895–1923 (1998). https://doi.org/10.1162/089976698300017197
11. Garcia, L.S., Jave, C.M., Cárdenas, M.E.H., López, P.A., Sánchez, G.B.: Pobreza y desnutrición infantil. PRISMA ONGD (2002)
12. Instituto Nacional de Estadística e Informática: Desnutrición Crónica Infantil en niñas y niños menores de cinco años disminuyó en 3.1 puntos porcentuales. https://gestion.pe/economia/disminuye-desnutricion-cronica-infantil-pais-revela-inei-114809. Accessed 6 July 2019
13. Instituto Nacional de Estadística e Informática: Desnutrición Crónica afectó al 12.2% de la población menor de cinco años de edad en el año 2018. https://www.inei.gob.pe/prensa/noticias/desnutricion-cronica-afecto-al-122-de-la-poblacion-menor-de-cinco-anos-de-edad-en-el-ano-2018-11370/. Accessed 6 July 2019
14. Mariños-Anticona, C., Chaña-Toledo, R., Medina-Osis, J., Vidal-Anzardo, M., Valdez-Huarcaya, W.: Determinantes sociales de la desnutrición cronica infantil en el Perú. Revista Peruana de Epidemiología **18**(1), 1–7 (2014)
15. Markos, Z., Doyore, F., Yifiru, M., Haidar, J.: Predicting under nutrition status of under-five children using data mining techniques: the case of 2011 Ethiopian Demographic and Health Survey. J. Health Med. Inform. **5**, 152 (2014)
16. Mehta, N.M., et al.: American Society for Parenteral and Enteral Nutrition Board of Directors. Defining pediatric malnutrition: a paradigm shift toward etiology-related definitions. J. Parenter. Enter. Nutr. JPEN **37**(4), 460–481 (2013)
17. Ministerio de Salud: Desnutrición Infantil Crónica y sus Determinantes de Riesgo, Lima, Perú, Marzo de 2010
18. Park, M., Kim, H., Kyung, S.: Knowledge discovery in a community data set: malnutrition among the elderly. Healthc. Inform. Res. **20**(1), 30–38 (2014). https://doi.org/10.4258/hir.2014.20.1.30

19. Prati, R.C., Batista, G.E., Monard, M.C.: Data mining with imbalanced class distributions: concepts and methods. Paper Presented at the IICAI (2009)
20. Sanap, S.A., Nagori, M., Kshirsagar, V.: Classification of anemia using data mining techniques. In: Panigrahi, B.K., Suganthan, P.N., Das, S., Satapathy, S.C. (eds.) SEMCCO 2011. LNCS, vol. 7077, pp. 113–121. Springer, Heidelberg (2011). https://doi.org/10.1007/978-3-642-27242-4_14
21. Sobrino, M., Gutiérrez, C., Cunha, A.J., Dávila, M., Alarcón, J.: Desnutrición infantil en menores de cinco años: tendencias y factores determinantes. Revista Panamericana de Salud Pública 35(2), 104–122 (2014)
22. Thangamani, D., Sudha, P.: Identification of malnutrition with use of supervised datamining techniques-decision trees and artificial neural networks. Int. J. Eng. Comput. Sci. 3(9), 8236–8241 (2014)
23. Tomek, I.: Two modifications of CNN. IEEE Trans. Syst. Man Commun. SMC–6(11), 769–772 (1976)
24. Wisbaum, W., et al.: DESNUTRICIÓN INFANTIL: Causas, consecuencias y estrategias para su prevención y tratamiento. Unicef, vol. 1, p. 21 (2011). https://old.unicef.es/sites/www.unicef.es/files/Dossierdesnutricion.pdf. Accessed 6 July 2019
25. World Health Organization: Malnutrición. https://www.who.int/es/news-room/fact-sheets/detail/malnutrition. Accessed 6 July 2019
26. Ye, F., et al.: Chi-squared automatic interaction detection decision tree analysis of risk factors for infant anemia in Beijing, China. Chin. Med. J. 129(10), 1193–1199 (2016). https://doi.org/10.4103/0366-6999.181955
27. Yilmaz, Z., Bozkurt, M.R.: Determination of women iron deficiency anemia using neural networks. J. Med. Syst. 36(5), 2941–2945 (2012). https://doi.org/10.1007/s10916-011-9772-4
28. Yu, C.H., Bhatnagar, M., Hogen, R., Mao, D., Farzindar, A., Dhanireddy, K.: Anemic status prediction using multilayer perceptron neural network model. In: 3rd Global Conference on Artificial Intelligence, GCAI, pp. 213–220 (2017)
29. Zheng, Z., Cai, Y., Li, Y.: Oversampling method for imbalanced classification. Comput. Inform. 34(5), 1017–1037 (2015)

Spanish Sentiment Analysis Using Universal Language Model Fine-Tuning: A Detailed Case of Study

Daniel Palomino$^{(\boxtimes)}$ [iD] and José Ochoa-Luna$^{(\boxtimes)}$ [iD]

Department of Computer Science, Universidad Católica San Pablo, Arequipa, Peru
{daniel.palomino.paucar,jeochoa}@ucsp.edu.pe

Abstract. Transfer Learning has emerged as one of the main image classification techniques for reusing architectures and weights trained on big datasets so as to improve small and specific classification tasks. In Natural Language Processing, a similar effect is obtained by reusing and transferring a language model. In particular, the Universal Language Fine-Tuning (ULMFiT) algorithm has proven to have an impressive performance on several English text classification tasks. In this paper, we aim at improving current state-of-the-art algorithms for Spanish Sentiment Analysis of short texts. In order to do so, we have adapted a ULMFiT algorithm to this setting. Experimental results on benchmark datasets show the potential of our approach.

Keywords: Sentiment Analysis · Natural Language Processing · Language Model · Transfer Learning

1 Introduction

Sentiment analysis allows us to perform an automated analysis of millions of reviews. With the rapid growth of Twitter, Facebook, Instagram and online review sites, sentiment analysis draws growing attention from both research and industry communities [16]. While it has been extensively researched since 2002 [13], it is still one of the most active research areas in Natural Language Processing (NLP), web mining and social media [25].

Polarity detection is the basic task in sentiment analysis [26]. This task allows us to determine whether a given opinion is positive, negative or neutral. Nowadays, this text classification problem is usually addressed by machine learning methods. Thus, training data and labelled reviews are used to define a classifier [13]. This machine learning approach relies heavily on feature engineering, although recent deep learning algorithms perform this task automatically [12].

In this paper we tackle the polarity detection task using a combined approach of Transfer Learning and Deep Learning. Moreover, we apply this approach on

This work was funded by CONCYTEC-FONDECYT under the call E041-01 [contract number 34-2018-FONDECYT-BM-IADT-SE].

© Springer Nature Switzerland AG 2020
J. A. Lossio-Ventura et al. (Eds.): SIMBig 2019, CCIS 1070, pp. 207–217, 2020.
https://doi.org/10.1007/978-3-030-46140-9_20

automated classification of Twitter messages in Spanish and its variant Peruvian Spanish (Spanish-PE). This is challenging because of the limited contextual information that Tweets normally contain.

Nowadays, in NLP it is common to use text input encoded as word embeddings such as Word2vec [18], Glove [22] and FastText [1]. When we reuse pretrained word embeddings in several tasks, we are indirectly employing a transfer learning scheme. In our work, we focus on another transfer learning approach: by pre-training a complete language model for a given language and then use it in text classification, we expect to transfer "knowledge" about the language that allows us to improve the task at hand. In this context, the Universal Language Fine-Tuning (ULMFiT) algorithm has proven to have an impressive performance on several English text classification tasks [10].

Our approach is based on ULMFiT within a deep learning architecture. This setup, which is novel for Spanish sentiment analysis, can be useful in several domains. Overall, our goal is to provide a general procedure that can be applied with less effort in other text classification works. The Deep Learning architecture used is composed by a Recurrent Neural Network [9] and a final dense layer. Those design choices allow us to obtain state-of-the-art results, in terms of F1, over the InterTASS 2017 dataset and competitive results over InterTASS 2018. These datasets were proposed in the TASS workshop at SEPLN. In the last seven years, this workshop has been the main source for Spanish sentiment analysis datasets and proposals [7,14,15].

The rest of the paper is organized as follows. In Sect. 2, related works are explained. Our methodology is presented in Sect. 3. Experiments and Results are described in Sect. 4. Finally, Sect. 5 concludes the paper and Sect. 6 shows some directions to future work.

2   Related Work

There is a plethora of related works regarding sentiment analysis. However, in this section we are only concerned with contributions for the Spanish language. Arguably one of the most complete Spanish sentiment analysis systems was proposed by Brooke et al. [2], which had a linguistically approach. Recent successful approaches for Spanish polarity classification have been mostly based on machine learning [6].

In the last seven years, the TASS at SEPLN Workshop has been the main source for Spanish sentiment analysis datasets and proposals [7,15]. Benchmarks for both the polarity detection and aspect-based sentiment analysis tasks have been proposed in several editions of this Workshop (Spanish Tweets have been emphasized).

Recently, deep learning approaches emerge as powerful computational models that discover intricate semantic representations of texts automatically from data without feature engineering. These approaches have improved the state-of-the-art in many sentiment analysis tasks including sentiment classification of sentences/documents, sentiment extraction and sentiment lexicon learning [25]. However, these results have been mostly obtained for the English Language.

Since 2015, there has been several Deep Learning architectures used for Spanish Twitter Sentiment Analysis, ranging from Multilayer Perceptron (MLP) [11], Recurrent Neural Networks (RNN) [8] and Convolutional Neural Networks (CNN) [24], to name a few. We refer to [19] in order to get an in-depth review of several deep Learning approaches for the Spanish language.

Our proposal is a deep learning approach but, unlike previous approaches, it uses a pre-trained language model to improve the polarity detection task. This setup is novel for the Spanish language.

3   Methodology

The process of Sentiment Analysis using Transfer Learning either of the type of Unsupervised, Inductive or Transductive as described by [21], comprises two steps:

1. The training of a first model on a source domain.
2. The reuse or adaptation of the first model within a second model for training a target domain.

In this sense, the classification task is divided in two sub-tasks, each one with its corresponding model and objective domain (also called dataset). Both of them are related by the weights that the first one provides to the second one when the transference occurs.

In this paper, the Inductive Transfer Learning approach will be used due to the source domain doesn't have labels whereas the target domain does. The source domain has a big dataset that can be used for training a model whose parameters will be after used for improving the training over the target domain. Moreover, in Sentiment Analysis, the source domain should encompass an exhaustive dataset and the target domain usually comprises a specific, small labelled dataset that allow us to classify sentences.

Recent works on text classification [10] highlight the use of an intermediate step which re-trains the first model using sentences of the target domain or a similar one. This process is called Fine-Tuning.

Thus, our pipeline is defined as follows:

– A first model corresponding to a Language Model (LM) which will be trained using sentences from the source domain so as to predict new words. The aim is to learn language essence and to extract deep information about sentence's composition.

  Also, due to the sequential nature of this sub-task [23], a good choice is resort to a Recurrent Neural Network (RNN) architecture. In particular, a suitable model is the weight-dropped AWD-LSTM [17]. AWD-LSTM is an architecture of stacked multi-layer LSTM which uses DropConnect on hidden-to-hidden weights so as to perform a recurrent regularization. In addition, a variation of the averaged stochastic gradient method, called NT-ASGD, is used.

– An intermediate step for fine-tuning which re-trains the parameters of the first model using the target domain.

- A second model which will be adapted from the first one, adding two layers for classification. This model takes advantage of the knowledge learned and will be trained on the labelled target domain.

This methodology to address general text classification problems [10] also proposes techniques such as gradual unfreezing, discriminative fine-tuning (Discr) and slanted triangular learning rate (STLR) for dealing with overfitting. The overall process is called: Universal Language Fine-Tuning (ULMFiT).

The initial pipeline is updated using ULMFiT, as shown in Fig. 1. The final three stages are:

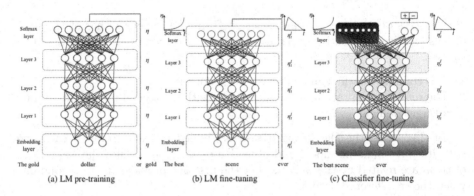

(a) LM pre-training   (b) LM fine-tuning   (c) Classifier fine-tuning

Fig. 1. Stages of updated pipeline using ULMFiT [10].

(a) The language model (LM) is trained on a general domain corpus to capture general features of the language in different layers.
(b) The full LM is fine-tuned on target task data using discriminative fine-tuning (Discr) and slanted triangular learning rates (STLR) to learn task-specific features.
(c) The classifier is fine-tuned on the target task using gradual unfreezing, Discr, and STLR to preserve low-level representations and adapt high-level ones (shaded: unfreezing stages; black: frozen).

This pipeline has shown to improve the state-of-the-art text classification on several datasets for English language. In this work, we have adopted the ULMFit pipeline for Sentiment Analysis on Spanish tweets datasets. Experiments show effectiveness of this approach for this task.

4   Experiments

A detailed setup about the hardware and software requirements for reproducing this paper are described in this section. In addition, we show hyperparameters tuned during experimentation by picking a learning rate that lead to convergence without overfitting and regularization.

4.1   Technical Resources

All experiments were carried out in Jupyter Notebooks running Python 3.6 kernel and Pytorch 0.3.1.

For a complete detail about dependencies used, the repository of the project is available at [20].

All models were trained on a Google Cloud VM with 2 vcpu, 13 GB of RAM and GPU K80 with 12 GB GDDR5.

4.2   Dataset

To train the entire model end to end, three data sources were used:

- **The General Language Model** was trained on a dump of the entire Spanish Wikipedia, from which only the top 100 million articles were kept and the vocabulary was limited to 60,000 tokens in accordance to the English setting approach.
- **The Specific Language Model** was trained on 136,286 unlabeled tweets for the Spanish language which were collected from Twitter using Tweepy (3.7.0).
- **The Specific Task Classifier** was trained on the dataset published by The Spanish Society for Natural Language Processing (SEPLN) for InterTASS (Task1) Competition 2017 [15] and InterTASS-PE (Task1/Sub-task 2) Competition 2018 [14].

The summarized data is shown in Tables 1a and b.

Table 1. Tweets distribution over InterTASS datasets.

(a) InterTASS 2017.

	Training	Development	Test
P	317	156	642
NEU	133	69	216
N	416	219	767
NONE	138	62	274
Total	1008	506	1899

(b) InterTASS-PE 2018.

	Training	Development	Test
P	231	95	430
NEU	166	61	367
N	242	106	472
NONE	316	238	159
Total	1000	500	1428

4.3   Pre-processing

Each corpus was pre-processed as follows:

- Twitter user references were replaced by the token "user_ref".
- URL references were replaced by the token "hyp_link".
- Hashtags comments were replaced by the token "hash_tag".
- Slang words were replaced by their formal equivalent, for example, "q" and "k" were replaced by the correct word "que".

- Interjections denoting laughter ("jaja", "jeje", "jiji", "jojo") were replaced by the token "risa_ja", "risa_je", "risa_ji", "risa_jo".
- Any other characters like "\n", "&lt", "&gt", "\xa0" were replaced by a space character.
- Redundant space character were removed.
- The text was converted to lowercase.

4.4 Architecture

The architecture for the General Language Model as well as the Specific Language Model [10] were comprised by a three-layer LSTM model with 1150 units in the hidden layer and embedding size of 400.

In the classifier, two linear blocks with batch normalization and dropout were added to the previous model. Rectified Linear Unit activations were used for the intermediate layer. A Softmax activation was used in the last layer.

4.5 Hyperparameters

For both training datasets, InterTASS (Task1) Competition 2017 [15] and InterTASS-PE (Task1/Sub-task 2) Competition 2018 [14], the hyperparameters are similar across all stages of the ULMFiT method.

The main hyperparameters shared for all models were:

- Backpropagation Through Time (BPTT): 70
- Weight Decay (WD): $1e-7$
- The batch size (BS) was limited by the available GPU memory.

Besides these parameters, the models used different configurations for the learning rate (LR), dropouts, cyclical learning rate (CLR) and slanted triangular learning rates (STLR). Additionally, gradient clipping (CLIP) was applied to the models.

Two configurations of dropout were used (see Table 2).

Table 2. Dropout configurations.

Dropout	ULMFiT [10]	AWD-LSTM [17]
Embedding dropout	0.02	0.10
Input dropout	0.25	0.60
Weight dropout	0.20	0.50
Hidden dropout	0.15	0.20
Output dropout	0.10	0.40

General Language Model. The hyperparameters for this model were directly transferred according Howard and Ruder work [10]. Scripts used were taken from the official Fastai repository [4] and ULMFiT repository [5].

Specific Language Model. A Learning Rate Finder (LRF) was used to determine suitable candidate learning rates, several values are depicted in Fig. 2.

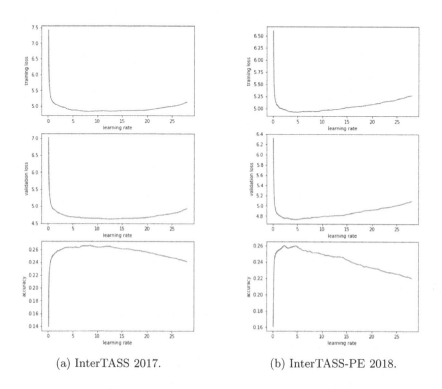

(a) InterTASS 2017.   (b) InterTASS-PE 2018.

Fig. 2. LRF for Specific Language Model.

With the information extracted from Fig. 2, a suitable learning rate (LR) was set to 12 for InterTASS 2017 and 5 for InterTASS-PE 2018 dataset.

Also, the gradient clipping (CLIP) was set to 0.92 and the dropout configuration (Table 2) was set to 0.8*ULMFiT.

Specific Task Classifier. Similar to the previous model, a learning rate finder (LRF) was used to determine suitable candidate learning rate (Fig. 3).

With the information extracted from Fig. 3, a suitable LR was set to $3e - 3$ for InterTASS 2017 and $2.5e - 3$ for InterTASS-PE 2018 dataset.

Also, the gradient clipping (CLIP) was set to 0.12 and the dropout configuration (Table 2) was set to 1.0*ULMFiT.

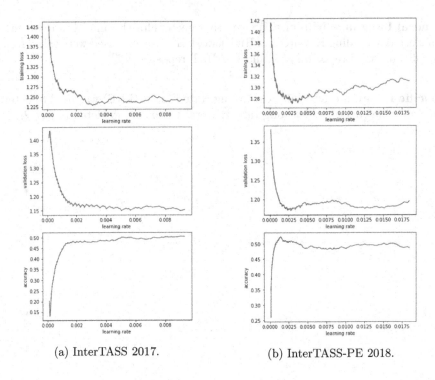

(a) InterTASS 2017.   (b) InterTASS-PE 2018.

Fig. 3. LRF for Specific Task Classifier

4.6 Results

The results for InterTASS (Task1) Competition 2017 [15] were better than
expected as shown in Table 3a, achieving the second best result, according to
M-F1 metric (the ELiRF-UPV team reached a M-F1 score of 0.493).

Table 3. Results over InterTASS Test datasets.

(a) InterTASS 2017.

Team	M-F1	Acc.
ELiRF-UPV-run1	0.493	0.607
Our proposal	**0.481**	**0.567**
RETUYT-svm_cnn	0.471	0.596
ELiRF-UPV-run3	0.466	0.597
ITAINNOVA-model4	0.461	0.476
jacerong-run-2	0.460	0.602
jacerong-run-1	0.459	0.608
INGEOTEC-evodag001	0.457	0.507
RETUYT-svm	0.457	0.583
tecnolengua-sentonly	0.456	0.582

(b) InterTASS-PE 2018.

Team	M-F1	Acc.
retuyt-cnn-pe-1	0.472	0.494
atalaya-pe-lr-50-2	0.462	0.451
retuyt-lstm-pe-2	0.443	0.488
retuyt-svm-pe-2	0.441	0.471
ingeotec-run1	0.439	0.447
elirf-intertass-pe-run-2	0.438	0.461
atalaya-mlp-sentiment	0.437	0.520
retuyt-svm-pe-1	0.437	0.474
Our proposal	**0.436**	**0.463**
elirf-intertass-pe-run-1	0.435	0.440

Likewise, results on InterTASS-PE (Task1/Sub-task 2) Competition 2018 [14], are shown in Table 3b. While they weren't the best, they are within the best nine results of the competition.

As depicted in Figs. 4a and b, the first 5 experiments on both benchmarks, during the fine-tuning process, used only train and development datasets for training the Specific Language Model which turned out poor results. Conversely, the next 5 experiments included tweets extracted using the Twitter API, as described in Subsect. 4.2. It is worth noting the improvement obtained after this addition.

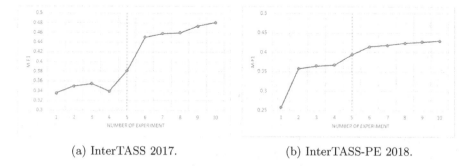

(a) InterTASS 2017.   (b) InterTASS-PE 2018.

Fig. 4. Evolution of results in test dataset for InterTASS competitions. The gray line indicates a before and after including the tweets extracted using the Twitter API for training the Specific Language Model.

In case of InterTASS-PE 2018, although there is a clear improvement, it is less impressive than InterTASS 2017. Perhaps, a tailored selection of Peruvian Tweets for training its Specific Language Model would have returned better results.

5 Conclusions

We have adapted ULMFit in order to perform sentiment analysis on Spanish Tweets—This approach is novel for this language. By using this setup we have achieved competitive results considering that the SEPLN datasets [14,15] are very challenging due to the limited contextual information provided.

Our best result (comparable to the state-of-the-art) was obtained on the InterTASS 2017 dataset. In contrast, we have experienced some difficulties using the InterTASS-PE 2018 dataset which is composed by Tweets in Spanish from the Peruvian dialect. These difficulties are due to the text used for training the Specific Language Model was mostly extracted from Castilian Spanish tweets. Thus, it is worth noting that training or fine-tuning the Specific Language Model with a relevant dataset has a positive impact in the classification task at hand.

6 Future Work

Recently, another transfer learning approach, called Bidirectional Embedding Representations from Transformers (BERT) [3], has emerged as the state-of-the-art in many NLP tasks. The use of this language model could enhance the performance of the pipeline presented in this work.

Also, there is a room for improvement if the language model approach is combined with data augmentation techniques. In this sense, new approaches for data augmentation such as the "BERT contextual augmentation" algorithm [27] could help us to improve our results if applied to our smalls datasets.

References

1. Bojanowski, P., Grave, E., Joulin, A., Mikolov, T.: Enriching word vectors with subword information. Trans. Assoc. Comput. Linguist. **5**, 135–146 (2017)
2. Brooke, J., Tofiloski, M., Taboada, M.: Cross-linguistic sentiment analysis: from English to Spanish. In: Proceedings of RANLP, vol. 2009, pp. 50–54 (2009)
3. Devlin, J., Chang, M., Lee, K., Toutanova, K.: BERT: pre-training of deep bidirectional transformers for language understanding. arXiv e-prints abs/1810.04805, arXiv:1810.04805, October 2018
4. Fastai: Fastai, May 2019. https://github.com/fastai/fastai
5. Fastai: ULMfit, May 2019. https://github.com/fastai/fastai/tree/master/courses/dl2/imdb_scripts
6. Garcia, M., Martinez, E., Villena, J., Garcia, J.: TASS 2015 – the evolution of the spanish opinion mining systems. Procesamiento de Lenguaje Nat. **56**, 33–40 (2016)
7. Garcia-Cumbreras, M.A., Villena-Roman, J., Martinez-Camara, E., Diaz-Galiano, M., Martin-Valdivia, T., Ureña Lopez, A.: Overview of TASS 2016. In: Proceedings of TASS 2016: Workshop on Sentiment Analysis at SEPLN, pp. 13–21 (2016)
8. Garcia-Vega, M., Montejo-Raez, A., Diaz-Galiano, M.C., Jimenez-Zafra, S.M.: Sinai in TASS 2017: tweet polarity classification integrating user information. In: Proceedings of TASS 2017: Workshop on Sentiment Analysis at SEPLN, pp. 91–96 (2017)
9. Graves, A.: Supervised Sequence Labelling with Recurrent Neural Networks. SCI, vol. 385. Springer, Berlin (2012). https://doi.org/10.1007/978-3-642-24797-2. https://cds.cern.ch/record/1503877
10. Howard, J., Ruder, S.: Universal language model fine-tuning for text classification. In: Proceedings of the 56th Annual Meeting of the Association for Computational Linguistics (Volume 1: Long Papers), pp. 328–339. Association for Computational Linguistics, Melbourne, July 2018. https://www.aclweb.org/anthology/P18-1031
11. Hurtado, L.F., Pla, F., Gonzalez, J.A.: EliRF-UPV at TASS 2017: sentiment analysis in twitter based on deep learning. In: Proceedings of TASS 2017: Workshop on Sentiment Analysis at SEPLN, pp. 29–34 (2017)
12. LeCun, Y., Bengio, Y., Hinton, G.: Deep learning. Nature **521**(7553), 436–444 (2015)
13. Liu, B.: Sentiment Analysis and Opinion Mining. Morgan and Claypool Publishers, San Rafael (2012)
14. Martinez-Camara, E., et al.: Overview of TASS 2018: opinions, health and emotions. In: Proceedings of TASS 2018: Workshop on Sentiment Analysis at SEPLN, pp. 13–27 (2018)

15. Martinez-Camara, E., Diaz-Galiano, M., Garcia-Cumbreras, M.A., Garcia-Vega, M., Villena-Roman, J.: Overview of TASS 2017. In: Proceedings of TASS 2017: Workshop on Sentiment Analysis at SEPLN, pp. 13–21 (2017)
16. McGlohon, M., Glance, N., Reiter, Z.: Star quality: aggregating reviews to rank products and merchants. In: Proceedings of Fourth International Conference on Weblogs and Social Media (ICWSM) (2010)
17. Merity, S., Keskar, N.S., Socher, R.: Regularizing and optimizing LSTM language models. CoRR abs/1708.02182, http://arxiv.org/abs/1708.02182 (2017)
18. Mikolov, T., Sutskever, I., Chen, K., Corrado, G.S., Dean, J.: Distributed representations of words and phrases and their compositionality. In: Burges, C.J.C., Bottou, L., Welling, M., Ghahramani, Z., Weinberger, K.Q. (eds.) Advances in Neural Information Processing Systems, vol. 26, pp. 3111–3119. Curran Associates, Inc. (2013). http://papers.nips.cc/paper/5021-distributed-representations-of-words-and-phrases-and-their-compositionality.pdf
19. Ochoa-Luna, J., Ari, D.: Deep neural network approaches for spanish sentiment analysis of short texts. In: Simari, G.R., Fermé, E., Gutiérrez Segura, F., Rodríguez Melquiades, J.A. (eds.) IBERAMIA 2018. LNCS (LNAI), vol. 11238, pp. 430–441. Springer, Cham (2018). https://doi.org/10.1007/978-3-030-03928-8_35
20. Palomino, D.: ULMFit implementation for TASS dataset evaluation, May 2019. https://github.com/dpalominop/ULMFit
21. Pan, S.J., Yang, Q.: A survey on transfer learning. IEEE Trans. Knowl. Data Eng. **22**(10), 1345–1359 (2010). https://doi.org/10.1109/TKDE.2009.191
22. Pennington, J., Socher, R., Manning, C.D.: Glove: global vectors for word representation. In: Empirical Methods in Natural Language Processing (EMNLP), pp. 1532–1543 (2014). http://www.aclweb.org/anthology/D14-1162
23. Rother, K., Rettberg, A.: ULMFit at GermEval-2018: a deep neural language model for the classification of hate speech in German tweets. In: Proceedings of the GermEval 2018 Workshop, pp. 113–119 (2018)
24. Segura-Bedmar, I., Quiros, A., Martínez, P.: Exploring convolutional neural networks for sentiment analysis of Spanish tweets. In: Proceedings of the 15th Conference of the European Chapter of the Association for Computational Linguistics: Volume 1, Long Papers, pp. 1014–1022. Association for Computational Linguistics (2017). http://aclweb.org/anthology/E17-1095
25. Tang, D., Wei, F., Qin, B., Yang, N., Liu, T., Zhou, M.: Sentiment embeddings with applications to sentiment analysis. IEEE Trans. Knowl. Data Eng. **28**(2), 496–509 (2016)
26. Turney, P.D.: Thumbs up or thumbs down?: Semantic orientation applied to unsupervised classification of reviews. In: Proceedings of the 40th Annual Meeting on Association for Computational Linguistics ACL 2002, pp. 417–424. Association for Computational Linguistics, Stroudsburg (2002). https://doi.org/10.3115/1073083.1073153
27. Wu, X., Lv, S., Zang, L., Han, J., Hu, S.: Conditional BERT contextual augmentation. CoRR abs/1812.06705, http://arxiv.org/abs/1812.06705 (2018)

Comparing Predictive Machine Learning Algorithms in Fit for Work Occupational Health Assessments

Saul Charapaqui-Miranda[1]([⊠])(iD), Katherine Arapa-Apaza[1]([⊠])(iD),
Moises Meza-Rodriguez[1]([⊠])(iD), and Horacio Chacon-Torrico[2]([⊠])(iD)

[1] Universidad Peruana Cayetano Heredia, Lima, Peru
{luis.charapaqui,katherine.arapa.a,moises.meza}@upch.pe
[2] Universidad Científica del Sur, Lima, Peru
hchaconto@ucientifica.edu.pe

Abstract. Some studies have tried to develop predictors for fitness for work (FFW). This study assessed the question whether factors used in the occupational medical practice could predict an individual fit for work result. We used a Peruvian occupational medical examination dataset of 33347 participants. We obtained a reduced dataset of 2650. It was split into two subsets, a training dataset and a test dataset. Using the training dataset, logistic regression, decision tree, random forest, and support vector machine models were fitted, and important variables of each model were identified. Hyperparameter tuning was an important part in these non-parametric models. Also, the Area Under the Curve (AUC) metric was used for Model Selection with a 5-fold cross validation approach. The results shows the Logistic Regression as the most powerful predictor (AUC = 60.44%, Accuracy = 68.05%). It is important to notice the best variables analysis in fitness to work evaluation by a Random Forest approach. Thus, the best model was logistic regression. This also reveals that the criteria associated with the workplace and occupational clinical criteria have a low level of prediction. Further studies should be done with imbalanced data to process bigger datasets, in consequence to obtain more robust models.

Keywords: Machine learning · Occupational health · Data science

1 Introduction

The role of Big data and machine learning in health care is an emerging area that enables the prediction and understanding of health determinants all along the continuum of care [1]. The main driver that has consistently facilitated its ever-increasing implementation is the ability to analyze huge volumes and varieties of structured and unstructured data not previously feasible. Epidemiological surveillance, signal detection and disease modelling are among the many examples researchers have developed [2]. Predictive algorithms are becoming transcendent in public health and epidemiology. Moreover, the transition from paper

© Springer Nature Switzerland AG 2020
J. A. Lossio-Ventura et al. (Eds.): SIMBig 2019, CCIS 1070, pp. 218–225, 2020.
https://doi.org/10.1007/978-3-030-46140-9_21

medical records to Electronic Health Records (EHR) has led to an exponential growth of data collection. As a result, big data provides wonderful opportunities for physicians, epidemiologists, and health policy experts to enhance data driven decisions that will ultimately affect health [3].

Occupational health aims to promote and maintain workers with the highest degree of physical, mental and social well-being. The prevention and control of occupational diseases has recently become a relevant problem. Globally, two million people die each year because of occupational accidents and work related injuries and illnesses [4,5]. Annually, work related diseases are estimated to occur in 160 million people, and approximately 58 million of them are to be absent during four workdays a year. Nonetheless, workplace accidents and injuries can be supervised and prevented with effective occupational health and safety policies [6]. The assessment of fitness for work (FFW) evaluates whether an individual is fit to execute his or her work tasks without risk to self or others [7]. These evaluation notes are documents issued by doctors that state the physical and mental fitness of an individual for work [8]. Thus, knowledge of both labour and health determinants is required to assess FFW evaluations. These documents are the cornerstone of occupational health assessment, for which patients have to surpass several general practitioners (GP), audiometric, ophthalmic, psychological and cardiological evaluations. Even when there are several guidelines and protocols for the FFW evaluation [9], reports indicate that physicians tend to rate heterogeneously these assessments [10].

The present study aims to develop and test machine learning models for FFW in an Peruvian urban occupational health medical evaluation dataset and compare their performance using several metrics. The best models obtained could be implemented in the occupational assessment as an aid for the physicians.

2   Methods

2.1   The Dataset

A comprehensive occupational health assessment raw dataset was prepared, analyzed and modelled for the algorithm construction. The data records come from an urban occupational medicine private clinic in Lima, Peru. Two excel files corresponding to the 2017 and 2018 data, with anonymized records and respective permissions, were physically delivered to the authors. This clinic provides occupational health consultations to third party businesses and firms that need their employees medically evaluated. Delivered data sets included all kind consultations and diagnosis registered during the aforementioned period. All recorded participants were adults between 18 and 88 years. The analyzed dataset is not publicly available.

Merged databases had 33,347 observations with 221 variables. Since the dataset included all types of consultations and results, most of the included fields contained missing values. Among the recorded categories in the dataset sociodemographics, consultation characteristics, laboratory and clinical evaluation fields were present. Most of the variables contained unstructured text including diagnosis, medical notes and recommendations. Only 14 variables contained no missing values and only 50 (22.6%) out of the 221 variables had 15% or less missing values.

2.2   Data Preparation

We choose work-entry occupational health assessment for the general model (n = 15,677) because the aim of this examination is to screen job applicants who may have an increase risk for occupational disease or injury in their work. Likewise many employers and other stakeholders believe that examinations prevent occupational diseases an sickness absence [11]. Considering an occupational health core evaluation that includes spirometric, muscle skeletal, audiometric and laboratory assessments, we dropped records that had missing values in these key components (see Fig. 1).

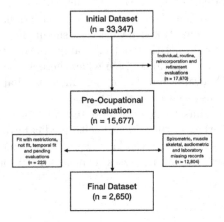

Fig. 1. Dataset preparation and record selection

2.3   Feature Selection

Even when the amount of variables provided in the dataset was large, the final features used for the predictive model was dramatically reduced. After we reduced the dataset we selected features that had no missing values. The final step used a heuristic feature selection where we kept the following variables:

"year", "id", "sex", "age", "job_type", "right_audiometry", "left_audiometry", "hearingloss_bilateral", "spirometry", "bmi", "hemoglobyn", "glucose", "bioq_cholesterol_total", "musculoskeletal"

Then for the purpose of the model construction we converted the columns that contained categorical values to numerical values by means of the One-hot-encoding algorithm.

2.4   The Outcome

A comprehensive systematic review of literature regarding FFW assessments described that less than 0.6% of the patients had their assessment as medical unfit for their duties [9]. Hence, we opted to select and filter (see Fig. 1) only two types of fitness for work status: Fit for work and Fit with recommendations. These dichotomization had a balanced distribution with 33.2% (n = 882) and 66.8% (n = 1768) fit and fit with recommendation results respectively.

2.5   Data Analysis

The correlation analysis between the data of the quantitative inputs (age, BMI, hemoglobin, glucose, cholesterol) showed no strong relationship between them. The final dataset (n = 2650) consisted on 14 features and the FFW outcome that is used to feed machine learning models such as Logistic Regression, Support Vector Machine (SVM), Random Forest and Decision Tree. We chose non-parametric methods because they presuppose less assumptions of the data distribution than parametric methods. We applied a 5-fold cross validation technique.

2.6   5-Fold Cross Validation

There are several methods to diagnose model performance but for our specific type of data, 5-fold cross validation was the best choice to avoid overlapping data processing and to diminish the pessimistic bias [12].

   We had to split the original dataset in training and test data to fit the model and evaluate the performance with unseen data, respectively. A good way to obtain a generalized model is to split it in training (70%) and testing (30%) portions. Subsequently, the training data is split in training and validation data according to the number of folds (k = 5) to evaluate the performance of each model. At last, the performance is processed by an arithmetic mean of each fold to obtain a robust metric such as Accuracy or Area Under the Curve (AUC) from the Receiver Operating Characteristics (ROC) curve to compare within models. The performance of non-parametric models depends on different parameter values called hyperparameters [13]. We can take advantage of cross validation to compare those with different methods. The hyperparameter tuning include C, kernel and gamma for Support Vector Classifier, max_depth, min_samples_split, min_samples_leaf d max_features for Decision Tree, Grid layout and Random layout in logistic regression.

3   Results

The final dataset was analyzed and processed using a Jupyter Notebook with Python version 3. The Scikit-Learn library provide machine learning models and the function to split the data in training and test data. The function Grid-SearchCV of the library Scikit-Learn saved us a lot of time on the model fitting and hyperparameter tuning. GridSearchCV contains these powerful features like k-fold cross-validation based on metrics evaluations and hyperparameter tuning. The best hyperparameters chosen are shown in the Table 1 [14]. Table 2 shows performance for each machine learning models based on accuracy and AUC-ROC, but the final evaluation for model selection to chose the best generalize model is the Logistic Regression with 60.44%. As it is shown graphically the AUC of each ROC curve in the Fig. 2.

Table 1. Machine learning models and its parameters

Machine learning model	Hyper parameters
Decision Tree	'max depth': 7, 'min samples split' = 350
Random Forest	'max depth': 7, estimators = 500, 'criterion': 'entropy'
Logistic Regression	'C': 1, 'penalty': l1
Support Vector Machine	'C': 10, 'gamma': 0.001

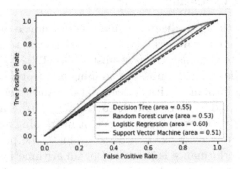

Fig. 2. ML models metrics evaluation

The hyper-parameter optimization of the models were selected by the Grid Search technique and the learning process was done by a k-fold cross validation approach [13]. Table 2 shows the Accuracy and the Area Under the Curve (AUC) evaluation metrics from the test dataset with its respective machine learning models. Those results are compared according to its metrics and the best model for FFW prediction is the Logistic Regression model.

Table 2. ML models metrics evaluation

Machine learning model	Accuracy	AUC-ROC
Decision Tree	67.30%	55.24%
Random Forest	66.92%	53.26%
Logistic Regression	68.05%	60.44%
Support Vector Machine	65.41%	51.04%

4 Discussion

In this case study, we used a non-parametric ensemble machine learning models for supervised learning [15]. As the problem in study was a binary classification, the outcome of this kind of models is a probability value between [0,1], then a threshold by the researcher is applied to determine the classification. The threshold value will affect greatly the final model results, so one option to surpass this kind of matter is to evaluate every threshold value in a curve called the ROC curve for every model. Evaluating ROC curve metrics has other benefits like knowing the rate of false positives and true positives. Finally, we measured the Area Under of the Curve (AUC) to quantitatively choose the best model.

We chose an evaluation metric such as the AUC because we add an evaluation metric like the area under the curve (classification problem where we depend on the probabilities of the models and a static threshold).

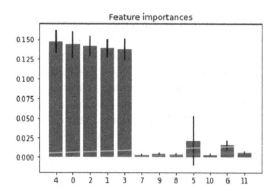

Fig. 3. ML models metrics evaluation

Fitness-to-work examination requires an objective assessment of the physical and mental health of employees. Occupational physicians have to be aware of the working conditions of characteristics of jobs, to ensure that the workers will not be a hazard to themselves or others. So there are factors like the working conditions and the health standards [16].

The variables we used to predict fitness for work were fit which meant the employee is able to perform the job without danger to self or others, without any restrictions. Likewise we considered fit subject to modifications, The reason why we used it is because we realized we had imbalanced data, (i.e. we had few unfit observations).

We analyzed occupational health work-entry assessments and their correlation with the variable fitness for work and found that it does not have a great predictive power. In future models this technique should be reassessed since this technique could encompass bias when large number of categorical and quantitative variables are found [17]. The Feature selection technique based on a Random Forest is very popular among data scientist practitioners, but the importance values of each variable are the bias when we use both numeric and categorical multi-class variables.

On the other hand, we analyzed determining health standards. We used the feature selection technique based on a random forest machine learning model technique, to predict the variables that have greater predictive power, finding that those with the highest predictive value were glucose, age, hemoglobin, BMI and cholesterol. As it is shown in Fig. 3. The binary classification problem has been done correctly according to the best practices in small datasets and avoiding overlapping data issues. Although, it would be interesting to use a larger datasets with imbalanced data since some useful techniques to approach this issue like re-sampling techniques currently exist [18].

5   Conclusion

We can conclude that the best model for binary classification problem for fitness for work was the logistic regression. Likewise the variables like occupation did not had a great predictive power but further studies can improve the feature selection techniques. We recommend to do further studies in larger data using re-sampling techniques in order to enhance the performance metrics as bioinformatics data is commonly imbalanced in classification problems and, also, implement other supervised learning models like Artificial Neural Network, Bayesian algorithms, Boosting approaches, etc.

No previous study to our knowledge has tested the prediction of FFW assessment in occupational health datasets. Since routinely occupational assessments are constantly required all around the globe, we think our models and results are relevant as a novel prediction approach to this matter and that could be further developed.

References

1. Murdoch, T.B., Detsky, A.S.: The inevitable application of big data to health care. JAMA 309(13), 1351–1352 (2013)
2. Kruse, C.S., Goswamy, R., Raval, Y.J., Marawi, S.: Challenges and opportunities of big data in health care: a systematic review. JMIR Med. Inf. 4(4), e38 (2016)

3. Char, D.S., Shah, N.H., Magnus, D.: Implementing machine learning in health care–addressing ethical challenges. New Engl. J. Med. **378**(11), 981 (2018)
4. Mona, G.G., Chimbari, M.J., Hongoro, C.: A systematic review on occupational hazards, injuries and diseases among police officers worldwide: policy implications for the South African police service. J. Occup. Med. Toxicol. **14**(1), 2 (2019)
5. Rommel, A., Varnaccia, G., Lahmann, N., Kottner, J., Kroll, L.E.: Occupational injuries in Germany: population-wide national survey data emphasize the importance of work-related factors. PLoS One **11**(2), e0148798 (2016)
6. Saifullah, H., Li, J.: Workplace employee's annual physical check-up and during hire on the job to increase health care-awareness perception to prevent diseases risk: a work for policy implementable option to global. Saf. Health Work **10**(2), 132–140 (2018)
7. Cox, R.A.F., Edwards, F., Palmer, K.: Fitness for Work: The Medical Aspects. Oxford University Press, Oxford (2000)
8. Coggon, D., Palmer, K.T.: Assessing fitness for work and writing a "fit note". BMJ **341**, c6305 (2010)
9. Serra, C., Rodriguez, M.C., Delclos, G.L., Plana, M., López, L.I.G., Benavides, F.G.: Criteria and methods used for the assessment of fitness for work: a systematic review. Occup. Environ. Med. **64**(5), 304–312 (2007)
10. Foley, M., Thorley, K., Van Hout, M.C.: Assessing fitness for work: GPs judgment making. Eur. J. Gen. Pract. **19**(4), 230–236 (2013)
11. Mahmud, N., et al.: Pre-employment examinations for preventing occupational injury and disease in workers. Cochrane Database Syst. Rev. (12), 1–46 (2010). https://doi.org/10.1002/14651858.CD008881. Article no. CD008881
12. Raschka, S.: Model evaluation, model selection, and algorithm selection in machine learning (2018)
13. Wong, J., Manderson, T., Abrahamowicz, M., Buckeridge, D.L., Tamblyn, R.: Can hyperparameter tuning improve the performance of a super learner? a case study. Epidemiol. (Cambridge, Mass.) **30**(4), 521 (2019)
14. Lee, J., Kim, H.R.: Prediction of return-to-original-work after an industrial accident using machine learning and comparison of techniques. J. Korean Med. Sci. **33**(19), 1–12 (2018)
15. Lindholm, A., Wahlström, N., Lindsten, F., Schön, T.B.: Supervised machine learning. http://www.it.uu.se/edu/course/homepage/sml/literature/lecture_notes.pdf. Accessed 31 May 2019
16. Cowell, J.: Guidelines for fitness-to-work examinations. CMAJ: Can. Med. Assoc. J. **135**(9), 985 (1986)
17. Zhou, Z., Hooker, G.: Unbiased measurement of feature importance in tree-based methods. arXiv preprint arXiv:1903.05179 (2019)
18. Konno, T., Iwazume, M.: Pseudo-feature generation for imbalanced data analysis in deep learning (2018)

Recognition of the Image of a Person, Based on Viola-Jones

Washington-Xavier Garcia-Quilachamin[1,2]([✉]), Luzmila Pro Concepción[1], Jorge Herrera-Tapia[2], and Richard José Salazar[2]

[1] Universidad Nacional Mayor San Marcos, Av. German Amezaga No. 375, Lima, Peru
profegarcia501@gmail.com
[2] Universidad Laica Eloy Alfaro de Manabí, Vía San Mateo, Manta, Ecuador

Abstract. In the field of image analysis, technological evolution is considered as an innovation through the application of algorithms in cameras for the detection and identification of objects and people, although these recognition tasks are complex for a computer. The general context of the application of the algorithms in the recognition of images is not known, therefore, the following research question is posed: What algorithm based on Viola-Jones allows the recognition of the image of a person? The objective of this investigation is to determine an algorithm based on Viola-Jones that allows to detect and identify the image of a person. This research was made through an algorithm comparison methodology, which allowed improving the recognition of a person's image pattern, based on the techniques and methods found in pattern recognition. The results obtained will serve as support for future studies, considering that the application of the Viola-Jones-based algorithm allowed the recognition and identification of a person's face in five different frontal perspectives, through a digital camera and was a fundamental basis to determine substantial improvements in the recognition of the image of a person.

Keywords: Algorithm detection · Viola-Jones algorithm · Person identification · Image recognition

1 Introduction

According to [1] pattern recognition systems are developed as part of a framework that allows continuous monitoring of human behavior in the area of assisted living, rehabilitation and entertainment, injury detection, sports, elderly care, energy efficiency lighting and surveillance in smart homes.

Within the contexts of technological evolution, there is the application of algorithms in cameras for the detection of objects, which is of great importance in development and innovation. There are several factors that motivate this research, being the optimization in the consumption of electric energy and the application for the safety of people among the most important.

In [2] object recognition is defined as the process of identifying a specific object, the class of objects in an image or video. Therefore, according to [3] this type of detection

© Springer Nature Switzerland AG 2020
J. A. Lossio-Ventura et al. (Eds.): SIMBig 2019, CCIS 1070, pp. 226–238, 2020.
https://doi.org/10.1007/978-3-030-46140-9_22

not only focuses on finding the kind of object to be detected, but also locating the extent of the object in an image.

From the study in the detection of objects, the innovation in the facial and people detection begins. According to [4] several researchers have developed methods and techniques to detect people in images, considering that the study of an effective method for the recognition of image patterns is continued.

The objective of this investigation is to determine an algorithm based on Viola-Jones that allows the re-knowledge of the image of a person, using a camera as video input. The methodology used is based on the analysis, comparison and verification of the algorithms found, allowing to identify the pattern of a person's image.

According to [5], the authors consider that facial recognition systems play a vital role in many applications, such as surveillance, biometrics and safety, for which the authors in [6] establish that the Viola-Jones algorithm is currently one of the most used to solve search problems of a person's face.

Recognition tasks according to [7] are considered complex for a computer because they have problems in the processes of object classification, border detection, movement tracking, etc. For this reason, there are different proposals for the recognition of objects, facial expressions, faces and human patterns. Thus, the authors argue in [8–10], that facial recognition methods based on local characteristics use information from the face (eyes, nose, mouth) to globally identify a person.

This research is based on the Viola-Jones algorithm and according to [11], the authors consider it as an integrated method for facial detection, monitoring and estimation of head postures. This article describes the research on the development and implementation of the algorithm that allows the identification of the face of a person and as a proposal for the result of this investigation, the algorithm that allows the recognition of the image of a person is detailed.

This document is organized as follows, in Sect. 2 the related works on our research are described. Section 3 focuses on the description of the methodology used in relation to the analysis of the algorithms found, considering the proposed question. Section 4 describes the results obtained and the development of the algorithm for the recognition of a person's face. Section 5 details the proposal that describes the algorithm for the recognition of a person's image. Finally, the conclusions of this investigation are presented.

2 Related Works

2.1 Background

The recognition works for images of human being have been proposed by several authors. Considering [6], they state that the Viola-Jones algorithm was created to look for the image of a person's face in a visible range as a radiation pattern and motivated by Viola, who considers in [12], that the selection of characteristics is achieved through a modification of the Ada-boost procedure and basic Haar functions. According to [13] the authors proposed a static vector image where the value of the vector at each point is a function of the motion properties in the spatial location, corresponding to a sequence of images represented in two templates with values for the recognition of the human being.

For the authors of [14] the recognition of different types of human activities such as running, limping, jumping, among others, has long been a subject of study in biomechanics, kinesiology, psychophysics and physical medicine. Due to the importance of this topic, from the research for the recognition of the different activities mentioned, other research topics arise, such as the recognition of colored object images and facials of a person.

There are various systems to perform facial recognition, according to [15] the most common is to include an enrollment phaser, during which images of the users' face are taken and used to create a template that is stored in a database (gallery images). Thus, the technology used in the recognition of patterns in people is related to the facial emotions of movement of the human pupil, according to [16] it is of great importance considering that the movement of the human eye is a rich source of information on behavior and human intention. There are studies that are based on the recognition of the face and objects of different shapes and colors, considering [17] the authors explain that the facial recognition of a person arises due to a wide range of real-life applications; for this reason, several face recognition algorithms have been developed through the years, in addition, algorithms were used in different branches of science that were adapted under the same concept to find the most effective. The authors of [18] consider that there are several ways to distinguish a person from another person: the face, the fingerprint, the gait and the iris are among the biometric properties, which are widely used for the recognition of people.

It is important to know that for now facial recognition is the main focus due to the inexpensive implementation and the non-intrusive nature of image acquisition, which is possible without the active participation of a subject. Therefore, there is no algorithm and model that is considered effective for the recognition of patterns in the detection of people. The following are the models, the techniques that served as the basis for this research for the development and application of the algorithm.

2.2 Models

In the review of related works, three models were found that allow the recognition of patterns, which are considered in this investigation.

(a) Hidden Markov (HMM): It is a statistical model to describe the characteristics of a stochastic process, according to [19] it is considered important in computational methods for the classification of human physical activity and the application in pattern recognition.

(b) Convolutional Neural Network (dCNN): It is a model that is used to classify images, group them by similarity and perform recognition of objects within scenes. The authors of [20] argue that this method allows a set of data to be formed and tagged with attributes. It is based on algorithms that can identify faces, people, traffic signs, tumors and aspects of visual data. This Convolutional Neural Network (dCNN) model can be implemented with Matlab and is available at Neural Network Toolbox™.

(c) Support Vector Machines (SVM): It is an algorithm model associated with learning that analyzes the data used for classification and backward analysis, as [21] assigns data from one or another category, making it a non-probabilistic binary linear classifier, this being a system of nonlinear human recognition, which effectively updates the classification parameters when a new framework is presented and classified. This method was first used in a pioneering document about the history of artificial vision [22]. Thus, Navneet Dalal and Bill Triggs introduced the characteristics of the Oriented Gradient Histogram (HOG) in 2005.

Of all the models, the SVM was chosen to be fully implemented in Matlab, because in real time it detects people not included in an upright position. In addition, this model is related to classification and regression problems; this will be used in our research through the algorithms described.

The SVM model is used to perform recognition of people in a real application [21], and with the criteria of the authors of [6], the implementation of the Viola-Jones algorithm allowed us to obtain in an integral way the representation of the original image frame of a person minimizing the amount and time of necessary calculations.

2.3 Techniques

Table 1 shows the techniques found and used by the recognition models described in item 2.2. According to [11], the Viola-Jones technique in some cases does not detect faces.

Table 1. Techniques found in recognition models

Techniques	HMM	dCNN	SVM	Ref.
Recognizes face images	x		x	[20, 23]
Recognizes images of objects		x	x	[20]
Effective monitoring and control in recognition	x		x	[21, 24]
Captures the image at an angle of 0° to 90°	x		x	[20, 23]
Captures the image at an angle of 90° to 180°			x	[23]
Captures the image at an angle of 180° to 270°			x	[21]
Captures the image at an angle of 270° to 360°	x		x	[20, 21]
Captures the image in a span of 1 to 5 min	x	x	x	[24–26]
Captures the image at a distance of 5 m			x	[25]
Detection of false objects and false faces	x	x	x	[25–27]
It does not capture the image having a lot of light on the place	x	x	x	[25–27]

2.4 Algorithms Found

Based on the research work carried out, Table 2 shows the algorithms that allow the recognition of an image with their advantages and disadvantages.

Table 2. Recognition Algorithms.

Algorithm	Description	Advantages	Disadvantages	Ref.
MCMC (Markov chain Monte Carlo)	Algorithm based on Hidden Markov's model. Applied to the HMM model, it is used for the recognition of human activities	Set of latent movements that are selectively shared between multiple trajectories and between different activities, they are learned efficiently by the MCMC algorithm	It has several limitations, for example the assumption of independence	[24]
WSMTAL (Weakly Supervised Multi-Type Attribute Learning)	Algorithm based on the Convolutional Neural Network (dCNN) model. It considers contextual signals and progressively increases accuracy using a limited number of people tagged data	Divides human attributes into multiple types, where each one contains several incompatible attributes and only one of them can be positive	Convolutional Neural Network (dCNN) does not need more training on target data sets. It is not so accurate	[20]
Viola-Jones	This algorithm is based on a series of weak classifiers called Haar-like-feactures that can be calculated efficiently from an integral image	This algorithm stands out for its low computational cost since it allows to be used in real time	Occlusion is a problem for this algorithm since it could not detect efficiently	[6, 28, 29]
EigenFaces	The EigenFaces algorithm is a facial recognition method based on the analysis component approaches	Evaluates images of size 23 × 28 pixels in an order to compare interpolarization	It is not yet coupled with (SVM) Support vector machine and (ANN) Artificial Neural Network	[30, 31]
Adaboost	Adaboost is a boosting algorithm presented by Freund and Sachapire in the generation of online learning	Used to select features, and train classifiers. This procedure dramatically increases the speed of the detector	Takes weak classifiers, calls them multiple times each time with different distribution over X	[28, 32]

2.5 Viola-Jones

The purpose of this investigation is to determine an algorithm based on Viola-Jones that allows to detect and identify the image of a person and their respective mathematical Eq. (1). Whereas this work is motivated in the detection of faces. According to [28] the detection of faces on real-time video on which the calculation of the integral image is based.

$$I(x, y) = \sum\nolimits_{xi<x,yi<y} i(x', y') \tag{1}$$

Where (x, y) is the integral image calculated in pixels, (x', y') is the original image. Using the integral image, any sum of a rectangular area ABCD can be calculated efficiently, (2):

$$\sum\nolimits_{(x,y)\in ABCD} i(x', y') = I(D) + I(A) - I(B) - I(C) \tag{2}$$

3   Methodology

3.1   Search Criteria

For the development of the proposed objective, the following question is asked: What algorithm based on Viola-Jones allows the recognition of the image of a person? which is considered as a criterion for the search of algorithms that allow to identify the pattern of recognition of the image of a person. The research was carried out through the search for information in several scientific repositories, using criteria such as:

(a)   Recognition of the pattern of the image of an object.
(b)   Algorithm for the recognition of the image of a person's face.
(c)   Recognition of the pattern of the image of an object AND Algorithm for the recognition of the image of a person's face.
(d)   Algorithm for the recognition of the image of a person's face patterns AND of the pattern of the image of an object.

Table 3. Results obtained from scientific repositories

Source	Elegible studies	Relevant studies	Main studies	%
ACM Digital Library	5936	20	11	22,92%
IEEE Xplore	305	34	6	12,50%
Science Direct	1042	92	18	37,50%
Springer	2840	38	13	27,08%
Total	10123	184	48	100,00%

In Table 3, 10123 articles related to the criteria are shown as a result of the search, of which 48 main articles based on pattern recognition research were considered. These were classified into models and techniques.

3.2 Framework of Work

The purpose of our research is to determine an algorithm that allows us to recognize the image of a person, so a framework was developed, in which the processes are described through the flowchart shown in Fig. 1.

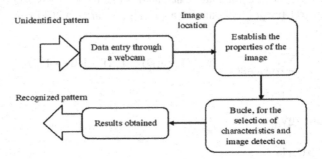

Fig. 1. Flowchart for image recognition

The hardware used to complement the improvement of the algorithms was a computer with 1.70 GHz CPU, Intel ® Core™ i3-4005U processor, RAM 4.00 GB, Windows 10 64-bit operating system, TOSHIBA Web-HD camera and as software used Matlab 2017b.

4 Results

Considering the objective of our investigation and the question, what algorithm based on Viola-Jones allows the recognition of the image of a person?. Algorithm 1 was found, described as a reference in this study and that through different tests and checks allowed us to obtain the algorithms listed in this document as a result.

4.1 Representation of Algorithm 1

As a result of our investigation, algorithm 1 was found, which was considered as a reference in this study for the respective verifications, development and application of the other algorithms.

4.2 Development of Algorithm 2

As a result of the research and respective tests, using Support Vector Machines to create real-time classifiers and pattern recognition in Matlab, Algorithm 2 was developed.

The improvement of Algorithm 2, applied in facial detection, was developed in five scenarios, using Matlab 2017b.

Algorithm 1: Reference

```
Data: image, detector people, imqdetec, imshow, frame, bboxes, f
image=vision.detectorpeople ( );
obj=imaq.VideoDevice ( );
set (obj);
    while (true)
        frame=step(obj);
        bboxes=step (faceDetector,frame);
        Imqdetect=insertObjectAnnotation(frame, ,bboxes,);
        imshow(Imqdetec)
        exit of imshow
        f=findobj();
    end
end
```

---

(1) Scenario 1. A person's face is detected through the webcam in real time.
(2) Scenario 2. The algorithm and through a webcam detects the face of a person 50 cm away. See Fig. 2.
(3) Scenario 3. The algorithm was improved so that the real-time video lasts until the user decides to stop or end the detection.
(4) Scenario 4. The algorithm detects the face of a person in a video in real time at a distance of 0.90 m. See Fig. 3.
(5) Scenario 5. The algorithm detects the face of a person in 5 different frontal positions with an angle of 15° Left-Right, within a real-time video, see Fig. 4.

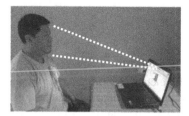

Fig. 2. Detection a 0.90 m

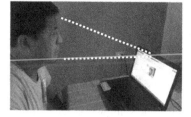

Fig. 3. Detection a 0.50 m

At the end of scenario 5, the facial recognition of a person in 5 different frontal perspectives with an angle of 15° in identification and left lateral detection and similarly 15° in identification and right lateral detection was obtained; See Fig. 4, which shows the capture of the face in a rectangle (frame).

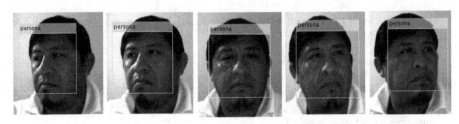

Fig. 4. Facial recognition of a person

Next, Algorithm 2 is represented, which allowed us to recognize a person's face, basing its design on Viola-Jones.

Algorithm 2: Facial recognition of a person

```
Data: video, faceDetector, obj, frame, bboxes, IFaces
faceDetector=vision.CascadeObjectDetector;
obj=imaq.VideoDevice;
  set (obj);
  figure ();
  while (true)
     frame=step(obj);
     bboxes=step (faceDetector,frame);
     IFaces=insertObjectAnnotation(frame, ,bboxes,);
     imshow(IFaces)
     f=findobj();
     if (isempty(f))
        close (gcf)
        break
     end
     pause (0.05)
  end
```

---

5   Proposal

Considering the analysis of algorithm 1 and development of Algorithm 2, it was possible to determine the proposed algorithm, which answers the question: What algorithm based on Viola-Jones allows the recognition of the image of a person?

The algorithm has been developed with an innovative factor for the detection of the image of a person in real time through a webcam, which is done through an infinite loop that captures each frame that the camera receives and through a command in Matlab, the person is detected. See Fig. 5.

For validation, the instructions are used to determine if an image exists using the face gradient histogram (HOG), classified in the support vector machine (SVM). The proposed algorithm was developed based on tests performed in two cases, considering the height of the person, see Table 4 and Table 5 respectively. The data obtained in the

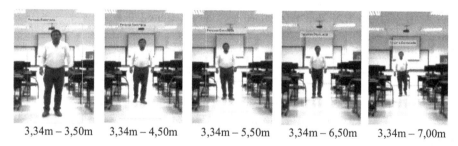

| 3,34m – 3,50m | 3,34m – 4,50m | 3,34m – 5,50m | 3,34m – 6,50m | 3,34m – 7,00m |

Fig. 5. Recognition of imagen of a person

recognition of the image of a person are related based on the parameters: height of the person, distance range, camera height, detection angle, recognition of the person.

Table 4. Data obtained, first case stature 1.65 m

Camera height (m)	Range distance (m)	Person stature (m)	Detection angle	Person recognition
0.88	0.0–3.34	1.65	28°	False
0.88	3.34–3.50	1.65	26°	True
0.88	3.34–4.00	1.65	24°	True
0.88	3.34–4.50	1.65	22°	True
0.88	3.34–5.00	1.65	20°	True
0.88	3,34–5.50	1.65	18°	True
0.88	3.34–6.00	1.65	16°	True
0.88	3.34–6.50	1.65	14°	True
0.88	3.34–7.00	1.65	12°	True

In Table 4, the data obtained allow us to determine how true the recognition of the image of a person is in a distance range of 3.34 m to 7.00 m considering the height of the person as 1.65 m and an angle of detection of 28°. The recognition of the image of the person in a range of 0 m to 3.34 m was also determined as False.

Table 5 shows the data obtained and described as True in relation to the recognition of the image of a person in a distance range of 4.28 m to 7.00 m considering the height of the person as 1.78 m and an angle of 16° for the detection. The recognition of the image of the person in a range of 0 m to 4.28 m will also be considered False.

5.1 Representation of the Proposed Algorithm

Next, the proposed algorithm for the recognition of the image of a person is described.

Table 5. Data obtained, second case stature 1.78 m

Camera height (m)	Range distance (m)	Person stature (m)	Detection angle	Person recognition
0.88	0.00–4.28	1.78	16°	False
0.88	4.28–4.50	1.78	14°	True
0.88	4.28–5.00	1.78	12°	True
0.88	4.28–5.50	1.78	10°	True
0.88	4.28–6.00	1.78	8°	True
0.88	4.28–6.50	1.78	6°	True
0.88	4.28–7.00	1.78	4°	True

Algorithm 3: Recognition of imagen of a person

```
Datos: video, peopleDetector, obj, frame, bboxes
peopleDetector = vision.PeopleDetector( )
obj=imaq.VideoDevice ( )
   set (obj);
   figure ( );
   while (true)
        frame=step(obj);
        bboxes=step (peopleDetector,frame);
        obj_p=insertObjectAnnotation (frame,bboxes);
        imshow(obj_p,)
        f=findobj( );
        pause (0.05)
   end
   release (obj)
end
```

---

6 Conclusion

After the respective investigations, tests and analysis of the algorithms studied, through their implementation and verification using the Image Acquisition Tool and Computer Vision System Toolbox tools of Matlab R2017b, its effectiveness and efficiency in pattern recognition could be verified. The functionality of the algorithm found and considered as a reference to distinguish and differentiate in recognition patterns was also verified. Finally, with the implementation of the second algorithm, it allowed us to detect and recognize the image of a person's face in 5 different frontal perspectives with an angle of 15° at a distance between 0.50 m to 0.90 m.

These analyzes were fundamental for the development and implementation of the proposed algorithm that allows answering the question and describing as true the recognition of the image a person based on Viola-Jones in a range of 3.34 m to 7.00 m and 4.28 m to 7.00 m, considering the angle of detection and the height of the person. Recognition in the range of 0 m to 3.34 m and 0 m to 4.28 m is considered false.

Data obtained as a result of the application of the proposed algorithm and the parameters considered for the validation in the detection of the image of a person are described, in which every 0.50 m increment was established as distances its analysis, which allowed to substantiate that the greater the distance, the smaller the angle in the detection, thus it was determined 7.00 m to be the final distance in the two cases considered for the analysis of the algorithm.

The results obtained in both cases, taking into account the height of a person, allow validating the algorithm to recognize a person in an established range and contribute to future research in performing a faster, simpler and less complex detection.

References

1. Nweke, H.F., Teh, Y.W., Al-garadi, M.A., Alo, U.R.: Deep learning algorithms for human activity recognition using mobile and wearable sensor networks: state of the art and research challenges. Expert Syst. Appl. **105**, 233–261 (2018)
2. Mathworks: Image Category Classification Using Bag of Features (2016)
3. Sinhal, K.: Object Detection using Deep Learning for advanced users (2017)
4. Santos, M.Y., et al.: A big data analytics architecture for Industry 4.0. In: Rocha, Á., Correia, A.M., Adeli, H., Reis, L.P., Costanzo, S. (eds.) WorldCIST 2017. AISC, vol. 570, pp. 175–184. Springer, Cham (2017). https://doi.org/10.1007/978-3-319-56538-5_19
5. Matai, J., Irturk, A., Kastner, R.: Design and implementation of an FPGA-based real-time face recognition system. In: Proceedings of IEEE International Symposium on Field-Programmable Custom Computing Machines, FCCM 2011, pp. 97–100 (2011)
6. Alyushin, M.V., Lyubshov, A.A.: The Viola-Jones algorithm performance enhancement for a person's face recognition task in the long-wave infrared radiation range. In: Proceedings of 2018 IEEE Conference of Russian Young Researchers in Electrical and Electronic Engineering, ElConRus 2018, pp. 1813–1816 (2018)
7. Lin, X.J., Wu, Q.X., Wang, X., Zhuo, Z.Q., Zhang, G.R.: People recognition in multi-cameras using the visual color processing mechanism. Neurocomputing **188**, 71–81 (2016)
8. Singh, A.K., Nandi, G.C.: Face recognition using facial symmetry, pp. 550–554 (2012)
9. Çarıkçı, M., Özen, F.: A face recognition system based on Eigenfaces method. Procedia Technol. **1**, 118–123 (2012)
10. Singh, K.R., Zaveri, M.A., Raghuwanshi, M.M.: Face identification under uncontrolled environment with LGFSV face representation technique. Open Comput. Sci. **3**(3), 129–148 (2013)
11. Murphy, T.M., Broussard, R., Schultz, R., Rakvic, R., Ngo, H.: Face detection with a Viola-Jones based hybrid network. IET Biomet. **6**(3), 200–210 (2016)
12. Viola, P., Jones, M.: Robust real-time face detection. In: Proceedings of Eighth IEEE International Conference on Computer Vision, ICCV 2001, vol. 2, pp. 747–747 (2001)
13. Bobick, A.F., Davis, J.W.: The recognition of human movement using temporal templates. IEEE Trans. Pattern Anal. Mach. Intell. **23**(3), 257–267 (2001)
14. Benabdelkader, C., Cutler, R., Nanda, H., Davis, L.: EigenGait : motion-based recognition of people using image self-similarity, pp. 284–294 (2001)
15. Bourlai, T., Cukic, B.: Multi-spectral face recognition: identification of people in difficult environments. In: ISI 2012 - 2012 IEEE International Conference on Intelligence and Security Informatics, pp. 196–201 (2012)
16. Jang, Y.M., Mallipeddi, R., Lee, S., Kwak, H.W., Lee, M.: Human intention recognition based on eyeball movement pattern and pupil size variation. Neurocomputing **128**, 421–432 (2014)

17. Liţă, L., Pelican, E.: A low-rank tensor-based algorithm for face recognition. Appl. Math. Model. **39**(3–4), 1266–1274 (2015)

18. Kamaruzaman, F., Shafie, A.A.: Recognizing faces with normalized local Gabor features and spiking neuron patterns. Pattern Recognit. **53**, 102–115 (2016)

19. Baca, A.: Methods for recognition and classification of human motion patterns – a prerequisite for intelligent devices assisting in sports activities, vol. 45, no. 2. IFAC (2012)

20. Su, C., Zhang, S., Xing, J., Gao, W., Tian, Q.: Multi-type attributes driven multi-camera person re-identification. Pattern Recognit. **75**, 77–89 (2018)

21. Lu, Y., Boukharouba, K., Boonært, J., Fleury, A., Lecœuche, S.: Application of an incremental SVM algorithm for on-line human recognition from video surveillance using texture and color features. Neurocomputing **126**, 132–140 (2014)

22. Kleinsmith, M.: Zero to hero: guide to object detection using deep learning: faster R-CNN, YOLO, SSD (2016). http://cv-tricks.com/object-detection/faster-r-cnn-yolo-ssd/

23. Huang, B.: FaceNet: a unified embedding for facerecognition and clustering, pp. 1–2 (2017)

24. Sun, S., Zhao, J., Gao, Q.: Modeling and recognizing human trajectories with beta process hidden Markov models. Pattern Recognit. **48**(8), 2407–2417 (2015)

25. Dastidar, J.G., Basak, P., Hota, S., Athar, A.: SVM based method for identification and recognition of faces by using feature distances. In: Bhateja, V., Coello Coello, Carlos A., Satapathy, S.C., Pattnaik, P.K. (eds.) Intelligent Engineering Informatics. AISC, vol. 695, pp. 29–37. Springer, Singapore (2018). https://doi.org/10.1007/978-981-10-7566-7_4

26. Zhang, Q.: Multiple Objects Detection based on Improved Faster R- CNN, pp. 99–103 (2016)

27. Sagayam, K.M., Hemanth, D.J.: Computers in Industry ABC algorithm based optimization of 1-D hidden Markov model for hand gesture recognition applications. Comput. Ind. **99**(March), 313–323 (2018)

28. Klette, R.: Concise Computer Vision (2014)

29. Tavallali, P., Yazdi, M., Khosravi, M.R.: An efficient training procedure for Viola-Jones face detector. In: Proceedings - 2017 International Conference on Computational Science and Computational Intelligence, CSCI 2017, pp. 828–831 (2018)

30. Rodavia, M.R.D., Bernaldez, O., Ballita, M.: Web and mobile based facial recognition security system using Eigenfaces algorithm. In: Proceedings of 2016 IEEE International Conference on Teaching, Assessment, and Learning for Engineering, TALE 2016, December, pp. 86–92 (2017)

31. Julián, F.G.C., Reyes, M.V., Sánchez, A.L., Ríos, C.A.J.: Reconocimiento Facial Por El Método De Eigenfaces. Pist. Educ. **127**(04), 66–81 (2017)

32. Febrero, P.: Adaboost con aplicación a detección de caras mediante el algoritmo de Viola-Jones Néstor Paz Febrero de 2009 (2009)

A Place to Go: Locating Damaged Regions After Natural Disasters Through Mobile Phone Data

Galo Castillo-López$^{(\boxtimes)}$, María-Belén Guaranda, Fabricio Layedra,
and Carmen Vaca

Facultad de Ingeniería en Electricidad y Computación,
Escuela Superior Politécnica del Litoral (ESPOL), Guayaquil, Ecuador
{gadacast,mguarand,fblayedr,cvaca}@fiec.espol.edu.ec

Abstract. Large scale natural disasters involve budgetary problems for governments even when local and foreign humanitarian aid is available. Prioritizing investment requires near real time information about the impact of the hazard in different locations. However, such information is not available through sensors or other devices specially in developing countries that do not have such infrastructure. A rich source of information is the data resulting from mobile phones activity that citizens in affected areas start using as soon as it becomes available post-disaster. In this work, we exploit such source of information to conduct different analyses in order to infer the affected zones in the Ecuadorian province of Manabí, after the 2016 earthquake, with epicenter in the same province. We propose a series of features to characterize a geographic area, as granular as a canton, after a natural disaster and label its level of damage using mobile phone data. Our methods result in a classifier based on the K-Nearest Neighbors algorithm to detect affected zones with a 75% of accuracy. We compared our results with official data published two months after the disaster.

Keywords: Mobile phones activity · Spatio-temporal analysis · Disaster management

1 Introduction

Natural disasters are unpredictable issues that worldwide governments need to face with a rising trend, each year. The United Nations [25], the World Bank [4,13] and others [3,15,16] have stated the importance of defining more effective ways of disaster management to overcome the consequences of the catastrophe in a time-fashioned way.

Large scale natural disasters involve budgetary problems for governments [5] even when local and foreign cash donations are available. Donations must be invested in a broad geographical area since extreme disasters usually affect a large number of neighboring zones. Prioritizing investment requires near real

© Springer Nature Switzerland AG 2020
J. A. Lossio-Ventura et al. (Eds.): SIMBig 2019, CCIS 1070, pp. 239–251, 2020.
https://doi.org/10.1007/978-3-030-46140-9_23

time information about the impact of the hazard in different locations [26]. Such information is not available through sensors or other devices specially in developing countries that do not have such infrastructure. Moreover, it has been observed that for disasters such as earthquakes, the relation between the country's income and damage is inverse, the less developed the country, the more damage will suffer [17]. In other words, people in developing countries will be more vulnerable. A rich source of information is the data resulting from mobile phone activity that citizens in affected areas start using as soon as they become available after the disaster, hours in some cases. We exploit such source of information in this work to conduct different analyses in order to infer the affected zones after the earthquake that took place in the Ecuadorian province of Manabi on April 16th, 2016. We characterize each of the cantons of Manabi using:

1. Network analysis applied to the towers the individuals who conduct mobile activity are connected to.
2. Temporal analysis to observe how the rythms of activity change after the disaster and;
3. Geographical analysis to propose the *Visitor Diversity Index*, an index based on the different towers involved in the mobile phone events generated by people located in a given area.

Using the aforementioned analyses we propose as our main contribution a classifier based on K-Nearest Neighbors to detect affected zones with a 75% of accuracy. We do so exploiting information of mobile phones activity generated in the following 24 h after the disaster and the results are compared with data collected through surveys and published officially two months after the disaster.

This article is organized as follows: Sect. 2 presents previous work regarding disaster management. Section 3 describes the datasets we analyze to build our model. Section 4 describes the metrics we propose as features to characterize each canton in the affected area, as well as the proposed classifier. Section 5 shows the results and discussion. Finally, Sect. 6 presents the conclusions and future work.

2   Related Work

There are many studies focused on defining new ways to deal with natural disasters, such as: wildfires [21], earthquakes [1,10,20,26], floods [7,9,22,24], typhoons [27], among others [8,18,28]. These previous works have proposed a wide variety of solutions going from tools to improve the management of the situation, to data analytics from different sources to extract insights to boost the decision-making process during the disaster.

In the field of disaster management tools, the concept of crowd-sourcing was introduced by the Global Earth Observation Catastrophe Assessment Network (GEO-CAN), formed to facilitate a rapid damage assessment after the 12 January 2010 Haiti earthquake [11]. The tool assisted in quantifying building damage through crowd-sourced imagery with spatial resolutions of up to 50 cm captured by DigitalGlobe, GeoEye, ImageCat and the Rochester Institute of Technology.

Another approach was presented by MacEachren et al. [19] with SensePlace2, a map-based web application that creates dynamic geographic, temporal, and thematic visualizations to enhance situational awareness using tweets as source. In the same line, Ashktorab et al. [2] developed Tweedr, a system to extract actionable information for disaster relief workers, analyzing the text of 17 million of tweets collected during 8 years and corresponding to 12 crisis events occurred in North America.

A lot of data sources have been used to address the issues of this research field, specifically the estimation of damage scale and identification of affected areas after the events. In [10], satellite, aircraft and unmanned aerial vehicles (UAVs) data were fused to estimate the damage scale of several incidents including the Haiti earthquake of 2010, Hurricane Irene of 2011, Hurricane Sandy of 2012 and the Illinois tornadoes of 2015. Oliveira et al. [21] characterized wildfire-affected areas in Portugal taking as resource: demographic data.

Social media data has also been widely used in this regard. For instance, Cerutti et al. [7] identify disaster affected areas after a flood in Italy in 2013, using geo-spatial footprints from Twitter. Following the same path, Cresci et al. [8] detect mentions of damage among emergency reports on Twitter employing a SVM classifier. Moreover, Yuan and Liu [29] demonstrated that the usage of social media to identify critical affected areas at the county level during disasters is viable. On the other hand, Wilson et al. [26] used Call Detail Records (CDRs) to estimate the displacement of people after the 2015 Nepal earthquake. Pastor-Escuredo et al. [22] calculated the impact of the 2014 France flooding using the same kind of data, just like Andrade et al. [1], with the metric RiSC, that quantifies the infrastructural damage of a region after the 2016 Ecuador earthquake.

Our work aims to continue with the promising results of [8] and [1] but mixing both techniques: a set of classifiers applied to this domain, and the characterization of the affected geographical zones using mobile phones activity.

3   Dataset

In this study, we used data from two different sources and nature, one for our analysis and the other one, as a ground truth.

3.1   Mobile Phones Activity Dataset

Published by a global Telecommunication provider operating also in Ecuador, in the form of CSV files. The purpose of this release was to generate insights regarding the earthquake that stroke Ecuador in April 2016. This dataset is the same used in [1]. These files contain 11 million records, of SMS (Short Message Service) messages and phone calls. The records correspond to two periods:

1. April 15th–18th: interval that match with one day before and three days after the earthquake.
2. July 15th–17th: interval that corresponds to 3 months after the catastrophe.

For the purpose of this study, we used records from the first period.

In order to explain what the entries of the dataset represent, the following concepts are needed:

1. Event: either a mobile phone call or a SMS. All the events in the dataset started in any city located in the province of Manabi.
2. Event tower (ET): this is the tower the user's device connected to when generating the *event*.
3. Home tower (HT): this is the tower where the user's device has been connected to most of the times, historically, when generating an *event*.

Events were aggregated by: canton, the nearest *ET*'s geographical coordinates, and the hour of the day when the 'event' took place. In particular, an entry portray the volume of *events* produced in the same date, hour, *event tower* and whose transmitters belong to the same *home tower* as shown in Fig. 1.

Fig. 1. Event tower where the *event* (either a call or a SMS) takes place and Home tower where the user starting the *event* belongs to as labeled by the Telecommunications provider. Taken from [6].

There are 11 thousand different cell towers, where 808 of them are positioned in the province of Manabi. The towers distribution in Manabi is presented in Fig. 2. Note that we do not posses information of the users generating the *events*, since the Telecommunication provider obeys privacy restrictions. Moreover, we do not know if a record corresponds to an SMS or a call.

3.2   Official Dataset

The *Secretaría Nacional de Planificación y Desarrollo (SENPLADES)* is an Ecuadorian government's entity in charge of the planning of strategies for the development and well-being of the country. They presented, two months after the disaster, an after-earthquake report including a map which identified the damaged cantons of the province of Manabi, in order to prioritize help to the most affected zones. This map is shown in Fig. 3

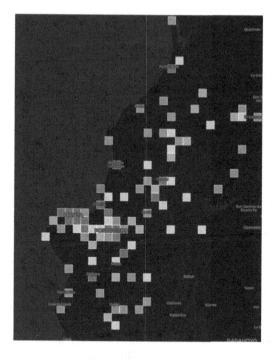

Fig. 2. Event towers distribution in Manabi. The red color represents a major concentration of towers, whereas yellow color represents a minor concentration. (Color figure online)

On the right side, only 3 intensity levels, colored differently, cover the province of Manabi. This is why in [12], a new map is generated, using just 3 levels for simplicity. This new map, as shown in Fig. 4, classifies cantons under 3 different levels of affectation. Level 1 (red color) points to the most damaged zones, and corresponds to level 8, yellow matches with level 7 and blue with level 6 in the EMS-98 scale [14].

This map helps us to label cantons according to their damage level. However, for the level 3 class, there are only two elements. Hence, the class 3 is underrepresented, and not useful for any machine learning model. Levels 2 and 3 have a similar affectation description, which is why we decided to merge levels 2 and 3. Thus, we have levels 1 (highly damaged) and 2 (moderately damaged), with 9 and 11 cantons respectively. These labels are used as ground truth for the validation of our proposed model.

4   Methods

The goal of this study is to automatically label a canton or any geographic unit, as highly or moderately damaged after a natural disaster. In order to detect

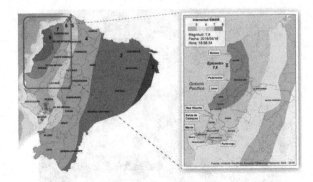

Fig. 3. Affectation intensity levels, corresponding to the province of Manabi, Ecuador. The red color represent an EMS-98 level of 8, while the yellow corresponds to level 6. Results from the Evaluation of the Seism of April 16th, 2016, by SENPLADES. (Color figure online)

the level of damage of a given canton, we developed three automated classifiers using records produced by mobile phone data and information that can be quickly calculated such as the distance from a canton to the earthquake epicenter. In this section we describe the methods we used to work with the aggregated mobile phone data described in Sect. 3. First, we propose three different approaches to characterize the activity presented in each of the Manabí's cantons: spatial, temporal and networks. In doing so, we calculate four metrics that later would be used as features to perform the classification task: visitors diversity index, distance to the earthquake epicenter, time series similarity and eigenvector centrality. Next, we perform three supervised learning algorithms: Linear Support Vector Classification (SVC), Logistic Regression and K-Nearest Neighbors (KNN); using the metrics previously calculated. Finally, we use a Leave-One-Out cross validation in order to evaluate our results.

4.1 Cantons Characterization

Temporal Analysis. Aggregating cell phone activity at canton level and by time spans of one hour, where the range of mobile phone events goes from 00h00 to 23h00, could finely represent the daily temporal behavior of the inhabitants of any canton. Whether it exists a significant difference on the activity of a canton between one day before and one day after a natural disaster, then it could be an indicator that it has occurred a disruptive event on that canton. For instance, the canton Manta, which was one of the most devastated cantons, showed an abruptly change in human mobile activity generation, as shown in Fig. 5.

Based on that premise, we examine the temporal behavior of Manabí's cantons, with the aim of identifying significant changes between the activity produced on April 15th and April 17th, since the catastrophe took place at the night of April 16th. We aggregate the amount of mobile phone events by canton and hour for each day to obtain the daily temporal series. Next, in order to

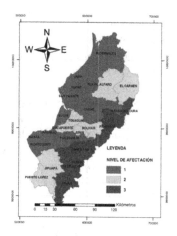

Fig. 4. Affectation intensity levels, corresponding to the province of Manabi, Ecuador. The red color corresponds to the most affected zones, while blue indicates the least affected ones. Taken from [12]. (Color figure online)

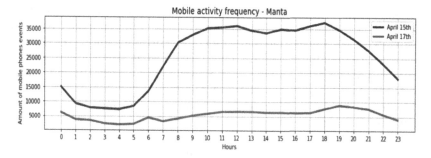

Fig. 5. Mobile activity frequency for April 15th (one day before the earthquake) and April 17th (the day after the catastrophe), of the canton of Manta.

discover how dissimilar the time series of both days are for each canton, we use the Euclidean distance as a metric for calculating the differences of both days on the time domain, as shown on Eq. 1.

$$dsm = \sqrt{\sum_{i=0}^{23}(a(t_i) - b(t_i))^2} \tag{1}$$

On Eq. 1, $a(t_i)$ and $b(t_i)$ represent two points of the two days time series at the same time slot. Through this metric, we can quantify the level of variation of the mobile phone activity for any two days of a particular canton and characterize the ones who present drastic changes in their activity, as well as later identify the causes that could lead to this.

Spatial Analysis. Natural disasters cause people to move from one place to another after such events, as mentioned in Sect. 1. People may move from close or far away places to another because of various reasons: to provide humanitarian aid, searching a safe place to stay, etc. The state-of-the-art has evidenced in a bunch of case studies where mobility patterns have been used to characterize the damage of a region after a natural disaster using cell phone activity. For instance, Andrade et al. [1] concluded that people who travel farther distances during the first 24 h after an earthquake, come from places that have been less affected than those who travel shorter distances. In a similar way, we propose *Visitors Diversity Index*, a tuned *Shannon Entropy*, which is a metric that explains the popularity of a place P_i in terms of the amount of different places where people, currently located in P_i, come from.

$$VDI(i) = \frac{-\Sigma_{a=1}^{A}\rho_{ia}log(\rho_{ia})}{log(\mathcal{A})} \qquad (2)$$

The *Visitors Diversity Index*, as shown in Eq. 2, is explained as follows: the factor ρ_{ia} is the proportion of an Event Tower i recording mobile phone events from people that have associated the a_{th} Home Tower, for A different Home Towers. A high *Visitors Diversity Index* implies that the area where the Event Tower is located, received people from many different geographic areas. We calculated the Visitors Diversity Index with data produced the day after the earthquake, to identify relevant locations post-disaster. However, the visitors diversity index is calculated for every Event Tower location and we need to characterize locations at canton level. Then we aggregate the indices by canton and calculate the cantonal geometric mean, which indicates the central tendency of a set of visitors diversity values for each canton. Finally, we obtain the Z *score* of the geometric means to normalize the cantonal visitors diversity indices.

Moreover, we also calculate the distance in kilometers between the location of the earthquake epicenter and every canton centroid according to the mobile phone towers locations that belong to each canton. We use the Haversine formula, as shown in Eq. 3, where $r_{\oplus} = 6,361$ km is Earth's average radius, ϕ_1, ϕ_2 and λ_1, λ_2 are the latitude and longitude of point 1 and 2 in radians, respectively.

$$d = \left[2\, r_{\oplus}\, \arcsin\left(\sqrt{\sin^2\left(\tfrac{\phi_1+\phi_2}{2}\right) + cos(\phi_1)cos(\phi_2)\sin^2\left(\tfrac{\lambda_1+\lambda_2}{2}\right)}\right)\right] \qquad (3)$$

Networks Analysis. Mobile activity is, by nature, represented as a communication network. Graphs that depict communication networks can give us actionable insights about the interactions between the entities involved in the network.

We filter records from April 17th, as we want to capture information from hours after the catastrophe. We build a directed graph $G = (V, E)$, where V is the set of vertexes that represent each Tower (Event or Home Tower) and E is the set of weighted edges, where an edge e_{ij} indicates that a group of k clients from a HT v_i made a call in the CT v_j. We assigned the weight w of the edges following the Eq. 4:

$$w_{eij} = \frac{log(k) * d}{max(d)} \tag{4}$$

Where d is the distance in kilometers between the nodes v_i, v_j. The weight w_{eij} takes into account the amount of users, as well as the shift in kilometers, for showing an edge as important. It is relevant whether if the shift was large (meaning the users moved large distances from their home) or if the amount of users is large (meaning the place is popular or received affected persons).

The main purpose of our graph analysis is to give a high score to the towers that have the highest influence in the network. For this, we select eigenvector centrality as a metric to extract the most important nodes. This algorithm stands that a node is important if it is linked to other important ones (this is, having a major number of entrant edges). For our case study, an important node represent a tower where mobile activity is generated by displaced people.

4.2 Model Training and Evaluation

To perform the classification task we use and compare the results of three supervised learning algorithms: Linear Support Vector Machine (SVM), Logistic Regression and K-Nearest Neighbors (KNN); using the set of features calculated on Sect. 4.1. Our aim, is to assign each of the 20 Manabí's cantons to a class: high damage or moderate damage. A k parameter of 5 neighbors presented the best performance when using KNN. All the algorithms we use to perform the classification task uses the four metrics previously calculated: visitors diversity index, distance to the earthquake epicenter, time series similarity and eigenvector centrality.

Due to the limited amount of data points we can use, since we only have information about 20 cantons, we perform a Leave-One-Out cross-validation to evaluate the classification. Leave-one-out cross-validation involves separating the data so that for each iteration we have a single sample for the test data and all the rest forming the training data. In that sense, we predict the damage label of every canton. To measure the classifier performance, we used the following metrics: *Accuracy*, defined in Eq. 5; *Recall*, as shown in Eq. 6; and the commonly used *F1-Score* defined in Eq. 7.

$$Accuracy = \frac{TP + TN}{TP + TN + FP + FN} \tag{5}$$

$$Recall = \frac{TP}{TP + FN} \tag{6}$$

$$F1 = \frac{2TP}{2TP + FP + FN} \tag{7}$$

where,

- **TP** is the number of cantons labeled as highly damaged correctly classified as highly damaged (True Positives).

- **TN** is the number of cantons labeled as moderately damaged correctly classified as moderately damaged (True Negatives).
- **FP** is the number of cantons labeled as moderately damaged erroneously classified as highly damaged (False Positives).
- **FN** is the number of cantons labeled as highly damaged erroneously classified as moderately damaged (False Negatives).

5   Results and Discussion

In this section we present the results of our study and briefly discuss the data, approach and limitations.

Table 1 shows the classification performance for all of our tested classifiers. We note that K-Nearest Neighbors presented the best results in all the performance metrics. Even though we obtained the same accuracy with Linear SVC and Logistic Regression, the SVC's recall metric outperformed the Logistic Regression's sensitivity. In fact, we could only correctly label as highly damaged 3 and 5, out of 9 highly damaged cantons using Logistic Regression and Linear SVC respectively. In contrast, we correctly identify 6 out 9 highly damaged cantons using K-Nearest Neighbors (KNN).

Table 1. Classifiers accuracy, recall and F1 score computations according to Eqs. 5, 6, and 7 respectively.

	Accuracy	Recall	F1 Score
Linear SVC	0.70	0.56	0.63
K-Nearest Neighbors	0.75	0.67	0.71
Logistic Regression	0.70	0.33	0.43

The recall metric, which tells us the percentage of total damaged cantons correctly classified, is of great importance for our framework. We note that KNN is capable of identifying a significant amount of regions that have suffered a high percentage of damage. KNN is a simple classification algorithm, and efficient for a few amount of elements as input. It does not make any assumptions on the data, for which it is useful the non-linear data we use. The poorest performance corresponds to logistic regression, which could mean that the dependent and independent variables relationship is not uniform [23]. The features could have a relationship a linear model cannot support or understand it. A limitation of our study is the amount of data per damage level. The model can be improved if there exists more data that represent each damage level. In addition, the original dataset was already aggregated; the scores values could have been affected by this aggregation, as the information is not so granular or specific to a single entity. Moreover, our ground truth only counts with labels at canton level, then we cannot perform any classification at a finer granularity (e.g. city level).

6 Conclusions and Future Work

In the present research work, we propose a novel model to detect and identify the most damaged zones by an earthquake, at a canton level. Even though other approaches have been focused on human mobility and behavior patterns, they have not dealt with the identification of the levels of affectation of regions. Moreover, there is little research applied to countries in means of development, such as Ecuador. Our approach proposes a machine learning model and four different scores or features that give a useful representation of the cantons and can be obtained after the first 24 h post-disaster. The model proposed, uses these scores in order to identify the level of damage of the cantons of Ecuador.

The results of this study can be used so that decision-makers at governments can effectively direct the humanitarian aid to places that are truly damaged. We show that our method can correctly label a highly damaged canton as "highly damaged" the 67% percent of times. Also, one of the main contributions of our work is that our method allows to identify highly damaged zones within the first 24 h after a natural disaster. This is greatly valuable for local governments, which have to prioritize the use of resources to the zones that urgently need them the most. Another contribution is the proposed *Visitors Diversity Index*, which is a tuned version of the popular *Shannon Entropy* metric. This index assigns a high popularity score to a place i in terms of the amount of different places where people, currently located in P_i, come from.

Future work could explore the creation of other metrics and scores, that help to represent the cantons and improve the performances of our methods. Furthermore, the proposed methods could be validated using other datasets corresponding to the same or other natural disaster, so to increase the robustness and inspect how general the model is. For this particular case of study, we could work at a canton level, but in other countries, this high granularity level does not exist. Thus, modifications and enhancements of the proposed methods should be considered. Also, since public institutions such as the Ecuadorian "Secretaría Nacional de Gestión de Riesgos" (Risk Management National Secretary), are interested in having information as the cantons classified by damage during the first eight or twelve hours post-disaster; exploring methods that work on those shorter time spans would be useful in the future. Finally, it is possible to use state-of-the-art algorithms of deep learning to improve the identification of the damage level of each canton.

References

1. Andrade, X., Layedra, F., Vaca, C., Cruz, E.: RiSC: quantifying change after natural disasters to estimate infrastructure damage with mobile phone data. In: 2018 IEEE International Conference on Big Data (Big Data), pp. 3383–3391. IEEE (2018)
2. Ashktorab, Z., Brown, C., Nandi, M., Culotta, A.: Tweedr: mining twitter to inform disaster response. In: ISCRAM (2014)

3. CDB: CDB, World Bank partner to increase disaster resilience through improved procurement (2018). https://www.caribank.org/newsroom/news-and-events/cdb-world-bank-partner-increase-disaster-resilience-through-improved-procurement
4. The World Bank: Disaster risk management (2019). https://www.worldbank.org/en/topic/disasterriskmanagement/overview
5. Cardona, O.D., Ordaz, M.G., Marulanda, M.C., Barbat, A.H.: Estimation of probabilistic seismic losses and the public economic resilience—an approach for a macroeconomic impact evaluation. J. Earthq. Eng. 12(S2), 60–70 (2008)
6. Castillo, G., Layedra, F., Guaranda, M.B., Lara, P., Vaca, C.: The silence of the cantons: estimating villages socioeconomic status through mobile phones data. In: 2018 International Conference on eDemocracy & eGovernment (ICEDEG), pp. 172–178. IEEE (2018)
7. Cerutti, V., Fuchs, G., Andrienko, G., Andrienko, N., Ostermann, F.: Identification of disaster-affected areas using exploratory visual analysis of georeferenced tweets: application to a flood event. Association of Geographic Information Laboratories in Europe, Helsinki, Finland, p. 5 (2016)
8. Cresci, S., Cimino, A., Dell'Orletta, F., Tesconi, M.: Crisis mapping during natural disasters via text analysis of social media messages. In: Wang, J., et al. (eds.) WISE 2015. LNCS, vol. 9419, pp. 250–258. Springer, Cham (2015). https://doi.org/10.1007/978-3-319-26187-4_21
9. De Albuquerque, J.P., Herfort, B., Brenning, A., Zipf, A.: A geographic approach for combining social media and authoritative data towards identifying useful information for disaster management. Int. J. Geogr. Inf. Sci. 29(4), 667–689 (2015)
10. Fernandez Galarreta, J., Kerle, N., Gerke, M.: UAV-based urban structural damage assessment using object-based image analysis and semantic reasoning. Nat. Hazards Earth Syst. Sci. 15(6), 1087–1101 (2015)
11. Ghosh, S., et al.: Crowdsourcing for rapid damage assessment: the global earth observation catastrophe assessment network (GEO-CAN). Earthq. Spectra 27(S1), S179–S198 (2011)
12. Gil, H.A.P.: Efectos del sismo del 16 de abril de 2016 en el sector productivo agropecuario de manabí. La Técnica (17), 30–42 (2017)
13. Giugale, M.: Time to insure developing countries against natural disasters (2017). https://www.worldbank.org/en/news/opinion/2017/10/11/time-to-insure-developing-countries-against-natural-disasters
14. Grünthal, G.: European macroseismic scale 1998. Technical report, European Seismological Commission (ESC) (1998)
15. Guha-Sapir, D., Hargitt, D., Hoyois, P.: Thirty years of natural disasters 1974–2003: the numbers. Presses univ. de Louvain (2004)
16. Hoeppe, P.: Trends in weather related disasters-consequences for insurers and society. Weather Clim. Extremes 11, 70–79 (2016)
17. Kellenberg, D., Mobarak, A.M.: The economics of natural disasters. Annu. Rev. Resour. Econ. 3(1), 297–312 (2011)
18. Kryvasheyeu, Y., et al.: Rapid assessment of disaster damage using social media activity. Sci. Adv. 2(3), e1500779 (2016)
19. MacEachren, A.M., et al.: SensePlace2: GeoTwitter analytics support for situational awareness. In: 2011 IEEE Conference on Visual Analytics Science and Technology (VAST), pp. 181–190. IEEE (2011)
20. Olen, S., Bookhagen, B.: Mapping damage-affected areas after natural hazard events using sentinel-1 coherence time series. Remote Sens. 10(8), 1272 (2018)

21. Oliveira, S., Zêzere, J.L., Queirós, M., Pereira, J.M.: Assessing the social context of wildfire-affected areas. The case of mainland Portugal. Appl. Geogr. **88**, 104–117 (2017)
22. Pastor-Escuredo, D., Torres, Y., Martinez, M., Zufiria, P.J.: Floods impact dynamics quantified from big data sources. arXiv preprint arXiv:1804.09129 (2018)
23. Ranganathan, P., Pramesh, C., Aggarwal, R.: Common pitfalls in statistical analysis: logistic regression. Perspect. Clin. Res. **8**(3), 148 (2017)
24. Rosser, J.F., Leibovici, D.G., Jackson, M.J.: Rapid flood inundation mapping using social media, remote sensing and topographic data. Nat. Hazards **87**(1), 103–120 (2017). https://doi.org/10.1007/s11069-017-2755-0
25. Schlein, L.: UN: most deaths from natural disasters occur in poor countries (2016). https://www.voanews.com/a/un-says-most-deaths-from-natural-disasters-occur-in-poor-countries/3548871.html
26. Wilson, R., et al.: Rapid and near real-time assessments of population displacement using mobile phone data following disasters: the 2015 Nepal eEarthquake. PLoS Curr. **8** (2016)
27. Yabe, T., Sekimoto, Y., Sudo, A., Tsubouchi, K.: Predicting delay of commuting activities following frequently occurring disasters using location data from smartphones. J. Disaster Res. **12**(2), 287–295 (2017)
28. Yu, M., Yang, C., Li, Y.: Big data in natural disaster management: a review. Geosciences **8**(5), 165 (2018)
29. Yuan, F., Liu, R.: Feasibility study of using crowdsourcing to identify critical affected areas for rapid damage assessment: Hurricane Matthew case study. Int. J. Disaster Risk Reduction **28**, 758–767 (2018)

Come with Me Now: New Potential Consumers Identification from Competitors

Hugo Alatrista-Salas, Miguel Nunez-del-Prado(✉), and Victoria Zevallos

Universidad del Pacífico, Lima, Peru
{h.alatristas,m.nunezdelpradoc,v.zevallosmunguia}@up.edu.pe

Abstract. The telecommunications industry is confronted more and more to aggressive marketing campaigns from competitor carriers. Therefore, they need to improve the subscriber targeting to propose more attractive offers for gaining new subscribers. In the present effort, a five steps methodology to find new potential subscribers using supervised learning techniques over imbalanced datasets is proposed. The proposed technique applies community detection to infers consumption information of competitors carriers subscribers within the communities. Besides, it uses a sampling technique to reduce the effect of a dominant class for an imbalanced classification task. The proposal is evaluated with a real dataset from a Peruvian carrier. The dataset contains one-month data, which is about 200 millions of transaction. The results show that the proposed technique is able to identify between two to ten times more new potential clients, depending on the sampling technique, as shows using the top decile lift value.

Keywords: Subscribers attraction · Imbalanced classification · Community detection

1 Introduction

Competition among telecom operator has radically increased in recent years in Latin America. As a result, operators are making significant investments in developing new strategies allowing them to increase their market share. These strategies have three different approaches. The first is to attract new users to the industry; the second, to attract customers of the competitors; and the third, in retaining the clients. While all fronts are important, the objective of the following study is to attract new clients from other telecom operators. This task presents considerable and interesting challenges due to the lack of information about the subscriber behavior from other telecom operators. Therefore, we rely on the information of the interaction these users maintain with the company's

---

Authors appear in alphabetical order, they contribute equally to the present paper.

© Springer Nature Switzerland AG 2020
J. A. Lossio-Ventura et al. (Eds.): SIMBig 2019, CCIS 1070, pp. 252–266, 2020.
https://doi.org/10.1007/978-3-030-46140-9_24

subscribers to determine their future behavior. The main objective is determining which clients belonging to another telecom operator are more likely to become new subscribers based on the analysis performed on the interactions in the telecommunications network.

To attain this objective, we use Call Detail Records (*i.e.,* call traffic and internet consumption) of Small Office Home Office and post-pay subscribers to determine whether a subscriber from another telecom operator will become a subscriber. We model the structure of the mobile social network as a directed graphs G(V,E), where the vertices are weighted by the internet consumption and edges by the volume of incoming and outgoing calls. Then, communities are detected to infer information about the subscribers' competitors behavior based on the attributes of the subscribers sharing the same community. Once information is completed, we compute some variables to qualify the changes in subscribers' attributes over time. Finally, a classification algorithm is applied to identify the most likely subscribers to migrate to the carrier running our methodology. Our approach achieves an accuracy value around 0.9. However, this classification is not trivial since the dataset is imbalanced. Therefore, we also performed a comparative analysis of resampling techniques to balance the dataset before performing the classification task.

The present work is organized as follows. Section 2 presents the related works. Section 3 introduces our methodology, while Sect. 4 describes the dataset we have used. Section 5 details the result of our experiments. Finally, Sect. 6 presents the conclusions and new research avenues.

2   Related Works

In this section, we list different studies on churn prediction, which is basically the same prediction task we perform. For instance, Columelli, Nunez-del-Prado and Zarate [2] introduce a methodology that summarizes churn risk score in telecommunication social networks. They rely on Fuzzy Logic system, combining the churn probability and the risk of the churner to leave the network with other subscribers. Their objective is classifying the possible deserters and calculate their influence analyzing the social network of an African telecommunication operator. First, they make a comparison between several classifiers, where the Extremely Random Tree algorithm obtains a better performance according to the lift curve. Then, they use metrics such as degree of centrality and page rank to measure the degree of influence issued and received from each possible churner. Finally, they apply a fuzzy logic system to obtain a unified metric of churn risk based on the measures of the probability of desertion, influence emitted (degree of centrality) and influence received (page rank) [2]. This paper has value because it proposes an interesting methodology to measure the risk of churn and makes a comparison between classification algorithms to predict the behavior of the users.

Pushpa and Shobha [10] propose to analyze the structure and behavior of a multi-relational network and the location of important elements to predict the churn of customers of a mobile operator in India. With this purpose, the social position of the users, represented by nodes, is evaluated based on the multiple connections they have with other users of the network (centrality degree). Then, this value is used to characterize the degrees of influence and importance of certain members. Finally, the REGE iterative algorithm based on regular equivalence (similarity between relationships) is used for classified users as deserters or non-deserters [10]. The value of this research relies on the analysis of the structure of the telecommunication network and the social importance of the nodes. This knowledge is then used to predict the churn, but it can also be used to attract customers more likely to leave the network of a competitor operator.

Amin et al. [1] propose a just in time classification technique using Naive Bayes. The idea behind this work is to use another company data to train a churn classifier for another company. Authors also test whether data transformation improves the precision of the prediction. They test their approach with publicly available data. The first dataset contains 20 features and 333 samples, and the second dataset has 250 features and 18000 customers. The metric they use to evaluate the performance of the Naive Bayes classification is the Area Under the ROC curve.

De Caigny, Coussement, and De Bock [3] compare Decision Tree, Logistic Regression, Random Forests and Logit Leaf Models for churn prediction. The idea behind LLM is that models constructed on different segments of the data rather than on the entire dataset predict better while maintaining the model interpretability. The LLM consists of two steps. In the first step, subscribers are segmented using decision rules. In the second step, a model is created for every leaf of the tree. The area under the receiver operating characteristics curve (AUC) and top decile lift (TDL) are used to measure the performance for which LLM scores significantly better than Logistic Regression and Decision Trees. It also performs as well as Random Forests and Logistic model trees. To perform the evaluations, the authors use 14 datasets from different industries of the Center for Customer Relationship Management Duke University.

3   Methodology

In the present section, we describe the methodology to attract new costumers from competitors in the telecommunications industry. The present effort allows telecommunication operators to determine which competitor operators subscribers are more likely to become new subscribers based on five different steps, as depicted in Fig. 1. Namely, graph modeling, community detection, variable generation, balanced classification, and feature analysis.

First, the *graph modeling* phase consist on building the social graph from the Call detail Records (*CDR*). The nodes stand for both *own subscriber* from the carrier running the analysis and subscribers from competitor carriers, while the edges represent social relations [10]. Thus, analyzing the social network provides essential information about the interaction of *own subscribers* and subscribers from competitors.

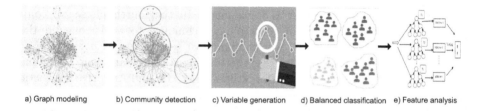

a) Graph modeling   b) Community detection   c) Variable generation   d) Balanced classification   e) Feature analysis

Fig. 1. Methodology process.

The *community detection* phase extracts the subgroup of the social network represented by a graph [10]; where the density of the connections is high within the community; while, the links between the nodes of different communities tend to be of low density [8]. The extraction of relevant communities in large social networks is a real challenge; however, it provides important information for making decisions about the structure and behavior of the subscribers in graph and subgraphs [11]. Therefore, we apply community detection to understand the competitors' subscribers behavior based on the characteristics of the *own subscribers* who belong to the same community. To accomplish this task, we rely on an adaptation of the Louvain algorithm. This variant consists on the change of the conventional modularity formula to work with directed graphs. This adjustment was proposed by Dugué and Perez *et al.* [4] based on Leicht and Newman work [6]. Hence, this algorithm allows to maintain the directionality and uses the computational effectiveness of Louvain algorithm to work with high dimensional networks.

$$Q_d = \frac{1}{m} \sum_{i,j} [A_{i,j} - \frac{d_i d_j}{2m}] \delta(c_i, c_j) \tag{1}$$

Where m is the number of edges in G, A_{ij} is the weight of the edge between nodes i and j, which is set to 0 if such edge does not exist, d_i is the number of neighbors of i (i.e. the degree of vertex of i), c_i is the community to which vertex i belongs and the $\delta(c_i, c_j)$ is defined as 1 if $c_i = c_j$, and 0 otherwise.

In the third phase of our methodology, we generate new variables to characterize competitors' subscribers, Accordingly, based on the social graph from the CDR, we build features like out-degree, in-degree, centrality out-degree, centrality in-degree and page rank. Also, we compute measures per community such as percentage of *own subscribers*, average number of consumed megabytes, average number of internet access, out-degree normalized, in-degree normalized, centrality out-degree normalized, and centrality in-degree normalized. In addition, we calculate ratios of the variables to quantify variation between weeks t and $t - 1$ as part of the characterization. These ratios are the variation of number of megabytes, number of internet access, out-degree normalized, in-degree normalized, centrality out-degree normalized, and centrality in-degree normalized. All these new variables are computed for each week to predict whether a competitor's subscriber could leave competitor carriers to become a client of the telecom operator running this proposal.

In our case, as the dataset is imbalanced. In the fourth phase we compare three different families of resampling techniques to avoid bias in the classification results [7]. Thus, we compare five techniques of *over-sampling* (*i.e.,* Naive random over-sampling, Synthetic Minority Oversampling Technique (SMOTE), Borderline-1 SMOTE, Borderline-2 SMOTE and Adaptive Synthetic (ADASYN)), seven techniques of *under-sampling* (*i.e.,* Random under-sampling, NearMiss-1, NearMiss-3, Edited Nearest Neighbor, All KNN, One Side Selection and Neighborhood Cleaning Rule), and a hybrid technique of *over-sampling and under-sampling* (*i.e.,* SMOTE Tomek).

The last phase uses the aforementioned variables and balancing techniques for identifying competitors' subscribers who will change their carrier from those who would not leave their current carrier in a certain period of time. With this objective, we use a binary classifier which uses the data of the first three weeks to train and the data of the last week to test the effectiveness of the model. To choose the classification algorithm, we rely on work of Columelli *et al.* [2]. Authors realized a comparative analysis between different classification algorithms, such as Extremely Random Trees, Naive Bayesian and Gradient Boosting, with the objective of predicting prepaid mobile subscribers desertion. The results show that the best classifier was Extremely Random Trees.

In the next section, we describe the dataset at our disposal to perform experiments.

4   Dataset Description

For the experiments, we use telecommunication anonymized data derived from a CDR of a Peruvian telecommunication operator. The data provides 121 310 940 call events and 106 400 759 internet connections of four weeks during June of 2018. It is worth noting that subscribers are tagged as *portability i.e.,* subscribers that came from a competitor carrier. From this data, we have split five different and complementary datasets as described below:

Table 1. Call traffic data example. Where *min* is the number of minutes of all calls; *Calls* is the Number of Calls; *Avg* is the average minutes per call

Caller Id	Callee Id	Direction	Date	Hour	Min	Calls	Avg	Type
948000000	948819472	IN	01/06/2018	18:32:29	394	9	43.77	ON-NET
948000000	950171864	OUT	01/06/2018	01:13:19	45	1	22	ON-NET
948011126	950171864	IN	02/06/2018	11:12:35	3	1	3	OFF-NET
948000000	951557467	OUT	04/06/2018	07:52:29	46	1	46	OFF-NET
948000000	951897248	IN	11/06/2018	12:03:09	8	1	8	OFF-NET

- **Call traffic data** is composed of Caller Id (*i.e.,* Subscriber Id), Callee Id, direction (incoming, outgoing), date, hour, duration in minutes, number of exchanged calls, average call duration, and type (On net, calls between subscribers of the same carrier; Off net, calls between subscriber and competitors' subscriber). We present an example of this dataset in Table 1.

- **Internet consumption data** contains only information about the subscribers but not from subscribers belonging to other carriers. It comprises Subscriber ID, date, hour, and number of consumed megabytes.

Table 2. Internet consumption data example. *Megabytes* is the consumed number of Megabytes

Subscriber Id	Date	Hour	Megabytes
948000000	11/06/2018	07:52:21	96
948000001	17/06/2018	10:23:09	85
948819472	19/06/2018	17:35:13	152
948000003	21/06/2018	21:12:51	157
950171864	30/06/2018	02:02:37	96

- **Portability data** identifies which subscribers came from a competitor operator. This variable is used to predict whether a client will change carrier from a competitor telecom operator (Table 3).

Table 3. Portability data example. Where *Portability* refers to subscriber who came from other carriers

Subscriber Id	Portability
948000000	0
948000001	0
948819472	1
948000003	1
950171864	0

- **Derived data from CDR**. Based in the first two data sets *i.e.,* Tables 1 and 2. We transform and summarize the variables in four weeks. Having as a result a dataset per week, Table 4.

Table 4. Derived data from CDR description.

Variable	Description
out_x	Out degree
in_x	In degree
cent_out_x	Centrality out degree
cent_in_x	Centrality in degree
pagerank_x	Page rank
%_own_subscribers_x	Percentage of own subscribers (*i.e*) in the community
megas_prom_x	Average number of megabytes used by own subscribers in the community
use_prom_x	Average number of times of internet use by own subscribers in the community
out_norm_x	Out degree normalized based on the community
in_norm_x	In degree normalized based on the community
cent_out_norm_x	Centrality out degree normalized based on the community
cent_in_norm_x	Centrality in degree normalized based on the community
ratio_megas_prom_x	Ratio between megas_prom_x of the week "t" and the megas_prom_x of the week "t-1"
ratio_use_prom_x	Ratio between use_prom_x of the week "t" and the use_prom_x of the week "t-1"
ratio_out_norm_x	Ratio between out_norm_x of the week "t" and the out_norm_x of the week "t-1"
ratio_in_norm_x	Ratio between in_norm_x of the week "t" and the in_norm_x of the week "t-1"
ratio_cent_out_norm_x	Ratio between cent_out_norm_x of the week "t" and the cent_out_norm_x of the week "t-1"
ratio_cent_in_norm_x	Ratio between cent_in_norm_x of the week "t" and the cent_in_norm_x of the week "t-1"

– **Social network data** is modeled as a graph $G(N, E)$ where the nodes are the subscribers and edges represents calls between subscribers. This information is extracted from Table 1. Thus, We construct three directed graphs weighted by the total number of minutes of calls, total number of calls, and average minutes per call. It is worth noting that the these graph are generated per week.

In the next section, we describe the the results of our experiments based on the described methodology and datasets.

5   Experiments

In the present section, we present the results of our experiments. First, we build the graph models weighting the edges by the number of calls, the amount of minutes and the average of minutes per calls for four weeks $S1$, $S2$, $S3$, and $S4$. Table 5 shows the size of the generated graphs.

Table 5. Graphs generated per week

Week	Nodes	Edges
S1	4 662 846	9 114 606
S2	4 704 090	9 080 917
S3	4 494 577	8 712 714
S4	4 198 888	7 939 203

Using the twelve generated graphs, we extract different variables taking the graphs weighted by the number of calls, the amount of minutes, and the average of minutes per calls. After applying community detection algorithm in each graph, we derived variables as summaries Table 4. It is worth noting that the x suffix in Table 4 is changed for c, m, or a when the variable is issued from the graph of calls, minutes and average minutes per call, respectively. For instance, out_c, out_m, and out_a are the out_degree values for the calls, minutes and average graphs. Once we have obtained all the variables, we apply different techniques to balance the dataset for classification. Thus, to evaluate the performance of the different models and determinate which resampling technique and data sets is the most appropriate for the proposed task we use the metrics presented below.

To evaluate a classification with imbalanced data, a recommended measure to use is the precision/recall curve (PCR) [9]. It measures the trade off between precision and recall (sensitivity). As complement the average precision metric (AP) calculates the average with weights reached in each threshold, where the increase in recall compared to the previous threshold is used as a weight [12]. Figure 2 presents a comparison between the PCR curves of the resampling methods applied to the datasets (*i.e.,* total number of minutes, total number of calls, average minutes per call, and union of the three data sets). We observe that the silhouette and AP values, in general, do not show optimal results for classification. This scenario is explained by the low value obtained by the models in precision, as consequence of the imbalanced test data.

Another important performance visualization tool is ROC curve, which measures the trade off between specificity and sensitivity (recall) [5]. In addition, it provides a performance metric called AUC, which measures the area under the ROC curve. The AUC is useful for evaluating the performance of different classifiers [9]. Figure 3 presents a comparative between the techniques of under-sampling, over-sampling, and the combination of over-sampling and

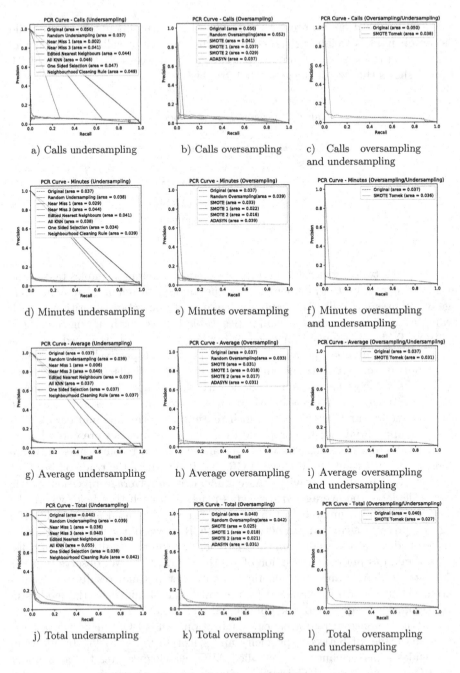

a) Calls undersampling

b) Calls oversampling

c) Calls oversampling and undersampling

d) Minutes undersampling

e) Minutes oversampling

f) Minutes oversampling and undersampling

g) Average undersampling

h) Average oversampling

i) Average oversampling and undersampling

j) Total undersampling

k) Total oversampling

l) Total oversampling and undersampling

Fig. 2. Precision/recall curve (PCR) curve.

under-sampling applied to each of the data sets. We observe that the best Under-sampling techniques are Random under-sampling and NearMiss-3, while, the best Over-sampling techniques are SMOTE and ADASYN. Comparing the AUC values, we note that the one obtaining the best results for the datasets of calls, average and total is the Random under-sampling (AUC = 0.96) and the best for the minutes dataset is NearMiss-3 (AUC=0.97).

Another adequate metric used in previous works to evaluate churn models is the Lift curve and value [2]. Lift measures the effectiveness of a predictive model calculated as the ratio between the results obtained with and without the predictive model. Figure 4 compares the performance of the models in terms of Lift curve and the value at 10%. On the one hand, the comparison between under-sampling techniques, the ones with the best lift value at 10% are Random under-sampling and NearMiss-3 with 9.9 for all the data sets. On the other hand, in the case of over-sampling techniques, the best one is ADASYN with a lift value at 10% of 8.9, 9.0, 8.6 and 8.1 for calls, minutes, average, and total, respectively.

In the case of the hybrid method SMOTE Tomek the lift value at 10% is 9.0, 8.6, 8.7, and 7.9 respectively. According to this results the best of all the models are Random under-sampling and NearMiss-3. Concerning the ground truth, we use the last week of the four weeks dataset. Therefore, we used the first three weeks to predict users who will come from other telecom operators and we observe whether those predicted subscribers become own subscribers in the last week of the dataset.

Figure 5 depicts the reports of the importance of estimators of the four best classification tasks applying Random under-sampling and the Extremely Random Trees classifier. We see that the most important characteristics for all models are the ratios of the variables derived from Internet consumption, such as the amount of consumed megabytes, and the frequency of use. It means that community detection improves the value to the classification process and therefore to work.

In summary, based on the presented metrics, the best model for classifying competitor carriers subscribers in those who will leave their carrier to become subscribers of the carrier running our methodology from those who would not is *Extremely Random Trees classifier*. This classification algorithm applied to the *total* dataset balanced with Random under-sampling technique out performs the other configurations. This result makes sense because this is the dataset that contains the all variables and therefore better identifies the behavior of the subscribers. It is worth noting that the difference in training the Extremely Random Trees classifier with the other datasets, such as calls, minutes or average after having applied the same resampling technique is not significantly different. Nevertheless, Ramdom Undersampling and Near-Miss 3 give slightly better results due to the majority points are near one to each other, which is the best scenario for both methods.

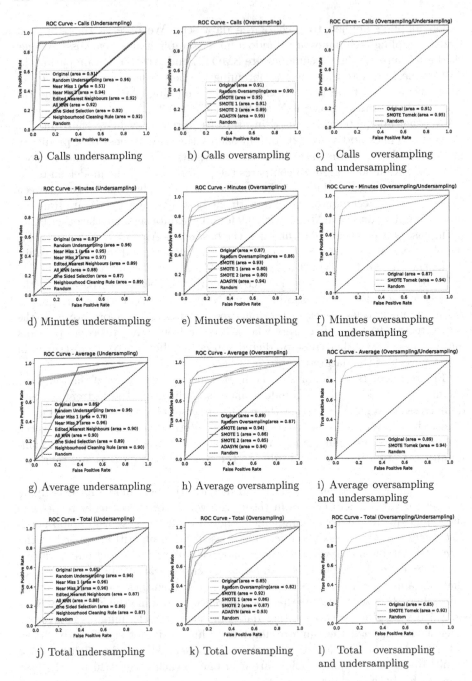

a) Calls undersampling

b) Calls oversampling

c) Calls oversampling and undersampling

d) Minutes undersampling

e) Minutes oversampling

f) Minutes oversampling and undersampling

g) Average undersampling

h) Average oversampling

i) Average oversampling and undersampling

j) Total undersampling

k) Total oversampling

l) Total oversampling and undersampling

Fig. 3. Receiver operating characteristic (ROC) curve.

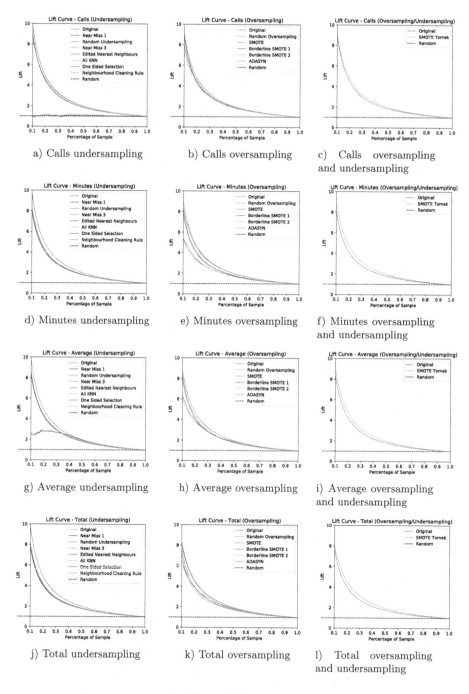

Fig. 4. Lift curve.

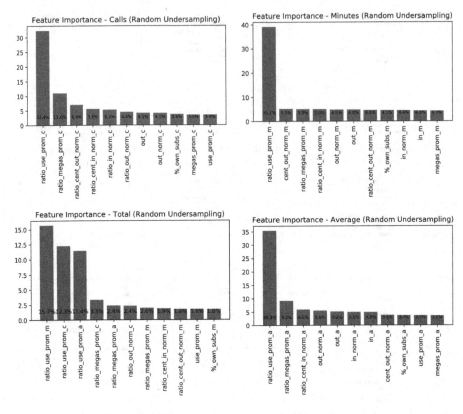

Fig. 5. Features importance analysis.

6   Conclusion

The construction of three graphs based on minutes, calls and average minutes per call as representations of the mobile telephone network allow us to analyze the interactions between subscribers. The value of this information relies especially on discovering the attributes and understanding the behavior of the competitors' customers. Based on these structures, important variables are generated for the classification of subscribers in those who will leave their carrier to become subscribers of the carrier running our methodology from those who would not. In addition, the community detection in the social graphs improve the characterization of subscribers from competitors carriers because we are able to infer certain consumption values (*e.g.*, consumed minutes, megabytes, among others) not visible in the dataset produced in the carrier running the proposed methodology. Also, it allows to obtain variables describing the behavior of the user in the community to which the subscriber belongs.

All the variables computed from subscriber interactions in the graph or in the community come together to characterize and obtain a refined individual subscriber profile. In addition, the time dimension is added, that is, how the attributes of the users vary between periods S1, S2, S3 and S4. Using these values, a complete characterization of the competitors subscribers behavior is obtained using. Therefore, this characterization takes into account the period as well as the evolution of these variables from one period to another. As observed in the results, the most significant variables for the best classifiers are the internet volume ratios and times (days) of consumption.

The selected Extremely Random Trees because classification algorithm uses bagging techniques of attributes and elements to perform the binary classification with interesting results. For the classification, the dataset from the first three periods S1, S2, and S3 are used to train the classifier. Subsequently, the performance of the model is measured with the fourth period S4. Note that due to the imbalance in the data, different resampling techniques are tested to balance classes and not bias the classifier by the majority class. Finally, based on the performance of the classifier after the application of a resampling technique, a comparative analysis is done. It is worth noting that our method could be applied to other industries when it is possible to model the clients interaction with competitor's clients in a graph form

The classifier evaluation attained good values for ROC curve, AUC, Lift curve, and Lift value. However, due to the imbalanced nature of the dataset, it is expected that not all the metrics reach desired values as shown in the PCR curve. Therefore, a low value in precision implies that not all subscribers identified as new potential subscribers will leave their current carrier. This opens new research opportunities to improve precision using deep learning and fuzzy logic techniques.

References

1. Amin, A., Shah, B., Khattak, A.M., Baker, T., Anwar, S., et al.: Just-in-time customer churn prediction: With and without data transformation. In: 2018 IEEE Congress on Evolutionary Computation (CEC), pp. 1–6. IEEE (2018)
2. Columelli, L., Nunez-del Prado, M., Zarate-Gamarra, L.: Measuring churner influence on pre-paid subscribers using fuzzy logic. In: 2016 XLII Latin American Computing Conference (CLEI), pp. 1–10. IEEE (2016)
3. De Caigny, A., Coussement, K., De Bock, K.W.: A new hybrid classification algorithm for customer churn prediction based on logistic regression and decision trees. Eur. J. Oper. Res. **269**(2), 760–772 (2018)
4. Dugué, N., Perez, A.: Directed Louvain: maximizing modularity in directed networks. Ph.D. thesis, Université d'Orléans (2015)
5. Fawcett, T.: An introduction to ROC analysis. Pattern Recognit. Lett. **27**, 861–874 (2006)
6. Leicht, E.A., Newman, M.E.: Community structure in directed networks. Phys. Rev. Lett. **100**(11), 118703 (2008)
7. Lemaître, G., Nogueira, F., Aridas, C.K.: Imbalanced-learn: a python toolbox to tackle the curse of imbalanced datasets in machine learning. J. Mach. Learn. Res. **18**(17), 1–5 (2017). http://jmlr.org/papers/v18/16-365.html
8. del Prado, M.N., Hendrikx, H.: Toward a route detection method base on detail call records. Working Papers, pp. 16–19. Centro de Investigación, Universidad del Pacífico, December 2016. https://ideas.repec.org/p/pai/wpaper/16-19.html

9. Saito, T., Rehmsmeier, M.: Precision-recall plot is more informative than the ROC plot when evaluating binary classifiers on imbalanced datasets. PLoS ONE **10**(3), 1–21 (2015)
10. Shobha, G., et al.: Social network classifier for churn prediction in telecom data. In: 2013 International Conference on Advanced Computing and Communication Systems, pp. 1–7. IEEE (2013)
11. Wu, X., Liu, Z.: How community structure influences epidemic spread in social networks. Physica A: Stat. Mech. Appl. **387**(2–3), 623–630 (2008)
12. Zhu, M.: Recall, precision and average precision. University of Waterloo (2004)

Global Brand Perception Based on Social Prestige, Credibility and Social Responsibility: A Clustering Approach

Rosario Medina-Rodríguez[1,2], Alvaro Talavera[1(✉)], Martín Hernani-Merino[1], Juan Lazo-Lazo[1], and Jose Afonso Mazzon[3]

[1] Universidad del Pacífico, Av. Salaverry 2020, Jesús María, Lima, Peru
{ra.medinar,ag.talaveral,mn.hernanim,jg.lazol}@up.edu.pe
[2] Pontificia Universidad Católica del Peru,
Av. Universitaria 1801, San Miguel, Lima, Peru
[3] Universidade de São Paulo (USP), São Paulo, Brazil
jamazzon@usp.br

Abstract. Towards the merchandising of a global brand, it is necessary to establish guidelines for marketing managers to define appropriate standardization/adaptation measures. Therefore, it is required to understand the construct of susceptibility to global consumer culture (SGCC) to position the brand according to the wishes and preferences of consumers belonging to specific segments of the global market. Based on three dimensions of the SGCI, proposed in literature: (i) social prestige; (ii) brand credibility; and (iii) social responsibility. This study aims to identify groups of global consumers; from different cultural backgrounds, ages, countries, among other characteristics; who share similar interests. For this purpose, an analysis and a comparison of four clustering algorithms are proposed. Besides, the best number of groups for each algorithm is calculated to find the groups that best explain the behavior of the global consumer. The results confirm the existence of a hybrid culture of global consumption, which produces companies to segment consumers from different countries based on similar or shared needs.

Keywords: Global brands · Clustering · Social prestige · Brand credibility · Social responsibility · Market segmentation

1 Introduction

Global brands have several definitions among the literature, in this work, a combination of them was adopted: "are brands that are sold, marketed and widely recognized under the same name in multiple countries with generally standardized and centrally coordinated marketing strategies." [9,21,29]. In emerging countries, global brands are perceived as a kind of passport to global citizenship [17,28]. Hence, global brands can express customers global identity; that is, consumers start to be considered part of the global consumer culture (GCC) [10].

© Springer Nature Switzerland AG 2020
J. A. Lossio-Ventura et al. (Eds.): SIMBig 2019, CCIS 1070, pp. 267–281, 2020.
https://doi.org/10.1007/978-3-030-46140-9_25

At the same time, the concept of susceptibility to GCC (SGCC) emerged, as "a desire or a tendency for the acquisition and use of global brands" with conformity to consumption trend, quality perception and social prestige serving as antecedents [34].

Given this context, Hernani et al. [14] proposed a model that represents a global brand, which is related to the intention to purchase global brands as a result of susceptibility and can differ from one consumer to another according to their culture. Consequently, this model can describe how a particular segment of global consumption perceives global consumption trends. It integrated the measures of SGCC with seven dimensions: (i) conformity to consumption trends; (ii) quality perception; (iii) social prestige; (iv) social responsibility; (v) brand credibility; (vi) perceived risk; and (vii) information costs saved. In order to know the behavior profiles of global brands consumers, some works using clustering algorithms have been proposed. Their methodology is based on gathering descriptive attributes of the customers to divide them into groups with similar behaviour related to a product under consideration [18].

Following this idea, in this paper, it is proposed an approach to analyse and discover the consumer behaviour and susceptibility to the consumption of global brands in different cultural settings, based on three dimensions of the model mentioned above. Social prestige reflected in consumer attributions of social status and self-esteem through the consumption of global brands. Also, it can indicate a high status for a product associated with that particular brand [10]. Consumers tend to perceive the consumption of a prestigious brand as an indicator of social status, self-esteem, wealth or power [14]. Brand credibility that refers to how credible the information about a branded product is. It resembles the respectability of the brand according to the customer based on its: reliability, expertise, honesty, attractiveness, trust-spreading, and what is advertised by the manufacturer [20]. Therefore, the content clarity and credibility of a brand might rise the product value, reduce material expenses, and perceived risk to the users; consequently, increasing the consumers buying intention [27]. Also, social responsibility that includes consumer perceptions of the social responsibility of the global brand. This concept was introduced by Bodur et al. to differentiate social responsibility efforts at corporate and product brand levels [11]. A favourable social responsibility image reflects brand associations that tend to have a positive effect on consumer attitudes [13]. Hence, a suitable social responsibility marketing strategy can produce significant results because it builds confidence in consumers.

In the search for market segments that identify with global consumption trends, the marketing literature highlights the importance of the use of cluster analysis [23] because this method helps to identify and define market segments that are at the center of the marketing strategy of multinationals [31]. This methodological approach is not commonly used in seeking to understand consumer behavior due to its operative complexity. In this way, the contribution of this paper, seeks to obtain the profiles of consumers (from different cultural backgrounds, ages, countries, among other characteristics) and their perception of global brands (according to the metrics of susceptibility to the global consumer culture). Thus, four clustering algorithms are analyzed and compared, looking for the best number of clusters for each algorithm and comparing the groups of the algorithms, looking for the clusters that best explain consumer behavior. In this way, the interpretation of the clusters is carried out concerning their impact on the commercialization of global brands.

This work is organized into five sections. Section 2 briefly describes the data set and the cluster algorithms. Section 3, presents the experimental results and discussion and Sect. 4, report the conclusions and future work.

2   Methods

In this section, we concisely recall the main aspects regarding the dataset and the cluster algorithms applied to this analysis, including a suitable parameter selection for each algorithm.

2.1   Dataset

As described in [14], the data was acquired through a questionnaire sent via email to United States, Brazil, Peru, France and the Czech Republic undergraduate students of business degrees (economics, administration and accounting) and MBA students. It is worth mentioning that after removing duplicate and incomplete questionnaires, the final sample is composed of 412 questionnaires, distributed as shown in Fig. 1. The ability scores of each of the seven dimensions of SGCC were estimated by applying the Item Response Theory (IRT). It should be noted that the ability score is normally expressed on a scale with an average of 0, standard deviation 1 and range of values between -3 and 3; which is a normalized score.

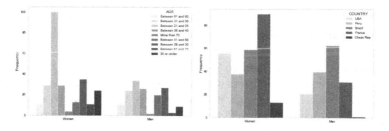

Fig. 1. Questionnaire participant's sex distribution according to age and country.

The variables considered from the model proposed in [14], are: (*i*) social responsibility; (*ii*) social prestige; and (*iii*) brand credibility. Once clusters have been founded, they need to be profiled using additional variables of interest, such as socio-demographic variables and behavioural variable [7]. In this case, we use age and gender; additionally, to incorporate the global consumer culture into the analysis, the consumers country was introduced.

2.2   Cluster Theory

Clustering is a method of unsupervised learning commonly used in many fields for statistical data analysis with the aim of grouping objects into classes of similar objects based on their locality and connectivity within an n-dimensional space [19,33]. Clustering algorithms partition data into a certain number of clusters (groups, subsets, or categories).

Mathematically given a set of input patterns $\mathbf{X} = \{\mathbf{x}_1, \ldots, \mathbf{x}_j, \ldots, \mathbf{x}_N\}$ where $\mathbf{x}_j = (x_{j1}, x_{j2}, \ldots, x_{jd})^T \in \Re^d$ and each measure x_{ji} is said to be a feature (attribute, dimension, or variable).

A (Hard) partitioning clustering attempts to seek a K partition of $\mathbf{X}, C = \{C_1, \ldots, C_K\}$ $(K \leq N)$, such that:

$$C_i \neq \phi, \; i = 1, \ldots, K; \tag{1}$$

$$\bigcup_{i=1}^{K} C_i = \mathbf{X}; \tag{2}$$

$$C_i \cap C_j = \phi, i, j = 1, \ldots, K \text{ and } i \neq j. \tag{3}$$

where N is the finite cardinality of the available representative data set and C_i is the total number of class types. For hard partitioning clustering, each pattern only belongs to one cluster. However, a pattern may also be allowed to belong to all clusters with a degree of membership, $u_{i,j} \in [0, 1]$, which represents the membership coefficient of the jth object in the ith cluster and satisfies the following two constraints:

$$\sum_{i=1}^{c} u_{i,j} = 1, \quad \forall j \quad \text{and} \quad \sum_{j=1}^{N} u_{i,j} < N, \quad \forall i \tag{4}$$

that is used in fuzzy clustering (see [15] and [25]).

For instance, it can be used to identify consumer segments, or competitive sets of products, or groups of assets whose prices co-move, or for geo-demographic segmentation. Therefore, its goal in marketing is to accurately segment customers in order to achieve more effective customer marketing via personalization. In this work, we chose four algorithms based on different ways of partitioning the space, described in Table 1.

3   Results and Discussion

In order to describe the results obtained from the clustering analysis, it is required first to select the best number of clusters to be used on each algorithm.

Table 1. List of the four well-known algorithms chose in our work, including a brief description based on [25,32].

Algorithm	Based on	Description
K-Means	Partition	The main idea is to update the center of the cluster which is represented by the center of data points, by iterative computation. The iterative process will be continued until some criteria for convergence (sum of squared Euclidean distances minimization) is met
Gaussian Mixture Models	Distribution	GMM consists of several Gaussian distributions from which the original data is generated. Then, the data obeying the same independent Gaussian distribution, is considered to belong to the same cluster. This algorithm employs an iterative scheme, where in each step, the likelihood is increased, ensuring that the algorithm usually converges
Fuzzy C-Means	Fuzzy Theory	The basic idea is that the discrete value of belonging label, $\{0,1\}$, is changed into the continuous interval $[0,1]$, in order to describe the belonging relationship among objects more reasonably. Then, FCM gets the membership of each data point to every cluster by optimizing an objective function
Kohonen Network	Neural Network Learning	The core idea is to build a mapping of dimension reduction from the input space of high dimension to output space of low dimension on the assumption that there exists topology in the input data [8,30]

Then, use the best model to visualize the consumer's segmentation, and finally, describe and discuss the clusters found and compare the algorithms results.

3.1 Selection of the Best Parameters and Number of Clusters

Determining the number of clusters is a challenging task when dealing with clustering algorithms. Besides, some algorithms have some additional parameters to be set in order to find the best model. Thus, we performed a grid search over the parameters listed in Table 2 (*Parameters*) optimizing the measure detailed in Table 2 (*Measure*). It is worth mentioning that we use a Python (scikit-learn) implementation to conduct our experiments.

Table 2. Clustering algorithm's parameters according to Python functions.

Algorithm	Function Name	Parameters	Measure
K-Means	KMeans (sklearn.cluster) [22]	n_clusters	Sum of squared distances
Gaussian Mixture Models	GaussianMixture (sklearn-mixture) [22]	n_components covariance_type	Bayesian information criterion
Fuzzy C-Means	fuzz.cluster.cmeans (scikit-fuzzy) [24]	n_clusters exponent_membership_function	Fuzzy partition coefficient
Kohonen Network	neurolab.net.newc (NeuroLab [1])	[input_neurons, min_max_values] output_neurons	Mean absolute error

For the K-Means algorithm, we use the Elbow method to find the best number of clusters. The Elbow method is based on the visualization of the value of a clustering criterion against the number of clusters ($n\_clusters$). As we keep increasing $n\_clusters$, there will be a decrease in the cost function. Then, a discontinuity in slope should correspond to the correct number of "natural" clusters [12]. As can be seen in Fig. 2, the optimal number of clusters using K-Means is two.

In order to find the best clustering model using Gaussian Mixture models, we performed a grid search using the number of clusters and the covariance matrix type, optimizing the Bayesian Information Criterion [26]. This criterion is used for model selection among a finite set of models where the model with the lowest BIC is preferred because it implies a better fit. According to Fig. 3, the best model uses a diagonal matrix and two clusters.

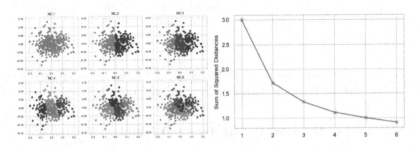

Fig. 2. Selection of the best number of clusters according to the Elbow method based on the sum of squared distances.

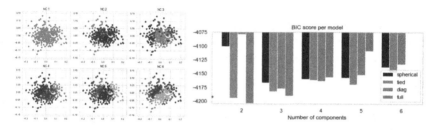

Fig. 3. Selection of the best number of clusters according to the lowest BIC measure using a diagonal covariance matrix.

The best model using the Fuzzy C-Means algorithm was found by performing a grid search over the number of clusters and the exponent of the membership function parameters; optimizing the Fuzzy Partition Coefficient (FPC) [4]. This coefficient is a metric which tells us how cleanly a particular model describes the data by measuring the amount of overlap between fuzzy clusters. It is defined on the range from 0 to 1, with one being best. Based on Fig. 4, the best model achieved a FPC of 0.7 using two clusters.

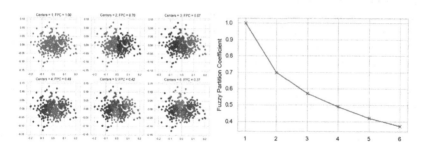

Fig. 4. Selection of the best number of clusters based on the highest Fuzzy Partition Coefficient, using two as the exponent of the membership function.

Regarding the parameters of the Kohonen Network, we trained it with two output neurons, as it was the best number of clusters found among the clustering algorithms described before. As can be seen in Fig. 5, it minimizes the mean absolute error in a small number of iterations, mapping the dataset into two clusters, each center is highlighted in orange color.

3.2 Cluster Validation Measures

An essential step in the segmentation process is to evaluate the partitioning quality to test the validity of the algorithm [18]. According to literature, the evaluation measures can be categorized into internal and external indices. Most of them take into consideration the compactness of the objects in the same

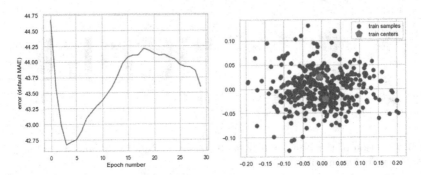

Fig. 5. Kohonen network training and the final position of the centers for each cluster. (Color figure online)

cluster and their separation in the distinct clusters [32]. In our experiments, we expressed the quality of the resulting clustering through two validity indices:

- Calinki-Harabasz, it is a "variance ratio criterion" giving some insight into the structure of the points [5]. The higher score relates to a model with better-defined clusters.
- Davies-Bouldin, it indicates the similarity of clusters which are assumed to have a data density which is a decreasing function of distance from a vector characteristic of the cluster [6]. A lower index relates to a model with better separation between the clusters.

As can be seen in Fig. 6, the algorithm which obtained the best validation measures, is the Fuzzy C-Means. In the following section, it is detailed the interpretation of the clusters resulting from each clustering algorithm according to global brands marketing.

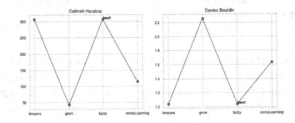

Fig. 6. Comparison of the validation indices obtained for the best number of clusters of each algorithm.

3.3   Results Interpretation from Each Clustering Algorithm

K-Means: From the results depicted in Fig. 7 (first row), it can be seen that this algorithm divides the dataset into two same-size clusters (206 for each group).

As detailed in Table 3, $C1$ has a majority presence of women and men participants from Peru and the United States, between 31 and 40 years old whereas that $C2$ includes both sex participants from Brazil, France and the Czech Republic between 21 to 30 years. It shows a marked age difference between both groups, where $C2$ represents the younger consumers and $C1$ the older ones. Regarding the dimensions analyzed, when comparing Social Responsibility from the resulting clusters, it can be seen that both groups tend to be critical to the companies practices regarding this dimension. However, $C1$ tends to accept the social responsibility practices of global brands unquestioningly. Additionally, we can see that younger people are the ones who claim for a better role of global companies in the well-being of society. Concerning the Social Prestige, $C2$ is more reluctant to accept that global brands transmit prestige, due to its lowest ability score is -2.78 when compared to $C1$, which value is -1.46. Thus, older consumers tend to buy global brands in order to improve their self-image. Meanwhile, about Brand Credibility, $C1$ perceives a global brand as believable in contrast with $C2$, where they usually question the information provided by global brand companies. To summarize, we can conclude that younger consumers ($C2$) are more concern about the social responsibility of the global brand companies which leads to a high/low brand credibility, rising/reducing the sales according to their positive/negative perception; because as they do not perceive global brands as a symbol of social prestige they can do without them.

Table 3. K-Means algorithm: ability scores, demographic and genre distribution based on the clusters found.

Cluster	Country	Sex	SR	SP	BC
C1	**USA (63.64%)** **Peru (64.10%)** Brazil (49.10%) France (34.71%) Czech Rep (35.71%)	Women and Men [31–40]	$[-1.75, 2.71]$	$[-1.46, 2.62]$	$[-0.83, 2.28]$
C2	USA (36.36%) Peru (35.90%) **Brazil (50.82%)** **France (65.29%)** **Czech Rep (64.29%)**	Women and Men [21–30]	$[-1.75, 0.88]$	$[-2.78, 1.42]$	$[-2.56, 1.38]$

Gaussian Mixture Models: From the second row of Fig. 7, we can conclude that $C2$ is almost included into $C1$. Furthermore, $C1$ groups 339 consumers including women between 21 and 25 years; and men with 21–40 years (see Fig. 4). It also is represented by consumers from Peru, France and the Czech Republic. Meanwhile, $C2$ (73 people) has 24.6% of the Brazilian consumers and 18.2% of the USA consumers. It is characterized by the presence of women from 26 to 40 years and men from under 20 to 40 years. Based on the three dimensions analyzed by the clustering algorithm, both groups are concern about the social responsibility of the global brand they are interested in buying. However, $C1$ is less agreeable that $C2$, since the high ability score for this dimension in 2.0 for $C1$ and 2.71 for $C2$. Likewise, according to the Social Prestige ability scores grouped by this algorithm, $C2$ perceive global brands as a sign of prestige. Besides, $C1$ is also less persuaded by global brands advertising.

Fuzzy C-Means: As can be seen in Fig. 7 (third row), the clustering algorithm groups 204 consumers in $C1$ and 208 in $C2$, respectively. Besides, as can be seen carefully in the dimension histograms, they are the same as the K-Means histograms. Moreover, comparing the ability scores from Tables 3 and 5, both clustering results share the same values. However, they differ in the age ranges, $C1$ (26–40 years) and $C2$ (21–25 years) consumers are younger than K-Means clusters, but they keep their perception towards the global brands. $C2$ consumers can increase their susceptibility to acquiring a global brand product according to positive brand credibility and social responsibility activities. Meanwhile, $C1$ consumers tend to buy global brands as a sign of their social prestige.

Table 4. Gaussian Mixture Models (GMM): ability scores, demographic and genre distribution based on the clusters found.

Cluster	Country	Sex	SR	SP	BC
C1	USA (81.82%) **Peru (84.62%)** Brazil (75.41%) **France (87.60%)** **Czech Rep (85.71%)**	Women [21–35] Men [21–40]	$[-1.75, 2.0]$	$[-2.78, 2.17]$	$[-2.56, 2.28]$
C2	USA (18.18%) Peru (15.38%) **Brazil (24.59%)** France (12.40%) Czech Rep (14.29%)	Women [26–40] Men [<20–40]	$[-1.75, 2.71]$	$[-1.67, 2.62]$	$[-0.83, 2.28]$

Table 5. Fuzzy C-Means: ability scores, demographic and genre distribution based on the clusters found.

Cluster	Country	Sex	SR	SP	BC
C1	**USA (62.34%)** **Peru (64.10%)** Brazil (49.18%) France (33.88%) Czech Rep (35.71%)	Women and Men [26–40]	$[-1.75, 2.71]$	$[-1.46, 2.62]$	$[-0.83, 2.28]$
C2	USA (37.66%) Peru (35.90%) **Brazil (50.82%)** **France (66.12%)** **Czech Rep (64.29%)**	Women and Men [21–25]	$[-1.75, 0.88]$	$[-2.78, 1.42]$	$[-2.56, 1.38]$

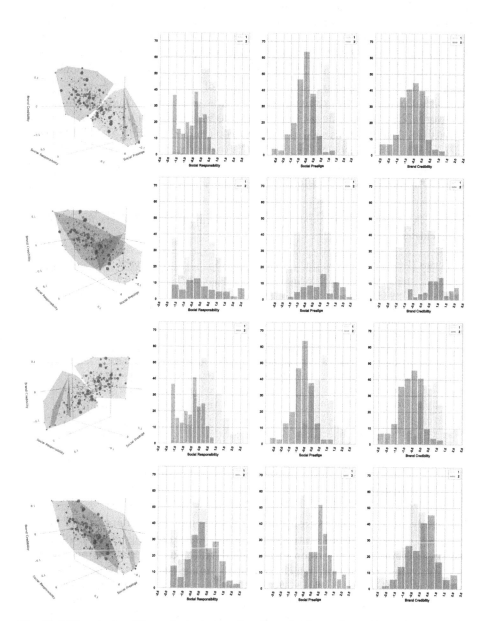

Fig. 7. Different algorithms cluster's visualization: the first column shows a 3D visualization of the clustering results, where cluster 1 is highlighted in green and Cluster 2 in red color, respectively. The second column depicts the histogram of the three variables of interest, part of the clustering analysis; where cluster 1 is highlighted in yellow and Cluster 2 in blue color. (Color figure online)

Kohonen Network: This algorithm grouped 220 consumers mostly from Brazil, France and the Czech Republic in $C1$; including women from under 20 to 50 years, and men between 21–30 years (see Table 6). In $C2$ there is a total of 192 consumers from the United States and Peru, grouped by women between 31–40 years and men between 36–60 years. According to the Social Responsibility dimension, $C1$ and $C2$ shared the lowest limit of the ability score (-1.75), which means that perceived this dimension as relevant before acquiring a global brand. However, $C2$ seems a little more persuadable when the company is not socially responsible. Moreover, the $C1$ represents consumers that buy global brands in order to achieve some social prestige level. Regarding the brand credibility, both clusters present the same upper limit (2.28); however, the $C2$ tends to trust more in what the brand offers to them.

Table 6. Kohonen Network: ability scores, demographic and genre distribution based on the clusters found.

Cluster	Country	Sex	SR	SP	BC
C1	USA (42.86%) Peru (48.72%) **Brazil (56.56%)** **France (59.50%)** **Czech Rep (57.14%)**	Women [<20–50] Men [21–30]	$[-1.75, 2.71]$	$[-2.78, 0.61]$	$[-2.56, 2.28]$
C2	**USA (57.14%)** **Peru (51.28%)** Brazil (43.44%) France (40.50%) Czech Rep (42.86%)	Women [31–40] Men [36–60]	$[-1.75, 2.51]$	$[-0.49, 2.62]$	$[-2.26, 2.28]$

4   Conclusions

This study aims to identify groups of global consumers who share similar behaviors based on three characteristics of the SCCG (social prestige, brand credibility and social responsibility). In order to achieve this goal, we analyze and compare four clustering algorithms, which allows obtaining the best number of groups for each algorithm and compare its solutions, to finally discover the best groups that explain the behavior of the global consumer. From the results, we can conclude that three clustering algorithms converged with the marketing theory (Kmeans, Fuzzy C-means and Competitive Learning). However, the Gaussian Mixture Model (GMM) algorithm does not reflect what is stated in the marketing literature.

As can be seen in the interpretation of the results, the three algorithms converge with the literature. The clustering takes place across the countries, separating the consumers into two groups: the youngest consumers (Brazilian,

French and Czech); and the consumers of mature age (Americans and Peruvians). This separation is justified by the conclusions of [2] and [16], where they conclude that businesses that operate at a global level should group target across different countries if they share similar preferences and needs. Therefore, it confirms the existence of a hybrid culture of global consumption [2].

Besides, in [2], the authors comment that the culture of global consumption represents a collection of common signs (e.g. products such as blue jeans and brands like iPod), which is understood and accepted by certain market segments, such as young people around the world. This situation is part of the obtained clustering results from three algorithms (K-means, Fuzzy C-means and Competitive Learning) which are valid in the literature because the ability scores for the analyzed dimensions for Brazilians, French and Czechs, tend to be more towards to the negative than to the positive. This circumstance denotes a greater acceptance by the proposals of global brands; unlike the Americans and Peruvians who show less acceptance and some questioning about the perceptions of the global brands. Our findings suggest that consumers in different countries develop common beliefs about global citizenship. It is a fact that consumers in favor of global brands are often younger [3]. Therefore, it is necessary to increase the intention to purchase global brands across groups that share perceptions on the characteristics of SGCC. Consequently, if the companies adopt the components of their branding programs according to the market and create conditions for each cluster identified of consumers; they could increase their benefits, for instance, cost savings.

References

1. Neurolab. https://pypi.org/project/neurolab/. Accessed 05 July 2019
2. Akaka, M.A., Alden, D.L.: Global brand positioning and perceptions: international advertising and global consumer culture. Int. J. Advert. **29**(1), 37–56 (2010)
3. Alden, D.L., Steenkamp, J.B.E., Batra, R.: Brand positioning through advertising in Asia, North America, and Europe: the role of global consumer culture. J. Mark. **63**(1), 75–87 (1999)
4. Bezdek, J.C.: Pattern Recognition with Fuzzy Objective Function Algorithms. Springer, Heidelberg (2013)
5. Caliński, T., Harabasz, J.: A dendrite method for cluster analysis. Commun. Stat.-Theory Methods **3**(1), 1–27 (1974)
6. Davies, D.L., Bouldin, D.W.: A cluster separation measure. IEEE Trans. Pattern Anal. Mach. Intell. **2**, 224–227 (1979)
7. Dolnicar, S., Grün, B.: Methods in segmentation. In: Dietrich, T., Rundle-Thiele, S., Kubacki, K. (eds.) Segmentation in Social Marketing, pp. 93–107. Springer, Singapore (2017). https://doi.org/10.1007/978-981-10-1835-0_7
8. Du, K.L.: Clustering: a neural network approach. Neural Netw. **23**(1), 89–107 (2010)
9. Dwivedi, A., Nayeem, T., Murshed, F.: Brand experience and consumers' willingness-to-pay (WTP) a price premium: mediating role of brand credibility and perceived uniqueness. J. Retail. Consum. Serv. **44**, 100–107 (2018)

10. Steenkamp, J.-B.E.M., Batra, R., Alden, D.L.: How perceived brand globalness creates brand value. J. Int. Bus. Stud. **34**(1), 53–65 (2003). https://doi.org/10.1057/palgrave.jibs.8400002

11. Guzmán, F., Davis, D.: The impact of corporate social responsibility on brand equity: consumer responses to two types of fit. J. Prod. Brand Manag. **26**(5), 435–446 (2017)

12. Hardy, A.: An examination of procedures for determining the number of clusters in a data set. In: Diday, E., Lechevallier, Y., Schader, M., Bertrand, P., Burtschy, B. (eds.) New Approaches in Classification and Data Analysis. STUDIES CLASS, pp. 178–185. Springer, Heidelberg (1994). https://doi.org/10.1007/978-3-642-51175-2_20

13. He, H., Zhu, W., Gouran, D., Kolo, O.: Moral identity centrality and cause-related marketing: the moderating effects of brand social responsibility image and emotional brand attachment. Eur. J. Mark. **50**(1/2), 236–259 (2016)

14. Hernani-Merino, M., Mazzon, J.A., Isabella, G.: Modelo de suscetibilidade para a cultura de consumo global. Revista Brasileira de Gestao de Negocios **17**, 1212–1227 (2015)

15. Höppner, F., Klawonn, F., Kruse, R., Runkler, T.: Fuzzy Cluster Analysis: Methods for Classification, Data Analysis and Image Recognition. Wiley, Hoboken (1999)

16. Huszagh, S.M.: Global marketing: an empirical investigation. Int. Executive **28**(3), 7–9 (1986)

17. Makri, K., Papadas, K.K., Schlegelmilch, B.B.: Global-local consumer identities as drivers of global digital brand usage. Int. Mark. Rev. **36**, 702–725 (2018)

18. Murray, P.W., Agard, B., Barajas, M.A.: Market segmentation through data mining: a method to extract behaviors from a noisy data set. Comput. Ind. Eng. **109**, 233–252 (2017)

19. Ornek, O., Subasi, A.: Clustering marketing datasets with data mining techniques. In: The 2nd International Symposium on Sustainable Development, Sarajevo, Bosnia and Herzegovina, vol. 3, pp. 408–412 (2010)

20. Othman, M., Kamarohim, N., Nizam, F.M.: Brand credibility, perceived quality and perceived value: a study of customer satisfaction. Int. J. Econ. Manag. **11**, 763–775 (2017)

21. Özsomer, A., Batra, R., Chattopadhyay, A., ter Hofstede, F.: A global brand management roadmap. Int. J. Res. Mark. **1**(29), 1–4 (2012)

22. Pedregosa, F., et al.: Scikit-learn: machine learning in Python. J. Mach. Learn. Res. **12**, 2825–2830 (2011)

23. Punj, G., Stewart, D.W.: Cluster analysis in marketing research: review and suggestions for application. J. Mark. Res. **20**(2), 134–148 (1983)

24. Ross, T.J., et al.: Fuzzy Logic with Engineering Applications, vol. 2. Wiley Online Library, Hoboken (2004)

25. Xu, R., Wunsch, D.: Survey of clustering algorithms. IEEE Trans. Neural Netw. **16**(3), 645–678 (2005)

26. Schwarz, G., et al.: Estimating the dimension of a model. Ann. Stat. **6**(2), 461–464 (1978)

27. Shteyneker, A., Isaac, O., Al-Shibami, A.H.: Factors influencing consumer purchasing intention within fashion luxury brand in Malaysia Int. J. Manag. Hum. Sci. **3**, 21–28 (2019)

28. Strizhakova, Y., Coulter, R.A., Price, L.L.: Branded products as a passport to global citizenship: perspectives from developed and developing countries. J. Int. Mark. **16**(4), 57–85 (2008)

29. Taylor, C.R., Okazaki, S.: Do global brands use similar executional styles across cultures? A comparison of US and Japanese television advertising. J. Advert. **44**(3), 276–288 (2015)
30. Vesanto, J., Alhoniemi, E.: Clustering of the self-organizing map. IEEE Trans. Neural Netw. **11**(3), 586–600 (2000)
31. Wedel, M., Kamakura, W.: Market Segmentation: Conceptual and Methodological Foundations. Kluwer Academic Publishers, Berlin (1999)
32. Xu, D., Tian, Y.: A comprehensive survey of clustering algorithms. Ann. Data Sci. **2**(2), 165–193 (2015)
33. Xu, R., Wunsch, D.: Clustering. Wiley-IEEE Press, Hoboken (2009)
34. Zhou, L., Teng, L., Poon, P.S.: Susceptibility to global consumer culture: a three-dimensional scale. Psychol. Mark. **25**(4), 336–351 (2008)

Using Embeddings to Predict Changes in Large Semantic Graphs

Damián Barsotti[✉] and Martín Ariel Domínguez[✉]

Group of Analysis and Processing of Large Social and Semantic Networks, FaMAF,
Universidad Nacional de Córdoba, Córdoba, Argentina
{damian,mdoming}@famaf.unc.edu.ar

Abstract. Understanding and predicting how large knowledge graphs change over time is as difficult as it is useful. An important subtask to address this artificial intelligence challenge is to characterize and predict three types of nodes: add-only nodes that can solely add up new edges, constant nodes whose edges remain unchanged, and del-only nodes whose edges can only be deleted. In this work, we improve previous prediction approaches by using word embeddings from NLP to identify the nodes of the large semantic graph and build a Logistic Regression model. We tested the proposed model in different versions of DBpedia and obtained the following prediction improvements on F1 measure: up to 10% for add-only nodes, close to 15% for constant nodes, and close to 22% for del-only nodes.

Keywords: Semantic graphs · Big Data · Graph embeddings · Machine learning

1 Introduction

We are interested in understanding and predicting how large knowledge graphs change over time to address various technological challenges, such as infrastructure needs related to data growth. An important subproblem is predicting which nodes within the graph will not have any edges deleted or changed (add-only nodes) or undergo any changes at all (constant nodes) and which ones will not have any edges added or modified (del-only). Predicting add-only nodes correctly has practical importance, as such nodes can then be cached or represented using a more efficient data structure. For example, we see parallelisms between our work and the track of changes in other large graphs, in particular the object graphs in garbage collection systems. State of the art garbage collection singles out objects that survive multiple garbage collections [12] and stops considering them for deletion. It is this type of optimizations that we expect detection of invariable nodes will help in the semantic graphs updates.

Definition. Given a multigraph G_0 with named edges such that each source node S is linked through an edge labeled V to a target node O, which we will

© Springer Nature Switzerland AG 2020
J. A. Lossio-Ventura et al. (Eds.): SIMBig 2019, CCIS 1070, pp. 282–290, 2020.
https://doi.org/10.1007/978-3-030-46140-9_26

call a *triple* $\langle S, V, O \rangle$, we will say a given node S is an *add-only node* if in a next version (G_1) of the multigraph, all triples starting on S in G_0 are also in G_1. That is, S is $add - only$ iff : $\forall v, o / \langle S, v, o \rangle \in G_0 \Rightarrow \langle S, v, o \rangle \in G_1$

Similarly, S is $del - only$ iff: $\forall v, o / \langle S, v, o \rangle \in G_1 \Rightarrow \langle S, v, o \rangle \in G_0$

Our intuition is that, in large scale semantic graphs holding an imperfect representation of the real world, there will be two types of changes, (1) model enhancements, where the truth about the world is better captured by the model and (2) model corrections, where the world has changed, and the model is updated. Updates of the first type result in new information added to the graph, without modifying existing data. Finding such nodes is the objective of our work.

In previous work [1], we show a logistic regression approach that, using binary attribute-values as features, achieves 90%+ precision on DBpedia[1] changes, we implement this model using Apache Spark. The present work improves those results by using a technique to represent a node in a large semantic ontology. This approach uses the **word2vec** word embeddings model [13] to represent the nodes in a large multi-graph as features to feed a Machine Learning (ML) model. The models obtained improve, in most cases, previous results considerably as we will see in the next sections.

This paper is structured as follows: in the next Section, we summarize related work. In Sect. 3 we discuss DBpedia, the semantic graph we used for our experiments. Our methods and results follow, closing with a conclusion, and possible research lines to continue.

2   Related Work

Mining graphs for nodes with special properties is not new to Big Data mining [4]. As DBpedia grows, much research is being conducted to exploiting this resource in AI-related tasks, and to model its changes. For example, there is research on modeling DBpedia's currency [14], that is, the age of the data in it and the speed at which those changes can be captured by any system. Although currency could be computed based on the modification/creation dates of the resources, this information is not always present in Wikipedia pages. To overcome this, the authors propose a model to estimate currency combining data from the original related pages and a couple of currency metrics measuring the speed of retrieval by a system and basic currency or timestamp. Their experiments suggest that entities with high system currency are associated with more complete DBpedia resources and entities with low system currency appear associated with Wikipedia pages that are not easily tractable (or that "could not provide real-world information" according with the authors). While both the authors and us look into variations in DBpedia, we are interested in changes that for the most part do not result from changes in the real-world, as Lehman and others are interested.

---

[1] http://dbpedia.org.

The need to account for changes in ontologies has long been acknowledged, given that they may not be useful in real-world applications if the representation of the knowledge they contain is outdated. Eder and Koncilia [6] present a formalism to represent ontologies as graphs that contain a time model including time intervals and valid times for concepts. They base their formalism on techniques developed for temporal databases, namely the versioning of databases instead of their evolution and they provide some guidelines about its possible implementation. Our work can be used to improve the internal representation of such temporal databases [2].

Another source of ontology transformation is spatiotemporal changes. Dealing with spatial changes in historical data (or over time series) is crucial for some NLP tasks, such as information retrieval [8]. In their research, the authors deal with the evolution of the ontology's underlying domain instead of its versioning or evolution due to developments or refinements. Their main result is the definition of partial overlaps between concepts in a given time series, which was applied to build a Finnish Temporal Region Ontology, showing promising results.

As far as we know, there are no approaches which predict the three types of nodes we use in our work, and test models using the complete DBpedia. For example, in [12], the authors only predict if an entity will change in the future. They obtained 66% and 75% of precision and recall, respectively, but the test set is a small subset of the DBPedia. In previous work [1] we developed models to predict add-only, constant, and del-only nodes. In that previous work, we obtain a logistic regression model, using binary characteristics to represent the nodes of interest, by the set of outgoing edge labels and the destination node. This work continues that line, with a different approach for the characterization of the nodes. To do so, the learned model represents nodes with vectors which correspond to the word embedding of labels from outgoing edges and labels from destination nodes. With this change, the resulting model achieves an improvement of up to 22%. The idea of this featurization was inspired in **node2vec** [7], an algorithmic framework for learning continuous feature representations for nodes in a graph. They define a flexible notion of the neighborhood of a node and design a biased random walk procedure. In our approach, we used this idea to generate an embedding model, which characterizes a node s by the embeddings of the outgoing verb and object from edges $< s, v, o >$. Those embeddings are used as features in ML models for add-only, constant and del-only nodes, more in deep details are given in Sect. 5.

3   Data

We use DBpedia, a large scale naturally occurring knowledge graph with a rich update history. It is a knowledge graph derived from the Wikipedia collaborative encyclopedia that started in January 2001 and, at present, it contains over 37 million articles in 284 languages.

Given that the content in Wikipedia pages is stored in a structured way, it is possible to extract and organize it in an ontology-like manner as implemented in the DBpedia community project. DBpedia contains knowledge from 111 different language editions of Wikipedia and, for English, the knowledge base consists of more than 400 million facts describing 3.7 million things [10]. A noble feature of this resource is that it is freely available to download in the form of *dumps* or it can be consulted using specific tools developed to query it. To perform our experiments, we consider all the DBpedia dumps available from 2010 to 2016[2].

These dumps contain the information in a language called Resource Description Framework (RDF) [9]. The WWW Consortium (W3C) has developed the RDF to encode the knowledge present in web pages, so that it is understandable and exploitable by agents during any information search. RDF is based on the concept of making statements about (web) resources using expressions in the subject-verb-object form. These expressions are known as triples, where the subject denotes the resource being described, the predicate denotes a characteristic of the subject and describes the relationship between the subject and the object.

A collection $s_i o_i v_i$ of such RDF declarations can be formally represented as a labeled directed multi-graph G, defined as set of labeled edges $< s_i, v_i, o_i >$, where s_i and o_i are nodes and v_i a label. This is naturally appropriate to represent ontologies.

Table 1, in column "source", shows the different years employed in this work. The DBpedia project obtains its data through a series of scripts run over Wikipedia, which on itself is a user-generated resource. Changes to the DBpedia scripts or to Wikipedia itself sometimes result in dramatic differences from one year to the next.

4 Methods

Our prediction system is implemented using Apache Spark[3], the Stellar-Random-Walk library[4], the **word2vec** implementation [13], and the distributed Logistic Regression package in MLlib [11].

This procedure consists of three phases: (1) Embedding model for node representation, (2) Building the prediction model, and (3) Prediction. The phases are described as follows:

– **Embedding model for node representation**: for this phase, we use the ideas from [7]. We build an embedding model to represent nodes based on **word2vec** embeddings [13], which associate each element in an RDF triple with a n-dimensional vector, for a given n. For NLP models, the training material to generate the embedding model is a set of NLP "sentences". Analogously, in our model, we generate "utterances" by random walks in the semantic graph. Formally, given a multi-graph G as described in the previous Section, for every subject s such that $< s, v, o > \in G$, we simulate a fixed

---

[2] https://wiki.dbpedia.org/develop/datasets.

[3] https://spark.apache.org/.

[4] https://github.com/data61/stellar-random-walk.

number n of random walks up to length l. Once we generate the random walks for all subjects s in the multigraph G, we get a collection of "sentences" M_G such that :

"s_0 v_0 $o_0 \ldots s_k$ v_k o_k" $\in M_G \iff < s_i, v_i, o_i > k \in G$ where: $s = s_0$, $o_i = s_{i+1}$, for $1 \leq i \leq$ and $k \leq l^5$.

Once, the collection M_G is completed, we run the **word2vec** training procedure, with a number N as input parameter, which returns an embedding model E_G that maps any s (subject), v (verb) or o (objet) with a vector of dimension N.

- **Building the prediction model**: In this phase, we generate three different Logistic Regression models: add-only LG_{add}, constant LG_{const}, and del-only LG_{del} nodes. As we describe in the previous Section, a list of dumps of DBpedia is available, each of them for a given date. Each dump defines a multi-graph G_i represented as a set of labeled edges $< s_i, v_i, o_i >$. We use two consecutive dumps as training material, and the third for evaluation. Let G_i and G_{i+1} be two consecutive dumps of DBpedia that we use as the training material. As any ML problem, we build a feature and target vectors. The feature vectors are the same for building LG_{add}, LG_{const} and LG_{del}. We first build an embedding as in the previous phase, let $E_{G_i \cup G_{i+1}}$ be the embedding for the union of graphs $G_i \cup G_{i+1}$. Then, for every subject $s \in G_i$, let $v_1, o_1 \ldots v_r, o_r$ be the verb and objects from the outgoing edges of node s. Then, we compute the maximum, average, and minimum of v_i, and also of o_i. In this way, using the average of vectors, the impact of the instability of **word2vec** models for unfrequent words is reduced. Also, during the **word2vec** training phase, terms with less than five occurrences are deleted. Finally, we concatenate those embedding vectors. Formally, that is:

$Av(E_{G_i \cup G_{i+1}}(v_1), \ldots, E_{G_i \cup G_{i+1}}(v_r)) \bullet Av(E_{G_i \cup G_{i+1}}(o_1), \ldots, E_{G_i \cup G_{i+1}}(o_r)) \bullet$
$Ma(E_{G_i \cup G_{i+1}}(v_1), \ldots, E_{G_i \cup G_{i+1}}(v_r)) \bullet Ma(E_{G_i \cup G_{i+1}}(o_1), \ldots, E_{G_i \cup G_{i+1}}(o_r)) \bullet$
$Mi(E_{G_i \cup G_{i+1}}(v_1), \ldots, E_{G_i \cup G_{i+1}}(v_r)) \bullet Mi(E_{G_i \cup G_{i+1}}(o_1), \ldots, E_{G_i \cup G_{i+1}}(o_r))$

Where $Av()$, $Ma()$ and $Mi()$ calculate the average, maximum and minimum between vectors, and $\bullet$ is the concatenation. The resulting feature vector has $6 * N$ dimensions, where N is the selected dimension for **word2vec** embeddings.

To obtain the binary target vector for a given node with subject s:

add-only: $\{(s, v_i, o_i) : (s, v_i, o_i) \in G_i\} \subseteq \{(s, v_i, o_i) : (s, v_i, o_i) \in G_{i+1}\}$
constant: $\{(s, v_i, o_i) : (s, v_i, o_i) \in G_i\} = \{(s, v_i, o_i) : (s, v_i, o_i) \in G_{i+1}\}$
del-only: $\{(s, v_i, o_i) : (s, v_i, o_i) \in G_{i+1}\} \subseteq \{(s, v_i, o_i) : (s, v_i, o_i) \in G_i\}$.

We feed the Mlib with these features and target vectors, and compute the three models LG_{add}, LG_{const} and LG_{del}.

- **Prediction**: Finally, in this phase we can predict add-only, constant, and del-only nodes in the unseen data from the next dump G_{i+2}.

Figure 1 shows a small example of feature and class extraction. A four-node graph G_i that we call OLD evolves into a five node graph G_{i+1} (NEW).

---

[5] Note that $k \leq l$ because o_k could be a literal, date for example, then it has no outgoing edges.

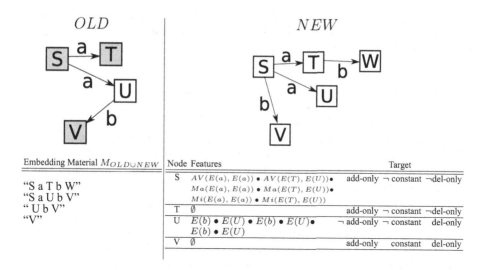

Fig. 1. Feature generation from an ontology *OLD* and *NEW*. In this example most nodes are add-only (shaded in *OLD*), only U loses a relation and it is thus del-only.

Table 1. Training in two consecutive years and evaluating on a third. Training maximizing F1.

Model	Train		Eval	System								
	Source		Target	Add-only			Constant			Del-only		
	G_{y1}	G_{y2}	G_{y3}	Prec.	Rec.	F_1	Prec.	Rec.	F_1	Prec.	Rec.	F_1
res-2018	2010-3.6	2011-3.7	2012-3.8	.57	.52	.55	.47	.19	.27	.78	.41	.54
d64				.60	.51	.55	.51	.23	.32	.81	.43	**.56**
d128				.62	.52	.56	.54	.25	**.34**	.84	.39	.54
d256				.61	.53	**.57**	.55	.24	.33	.84	.40	.54
res-2018	2011-3.7	2012-3.8	2013-3.9	.73	.67	.70	.68	.67	.68	.81	.83	.82
d64				.70	.68	.69	.67	.71	.69	.81	.90	**.85**
d128				.71	.70	.70	.71	.69	**.70**	.81	.89	**.85**
d256				.77	.68	**.73**	.75	.66	**.70**	.80	.77	.79
res-2018	2012-3.8	2013-3.9	2014	.37	.94	.53	.29	.92	.44	.39	.95	.55
d64				.36	.98	.53	.33	.97	**.49**	.40	.98	.57
d128				.38	.97	**.55**	.32	.96	**.49**	.41	.97	**.58**
d256				.38	.98	**.55**	.29	.96	.45	.41	.97	**.58**
res-2018	2013-3.9	2014	2015-04	.30	.91	.45	.39	.83	.53	.76	.61	.68
d64				.33	.94	.48	.48	.87	.62	.83	.63	.72
d128				.33	.95	**.49**	.49	.89	**.63**	.85	.63	.72
d256				.32	.96	.48	.47	.88	.61	.86	.63	**.73**
res-2018	2014	2015-04	2015-10	.63	.79	.70	.63	.58	.60	.72	.64	.68
d64				.76	.78	.77	.75	.73	.74	.70	.82	.75
d128				.73	.86	.79	.74	.77	.75	.73	.81	.77
d256				.74	.86	**.80**	.75	.76	**.75**	.78	.79	**.80**
res-2018	2015-04	2015-10	2016-04	.92	.42	**.58**	.90	.39	**.55**	.94	.42	.58
d64				.94	.35	.51	.92	.31	.47	.94	.65	.77
d128				.93	.38	.54	.92	.34	.49	.94	.67	.78
d256				.93	.39	.55	.92	.35	.50	.95	.68	**.79**

The target for each node is computed over OLD, using three binary features. The features are calculated from the resulting embedding model $E_{OLD \cup NEW}$ (renamed as E) computed from $M_{OLD \cup NEW}$ training material.

5   Results

Using the machine learning method described in the previous section we take three consecutive years, $G_{y_1}, G_{y_2}, G_{y_3}$, build a model M on $G_{y_1} \cup G_{y_2}$, apply M on G_{y_2}, obtaining G'_{y_3} and evaluate it by comparing it to G_{y_3}. For features generation, we use random walks with a maximum of 10 walks per node, and a maximum depth of 80. We generate prediction models M for 64, 128, 256 dimensions of embedding models. Table 1 shows the results compared with the baseline results, labeled as "res-2018", obtained in previous work [5]. The comparison is performed with the new prediction models calculated by using embedding vectors of dimensions 64, 128, and 256. We can see that for del-only nodes the improvement varies between 2% to 20%, depending on the years predicted. For add-only and constant nodes, the increase ranges from 1% to 10%. For del-only nodes, we achieve the best improvements, even for the last dump (2016), where the other models decrease their performance about 5%.

From the table, we can also see that detecting constant nodes, on the other hand, is a much more difficult task that might be ill-defined given the nature of the updates discussed in the introduction. Finally, in Table 2, we show some examples of right prediction and mispredictions for add-only nodes.

Table 2. Example of predictions and mispredictions, using 2015-04 → 2015-10 as training and tested on 2016-04 with model 'd128'.

Correctly predicted add-only	
USS_Breakwater_(SP-681)	*constant*
Interborough_Handicap	*constant*
Thode_Island	*added* archipelago→Marshall_Archipelago
Colonel_Reeves_Stakes	*added* location→Perth
	added location→Australia
Incorrectly predicted as add-only	
Beverly_Hills_Handicap	*disappears due to name change*
First_Ward_Park	*disappears due to name change*
Basie_Land changes	*changes* previousWork → On_My_Way_and_Shoutin'_Again!
	to previousWork→Ella_and_Basie!
Correctly predicted as not add-only node	
2012_Shonan_Bellmare_season	*changes* league→2012_J._League_Division_2
	to to league→2012_J.League_Division_2

6 Conclusions and Future Work

In this work, we improve the performance of the results obtained in previous work [1] for predicting node changing in different temporal dumps of DBpedia. For this purpose, we use a novel way to characterize the nodes of a large semantic graph using NLP concepts: word embedding. With this way of mining the graph, in most cases, we obtain significant improvements, up to 22%, while we get a small drop in performance for add-only and constant nodes for the last available dump in the conventional DBpedia. We think that this model has less performance than all previous ones, due to the training material have less variability. The reason is that the DBpedia dumps used to obtain the classifier belongs to the same year, and for all previous cases it used different years.

There are several possible lines of work to continue this publication. In this sense, to further improve the models, we plan to conduct research about the convolution function for node embeddings. We have used a simple average of the vectors of the component words, but there are other more sophisticated functions, such as the weighted average by the inverse document frequency (IDF) [15].

Another possibility of improving the results is to use an end-to-end graph-based neural network model, including Recurrent Neural Networks for the node representation. This approach solves an NLP task, the relation extraction in a text, see [3].

Besides, we are interested in testing DBpedia dumps after 2016, which are available in a new version called DBpedia Live. This new version makes it possible to obtain dumps on the desired date and offers pre-calculated dumps after 2016 [6].

On the other hand, we plan to use these results in other lines of research. In [5] we presented experiments on two types of entities (people and organizations) and, using different versions of DBpedia, we found that robustness of the tuned algorithm and its parameters do coincide, but more work is needed to learn these parameters from data in a generalizable fashion.

In [5], we explored the robustness for the particular case of Referring Expressions Generation (REG) algorithms through different versions of an ontology. Our current work is part of a plan to simulate natural perturbations on the data to find the conditions in which REG algorithms start to fail (for example, a simulated DBpedia of 25 years in the future). For general changes prediction of DBpedia, we started using the ideas of "Disentangled" representation as in [16], we split large scale graph evolution in simple problems, add-only, constant and del-only nodes prediction.

References

1. Barsotti, D., Dominguez, M.A., Duboue, P.A.: Predicting invariant nodes in large scale semantic knowledge graphs. In: Lossio-Ventura, J.A., Alatrista-Salas, H. (eds.) SIMBig 2017. CCIS, vol. 795, pp. 48–60. Springer, Cham (2018). https://doi.org/10.1007/978-3-319-90596-9_4

---

[6] https://databus.dbpedia.org/dbpedia/mappings.

2. Cheng, S., Termehchy, A., Hristidis, V.: Efficient prediction of difficult keyword queries over databases. IEEE Trans. Knowl. Data Eng. **26**(6), 1507–1520 (2014)
3. Christopoulou, F., Miwa, M., Ananiadou, S.: A walk-based model on entity graphs for relation extraction. In: Proceedings of the 56th Annual Meeting of the Association for Computational Linguistics (Volume 2: Short Papers). ACL, Melbourne (2018)
4. Drury, B., Valverde-Rebaza, J.C., de Andrade Lopes, A.: Causation generalization through the identification of equivalent nodes in causal sparse graphs constructed from text using node similarity strategies. In: Proceedings of SIMBig 2015, pp. 58–65 (2015)
5. Duboue, P.A., Domínguez, M.A.: Using robustness to learn to order semantic properties in referring expression generation. In: Montes-y-Gómez, M., Escalante, H.J., Segura, A., Murillo, J.D. (eds.) IBERAMIA 2016. LNCS (LNAI), vol. 10022, pp. 163–174. Springer, Cham (2016). https://doi.org/10.1007/978-3-319-47955-2_14
6. Eder, J., Koncilia, C.: Modelling changes in ontologies. In: Meersman, R., Tari, Z., Corsaro, A. (eds.) OTM 2004. LNCS, vol. 3292, pp. 662–673. Springer, Heidelberg (2004). https://doi.org/10.1007/978-3-540-30470-8_77
7. Grover, A., Leskovec, J.: node2vec: scalable feature learning for networks. CoRR (2016)
8. Kauppinen, T., Hyvönen, E.: Modeling and reasoning about changes in ontology time series. In: Sharman, R., Kishore, R., Ramesh, R. (eds.) Integrated Series in Information Systems, pp. 319–338. Springer, Boston (2007)
9. Lassila, O., Swick, R.R., Wide, W., Consortium, W.: Resource description framework (RDF) model and syntax specification (1998)
10. Lehmann, J., et al.: DBpedia - a large-scale, multilingual knowledge base extracted from Wikipedia. Semant. Web J. **6**(2), 167–195 (2015)
11. Meng, X., et al.: MLlib: machine learning in apache spark. J. Mach. Learn. Res. **17**(1), 1235–1241 (2016)
12. Meroño-Peñuela, A., Guéret, C., Schlobach, S.: Release early, release often: predicting change in versioned knowledge organization systems on the web. CoRR abs/1505.03101 (2015)
13. Mikolov, T., Chen, K., Corrado, G., Dean, J.: Efficient estimation of word representations in vector space. In: Proceedings of NIPS13 (2013)
14. Rula, A., Panziera, L., Palmonari, M., Maurino, A.: Capturing the currency of DBpedia descriptions and get insight into their validity. In: Proceedings of the 5th International Workshop on Consuming Linked Data (COLD 2014) (2014)
15. Arora, S., Liang, Y., Ma, T.: A simple but tough-to-beat baseline for sentence embeddings. In: Proceeding of International Conference on Learning Representations, ICLR 2017, 24–26 April, Toulon, France (2017)
16. Whitney, W.: Disentangled representations in neural models. CoRR abs/1602.02383 (2016)

Super Resolution Approach Using Generative Adversarial Network Models for Improving Satellite Image Resolution

Ferdinand Pineda[1,2]([envelope]) [ID], Victor Ayma[1]([envelope]) [ID], Robert Aduviri[1] [ID], and Cesar Beltran[1] [ID]

[1] Pontifical Catholic University of Peru, Lima, Peru
grpiaa@pucp.edu.pe, vaaymaq@pucp.pe
[2] Altiplano National University, Puno, Peru
ferpineda@unap.edu.pe
http://www.pucp.edu.pe, http://www.unap.edu.pe

Abstract. Recently, the number of satellite imaging sensors deployed in space has experienced a considerable increase, but most of these sensors provide low spatial resolution images, and only a small proportion contribute with images at higher resolutions. This work proposes an alternative to improve the spatial resolution of Landsat-8 images to the reference of Sentinel-2 images, by applying a Super Resolution (SR) approach based on the use of Generative Adversarial Network (GAN) models for image processing, as an alternative to traditional methods to achieve higher resolution images, hence, remote sensing applications could take advantage of this new information and improve its outcomes. We used two datasets to train and validate our approach, the first composed by images from the DIV2K open access dataset and the second by images from Sentinel-2 satellite. The experimental results are based on the comparison of the similarity between the Landsat-8 images obtained by the super resolution processing by our approach (for both datasets), against its corresponding reference from Sentinel-2 satellite image, computing the Peak Signal-to-Noise Ratio (PSNR) and the Structural Similarity (SSIM) as metrics for this purpose. In addition, we present a visual report in order to compare the performance of each trained model, analysis that shows interesting improvements of the resolution of Landsat-8 satellite images.

Keywords: Super Resolution · SR-GAN · Landsat-8 · Sentinel-2

1 Introduction

According to [1], currently, there is an increasing demand for obtaining high resolution images, so the applications in different research areas, such as computer vision, remote sensing, medical, among others, could take advantage of the quality of that type information and be able to improve its results; however,

J. A. Lossio-Ventura et al. (Eds.): SIMBig 2019, CCIS 1070, pp. 291–298, 2020.
https://doi.org/10.1007/978-3-030-46140-9_27

this particular scenario (of working with high resolution images) can not always be ensured, and that is the case of remote sensing applications, in which, huge amounts of information (images) provided by the satellites around the Earth is provided, but only a few proportion of that images are available at higher resolutions. One way to overcome this problem is through the applications of digital image processing techniques, such as Super Resolution (SR), which is the process of generating high resolution (HR) images from low resolution (LR) images [16].

Classic models of SR techniques use linear, cubic splines, lanczos, filtering, among other approaches, as interpolation methods to improve image resolution; but these techniques have major problems in processing the fine details in the images, such as those representing curves, edges and abrupt intensity variations between neighboring pixels [2]. As an alternative, these classical methods can be replaced by models based on deep learning approaches [3–5]; however, there is still a problem when dealing with complex textures. According to [6], those problems can be solved by performing the SR process using a Generative Adversarial Network (GAN) combined with convolutional networks (hereafter referred as SR-GAN), so the textures or complex details in the image can be likewise improved.

In this work we replicated the methodology proposed at [6]. This work is a first approximation in the use of this type of techniques in the improvement of the resolution of satellite images of low resolution. So we could exploit the large volume of images currently available in the dataset used in that work. We used that model as baseline to train our specific model, adjusting it with Sentinel-2 satellite images, so these technique, SR-GAN, could be used to improve the low resolution of Landsat-8 satellite images for its use in different remote sensing applications. For this purpose, we have created a new and different datasets for training and validating the model to improve Landsat-8 satellite images towards its reference provided by the Sentinel-2 satellite images.

The remaining of this work is organized as follows, the creation and preprocessing of the dataset is described in Sect. 2; the experimental design and the results are presented in Sect. 3; finally, conclusions and guidelines for future research in this area are discussed in Sect. 4.

2   Methodology

The following sub sections discuss the methodology proposed for preprocessing the images used in this work, from DIVerse2k dataset and Sentinel-2 images; in addition, a briefly description of the deep learning model architecture is also presented.

2.1   Dataset

DIVerse2k Dataset. (DIV2K) is conformed by a large diversity of high resolution images collected from Internet [10], all the images are 2 K resolution, that is, they have 2 K pixels on at least one of its axes (vertical or horizontal), the images are of high quality in the terms of small amounts of noise. High resolution images help in classification or segmentation processes to extract information from these images, as in the cases of deforestation, land use, urban growth, natural disasters. For our work, we used 900 images of different contents. The network implementation, used for improving the satellite images resolution with the SR technique, was trained using 800 images for training and 100 images for validation.

Sentinel2-512 Dataset. Sentinel-2 is a European mission, consisting of two twin satellites, each carrying a Multi-Spectral Instrument (MSI). Each satellite passes the same zone every 10 days [7]. Sentinel-2 is in a low 290 km orbit, its optical instruments consist of 13 spectral bands, 4 bands with 10 m of resolution, 6 bands with 20 m resolution and 3 bands with 60 m of resolution, providing images covering 100 km × 100 km [7]. For this work we used bands 2, 3 and 4, with 10 m resolution each.

For creating the Sentinel2-512 dataset, we obtained 24 images from Sentinel-2 satellite, corresponding to period from December 2018 to March 2019, those images were processed to generate the Sentinel2-512 dataset. The bands 2, 3 and 4 of each Multi-Spectral satellite image were extracted and joined into a new multichannel image with 10980 × 10980 pixel resolution. Each new image were divided in 43 tiles of 512 × 512 pixels, 21 tiles of 228 × 288 pixels, 21 of 228 × 512 pixels and 1 of 228 × 228 pixels, providing a total of 484 tiles per image. We discarded tiles with the presence of clouds and tiles with missing information (as those belonging to the extremes of the satellite image), remaining 2192 images, and we used 2000 images for training our model, and the rest for validating it.

For testing the performance of our model, when applied in a real problem, we use a Landsat-8 satellite image. Landsat-8 is part of a global research program known as NASA's Science Mission Directorate, with an orbit of 705 km at the equator, it passes the same zone every 16 days [12]. Landsat-8 is composed of nine shortwave spectral bands, 8 bands at 30 m and 1 band at 15 m of resolution. For this work, we used bands 2, 3 and 4, each at 30 m resolution.

2.2 SR-GAN Approach

As previously introduced, Super Resolution (SR) is the process of generating high resolution (HR) images from low resolution (LR) images. Since the last three decades many techniques have been proposed for performing SR processes [14,15]. More recently, Jianchao Yang [14] explore diverse SR techniques such as image observation models, processing at frequency domain, interpolation-restoration by non-iterative approaches, until statistical approaches. Currently, as an alternative, these classical SR methods can be replaced by models based on deep learning approaches, such as Generative adversarial network (GAN).

GAN was introduced by Ian Goodfellow [11], it proposes a new framework for estimating generative models via an adversarial process, in which two models are simultaneously trained: a generative model "G", that captures the data distribution, and a discriminative model "D", that estimates the probability that a sample belongs to the training data rather than a sample provided by G. The training procedure for G is to maximize the probability of D making a mistake.

Super Resolution techniques using Generative Adversarial Network models (SR-GAN) are based on the work of [6] and implemented by [8]. The architecture proposed by [6] is shown in the Fig. 1. This architecture uses two convolutional layers in the generator with 3×3 small kernels, 64 feature maps, followed by batch-normalization layers and a Parametric ReLU as activation function. Finally, the model increase the resolution of the input image applying 2 convolutional sub-pixel layers.

After performing the generative process, the discriminator process is applied to discriminate the images obtained from the generator. In the discriminator this architecture uses Leaky ReLU as an activation function and avoids the max-pooling throughout the network. The network contains 8 convolutional layers with an expanded number of 3×3 filter kernels, increasing by a factor of 2 from 64 to 512 kernels as a VGG network. The resulting 512 feature maps, then are processed by two dense layers and a final sigmoid activation function.

As presented in Fig. 1, for the SR-GAN architecture, the objective of the discriminator D is to discriminate if the ISR image produced by the generator G is a high resolution image, to achieve this the discriminator D is trained with the IHR images at high resolutions. The objective of the generator G is to obtain a satellite image at super resolution (ISR), based on an input image at low resolution (ILR).

3   Experiments and Results

This section describes the experiments that have been conducted and the results that were obtained. This work proposed to apply the SR-GAN models for processing Landsat-8 satellite images in order to increase its resolution, using two different deep learning networks for that purpose, one trained with high resolution satellite images from Sentinel2-512 dataset, and the other trained with common images from DIV2K dataset.

In this work the model proposed by [6] and implemented by [8] was replicated as the base model and proof of concept. The training was performed using and NVIDIA TITAN XP GPU.

The training of the network using both datasets, the Div2K and Sentinel2-512, was performed using a batch size of 128 with 100 epochs and a scaling factor of 4. On the trained network, we use a Landsat-8 satellite image as input in order to assess the performance of each approach.

To evaluate the quality of our results, we use the PSNR and SSIM metrics for assessing the quality of the super resolution images. For PSNR metric, it value approaches infinity as the Mean Square Error (MSE) approaches zero; this shows that higher PSNR values defines higher image qualities. Correspondingly, a small value of PSNR implies higher numerical MSE values, defining higher differences between images. The SSIM is a well-known quality metric used to measure the similarity between two images; possible values of the SSIM index

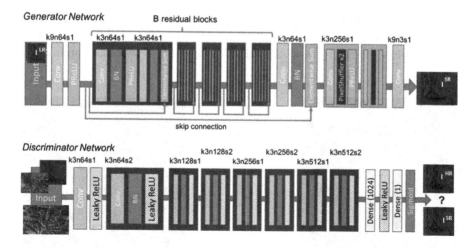

Fig. 1. Generator and discriminator models at the SR-GAN architecture, adapted of Ledig, kernel size(k), number of feature map (n), stride (s)

are in [0,1] range. A value of 0 means no correlation between images and 1 means that images are similar [13].

At the training stage, the SR-GAN results were analyzed by comparing the outcomes from the models trained with the two datasets, using the PSNR and SSIM as metric for its evaluation at each epoch, the results are shown in Fig. 2. At the validation stage, the results are summarized in the Table 1, and are those related to the comparison between the Sentinel-2 image against the two outcomes from the SR-GAN models processing a Landsat-8 image. We had a better result with the dataset Sentinel2-512.

Table 1. Testing results with the SR-GAN models when processing a Landsat-8 image

	Sentinel2-512	DIV2k
PSNR	29.391	24.149
SSIM	0.803	0.749

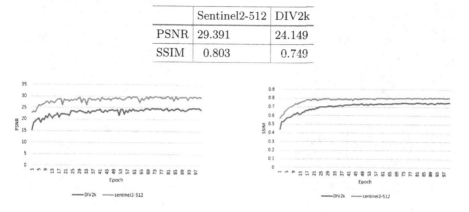

Fig. 2. PSNR and SSIM metrics at the SR-GAN models training stage using DIV2K and Sentinel2-512 datasets

From a visual analysis, the images presented in Fig. 3 shows a tile of a Landsat-8 and a Sentinel-2 images, from the Northern Coast of Piura, in Peru; and the results obtained by processing the Landsat-8 image with both approaches

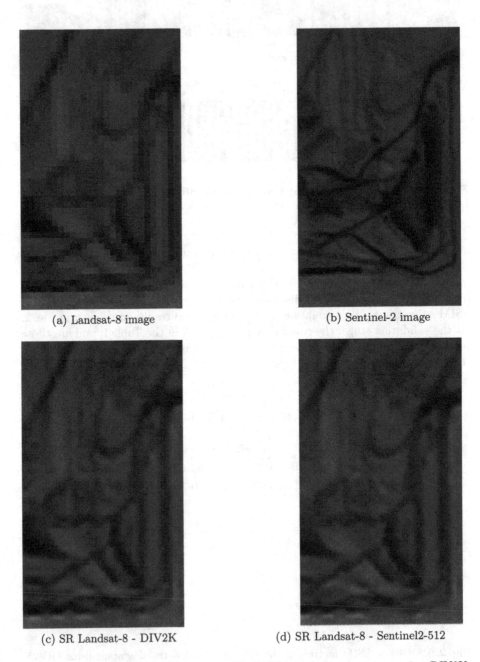

(a) Landsat-8 image   (b) Sentinel-2 image

(c) SR Landsat-8 - DIV2K   (d) SR Landsat-8 - Sentinel2-512

Fig. 3. PSNR and SSIM metrics at the SR-GAN models training stage using DIV2K and Sentinel2-512 datasets

of the SR-GAN trained models. As it can be seen in the figure, both trained SR-GAN models achieved an increase in its resolution with respect to the original input image of the Landsat-8 satellite, with a very similar approach to the Sentinel2 image.

4 Conclusions

This works shows that the application of Super Resolution techniques based on Generative Adversarial Network models (SR-GAN) in the improvement of the resolution of Landsat-8 satellite images is indeed possible; however we believe that this results can be improved by using 16 bit images in Tiff format. In terms of architecture as future work, the use of recent pre-trained networks, satellite images at higher resolutions, and the use of panchromatic images, could lead to a greater improvement of the resolution of Landsat-8 images. This work open lines of application, which not only serve to improve the resolution of the images of the visible spectrum of LANDSAT, but for all its bands, and even extend these approaches to images of different nature such as SAR.

Acknowledgments. The authors acknowledge the support provided by SENCICO(Servicio nacional de capacitación para la Industria de la Construcción) and FONDECYT (Fondo Nacional de Desarrollo Científico, Tecnológico y de Innovación Tecnológica) in the scope of the project under the financing agreement No. 131-2018-FONDECYT-SENCICO.

References

1. Keshk, H.M., Abdel-Aziem, M.M., Ali, A.S., Assal, M.A.: Performance evaluation of quality measurement for super-resolution satellite images. In: Proceedings of 2014 Science and Information Conference, SAI 2014, pp. 364–371 (2014). https://doi.org/10.1109/SAI.2014.6918212
2. Singh, S.: Enhanced deep image super-resolution. In: 2018 International Conference on Advances in Computing, Communications and Informatics (ICACCI), pp. 1207–1211 (2018)
3. Zhao, L., Sun, Q., Zhang, Z.: Single image super-resolution based on deep learning features and dictionary model. IEEE Access **5**, 17126–17135 (2017). https://doi.org/10.1109/ACCESS.2017.2736058
4. Dong, C., Loy, C.C., He, K., Tang, X.: Image super-resolution using deep convolutional networks. IEEE Trans. Pattern Anal. Mach. Intell. **38**(2), 295–307 (2016). https://doi.org/10.1109/TPAMI.2015.2439281
5. Ghosh, V.C.A., Thulasidharan, P.P.: A deep neural architecture for image super resolution. In: 2018 International Conference on Data Science and Engineering (ICDSE), pp. 1–5 (2018)
6. Ledig, C., et al.: Photo-realistic single image super-resolution using a generative adversarial network. In: Proceedings - 30th IEEE Conference on Computer Vision and Pattern Recognition, CVPR 2017, January 2017, pp. 105–114 (2017). https://doi.org/10.1109/CVPR.2017.19

7. ESA: SENTINEL-2 User Handbook Sentinel-2 User Handbook SENTINEL-2 User Handbook Title Sentinel -2 User Handbook SENTINEL-2 User Handbook, no. 1, pp. 1–64 (2015). https://sentinel.esa.int/documents/247904/685211/Sentinel-2-User-Handbook

8. Hao, R.: A pytorch implementation of SRGAN based on CVPR 2017 paper"photo-realistic single image super-resolution using a generative adversarial network" (2018). e1f9fdb7dbbb7a023ddbd19340e82101ae9147fa

9. Everingham, M., Van Gool, L., Williams, C.K.I., Winn, J., Zisserman, A.: The PASCAL Visual Object Classes Challenge 2012 (VOC2012), Results. http://www.pascal-network.org/challenges/VOC/voc2012/workshop/index.html

10. Agustsson, E., Timofte, R.: NTIRE 2017 challenge on single image super-resolution: dataset and study. In: IEEE Computer Society Conference on Computer Vision and Pattern Recognition Workshops, July 2017, pp. 1122–1131 (2017). https://doi.org/10.1109/CVPRW.2017.150

11. Goodfellow, I.J., et al.: Generative Adversarial Networks, pp. 1–9 (2014). https://doi.org/10.1017/CBO9781139058452

12. USGS: LANDSAT 8 (L8) DATA USERS HANDBOOK Version 1.0 June 2015. Departament of the Interior U.S. Geological Survey, vol. 8, June 2015

13. Horé, A., Ziou, D.: Image quality metrics: PSNR vs. SSIM. In: Proceedings - International Conference on Pattern Recognition, August, pp. 2366–2369 (2010). https://doi.org/10.1109/ICPR.2010.579

14. Huang, T., Yang, J.: Image super-resolution: historical overview and future challenges. Super-Resolution Imaging, pp. 19–52 (2010)

15. Irani, M., Peleg, S.: Super resolution from image Sequences.pdf, pp. 115–120. IEEE (1990)

16. Keshk, H.M., Yin, X.C.: Satellite super-resolution images depending on deep learning methods: a comparative study. In: 2017 IEEE International Conference on Signal Processing, Communications and Computing, ICSPCC 2017, January 2017, 1–7 (2017). https://doi.org/10.1109/ICSPCC.2017.8242625

Computer-Assisted Learning for Chinese Based on Character Families

John Lee$^{(\boxtimes)}$ and Chak Yan Yeung

Department of Linguistics and Translation, City University of Hong Kong,
Kowloon Tong, Hong Kong SAR
jsylee@cityu.edu.hk, chak.yeung@my.cityu.edu.hk

Abstract. We describe a computer-assisted language learning (CALL) approach for Chinese that is based on character families. This approach exploits word and character embeddings to construct character families that highlight the phonetic regularity and semantic regularity of their member characters. We apply these families in a CALL game where players attempt to combine sub-character components to form characters within a family.

Keywords: Computer-assisted language learning · Chinese · Character families · Word embeddings

1 Introduction

Chinese language pedagogy is a research area that has been attracting considerable interest [9,10]. Over 80% of Chinese characters are compound characters, formed by sub-character components called *radicals* [16]. It is therefore advantageous to exploit one's knowledge of the radicals when learning new characters. Indeed, in order to foster awareness of this structural regularity, many computer-assisted language learning (CALL) systems for Chinese offer Scrabble-like games, where players attempt to manipulate radicals to form characters.

As building blocks for characters, some radicals serve as *phonetic radicals* to provide pronunciation cues, and others serve as *semantic radicals* to give hints to the characters' semantic category. Table 1 shows an example. For a systematic review of characters that are phonetically or semantically similar, one can therefore organize characters into "character families" according to phonetic radical or semantic radical [1]. More precisely, members of a "phonetic character family" share a common phonetic radical, and should have identical or similar pronunciation as the radical (Table 2a); members of a "semantic character family" share a common semantic radical, and should be semantically close to the

---

This work is partially supported by an Applied Research Grant (#9667175) at City University of Hong Kong, and by the Innovation and Technology Fund (Ref: ITS/389/17) of the Innovation and Technology Commission, the Government of the Hong Kong Special Administrative Region. We thank Lam Xing for implementing the mobile app.

J. A. Lossio-Ventura et al. (Eds.): SIMBig 2019, CCIS 1070, pp. 299–305, 2020.
https://doi.org/10.1007/978-3-030-46140-9_28

radical (Table 2b). This pedagogical approach is taken, for example, by the *Chinese Radical-Based Character-Family E-Learning Platform*.[1] Empirical studies have shown the benefits brought by knowledge of phonetic and semantic radicals to Chinese language learning [8,10,14].

Our goal is to develop a CALL game for Chinese based on phonetic and semantic character families. The game objective is to recognize a character family by examining the radicals that appear in its member characters. To optimize pedagogical effectiveness, it is important to select character families that exhibit a high degree of phonetic or semantic regularity. Not all radicals, however, are reliable in this regard. Only about 38% of the phonetic radicals yield characters with regular pronunciation [18]; only 39% to 58% of the characters are semantically transparent, according to an analysis of primary school materials [2]. As a result, most existing CALL tools had to rely on manual selection. To build a comprehensive game covering a larger number of characters, it would be more efficient to perform automatic selection for character families.

This paper proposes selection methods that exploit word and character embeddings, reports their application in a prototype game, and presents preliminary evaluations. After giving some background on semantic-phonetic compounds and previous work (Sect. 2), we describe our dataset (Sect. 3) and game design (Sect. 4). We then discuss our methods for character family selection (Sect. 5) and conclude (Sect. 6).

Table 1. An example semantic-phonetic compound, 晴 *qíng* 'sunny', decomposed into its phonetic radical and semantic radical.

Compound	Semantic radical	Phonetic radical
晴	日	青
qíng	*rì*	*qīng*
'sunny'	'sun'	'blue, green'

Table 2. Example phonetic and semantic character families.

(a) Phonetic character family	(b) Semantic character family
All members have the phonetic radical 青 *qīng* 'blue, green'	All members have the semantic radical 日 *rì* 'sun'
晴 *qíng* 'sunny';	晴 *qíng* 'sunny';
蜻 *qīng* 'dragonfly';	暉 *huī* 'sunshine';
請 *qǐng* 'please';	曉 *xiǎo* 'dawn';
...	...

---

[1] Accessed at http://other.allad.com.tw/chinese2/fonts.php.

2   Background

After a discussion on semantic-phonetic compounds (Sect. 2.1), which form the focus of our CALL game, we characterize different degrees of phonetic and semantic similarity (Sect. 2.2) and review existing games (Sect. 2.3).

2.1   Semantic-Phonetic Compounds

Among the characters listed in *Shuowen Jiezi*, a Chinese dictionary, 82.5% are semantic-phonetic compounds [7]. It has also been estimated that 81% of the most frequent Chinese characters are semantic-phonetic compounds [11].

A semantic-phonetic compound consists of a semantic radical, which indicates the semantic category of the character; and a phonetic radical, which cues the pronunciation of the character. In the example shown in Table 1, the character 晴 *qíng* 'sunny' is made up of two radicals: its left side is the semantic radical 日 *rì* 'sun', which has a closely related meaning; its right side is the phonetic radical 青 *qīng* 'blue, green', whose pronunciation is similar.

2.2   Phonetic and Semantic Regularity

Each Chinese character corresponds to one syllable, which consists of an onset (or *initial*) and a rime (or *final*). Previous studies classified phonetic similarity into four categories [3]: Two characters may have the same phonemes and same tone (e.g., 青 *qīng* and 清 *qīng*); same phonemes but different tones (e.g., *qīng* and 請 *qǐng*); same rime (e.g., *qīng* and 精 *jīng*); same onset, i.e., alliterating (e.g., *qīng* and 恰 *qià*); or no similarity. In a study on the 3,027 most frequent left-right structured characters, about 33% of these compounds are classified as "same phonemes and same tone" [6].

The spectrum of semantic similarity has also been analyzed, for example as six levels of semantic transparency [2]. A character is considered transparent when its meaning is the same as or directly related to the semantic radical (e.g., 櫃 'wardrobe' and its radical 木 'wood'), or when it belongs to the category of the semantic radical (e.g., 姐 'elder sister' and its radical 女 'female'). A character is semi-transparent when its meaning is only indirectly or loosely related to the radical (e.g., 煙 'smoke' and its radical 火 'fire').

2.3   CALL Games for Chinese

The objective in most CALL games for Chinese characters is to form characters using a set of radicals [8]. The board game *Zhōngwén pīnzì yóuxì*[2], for example, offers tiles of radicals in left-right and top-bottom structures that can be combined to form over 2,200 characters. Since these games are designed to review structural regularity, the selection of radicals is primarily based on their

---

[2] 中文拼字遊戲, published by Sun Ya Publications (HK) Ltd.

productivity and frequency, rather than their ability to highlight phonetic or semantic patterns among characters. While our proposed approach features a similar game objective, it is distinguished in optimizing the choice of radicals to yield characters that illustrate phonetic and semantic regularities.

3   Data

We constructed a pool of 4,214 characters from the vocabulary lists of the *Hanyu Shuiping Kaoshi* [5] and *Test of Chinese as a Foreign Language* [15], two popular schemes for Chinese pedagogy; as well as from characters that appear in the 40,000 most frequent words in Chinese Wikipedia. We used traditional characters and decomposed them into radicals with HanziJS[3] with the decomposition types "left-right", "top-bottom" and "inside-outside". Of the 4,214 characters, 3,535 were decomposed and they formed the basis of the character families.

We identified the two radicals of each character, and then assigned the character to their respective families. This procedure yielded 616 candidate character families[4], each with an average of 11.1 member characters.

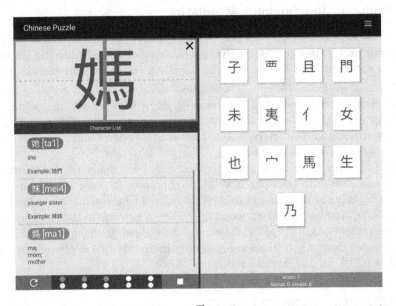

Fig. 1. Two radicals, 女 *nǚ* 'female' and 馬 *mǎ* 'horse', have been dragged from the Radical Panel (right) to the Character Box (top left) to form the character 媽 *mā* 'mother'. The Character List (bottom left) displays the valid characters formed so far.

---

[3] https://github.com/nieldlr/hanzi.
[4] We included three additional families taken from the appendix of [12].

4   Game Design

Adopting the context-sensitive, just-in-time paradigm for language learning [4], the app randomly chooses a character that appears in the name of the player's current location, as detected by the Google Map API.[5] It then selects either the phonetic or semantic character family (Table 2) of the character.

The member characters of the selected family serve as the "answer set" for the current round of game. The "Radical Panel" displays tiles for all radicals that appear in the answer set, and for a few other radicals that serve as distractors (Fig. 1). The player may long-press on any tile to see the English gloss of the radical.[6] Similar to the design of the Upwords variant of Scrabble, the player can drag-and-drop any radical tile to the "Character Box" to stack it on another tile.

The player is to form as many characters and as quickly as possible. When a valid character is formed in the Character Box, it is inserted into the "Character List" (Fig. 1) and the player scores. In case of a phonetic family, the score is correlated to the character's category of phonetic regularity (Sect. 2.2); in case of a semantic family, the score is derived from cosine similarity (Sect. 5.2). At the end of a round, a summary page shows the total score and the characters formed and missed by the player.

5   Character Family Selection

Among the candidate character families in our dataset (Sect. 3), we automatically selected those that best illustrate phonetic regularity (Sect. 5.1) and semantic regularity (Sect. 5.2).

5.1   Phonetic Character Families

We compare the pronunciation of each character to the phonetic radical of its family. If the candidate family has at least three member characters with the same phonemes or same rime as the radical, it is accepted for use in the game. Another member character with less phonetic similarity (and hence lower score) is also randomly chosen for inclusion in the answer set.

Evaluation. To gauge the difficulty of the game, we conducted a study on 19 students, all native Chinese speakers, at a university in Hong Kong. During a 10-minute period, the subjects played three rounds of game with randomly chosen phonetic character families. The subjects were able to form 50.3% of the characters in the answer set (Table 3). They were more likely to recognize characters with a higher degree of phonetic regularity: 72.2% among characters with the same phonemes or rime, compared to 48.8% among the rest. These results suggest that our game offers a level of difficulty that is sufficient for players to benefit from reviewing the missed characters.

---

[5] The player can also override the app and directly input the desired character.

[6] The gloss is taken from CC-CEDICT, which was accessed at https://www.mdbg. net/chinese/dictionary?page=cedict.

Table 3. Average proportion of characters formed by subjects during games with phonetic character families.

Characters	% of characters formed
Same phonemes or same rime	72.2%
Other	48.8%
Overall	50.3%

5.2 Semantic Character Families

We estimate the semantic similarity between a character and its family. Compared to one-hot representations, distributed word representation—representing a word as a vector in a continuous vector space—has been shown to better encode semantic information [13]. We hence derived the character vector and the "family vector", the representation of the character family, by training word, character and component embeddings with a state-of-the-art algorithm [17].

We defined the family vector to be the average of the embeddings of all member characters, since the component embeddings in [17] did not cover all semantic radicals. As for the character vector, we averaged the embeddings of the 5 most frequent words that contain the character. Compared to the character embeddings already computed in [17], this average led to better performance, likely because it captures the dominant meaning of polysemous characters.

We then computed the cosine similarity score between the character vector and the family vector. The family is accepted for use in the game if it has at least three member characters whose score exceeds 0.5. A character with a lower score is also randomly chosen for inclusion in the answer set.

Evaluation. We used the 214 standard semantic radicals in Chinese dictionaries as the gold set of semantic character families. For each candidate character family (Sect. 3), we computed the average cosine similarity score of its top 10 member characters. The family is accepted if the average score is above a minimum threshold. A threshold of 0.5 produced the best results, at 0.31 precision and 0.95 recall, suggesting that the embeddings trained with [17] are capable of recognizing families with high semantic regularity. Informal analysis on the false positives showed that some of these families also contain member characters with high semantic transparency. This method can thus potentially facilitate the expansion of character learning materials beyond the standard radicals.

6   Conclusion

We have presented a computer-assisted language learning (CALL) approach for Chinese that is based on character families. We described automatic methods to select families whose members are phonetically or semantically similar, and reported preliminary evaluation results. To the best of our knowledge, this is the first effort to design and build a CALL game that highlights both phonetic regularity and semantic regularity among Chinese characters.

References

1. Chen, H.C., Chang, L.Y., Chang, K.E., Chiou, Y.S., Sung, Y.T.: Chinese orthography database and its application in teaching chinese characters (in Chinese). Bull. Educ. Psychol. (Spec. Issue Reading) **43**, 269–290 (2011)
2. Chung, F.H.K., Leung, M.T.: Data analysis of Chinese characters in primary school corpora of Hong Kong and mainland China: preliminary theoretical interpretations. Clin. Linguist. Phonetics **22**(4–5), 379–389 (2008)
3. DeFrancis, J.: Visible Speech: The Diverse Oneness of Writing Systems. University of Hawaii Press, Honolulu (1989)
4. Edge, D., Searle, E., Chiu, K., Zhao, J., Landay, J.A.: MicroMandarin: mobile language learning in context. In: Proceedings SIGCHI Conference on Human Factors in Computing Systems (2011)
5. Hanban: International Curriculum for Chinese Language and Education. Beijing Language and Culture University Press, Beijing (2014)
6. Hsiao, J.H., Shillcock, R.: Analysis of a Chinese phonetic compound database: implications for orthographic processing. J. Psycholinguist. Res. **35**, 405–426 (2006)
7. Lai, M.D.: Huayuwen Jiaoxue Hanzi Xingshengzi Jiegou Fenxi (in Chinese). World Chinese Lang. **117**, 169–175 (2016)
8. Lam, H.C., et al.: Designing CALL for learning Chinese characters. J. Comput. Assist. Learn. **17**, 115–128 (2001)
9. Lam, H.C.: A critical analysis of the various ways of teaching Chinese characters. Electron. J. Foreign Lang. Teach. **8**(1), 57–70 (2011)
10. Leong, C.K., Tse, S.K., Loh, K.Y., Ki, W.W.: Orthographic knowledge important in comprehending elementary Chinese text by users of alphasyllabaries. Reading Psychol. **32**(3), 237–271 (2011)
11. Li, Y., Kang, J.S.: Analysis of phonetics of the ideophonetic characters in modern Chinese. In: Chen, Y. (ed.) Information Analysis of Usage of Characters in Modern Chinese (in Chinese), pp. 84–98. Shanghai Education Publisher, Shanghai (1993)
12. Liow, S.J.R., Tng, S.K., Lee, C.L.: Chinese characters: semantic and phonetic regularity norms for China, Singapore, and Taiwan. Behav. Res. Methods Instrum. Comput. **31**(1), 155–177 (1999)
13. Mikolov, T., Chen, K., Corrado, G., Dean, J.: Efficient estimation of word representations in vector space. In: Proceedings International Conference on Learning Representations (ICLR) (2013)
14. Tse, S.K., Marton, F., Ki, W.W., Loh, E.K.Y.: An Integrative Perceptual Approach to Teaching Chinese Characters. Instr. Sci. **35**, 375–406 (2007)
15. Tseng, W.H.: Huayu baqianci ciliang fenji yanjiu (Classification on Chinese 8000 Vocabulary). Huayu Xuekan **6**, 22–33 (2014)
16. Wang, S.Y.: The Chinese language. Sci. Am. **228**, 50–63 (1973)
17. Yu, J., Jian, X., Xin, H., Song, Y.: Joint embeddings of Chinese words, characters, and fine-grained subcharacter components. In: Proceedings Conference on Empirical Methods in Natural Language Processing (EMNLP), pp. 286–291 (2017)
18. Zhou, Y.G.: Xiandai hanzihong shengpangde biaoyin gongneng wenti [To what degree are the "phonetics" of present-day Chinese characters still phonetic? Zhongguo Yuwen **146**, 172–177 (1978)

Controlling Formality and Style of Machine Translation Output Using AutoML

Aditi Viswanathan$^{(\boxtimes)}$ ⓘ, Varden Wang$^{(\boxtimes)}$ ⓘ, and Antonina Kononova$^{(\boxtimes)}$

Google, Mountain View, USA
{aditiv,varden,akononova}@google.com

Abstract. An often overlooked difficulty of machine translation is producing a consistent formality (or register) in the target language. This is especially hard when the source language may have fewer levels of formality than the target language. We take a transfer learning approach using Google's AutoML Translate to train custom neural machine translation (NMT) models to consistently produce a specific formality. We experiment with formality levels for English to Spanish, English to French and English to Czech. This approach makes it possible to have better and more consistent in-context translation while still leveraging the strength of a general purpose machine translation system.

Keywords: Machine translation · Domain adaptation · Formality

1 Introduction

An important aspect of using machine translation (MT) in a business setting is maintaining a **consistent** tone and style–often called register [1] (or degree of politeness). Often, organizations want to translate text for a particular type of customer, situation or market where register is important. For example, translations for diplomatic communications differ in register from those for social media; or translations targeted at consumers are generally less formal than translations for business customers.

The style and tone of the MT output in these cases can be as important to businesses as meaning preservation and fluency. Furthermore, often the source text does not indicate the formality level of the target translation. English, for example, has fewer levels of formality [13] than many other languages, such as French or Korean–which has at least six levels of formality [11]. Consequently, there is inconsistency in using a generic MT system between these language pairs, where some sentences may be translated using formal grammatical markers while others get translated with informal grammatical markers. This leads to a loss of context across a series of sentences and is a significant impediment to the use of general purpose MT in business settings.

J. A. Lossio-Ventura et al. (Eds.): SIMBig 2019, CCIS 1070, pp. 306–313, 2020.
https://doi.org/10.1007/978-3-030-46140-9_29

In this experiment, we do not seek to model the full range of variability that registers may cover. Such an experiment would be quite complicated and would require us to parse out many different sociolinguistic situations. Instead, we focus on the register associated with personal pronouns in the phenomena of **T-V distinctions** [2], which is an important factor in formality, especially for Romance languages [8] like French and Spanish. In the case of Spanish, the second person *tú* ("you") is used when communicating with those familiar with the speaker while the more respectful form is the second-person *usted*.

In this paper we explore a simple and fast non-rules based technique for developing custom machine translation models that produce translations consistently in the desired style or formality/register using the Google Cloud AutoML Translation framework [14]. This can be seen as a special case of domain adaptation.

2   Related Work

Previous work on Formality-Sensitive Machine Translation [5] were developed using standard phrase-based MT architecture implemented as an n-best re-ranking system. Other explored techniques include style transfer after translation [6,9], but this technique requires already having an adequate translation available.

Sennrich et al. [10] proposed a method using *side constraints*–additional markers for input features such as politeness or formality. This approach relies on annotating politeness in the training set to obtain the politeness feature. Results are effective with English to German showing that translations constrained to be polite were in fact labelled polite or neutral 96% of the time and labelled informal or neutral when constrained to be informal 98% of the time. However, this method relies on passing in special tokens to mark politeness as part of the source input.

Similar approaches using domain adaptation [4] focus upon reflecting personal traits of the source speaker in the target translation. The aforementioned method proposes to learn speaker-specific parameters, which the authors cast as extreme domain adaptation. Our framing of the problem is orthogonal to this as we seek a consistent and uniform stylistic translation output regardless of any personal traits of the speaker or source input.

3   System and Training

Neural machine translation (NMT) is an approach to machine translation that uses a large artificial neural network to predict the likelihood of a sequence of words, typically modeling entire sentences in a single integrated model.

To create a general purpose formality model, we choose AutoML Translate[1], a Google Cloud AI product for customizing NMT engines for specific industries

---

[1] See https://cloud.google.com/translate/automl/docs/ for official Google documentation.

and domains. The AutoML Translation framework uses transfer learning and neural architecture search [14] to train new models on the basis of preexisting NMT models. In particular, it leverages the Google NMT (GNMT) system—a sequence-to-sequence neural machine translation system consisting of a deep LSTM network [3,12] as the baseline model. This framework is well suited to creating domain-specific customized models from in-domain input datasets that can also generalize well to different tasks.

3.1 Model Development

We create training, test and validation datasets by filtering parallel text for a set of seed words that are markers for informal and formal registers (T-V) in that language (see Table 1). These markers are chosen based on linguistic rules for the language, and are chosen such that they create sufficient (not necessary) conditions to determine the T-V register for that language. We create datasets based on these conditions[2] from Google's bilingual data (see Table 4 for details on the dataset sizes per model).

Table 1. Formality-specific markers are used to create datasets that are then used to train and evaluate custom models. (T) = Informal, (V) = Formal

Spanish (T)	Spanish (V)	French (T)	French (V)	Czech (V)
tú	él	tu	vous	vy
tu	ella	te	votre	vás
tus	Ud.	toi	vos	vám
ti	se	ton	vôtre	vámi
tuyo	usted	tes	vôtres	váš
tuyos	suyo	ta		vaše
tuya	suyos	tien		vašeho
tuyas	suya	tiens		vašemu
te	suyas	tienne		vaší
contigo		tiennes		vaším
				vašem

---

[2] For example, in Spanish, if a target segment contains any of the words listed in Column 1 of Table 1, it is a sufficient condition to determine that its register is informal (T). However, determining that a target segment is of the formal register (V) is more challenging because some of the words that signify the formal register are also used to refer to the 3rd person (e.g. Spanish *suyo* can mean English formal *yours* or 3rd person *his*). To solve for this, we filter segment pairs where the target segment contains (V) markers **and** the source segment contains any English inclusion words like 2nd person pronouns (e.g. "you", "yours") **and** does **not** contain any English exclusion words like 3rd person pronouns (e.g. "her", "she", "them"). This combined rule is a sufficient condition to determine that the register of the target segment is formal (V).

We then use these formality-specific datasets to train custom models that are biased towards the respective registers using AutoML Translate. We initially use the generic GNMT model [12] as the base model and train a custom model on top of the base per formality register and language pair. We repeat this step multiple times, each time using the custom model trained in the previous step as the base model for the current step. The training data at each step remains the same–the intention with this approach is to force a strong bias on either the T or V form, while retaining the ability to generalize well (see Table 3 for example model outputs). We see significant incremental improvement in formality biasing with this iterative warm start approach. For French and Spanish, we observe that running the training 2–3 times performs the best in biasing towards a specific formality register while preserving meaning and fluency. We expect that further experimentation can help identify the optimal number of "warm re-starts" per register and language pair.

4   Evaluation

Setup. In order to evaluate whether the translation models successfully produce the desired register, we ask human translators to develop translation references of differing formality registers (formal and informal) from the same source segments[3] (see example Table 2). We use 400 source segments that are drawn randomly from the WMT '11 and '12 Translation Task test sets.

The evaluation sets are then divided by formality level. The formal set will be used to evaluate the formal models and the informal set used to evaluate the informal models. The translated segments from each formality level–from both human translation and machine translation–is then sent through human evaluation to rate the quality and formality of the translations.

For automatic evaluation, we use larger evaluation sets of 10000 segments for each language and formality register. These evaluation sets are created using the same methodology used to create the training datasets (see Table 1).

Table 2. Use of formal singular 'you' vs informal singular 'you' with verb agreement.

English	Formal (V)	Informal (T)
Juan, how are you?	Juan, cómo está **usted**?	Juan, cómo estás?
Do you know where the house is?	Sabe **usted** dónde está la casa?	Sabe**s tú** dónde está la casa?

4.1   Automatic Evaluation

We use the standard automatic machine translation evaluation metric BLEU [7], with single references, to baseline the formality biased models relative to the

---

[3] Segments may consist of either a single sentence or multiple sentences.

Table 3. Example model outputs from Spanish custom models

English	Generic MT	Formal Bias Model	Informal Bias Model
However, you can get the second one for free	Sin embargo, **puede** obtener el segundo de forma gratuita. (V)	Sin embargo, **usted puede** conseguir el segundo de forma gratuita	Sin embargo, **te puedes** conseguir el segundo gratis
You will just sleep better	Sólo dormirás mejor. (T)	**Usted** sólo dormirá mejor	Sólo dormirás mejor

Table 4. Comparison of BLEU scores across English to French and English to Spanish models

Language	Evaluation Set Register	Dataset Size (segment pairs)	Formal Bias Model	Informal Bias Model	Google Translate (GT)	Performance Gain over GT
French	Formal	33M	**62.362**	39.668	57.28	+5.082
	Informal	5.6M	29.972	**50.699**	40.844	+9.855
Spanish	Formal	33M	**54.394**	36.449	42.603	+11.791
	Informal	33M	37.165	**65.686**	46.476	+19.21
Czech	Formal	4K	**51.117**	–	33.75	+17.367
	Formal	2.3M	**56.323**	–	33.004	+23.319

base Google NMT provided by AutoML. BLEU has reasonably high correlation with human judgments of quality. It helps us understand how well the model is biasing towards a specific formality as matching markers in the model output should be reflected in the reference set. While BLEU should never be used as the only metric to assess translation quality, it provides a quick and useful measure for rapidly iterating and improving systems.

Results. Table 4 exhibits our BLEU scores for French, Spanish and Czech formality models on Formal/Informal register evaluation datasets. As expected, the custom AutoML model with a formal bias does better than generic MT on evaluation sets that have a formal register; and the custom AutoML model with an informal bias does better on evaluation sets that have an informal register. The BLEU score performance differences are especially significant for English to Spanish and English to Czech models.

4.2   Human Evaluation

Human evaluation of translations tend to be a more reliable and authoritative method in measuring machine translation quality. So, in addition to using BLEU scores–which may conflate translation errors and formality mismatches–we ask bilingual human raters to rate the machine translation output on both the traditional measures of fluency and meaning, but also level of formality. For the languages we have chosen we ask raters to rate the formality as formal, informal, or neutral. The raters are bilingual native speakers of the target language.

EN to FR

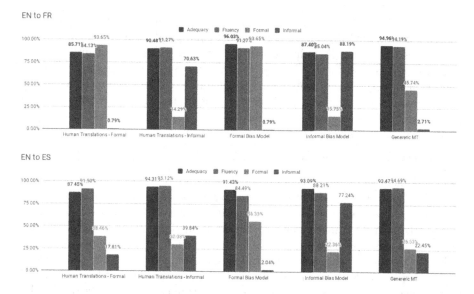

EN to ES

Fig. 1. Comparison of Adequacy, Fluency and Formality across models. Neutral formality ratings are not shown. In general, our models are able to bias the source text to the desired formality. Furthermore, our adequacy and fluency ratings are comparable to both human translations and Generic MT.

Results. Adequacy is rated on a 4 point scale going from None, Little, Most, All. Fluency is also rated on a 4 point scale going from Nonsense, Poor, Good, Flawless. Formality was rated as Informal, Neutral, or Formal. In Fig. 1: Adequacy is shown as percentage of segments in the evaluation set receiving adequacy ratings of Most or All meaning preserved; Fluency is shown as a percentage of segments in the evaluation set receiving fluency ratings of Good or Flawless.

Interestingly, we suspect that the dramatic difference between the French and Spanish systems in the human evaluation results for formality in the Human Translations-Formal evaluation and the Formal Bias Model evaluation may have to do with the consistency and source of the training data we used. The data for our French models came primarily from parallel text aimed towards the variation of French in France. The data used for the Spanish translation models came from a larger variety of locales including different Latin American varieties of Spanish as well as Spanish from Spain. Therefore, we surmise that agreement on formality may be lower due to local differences on what is considered formal or informal.

Human evaluation for Czech was only performed for the 2.3M Formal Czech model. Adequacy and fluency were 89% and 87% respectively, with 98.3% of the segments rated as formal.

5 Conclusion

In this paper, we use a domain adaptation technique to bias a model to produce translations according to a desired formality or register while still maintaining a high level of fluency and meaning. After proper training, translations with unintended formality levels have been almost eliminated from our models. Additionally, the Czech models indicate that by leveraging transfer learning from the base model, it is possible to develop a formal model by tuning with a dataset of fewer than 5 thousand sentences. Our evaluation shows the effectiveness of this technique in producing consistent in-context translations with a specific formality register, without a significant loss in translation quality.

5.1 Further Experiments

We would like to extend our technique to other languages. Languages like Korean are said to have at least six levels of formality. It would be interesting to see how well this technique captures the differentiation between them. In a few cases, our models produce translations with mixed formalities. Reducing or detecting such errors is also an interesting basis for future work on this technique.

Lastly, we want to expand this technique beyond just T-V distinctions. Based on some experiments we've run on French to English parallel text from 12 Shakespearean comedies (see Table 5 for example output), it is possible to use this technique to create domain-adapted custom models that reflect a personality or language style.

Table 5. Example model outputs from an experiment on French to English Shakespearean data

French	Generic MT	Custom Shakespearean Model
Qu'est-ce que tu fais?	What are you doing?	What art thou doing?
Oui! C'est toi que je veux dire.	Yes! It's you I want to say	Aye! I mean thee
Comment on est aujourd'hui?	How are we today?	How now?

References

1. Biber, D., Finegan, E.: Sociolinguistic Perspectives on Register. Oxford University Press on Demand, Oxford (1994)
2. Brown, R., Gilman, A., et al.: The pronouns of power and solidarity. Bobbs-Merrill, Indianapolis (1960)
3. Chen, M.X., et al.: The best of both worlds: combining recent advances in neural machine translation. arXiv preprint arXiv:1804.09849 (2018)
4. Michel, P., Neubig, G.: Extreme adaptation for personalized neural machine translation. arXiv preprint arXiv:1805.01817 (2018)
5. Niu, X., Martindale, M., Carpuat, M.: A study of style in machine translation: controlling the formality of machine translation output. In: Proceedings of the 2017 Conference on Empirical Methods in Natural Language Processing, pp. 2814–2819 (2017)
6. Niu, X., Rao, S., Carpuat, M.: Multi-task neural models for translating between styles within and across languages. arXiv preprint arXiv:1806.04357 (2018)

7. Papineni, K., Roukos, S., Ward, T., Zhu, W.J.: Bleu: a method for automatic evaluation of machine translation. In: Proceedings of the 40th Annual Meeting on Association for Computational Linguistics, ACL 2002, Association for Computational Linguistics, Stroudsburg, PA, USA (2002), pp. 311–318. https://doi.org/10.3115/1073083.1073135

8. Posner, R.: The Romance Languages. Cambridge University Press, Cambridge (1996)

9. Rao, S., Tetreault, J.: Dear sir or madam, may i introduce the GYAFC dataset: corpus, benchmarks and metrics for formality style transfer (2018)

10. Sennrich, R., Haddow, B., Birch, A.: Controlling politeness in neural machine translation via side constraints. In: Proceedings of the 2016 Conference of the North American Chapter of the Association for Computational Linguistics: Human Language Technologies, pp. 35–40 (2016)

11. Sohn, H.M.: The Korean Language. Cambridge University Press, Cambridge (2001)

12. Wu, Y., et al.: Google's neural machine translation system: bridging the gap between human and machine translation. CoRR abs/1609.08144 (2016). http://arxiv.org/abs/1609.08144

13. Xiao, Z., McEnery, A.: Two approaches to genre analysis: three genres in modern american english. J. Eng. Ling. **33**(1), 62–82 (2005)

14. Zoph, B., Le, Q.V.: Neural architecture search with reinforcement learning. arXiv preprint arXiv:1611.01578 (2016)

Linguistic Fingerprints of Pro-vaccination and Anti-vaccination Writings

Rebecca A. Stachowicz[✉]

Montclair State University, Montclair, NJ 07043, USA
stachowiczr1@montclair.edu

Abstract. Vaccination hesitancy has been gaining public attention as a global health threat. With the echo chamber effect of social media and the prevalence of misinformation, it is becoming more important to understand all aspects of anti-vaccination attitudes, especially when facts to the contrary can solidify rather than change beliefs. Starting with the question of what might drive anti- or pro-vaccination views, this paper describes a new, balanced corpus of vaccination writings. In order to gather all the linguistic signals, corpus analysis as well as feature selection and classification tasks are used to explore themes and motivations that define each class. Our results reveal that anti-vaccination writings are typically less formal. Results also indicate the possibility that the authors of such writings are processing trauma. These findings suggest that future health promotion efforts should make attempts not to talk down to individuals and should stem from a place of understanding.

Keywords: Language · Vaccination · Health · Autism · LIWC

1 Introduction

Vaccination has been gaining recognition worldwide as a global health priority. The World Health Organization's 2019 list of ten threats to global health includes vaccine hesitancy [1]. With the echo chamber effect of social media and the prevalence of misinformation, it is becoming more important to understand all aspects of anti-vaccination attitudes, especially when facts to the contrary can solidify rather than change beliefs [2–4, 19].

Anti-vaccination sentiment is nothing new. Resistance to vaccination became organized when The Vaccination Act of 1853 required Edward Jenner's smallpox vaccine by law in England. A group was formed called the Anti-Vaccination League.

Years later, Wakefield [5] claimed a link between the measles, mumps, rubella (MMR) vaccine and autism. Spurred on by this fraudulent study, anti-vaccination sentiment has grown since. Occurrence of measles, which is preventable by vaccine, increased 30% in 2017, and, "countries close to eliminating the disease have seen a resurgence" [1, 6].

According to the Centers for Disease Control (CDC) no link exists between vaccines and autism (2019). The British Journal, Lancet, the original publisher of the infamous study, has since retracted Wakefield [5, 7]. There has also been an abundance of research

J. A. Lossio-Ventura et al. (Eds.): SIMBig 2019, CCIS 1070, pp. 314–324, 2020.
https://doi.org/10.1007/978-3-030-46140-9_30

conducted since that disproves the spurious link between vaccines and autism [8–11]. However, due to media attention in the UK, US, and worldwide, in addition to celebrity endorsement, Wakefield's study is not universally considered to be misinformation, and many parents still see vaccination as a personal choice. [12, 13].

The idea that there is a connection between vaccines and autism has taken root in many communities, and it has grown into a movement. Just like the Anti-Vaccination League of 1853, people today, often labeled *anti-vaxxers*, are refusing to vaccinate their children. The total number of people infected with measles in 2018 was three times the number in 2017 [1], and the percentage of children under 2 years old in the United States who haven't received any vaccinations has quadrupled in the last 17 years [14]. Central to the anti-vaccination movement are a series of core beliefs, among them: vaccines contain harmful substances, vaccination is a personal choice, and vaccines cause autism in children. The latter two are especially harmful given that "herd immunity" is necessary to support individuals who cannot be vaccinated and how autism, and autistic people are often framed in anti-vaccination narratives.

Given the dangers of this global crisis, changing anti-vaccination attitudes has become a public health issue. Research has shown that confirmation bias can often thwart efforts to convince parents to vaccinate using facts [15, 19]. Therefore, new and different approaches to this complex problem are not only welcome, but also necessary in the current climate.

1.1 Background

As facts continue to fall short, it is imperative that we explore other methods to ensure vaccination coverage. Previous research has focused on creating a profile of individuals with anti-vaccination attitudes [12, 16], and previous studies have solidified the assumption that users of social media primarily consume information that reinforces their own beliefs [4, 15]. Attitudes towards autism and vaccination are also reinforced through other online content [17]. Terms, themes, and figures that define the vaccination debate have also been identified [18]. Language use has also been compared across these insular groups, but until now, this research has focused only on social media platforms within the limited context of comment threads, shares, and re-posts [3, 17].

Research has also come to light describing the often stigmatizing nature of labeling neuro-divergent individuals [20]. While the validity of person-first language is still debated among the Autism community [21], understanding the kinds of labels and language used in both the anti-vaccination and pro-vaccination communities provides insight into each group's perception of autistic individuals. This may prove essential to public health interventions especially when autistic children and their siblings are under vaccinated [22].

1.2 Current Study

In this paper we aim to investigate the language used in web-based writings outside of social media and across genres on the subject of vaccination. This corpus analysis, as well as feature selection and classification tasks are designed to provide a tool to better understand anti-vaccination writings and the psychological aspects of the language surrounding this movement with the ultimate aim of aiding future health promotion efforts.

The goals of the study were twofold. Part 1 explored terms and Linguistic Inquiry and Word Count (LIWC) features. LIWC is a text analysis program that evaluates the degree to which various types of words are used in a piece of writing. The results of LIWC analysis provide insight into the psychological meaning behind specific language choices [23]. The hierarchical structure of LIWC enabled us to hone in on specific categories of words. To illustrate, the LIWC category Relativity includes words such as, area, bend, exit, and stop, and one of its subcategories Space includes the language items, down, in and thin among others. These LIWC features and other terms in this corpus were analyzed for frequency as well as how each differed across writings. Part 2 looked at collocations and n-grams to determine relevant themes as well as the extent to which various labels are used to describe Autistic individuals in each community.

2 Procedure

We compiled a corpus of web-based writings on the subject of vaccination and annotated for two classes: pro-vaccination and anti-vaccination. We started with basic corpus analysis, such as keywords, collocations, and n-grams. Then we explored automatic approaches to distinguish between anti- and pro-vaccination texts using psychometric word analysis with LIWC [23] combined with feature selection and classification tasks.

Corpus Collection. A master corpus of 124 separate documents was created primarily focused on the subject of vaccination, with a secondary focus of autism. The corpus was compiled by searching the terms vaccination, vaccinate, vaccine(s), vaccine dangers, anti-vaccine, autism vaccine, vaccine risks on the CDC webpage, EBSCOhost, Generation Rescue, Google, Google Scholar, WHO, and on a variety of news websites purpose chosen to span a variety of political ideologies (e.g. ABC, BBC, Breitbart, CNN, Fox). The writings were converted into plain text files, cleaned by hand, and standardized to American English (to improve corpus analysis results).

A human annotator proofread the corpus and eliminated irrelevant material. Our final corpus contains 59 anti-vaccination documents with 92,866 total work tokens and 9,446 word types and 65 pro-vaccination documents with 84,443 word tokens and 8,307 word types.

2.1 Vaccination Sentiment Annotation

Each piece of writing was read and categorized as either pro-vaccination: encouraging vaccination efforts and/or discussing the benefits of vaccination, or anti-vaccination: discouraging vaccination and/or discussing the risks. Writings that did not seem to fit either category were discarded. Documents were then sorted into one of five genres: news, testimonial, blog, information, or research study. These five categories were created to ensure that each class was composed of a balanced representation of writing styles so it could be safely compared.

The categories were assigned as follows. News was assigned if a piece of writing was an impersonal (to the author) story about an event or series of events. A testimonial was assigned if a piece of writing illustrated a personal experience or the experience of a person with a close relationship to the author. Blog was assigned to writings with a clear position written as a personal opinion or the opinion of an organization or cause. Information was assigned if a document shared information proven to be factual or believed to be factual and/or methods for accomplishing something. Research study was assigned if an academic writing was based around an experiment, literature review, or policy.

Corpus Analysis. Collocations (within five words to the left or right: 5L, 5R) were found in each corpus surrounding the terms: autism, autistics, had autism, has autism, is autistic, with autism, child, children, parent, parents, person, people, vaccine, vaccines Collocates were found using (MI) Mutual Information and T-Score [24]. Common n-grams (trigrams, 4-grams, and 5-grams) were also extracted.

We used part of a general-purpose corpus of contemporary American English (COCA) [25] to define keywords. Spoken texts were removed in order to reflect the genre variation of our corpora, which did not include spoken items. Keywords and the terms from each class with a relative frequency over 4 were tested for significance using tf-idf weights.

2.2 Feature Selection

We extracted 95 features using LIWC2015 [23]. Linguistic Inquiry and Word Count (LIWC) is an "efficient and effective method for studying the various emotional, cognitive, and structural components present in individuals' written speech samples" [26]. By using LIWC features, we endeavor to explain and compare motivations behind the language use of pro-vaccination and anti-vaccination advocates.

We applied six different feature selection (Information Gain, Cfs Subset, Wrapper Subset, Chi Squared, Gain Ratio, Symmetrical Uncertainty) algorithms to our data and chose only those on which all six agreed. These 16 LIWC features, Words/sentence, 1st person singular, 3rd person singular, Cognitive processes, Insight, Differentiation, Body, Relativity, Space, Swear words, Periods, Commas, Question marks, and Exclamation marks, were used for the majority of our classification experiments.

Table 1. Classification task performance.

Features	Model	Accuracy	Precision	Recall	F1
ALL (95)	Baseline	**0.52**	0.28	0.36	**0.47**
	NaivesBayes	0.69	0.69	0.69	0.68
16	J48	0.68	0.68	0.68	0.68
	DecisonTable	0.69	0.69	0.69	0.69
	NaïveBayes	**0.77**	0.80	0.77	**0.77**

Tasks with other classification algorithms were attempted and yielded less notable results.

2.3 Classification

Due to our balanced corpus, we chose a simple majority class classifier for our baseline. We also experimented with other classification algorithms and with different feature sets. Our results are summarized in Table 1.

The Naive Bayes classifier produced promising results (77%) and significantly improved over the baseline (52%) when used with the 16 features described above and 10-fold cross-validation.

Table 2. Keywords by class.

Rank	Anti-vaccination	Pro-vaccination
1	Vaccine	Vaccine
2	Vaccines	Vaccines
3	Autism	Vaccination
4	Vaccination	Measles
5	Vaccinations	Autism
6	Immune	Vaccinated
7	Mercury	Immunity
8	Vaccinated	Rubella
9	Thimerosal	MMR

3 Results

The most frequent words across corpora were similar. As seen in Table 2, 11 of the top 20 words are shared between the pro- and anti-vaccination categories. However, tf-idf weights revealed fewer similarities across categories (Table 3).

Looking at tf-idf weights, *DNA* has the most weight in the anti- vaccination corpus. This aligns with the mistaken belief in the anti-vaccination community that vaccines made using human embryo cells can cause harm to patients [27]. This term along with *flu* highlights the prevalence of misinformation beyond the vaccine-autism link. Whereas *thimerosal* (a mercury-containing organic compound used as a preservative in some vaccines), *mercury*, and *autism*, which also show up in the keywords and most frequent words, are clear references to the beliefs brought on by Wakefield [5]. The high rank of *I* and *he* are in line with the LIWC feature categories 1st person singular, and 3rd person singular in this corpus, which through multiple feature selection and classification tasks were determined to be significant.

In the pro-vaccination corpus the highest tf-idf weights were *sliv* (school-located influenza vaccination), *consent*, *influenza*, and *herd*. These terms highlight the policy efforts of pro-vaccination proponents to lower the age of consent for vaccination. Vaccination in schools leverages higher coverage to improve herd immunity, as school children

Table 3. tf-idf weight by class.

Rank	Anti-vaccination		Pro-vaccination	
1	Dna	11.16	Sliv	27.78
2	i	7.54	Consent	13.59
3	Thimerosal	7.49	Influenza	11.50
4	Pregnancy	7.37	Herd	10.36
5	Mercury	6.86	Exemption	9.44
6	Flu	6.47	HPV	9.03
7	Cell	6.32	Schools	8.50
8	He	6.06	Exemptions	8.38
9	Cells	5.86	Immunity	8.21
10	Autism	5.79	Participants	7.80

sliv refers to school-located influenza vaccination

have the highest rates of infection. These terms along with *schools* and *immunity*, show that vaccine coverage in schools and herd immunity awareness are issues central to vaccination advocates' efforts.

Table 4. Most frequent words by class.

Instances of word in corpus (rank)		
Word	Pro-vaccination	Anti-vaccination
Vaccine	905 (1)	1001 (1)
Vaccination	626 (2)	225 (6)
Vaccines	559 (3)	671 (2)
Children	475 (4)	466 (3)
Measles	454 (5)	–
Autism	270 (8)	378 (4)
Health	286 (7)	279 (5)
Parents	312 (6)	184 (9)
Medical	–	199 (7)
Child	–	195 (8)
People	260 (9)	130 (18)130 (18)
Disease	206 (13)	162 (10)
Vaccinated	220 (10)	–

4 Discussion

The high term frequency words, keywords, and tf-idf representations in our pro-vaccination corpus are in line with the results of Kang et al. [17] with respect to pro-vaccination writings. Their positive network included the concepts: measles, autism, HPV vaccine, vaccine-autism link, meningococcal disease, and MMR vaccine. Their negative network referred to the CDC, vaccine industry, doctors, mainstream media, pharmaceutical companies, and United States. While the frequent words (Table 4), key-words, and tf-idf in our anti-vaccination corpus were not consistent with these findings, as they included more language focused on vaccine ingredients and the purported neg-ative effects of vaccination, the n-grams revealed terms in line with these concepts and agencies.

However, the pro-vaccination n-grams also largely referenced the United States and CDC as well. There was a notable lack of mentions of pharmaceutical companies across both corpora. Possible reasons for these differences could be the addition of autism as a search term during our corpus compilation, and the exclusive use of news articles in Kang et al.'s study contrasted with our inclusion of other genres.

As far as punctuation, the anti-vaccination texts contained more question marks and exclamation marks than the pro-vaccination texts (see Fig. 1). The use of exclama-tion marks in anti-vaccination texts was also notably ten times the amount of baseline LIWC tests [26]. This is indicative of stylistic differences that may be the result of the prevalence of funded non-profit organizations' writings in the pro vaccination corpus. Such organizations would have the resources for widespread quality control (i.e. proof-reading). In contrast, most anti vaccination writing were published by individuals or online-community interest groups that, with the exception of Generation Rescue, would not have such resources. Informality was also evidenced by more than six times the amount of swear words in the anti class than the pro. The combined vaccination corpus, however, contained far less profane words than baseline. Pro-vaccination writings also contained more periods and commas than anti vaccination writings. The role of punc-tuation may be related. The accessibility of resources mentioned above as well as the tendency for academic writing to contain more periods and commas than are typically found in less formal styles due to in text citations.

Pro-vaccination writings made more references to relativity and space (Fig. 1), per-haps a result of advocates' reporting on regions of outbreak, spread of disease, and resurgences as well as the tendency to explore best practices for vaccination coverage which include location and strategy. The anti-vaccination class made fewer references to words in these categories, and far less than baseline, indicating that perhaps location and movement is less important to their cause.

Anti-vaccination texts contained twice the mentions of body-associated words when compared to pro, which surprisingly contained less than baseline. These findings agree with those of Faasse and Chapman [3], which describe anti-vaccine Facebook comments as having more body references than pro-vaccine comments. Past research has shown that the typical person with anti-vaccination attitudes is more disgusted by blood and needles than a person without such beliefs [12]. Perhaps a larger percentage of body related words reflect these fears. Anti-vaccination results also support findings from that anti-vaccine comments make more references to money [3]. Pro-vaccination results run

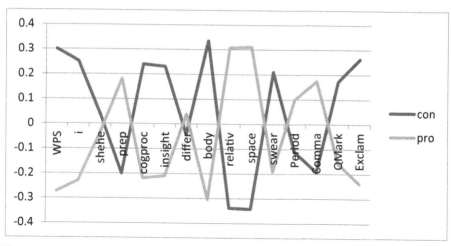

Fig. 1. Normally distributed values across LIWC features of interest for pro-vaccination and anti-vaccination classes.

counter to Faasse and Chapman [3], as anti-vaccination writings made slightly more references to family, though both contained a much higher percentage of family words than baseline.

Cognitive process words ranked higher, in anti-vaccination writings, as well as its subcategory insight. Use of insight words while detailing past events implies the processing of trauma [28]. One reason there may be a larger percentage of such words is that many anti-vaccination advocates are grieving. The term SIDS (sudden infant death syndrome) ranked high (14th of anti 4-grams, and a frequency of 23) in several metrics. These LIWC insight percentages may be indicative of a grieving process that many parents are going through. Some parents even consider having an autistic child as a loss. In a 2010 interview with PBS Frontline, Jenny McCarthy, anti-vaccination advocate, is quoted as saying, "Ask 99.9 percent of parents who have children with autism if we'd rather have the measles versus autism, we'd sign up for the measles." Whether overt, or subtler, the grieving process is a possible reason for a larger percentage of cognitive process words. In pro-vaccination writings where it is less common to see themes of trauma and loss, these cognitive process words are less prevalent. A heightened percentage of cognitive processes terms is also a quality of more complex language, but so are prepositions of which the pro-vaccination writings contained slightly more [29].

Anti-vaccination writings contained more 1st person pronouns than pro-vaccination and baseline. These findings are consistent with Kowalski [30] who found that victim-focused language used more 1st person singular pronouns than language where the writer is at fault. This is consistent with the "vaccines as the villain" narrative found in many anti-vaccination writings. Greater use of 1st person also corresponds to emotion and informal language and 3rd person to social interests and support [26]. Considering that the majority of anti-vaccination writings came from sources with less resources, it may be the case that they would contain more emotional and less formal language, and read as if from a social interest or support group.

Table 5. Label collocations across classes.

Phrase	Has autism	Had autism	Is autistic	With autism	Autism	Autistic
Anti collocates	Skeparent	Exhausting	Eldest	Children	Spectrum	Children
	Blogher	Son	Complications	Leucocytes	adhd	
	Vaccinate	Mccarthy	Son	Exploration	Relationship	
	Medicine	Jenny	Autistic	Anomalies	Prevalence	
	Based	Never	Reasons	Accommodations	Disorder	
Pro collocates		Result		Toddler	Trigger	Undisclosed
		Never		Subsets	Spectrum	Transpired
		Three		Spurious	Disorder	Integrating
		Being		Rarer	Cause	Hating
		Vaccinated		Proportionally	Link	Faces

Blank space indicates a lack of statistically significant collocates outside of function words.

Though a larger corpus is needed to comprehensively evaluate the impact of labels in vaccination writings, there is evidence of a higher percentage of noun labels within anti-vaccination writings when compared with pro-vaccination sources (Table 5). While any label can be harmful, noun labels have been shown to most negatively influence others' perceptions of neuro-divergent individuals [20].

5 Conclusion

Overall, the main divisions that categorize anti-vaccination writings from pro-vaccination tend to concern formality and narrative structure: mostly notably use of punctuation, pronouns, and cognitive process words. Themes and key terms were concurrent to past research with one exception. However, more research is needed to see if individual genres within the subject of vaccination have unique qualities. By compiling a larger corpus, future studies could explore differences across categories of writing, and perhaps uncover further relevant LIWC features. Evidence suggests that future health promotion efforts should make attempts not to talk down to individuals, given the writings' less academic qualities and should stem from a place of understanding, considering the grieving process many anti-vaccination advocates may be experiencing.

Waning vaccination coverage and recent resurgences of once "eradicated" diseases have drawn the attention of public health officials, policy makers, and governments worldwide. As anti-vaccination sentiment continues to flourish, understanding the attitudes of its supporters and the nuances of the movement's misinformation become an essential to health promotion efforts. Further research that expands upon this pilot study is cogent to these efforts. Anti-vaccination attitudes have a long history, but with new strategies and new information, research of this kind can only serve to enrich the fight for maximum vaccination coverage, herd immunity, and a healthier world.

Acknowledgments. Thank you to Lauren Covey, Anna Feldman, and Susana Sotillo for teaching me and supporting this process. R. Claire Lingenfelter, thank you for the moral support and Vikki Fiore for the moral and technical support.

References

1. Ten Threats to Global Health in 2019. World Health Organization website, January 2019. https://www.who.int/emergencies/ten-threats-to-global-health-in-2019. Accessed 3 Mar 2019
2. Jolley, D., Douglas, K.M.: The effects of anti-vaccine conspiracy theories on vaccination intentions. PLoS ONE **9**(2), e89177 (2014)
3. Faasse, K., Chatman, C.J., Martin, L.R.: A comparison of language use in pro-and anti-vaccination comments in response to a high profile Facebook post. Vaccine **34**(47), 5808–5814 (2016)
4. Schmidt, A.L., Zollo, F., Scala, A., Betsch, C., Quattrociocchi, W.: Polarization of the vaccination debate on Facebook. Vaccine **36**(25), 3606–3612 (2018)
5. Wakefield, A.J., et al.: RETRACTED: ileal-lymphoid-nodular hyperplasia, non-specific colitis, and pervasive developmental disorder in children. Lancet **352**(9123), 234–235 (1998)
6. Monitoring Measles Cases. Centers for Disease Control website, 17 August 2018. https://www.infectioncontroltoday.com/public-health/cdc-monitoring-measles-cases. Accessed 3 Mar 2019
7. Caplan, A.L.: Retraction—ileal-lymphoid-nodular hyperplasia, non-specific colitis, and pervasive developmental disorder in children. In: The Weekly Epidemiological Record, vol. 84, pp. 301–308 (2009)
8. Hviid, A., Hansen, J.V., Frisch, M., Melbye, M.: Measles, mumps, rubella vaccination and autism: a nationwide cohort study. Ann. Intern. Med. **170**(8), 513–520 (2019)
9. Madsen, K.M., et al.: A population-based study of measles, mumps, and rubella vaccination and autism. New England J. Med. **347**(19), 1477–1482 (2002)
10. Stratton, K., Gable, A., Shetty, P., McCormick, M.: Institute of Medicine (US) Immunization Safety Review Committee. Immunization Safety Review: Measles-Mumps-Rubella Vaccine and Autism. National Academies Press (2001)
11. Taylor, B., et al.: Autism and measles, mumps, and rubella vaccine: no epidemiological evidence for a causal association. Lancet **353**(9169), 2026–2029 (1999)
12. Hornsey, M.J., Harris, E.A., Fielding, K.S.: The psychological roots of anti-vaccination attitudes: A 24-nation investigation. Health Psychol. **37**(4), 307 (2018)
13. Backus, F., De Pinto, J., Dutton, S., Salvanto, A.: CBS News poll on vaccines and the measles outbreak. CBS News. 20 February 2015. https://www.cbsnews.com/news/cbs-news-poll-on-vaccines-and-the-measles-outbreak. Accessed 3 Mar 2019
14. Hill, H.A., Elam-Evans, L.D., Yankey, D., Singleton, J.A., Kang, Y.: Vaccination coverage among children aged 19–35 months—United States, 2016. MMWR Morb. Mortal. Wkly Rep. **66**(43), 1171 (2017)
15. Horne, Z., Powell, D., Hummel, J.E., Holyoak, K.J.: Countering antivaccination attitudes. Proc. Natl. Acad. Sci. **112**(33), 10321–10324 (2015)
16. Joslyn, M.R., Sylvester, S.M.: The determinants and consequences of accurate beliefs about childhood vaccinations. Am. Polit. Res. **47**(3), 628–649 (2019)
17. Kang, G.J., et al.: Semantic network analysis of vaccine sentiment in online social media. Vaccine **35**(29), 3621–3638 (2017)
18. Arif, N., et al.: Fake news or weak science? Visibility and characterization of anti-vaccine webpages returned by Google in different languages and countries. Front. Immunol. **9**, 1215 (2018)
19. Nyhan, B., Reifler, J., Richey, S., Freed, G.L.: Effective messages in vaccine promotion: a randomized trial. Pediatrics **133**(4), e835–e842 (2014)
20. Cuttler, C., Ryckman, M.: Don't call me delusional: stigmatizing effects of noun labels on people with mental disorders. Stigma Health **4**(2), 118 (2019)

21. Brown, L.: Identity-first language. Autistic Self Advocacy Netw. **2** (2012). https://autisticadvocacy.org/about-asan/identity-first-language. Accessed 10 Apr 2019
22. Zerbo, O., et al.: Vaccination patterns in children after autism spectrum disorder diagnosis and in their younger siblings. JAMA Pediatr. **172**(5), 469–475 (2018)
23. Linguistic Inquiry and Word Count: LIWC2015. Pennebaker Conglomerates, Austin, TX (2015)
24. Stubbs, M.: Collocations and semantic profiles: On the cause of the trouble with quantitative studies. Funct. Lang. **2**(1), 23–55 (1995)
25. Davies, M.: The Corpus of Contemporary American English as the first reliable monitor corpus of English. Literary Linguist. Comput. **25**(4), 447–464 (2010)
26. Pennebaker, J.W., Boyd, R.L., Jordan, K., Blackburn, K.: The development and psychometric properties of LIWC2015 (2015)
27. Yang, H.: Establishing acceptable limits of residual DNA. PDA J. Pharm. Sci. Technol. **67**(2), 155–163 (2013)
28. Pennebaker, J.W., Mayne, T.J., Francis, M.E.: Linguistic predictors of adaptive bereavement. J. Pers. Soc. Psychol. **72**(4), 863 (1997)
29. Hartley, J., Pennebaker, J.W., Fox, C.: Abstracts, introductions and discussions: How far do they differ in style? Scientometrics **57**(3), 389–398 (2003)
30. Kowalski, R.M.: "I was only kidding!": Victims' and perpetrators' perceptions of teasing. Pers. Soc. Psychol. Bull. **26**(2), 231–241 (2000)

Design of Cognitive Tutor to Diagnose the Types of Intelligence in Preschool Students from Ages 3 to 5

Flor de María Olivares Ramos(✉)

Universidad Nacional de Ingeniería, Lima, Peru
flor.olivares@gmail.com

Abstract. The relationships between preschool, employment and economic pro-ductivity, as well as cost-benefit studies in this field, show a potential high return on investment in the early years of childhood. Preschool is the main base of the educational structure according to the Peruvian Ministry of Education. However, investment in this type of education is on average about 250 soles ($77) per student. On average there is one teacher per 18 students and just 60% of these teachers are specialized in preschool education (Escale 2015). In this context, talking about equal opportunities have been contradictory because these kinds of students have been part of the population that has not generated productivity in the country. On the other hand, when talking about the productivity of people, this could have a direct correspondence with the innate capacity that people have (Cerquín Cortez 2017), which are call like intelligences according to Howard Gardner in the theory of seven intelligences. Could you imagine that we can detect these intelligences in the first years of a child? This gives us an opportunity to improve our abilities in the coming years. For several years, student abilities have gone unnoticed because of curricular education and even now continue to remain the same. Although there are current methodologies designed for the diagnosis of these types of intelli-gences in early education, this could go unnoticed given the inexperience of the teacher and excessive workload as well as the need of psychologists for its proper application. In contrast, increasing the use of technology could be to our benefit. This work proposes the development of a cognitive tutor to diagnose the types of intelligence in preschool aged children in rural areas with teachers without an educational degree and little to no presence of psychologists.

Keywords: Artificial intelligence · Expert system/cognitive tutor · Model of intelligence types · Cognitive science · Preschool education

1 Introduction

The research proposes a change of context in the curricular plan of early childhood education, in children aged 3 to 5 years, who have put aside the traditional school practice of prioritizing linguistic and logical mathematical skills over the rest of the skills a human can display and develop. This traditional school practice led to diagnose and evaluate students based on these types of skills which in turn led to overseeing the abilities of

© Springer Nature Switzerland AG 2020
J. A. Lossio-Ventura et al. (Eds.): SIMBig 2019, CCIS 1070, pp. 325–332, 2020.
https://doi.org/10.1007/978-3-030-46140-9_31

several students who did not fit the traditional system well (Granado Alonso et al. 2004). Because some students could have been high-lighted in other areas of abilities, reveals the high rates of injustice in primary and secondary education (Minedu 2019). Inequality is more prominent in rural contexts due to high poverty rates generating clear differences in the level of learning provided in each social sector (Escale 2015).

According to several analyses, poverty was one of the variables. It was found that poor students have less access to education and attend schools that do not offer all the basic services and whose teachers do not have enough training, which generates gaps in educational outcomes (Cueto 2019). For this reason, education must combat the large educational gap based on poverty levels that causes an inequity in the quality of education which does not differentiate the scarce resources for a large percentage of the population. In the same way, considering one of the six objectives of the National Educational Project and the Educational Policy guidelines that are mentioned in the Peru Plan by 2021, created by the National Center for Strategic Planning (CEPLAN) which provides the guidelines of the educational policy intended to eliminate the gaps between public and private education, and between rural and urban education, addressing cultural diversity (Minedu 2019). According to the general context described, the problem that the thesis aims to solve is the inequity in the quality of education for all, thus eliminating the gap between public and private education. For which, the main components will be technology and Internet access which the largest number of Peruvian populations currently possesses (INEI 2012). The thesis aims to develop a cognitive tutor that supports the work of preschool teachers. The researcher considers preschool education as one of the main pillars given the current structure of education (Minedu 2019). Artificial intelligence (AI) technology, developed by IBM Watson, is an open and multi-cloud platform that allows you to automate the life cycle of the AI will be used to design the cognitive tutor. Powerful models will be created from scratch or to save time, preconfigured business applications may be used. The main objective of this thesis is to enhance education using technology; it is not a thesis of education itself. We will use a model of intelligence types previously validated in the thesis from the University of Seville, Spain, entitled "INTELIGENCIAS MÚLTIPLES EN LA EDUCACIÓN INFANTIL" (MULTIPLE INTELLIGENCES IN CHILDHOOD EDUCATION). Consequently, the validation of the methodology of the model is not subject of this investigation. The processing model in the cognitive tutor using Watson, will be carried out with a personalized design using the expert system. AI will be used to generate knowledge in Watson allowing the cognitive tutor to identify intelligence types based on the criteria of the teacher which in turn will be validated through the future interaction with the child.

2 Problem

The research will attempt to resolve the problem of inequity in the quality of education as the main cause to learning problems in early child-hood education. For more than 10 years, incentives to improve education have increased because of the participation of public and private entities who consider education as a key to achieve cultural change in Peruvian society (Cueto 2019). However, inequality remains due to the poverty variable detected in different investigations, where the number of children and young people involved is 1.3 million in initial education, 3.7 million in primary education and 2.5 million in secondary education, of which 79% of them are enrolled in public educational institutions (Guadalupe et al. 2017).

In initial education (pre-school and kindergarten), there are more than 11,000 state educational centers and more than 18,000 non-governmental programs that serve 994 thousand children under the age of six. In contrast, the number of qualified teachers (teachers with a teaching degree associated with the level that they teach) working in these educational centers is 60% work in preschool (INEI 2012). In a State that promotes equality, the most qualified teachers should teach children who belong to vulnerable groups. The Teacher Reform encourages the participation of teachers in educational institutions of EIB (Education International Bilingual). However, it does not generate enough incentives for the most qualified teachers to teach in institutions that underprivileged students attend. It is in this context that initiatives to eliminate the gaps between public and private education, and between rural and urban education will take place. Addressing cultural diversity should be a priority from all existing professional fronts as well as using existing advanced technological resources such as an Artificial Intelligence (AI) program. AI is one of the main tools that could support the simulation of a psychologist to reinforce the student's education with minimal cost alleviating the need for a psychologist for each student.

2.1 Problem Formulation

The problem is clearly formulated by posing the following research question:

What is the impact of cognitive tutor to diagnose the types of intelligence in the education of students from ages 3 to 5 in childhood education?

General Objectives. Evaluate the impact of a cognitive tutor to diagnose the types of intelligence in students from ages 3 to 5 in childhood education.

Specific Objectives
Reproduce the diagnostic methodology of the types of intelligence using a cognitive tutor program in IBM IA Watson.

Testing the prototype of the cognitive tutor to diagnose the types of intelligence in students from ages 3 to 5 in childhood education.

Evaluate the impact of the cognitive tutor to enhance the types of intelligence in students from ages 3 to 5 in childhood education.

3 Theoretical Basics

Research about the recognition of mathematical talent (Pavlekovic 2007) concludes that recognition of this talent needs the joint work of a psychologist and the teacher. Schools do not usually have the possibility of hiring both professionals due to different factors. Therefore, an expert system was developed with the objective to enhance teacher decision making by simulating previously defined knowledge of psychologists. In conclusion, the use of the expert system to support the decision making of a teacher could achieve an increase in the recognition of mathematical talent in students. Likewise, the use of similar AI programs is recommended for learning development in schools.

The integration of two AI methods such as: Expert Systems and Artificial Neural Networks, as a decision support tool for teachers in the recognition of gifted children were tested and produced similar results. These tools are usually used in tutoring systems to support learning or to teach a specific topic and are rarely considered for the diagnosis of skills (Pavlekovic and Zekic-Susac 2008). In conclusion, other research supports using the methodology of neural networks and fuzzy logic for the process of diagnosing a gifted student in an educational system with the objective to simulate the evaluation of the teacher to identify the characteristics of a student for the selection of a learning system that suits him (Stathacopoulou et al. 1999).

4   Theoretical Framework

4.1   Artificial Intelligence

It is a field that aims to solve complex problems with the following areas of interest: Vision, Natural Language, Expert System, Reading Compression, Robotics, Speech and Neural Networks (Giarratan 1998) and (Lahoz-Beltrá 2004b).

4.2   Expert System

Responsible for reproducing the knowledge of a specialist or specialized professional in a specific branch to solve complex problems (Giarratan 1998) and (Kendall 2011).

The traditional elements of an expert system are (Giarratan 1998):

User Interfaces: allows communication between the system and the user

Means of Explanation explains to the user the reasoning of the system

Active Memory: a global database of the facts used by the rules

Mechanism of Inference makes inference to decide which rules meet the facts or objects; gives priority to the rules met

Agenda: a list of priorities assigned to the rules created by the inference mechanism, whose patterns satisfy the facts or objects of active memory

Medium for the Acquisition of Knowledge: automatic way for the user to introduce data to the system without needing an engineer to code this explicitly

4.3 Multiple Intelligence

This theory, according to the author, proposes seven intelligences which have been widely investigated and documented (Granado Alonso et al. 2004):

Musical Intelligence includes sensitivity to rhythm, tone, melody, timbre and pitch.

The Kinetic-Body Intelligence appeals to multiple skills such as the ability to use the body to express ideas or feelings, to overcome obstacles, or to achieve certain objectives in various situations and includes manual skills to build or transform things and handle objects with dexterity.

Logical-Mathematical Intelligence includes sensitivity to schemas and logical relationships, affirmations and propositions (if-then, cause-effect), functions, inferences, abstractions.

Linguistic Intelligence implies sensitivity to sounds or phonemes, syntax or structure of language, semantics or meanings of language and different uses of language, such as rhetoric or persuasion.

Space Intelligence is the ability to perceive the visual-spatial world and to realize transformations based on that perception.

Intrapersonal Intelligence refers to self-knowledge and the ability to adapt to one's own ways of acting.

Interpersonal Intelligence is the sense of oneself and constitutes a mixture of intrapersonal and interpersonal components.

4.4 Cognitivism and Theory of Information Processing

Studies of internal processes during learning and memory structures are proposed and subjected to validation models that explain how the human mind learns and retains that information. The theories of information processing are based on analogies with computational machines. Memory is a structure of interrelated knowledge which can be schematically visualized as a network in which each union (node) is a fact of and each arrow represents the interrelation with another fact of. An act of learning consists of three things (Norman 1980):

Initially, there is existing knowledge at a given moment.

New knowledge, C1 and C2, is interconnected by the relationship R but not yet assimilated and accommodated in the memory structure.

The new knowledge, it has been properly connected with the previous one, which can now be distinguished between the new and previously existing knowledge. Now be distinguished between the new and previously existing knowledge (Fig. 1).

Learning from this perspective focuses on incorporating new learning into the memory structure and being able to repair and use it when necessary. This form of teaching, therefore, focuses on ensuring that the student will fill in the gaps in that memory structure.

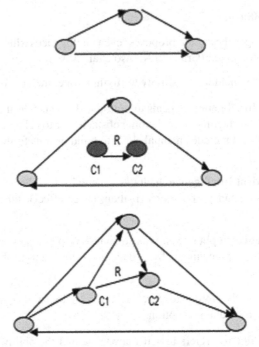

Fig. 1. Process to improve the knowledge

5   Contributions of the Author

Currently the use of artificial intelligence is cogitating a high visibility from different areas of business, given the optimization of human resources that causes. Considering also the easiest Internet access to which children begin to access. As a thesis student, I think it is important to raise the use of AI to simulate the profiles of different critical experts to improve a child's education. Especially at an early age. So, the direct contribution of my thesis is to try to prototype the knowledge of a psychologist embodied in a methodology to detect types of intelligence in a child in pre-school education. Trusting to continue with the work already done by different experts to use technology in education and trusting to impact other colleagues who could continue to implement technology in our education that needs to take more and more giant steps so as not to fall behind in a century like the actual.

6   Research Method

The research will simulate the diagnostic methodology of multiples intelligences using a cognitive tutor.

Phase 1: To achieve the re-production of the diagnostic methodology of the types of intelligence in a cognitive tutor using IBM IA Watson, the following activities must be carried out:

Representation of the diagnostic methodology of the types of intelligence in a sematic network used by a cognitive tutor.

Preparation of a related database for the registration of facts that match with knowledge to generate new facts.

Determine the actions for the inference engine for the cognitive tutor using IBM IA Watson.

Development of interface to interact with the user.

Phase 2: To test the prototype of the cognitive tutor to diagnose the types of intelligence in students from ages 3 to 5, the teacher should carry out the following activities:

Student registration.

Determination of the suggested profile of the student by types of intelligence.

Create an activity plan according to the student's profile.

Registration of interaction with activities suggested by the profile.

Registration of interaction with activities not suggested by the profile.

Determination of the user's profile by intelligence types according to interaction with the system.

Phase 3: To evaluate the impact of the cognitive tutor to boost the types of intelligence in students from ages 3 to 5 in childhood education, the following activities must be performed:

Comparison of the profile according to interaction with the system of intelligence types.

Comparison of average profile matches.

Suggested and the profile according to interaction with the system of intelligence types.

References

Escale: Estadística de plan educativo 2019 (2015). de Ministerio de educación Sitio web: http://escale.minedu.gob.pe/ueetendencias20002015

Cerquín Cortez, S., Roncal Rojas, J.T.: Relación de la gestión del talento humano con la productividad laboral en los trabajadores del consorcio Cajabamba S.A.C. Boticas Diana, Cajamarca. (Tesis Parcial) (2017)

Van Leeuwen, J.: Playability in Actions Videogames. Gamasutra Game Developer. http://gamasutra.net/playability.html. Accessed 13 Feb 2008

Proposal of educational goals and Indicators to 2021. [Proposal] Ministerio de Educacion del Perú (Minedu), I. Lima (2019)

Guadalupe, C., León, J., Rodríguez, J.S., Vargas, S.: La educación peruana en contexto: tendencias, permanencias y cambios. En Análisis y perspectivas de la educación básica (44). GRADE, Lima (2017)

Granado Alonso, C.: Inteligencias múltiples en la educación infantil. Grupo de Investigación Didáctica/Universidad de Sevilla, vol. 1, pp. 5–30 (2004)

Cueto, S.: Research for development in Peru [E-book], 1st edn, pp. 55–80. Analysis Group for Development (GRADE), Peru (2019)

National Institute of Statistics and Informatics (INEI): Expenditure allocated by the central government to the education sector, Lima, Perú, 1 January 2012

Pavlekovic, M.: Expert system to detect mathematical talent. The Institute of Electrical and Electronic Engineering (IEEE), pp. 98–116 (2007)

Pavlekovic, M., Zekic-Susac, M.: Integration of an expert system and neural networks to recognize a child's mathematical talent. The Institute of Electrical and Electronic Engineering (IEEE), pp. 557–562 (2008)

Stathacopoulou, R., Magoulas, G., Grigoriadou, M.: Neural network-based fuzzy modeling of the student in intelligent tutoring systems. In: International Joint Conference on Neural Network, vol. 5, pp. 3517–3521 (1999). https://doi.org/10.1109/ijcnn.1999.836233

Giarratano, J.C.: Expert Systems: Principles and Programming, 3rd edn. Course Technology, México (1980)

Lahoz-Beltrá, R.: Bioinformática: simulación, vida artificial e inteligencia artificial (ed. rev.). Díaz de Santos, Madrid (2004b)

Kendall, E., Kendall, K.E.: Análisis y Diseño de Sistemas, 8th edn. Pearson Educación, México (2011)

Norman, D.A.: Doce temas para la ciencia cognitiva. Cienc. Cogn. **4**, 1–32 (1980). https://doi.org/10.1207/s15516709cog0401_1

Fake News in Spanish: Towards the Building of a Corpus Based on Twitter

Braulio Andres Soncco Pimentel[1](✉) and Roxana L. Q. Portugal[2](✉)

[1] UNSAAC, Cusco, Peru
992182@unsaac.edu.pe
[2] PUC-Rio, Rio de Janeiro, Brazil
rportugal@inf.puc.rio.br

Abstract. Nowadays, we can use various techniques to detect fake news that depends mainly on supervised models that trained a corpus of true and fake news in English. However, these models are not suited to classify news in Spanish. On the other hand, very few is known about the provenance of news in existing corpora. This work presents a strategy to create a Corpus of news in Spanish for fake new detection purposes. We propose Twitter as a mediator to find relevant sources of where to take the news. As such, we report the work in progress performed to characterize Twitter as a means to retrieve the news.

Keywords: Corpus · Fake news · Politics · Social networks

1 Introduction

Fake news is a common term in these days, however even we are conscious of its existence, we, as humans, are not as accurate to detect lies [1]. Shu et al. [2] cites that human is vulnerable to identify fake news due two factors: Naive Realism and Confirmation Bias. The first when readers believe as accurate information the ones aligned with their point of view, and the second when readers are abler to receive content that confirms their view.

Several efforts emerged to tackle the automated identification of fake news in different areas, particularly in politics [3–8]. However, such solutions are not as effective for classifying true and fake news in languages other than English. That is, the language characteristics influence in automated classifiers [9]. We verified few work creating Spanish corpora [10, 11]. One of them [11] corroborates [9] stressing the importance of a corpus creation as a first step to deal with fake news. On the challenges to building a corpus, Tschiatschek et al. [12] indicate the lack of corpora pointing the provenance of news, as well as the subjectivity in annotations of news.

Fake news proliferates rapidly on social networks [4, 9, 12], as readers share the news without paying attention if they are fake [2, 12]. Less attention is paid to the sources generating fake news [12]. A principle towards the building of a corpus [13] indicates

© Springer Nature Switzerland AG 2020
J. A. Lossio-Ventura et al. (Eds.): SIMBig 2019, CCIS 1070, pp. 333–339, 2020.
https://doi.org/10.1007/978-3-030-46140-9_32

that the Universe of Discourse (contents) should be properly selected to support the purpose. However, existing corpora is created by crawling news from the most established newspapers [4, 9] leaving out other digital sources such as new digital newspapers and blogs.

A strategy to find relevant sources of fake news may be to identify the most widespread news on social networks such as Twitter. That is, by finding the comments that impact more on a topic, it is possible to trace the comments with URLs. Although there is a growth in the detection of fake news using the content of Twitter itself [14–16], this work proposes its use only as a mediator due to the nature of the tweets, which are short, fragmented and decontextualized [17].

This work presents the work in progress towards the building of a Spanish corpus for fake news identification. The paper is organized as follows. In Sect. 2, we explain the research goals. Section 3 details the progress to characterize Twitter in the strategy. Section 4 concludes and summarizes future work.

2 Research Objectives

To define our strategy, we elicit fake-news works [3–12] to know more about the definitions that we summarized in Table 1. We looked for the pros and the perils of Artificial Intelligence techniques, as such some authors stress the importance of explainable data when using AI techniques [18, 19], that is, we should not rely on predictive models that do not show us their rationale.

Table 1. Eliciting concepts about fake news

Technical concepts	Topics
Linguistic features, Machine learning, Veracity assessment, news verification, SVM, Knowledge networks, Predictive modelling, Feature extraction, Linguistics correlation, Visualization, Metadata	Politics, Sports, Technology, Show Business

To delineate a strategy to find relevant sources in Twitter messages, we found necessary the understanding of the paradigm of this environment. However, few details are given. The main focus is the influence of Twitter in the dissemination of news. By using Google Scholar, we searched the query *allintitle: twitter paradigm*, with which we found eight papers and selected four by its title [21–24]. We elicit the frequent topics: politics, sports and nursing. An important fact is mentioned, that is, a single person can easily reach thousands of contacts through a topic of interest. However, while Twitter metadata such as *tweets, retweets, hashtags*, among others are implicit, works [21–24] lack details about the interactions among the actors, as well as details on how a topic becomes relevant (a trend).

Following, we developed two hypotheses to tackle our main goal, which is the identification of fake news in Spanish. (1) A corpus of news in Spanish needs to be reliable, and (2) Twitter can be useful as a mediator to find of news. This hypothesis answers two questions:

What Would Be a Reliable Corpus of News?

Any fake-news work has to build or rely on a dataset based on a corpus. A corpus creation takes time because it is needed to ensure the quality of information when collecting and classifying data. In this regard, few works [4, 9, 20, 21] report on process and data provenance to build a classified corpus. Some authors [18, 19] stress that AI approaches need to be explainable from the inputs to outputs. Such is that an AI system is classified as opaque, interpretable, and comprehensible [19]. A corpus comes to be the input of an AI system, and, by exposing their contents' sources and the process to select them and annotate, the corpus can be less opaque.

Another aspect to consider when building a corpus is a principle stated by Sinclair and Wynne [13]: "The contents of a corpus should be selected regardless of their language, but according to their communicative function in the community in which they occur". Thus, contents of a Corpus shouldn't be selected arbitrarily but pointing a communicative function be it a topic (e.g. politics) or a type of information (e.g. news).

Therefore, we consider a reliable corpus to be one that makes its construction process transparent, as much as it characterizes a Universe of Information (UdI).

Why Twitter Is Relevant as a Means of Information?

Twitter is the ultimate way to get real-time information about various events, from politics, health, sports or natural phenomena. In the particular case of politics, authorities transmit their decisions, opinions and communicate to the population about their management. The journalists also show not only their journalistic line, but also their personal opinion [8]. Messages on Twitter, called *tweets,* are concise and easy to read and interpret. There is a notion of *hashtags*, which serves to broaden and spread all messages related to a certain topic. Such spread, when carried out by relevant political actors, can influence the people's decision [15]. There is also the citizen side, who are information consumers, who decide to accept, deny or ask questions about the *tweets* [7]. Twitter is used to generate political polarization [25], a situation that can be envisaged [26, 27].

Some particular scenarios are the political choices of countries; political campaigns are transferred to social networks, reaching connected users. The best-known cases are the 2008 presidential election in the United States [28], and the influence of Facebook in the US presidential election [14].

Research Strategy

We defined seven steps towards the detection of fake news in Spanish:

1. Understand Twitter paradigm
2. Select a UdI to extract trends from Twitter
3. Identify UdI trends in the last 3 years
4. Identify at least ten relevant media in the last 3 years
5. Retrieve news from relevant media.
6. Classify true and false news using literature techniques.
7. Verify results against human review.

3   Work in Progress

So far, we have reach three steps from our strategy, despite technical constraints of Twitter. To identify the relevant tweets that may anchor the URLs of news, we modeled the Twitter actors involved in spreading the news. A script to collect the trends (*hashtags*) is made available.

3.1 Twitter Paradigm

As our focus is to investigate the spreading of fake-news on Twitter, so that we design a strategy to find relevant tweets, we depart by identifying the actors and interaction involved. By using the intentional modeling language i* [29] (Fig. 1) we were able to show the different roles that Twitter user can perform, that is, in the fake-news context, we identified four social actors: politicians, journalists, citizen and anonymous. Each one can cover the place of a software agent called Twitter user. Any Twitter user can become an influencer or a troll, or both at the same time. A troll is an internet user who intentionally provokes other users, often using offensive language to attack an argument or a person. Trolls can work alone or together. A group of trolls can easily spread fake news [30]. An Influencer is a person who possesses a set of personal and social attributes so that he can reach others quickly [31]. According to [7], any Twitter user, as information consumers, decide to occupy a position: accept, deny or ask questions about the *tweets*.

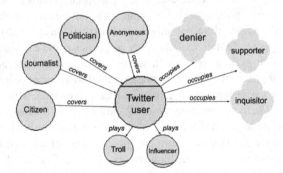

Fig. 1. Actors in Twitter.

3.2 Recovering Twitter Trends

One way to filter the relevant *tweets* may be the identification of trends so we can anchor the tweets with more impact and through them to know the sources (URLs), as well as actors spreading the news. However, the Twitter API does not provide a method to get the *hashtags* that occurred in a set of time. As such, by using web-scraping techniques (https://github.com/soncco/hashtag-scraper) we collect them from Trendogate.com. This site keeps a trend archive of different locations since March 2015. Thus, we can recover a set of *hashtags* given a UdI: [Location, Time interval].

As a sample, in Fig. 2, we configured the UdI: Lima-Peru from March 2018 to March 2019. After recovering, we ordered the hashtags by frequency and selected the top 100. From them, we manually selected the ones related to the political topic.

'César Villanueva', 'Alberto Fujimori', 'Daniel Salaverry', 'Pedro Chávarry', '#NiUnaMenos', 'Edwin Oviedo', '#Elecciones2018', 'Luz Salgado', '#GlatzerTuesta', '#LavaJato', 'Rosa Bartra', 'Kenji Fujimori', '#Congreso', 'Presidente Vizcarra', 'Fuerza Popular', 'Alejandro Toledo', 'Fiscalía', 'Yesenia Ponce', 'Mesa Directiva'

Fig. 2. Hashtags about politics in Lima-Perú, from March 2018 to March 2019

Twitter Constraints

The Twitter API provides a way to get *tweets* according to premium[1] parameters and operators for accessing data. One can get *tweets* from the beginning of Twitter (2006) to the present by combining them. However, a free developer account only allows 50 queries per month, as well as limiting the use of some operators.

4 Conclusion

This work presents the steps achieved to build a reliable corpus of news in Spanish for fake-news detection. We describe the strategy to cope with Twitter data as a mediator to find sources of news. As *hashtags* are a means to find relevant tweets, we have worked in an automated way to retrieve them.

Future work is focused on strategies to semi-automate the *hashtags* filtering given a topic (Fig. 2), as well as modeling each actor intentions in the spreading of news (Fig. 1). By modeling the Twitter paradigm in the fake-news context, we will be able to create heuristics to identify relevant sources. In parallel, given the restrictions of the Twitter API, we will work on mechanisms to create efficient queries with the *hashtags* that will lead us to retrieve relevant tweets.

Acknowledgment. Portugal acknowledges the support of Cnpq scholarship 146372/2018-2.

References

1. Bond Jr., C.F., DePaulo, B.M.: Accuracy of deception judgments. Pers. Soc. Psychol. Rev. **10**(3), 214–234 (2006)
2. Shu, K., Sliva, A., Wang, S., Tang, J., Liu, H.: Fake news detection on social media: a data mining perspective. ACM SIGKDD Explor. Newsl. **19**(1), 22–36 (2017)
3. Karimi, H., Roy, P., Saba-Sadiya, S., Tang, J.: Multi-source multi-class fake news detection. In: Proceedings of the 27th International Conference on Computational Linguistics, pp. 1546–1557, August 2018
4. Pérez-Rosas, V., Kleinberg, B., Lefevre, A., Mihalcea, R.: Automatic detection of fake news. arXiv preprint arXiv:1708.07104 (2017)

---

[1] https://developer.twitter.com/en/docs/tweets/search/guides/standard-operators.

5. Shu, K., Wang, S., Liu, H.: Understanding user profiles on social media for fake news detection. In: 2018 IEEE Conference on Multimedia Information Processing and Retrieval (MIPR), pp. 430–435. IEEE, April 2018
6. Choraś, M., Giełczyk, A., Demestichas, K., Puchalski, D., Kozik, R.: Pattern recognition solutions for fake news detection. In: Saeed, K., Homenda, W. (eds.) CISIM 2018. LNCS, vol. 11127, pp. 130–139. Springer, Cham (2018). https://doi.org/10.1007/978-3-319-99954-8_12
7. Zubiaga, A., Aker, A., Bontcheva, K., Liakata, M., Procter, R.: Detection and resolution of rumours in social media: a survey. ACM Comput. Surv. (CSUR) **51**(2), 32 (2018)
8. Tumasjan, A., Sprenger, T.O., Sandner, P.G., Welpe, I.M.: Predicting elections with twitter: what 140 characters reveal about political sentiment. In: Fourth International AAAI Conference on Weblogs and Social Media, May 2010
9. Monteiro, R.A., Santos, R.L.S., Pardo, T.A.S., de Almeida, T.A., Ruiz, E.E.S., Vale, O.A.: Contributions to the study of fake news in Portuguese: new corpus and automatic detection results. In: Villavicencio, A., et al. (eds.) PROPOR 2018. LNCS (LNAI), vol. 11122, pp. 324–334. Springer, Cham (2018). https://doi.org/10.1007/978-3-319-99722-3_33
10. Posadas-Durán, J.P., Gómez-Adorno, H., Sidorov, G., Escobar, J.J.M.: Detection of fake news in a new corpus for the Spanish language. J. Intell. Fuzzy Syst. **36**(5), 4869–4876 (2019)
11. Blázquez-Ochando, M.: El problema de las noticias falsas: detección y contramedidas (2018)
12. Tschiatschek, S., Singla, A., Gomez Rodriguez, M., Merchant, A., Krause, A.: Fake news detection in social networks via crowd signals. In: Companion of the The Web Conference 2018 on The Web Conference 2018, pp. 517–524. International World Wide Web Conferences Steering Committee, April 2018
13. Sinclair, J., Wynne, M.: Corpus and text-basic principles' in developing linguistic corpora: a guide to good practice (2004)
14. Allcott, H., Gentzkow, M.: Social media and fake news in the 2016 election. J. Econ. Perspect. **31**(2), 211–236 (2017)
15. Bastos, M.T., Raimundo, R.L.G., Travitzki, R.: Gatekeeping Twitter: message diffusion in political hashtags. Media Cult. Soc. **35**(2), 260–270 (2013)
16. Buntain, C., Golbeck, J.: Automatically identifying fake news in popular twitter threads. In: 2017 IEEE International Conference on Smart Cloud (SmartCloud), pp. 208–215. IEEE, November 2017
17. Gounari, P.: Authoritarianism, discourse and social media: Trump as the 'American Agitator'. In: Critical Theory and Authoritarian Populism, p. 207 (2018)
18. Doran, D., Schulz, S., Besold, T.R.: What does explainable AI really mean? A new conceptualization of perspectives. arXiv preprint arXiv:1710.00794 (2017)
19. Ghosh, P.: AAAS: Machine learning "causing science crisis" 16 February 2019. https://www.bbc.com/news/science-environment-47267081. Accessed 12 June 2019
20. Portugal, R.L.Q., Roque, H., do Prado Leite, J.C.S.: A corpus builder: retrieving raw data from GitHub for knowledge reuse in requirements elicitation. In: SIMBig, pp. 48–54 (2016)
21. Moulai, H., Drias, H.: Towards the paradigm of information warehousing: application to Twitter. In: Demigha, O., Djamaa, B., Amamra, A. (eds.) CSA 2018. LNNS, vol. 50, pp. 147–157. Springer, Cham (2019). https://doi.org/10.1007/978-3-319-98352-3_16
22. Basaille, I., Kirgizov, S., Leclercq, É., Savonnet, M., Cullot, N.: Towards a Twitter observatory: a multi-paradigm framework for collecting, storing and analysing tweets. In: 2016 IEEE Tenth International Conference on Research Challenges in Information Science (RCIS), pp. 1–10. IEEE, June 2016
23. Sheffer, M.L., Schultz, B.: Paradigm shift or passing fad? Twitter and sports journalism. Int. J. Sport Commun. **3**(4), 472–484 (2010)

24. Lesen, A.E.: A new paradigm for science communication? Social media, Twitter, science, and public engagement: a literature review. In: Scientists, Experts, and Civic Engagement: Walking a Fine Line, p. 111 (2015)
25. Conover, M.D., Ratkiewicz, J., Francisco, M., Gonçalves, B., Menczer, F., Flammini, A.: Political polarization on Twitter. In: Fifth International AAAI Conference on Weblogs and Social Media, July 2011
26. Colleoni, E., Rozza, A., Arvidsson, A.: Echo chamber or public sphere? Predicting political orientation and measuring political homophily in Twitter using big data. J. Commun. **64**(2), 317–332 (2014)
27. Conover, M.D., Gonçalves, B., Ratkiewicz, J., Flammini, A., Menczer, F.: Predicting the political alignment of twitter users. In: 2011 IEEE Third International Conference on Privacy, Security, Risk and Trust and 2011 IEEE Third International Conference on Social Computing, pp. 192–199. IEEE, October 2011
28. Cogburn, D.L., Espinoza-Vasquez, F.K.: From networked nominee to networked nation: examining the impact of Web 2.0 and social media on political participation and civic engagement in the 2008 Obama campaign. J. Polit. Mark. **10**(1–2), 189–213 (2011)
29. Yu, E.: Strategic modelling for enterprise integration. In: Proceedings of the 14th World Congress of the International Federation of Automatic Control, pp. 5–9, July 1999
30. Dalton, M.D., Luke, J.S.: U.S. Patent No. 9,961,115. U.S. Patent and Trademark Office, Washington, DC (2018)
31. Bakshy, E., Hofman, J.M., Mason, W.A., Watts, D.J.: Everyone's an influencer: quantifying influence on twitter. In: Proceedings of the Fourth ACM International Conference on Web Search and Data Mining, pp. 65–74. ACM, February 2011

Author Index

Printed in the United States
by Baker & Taylor Publisher Services